By Herbert Weinstock

CHOPIN: *The Man and His Music* (*1949*)

HANDEL (*1946; Handel Bicentenary Edition, 1959*)

TCHAIKOVSKY (*1943*)

These are BORZOI BOOKS
published by ALFRED A. KNOPF in New York

CHOPIN

CHOPIN

THE MAN
AND HIS MUSIC

HERBERT WEINSTOCK

NEW YORK : ALFRED · A · KNOPF

1959

THIS IS A BORZOI BOOK,
PUBLISHED BY ALFRED A. KNOPF, INC.

PUBLISHED MARCH 7, 1949
SECOND PRINTING, JUNE 1959

Preface

WITH REGARD to the music of Chopin the problem of a reliable edition has never been satisfactorily solved. The Breitkopf & Härtel collected edition, edited and critically revised by Bargiel, Brahms, Franchomme, Liszt, Reinecke, and Rudorff, was excellent for its day. But it is excessively rare, and its day was not our day, which has at its disposal far more information. The editions supervised or edited by Debussy, Joseffy, Klindworth, Mikuli, and several others are reliable only in part. Similarly the renowned Oxford Edition, edited by Édouard Ganche, is excellent in part; it is, in fact, the best of a not very satisfactory lot.

The truth is that a satisfactory edition of Chopin would have to be a variorum edition. Not only was the composer careless in his notation; he also several times wrote down widely varying versions of the same piece. In many cases it is literally impossible to establish one version as definitive. I have pointed out numerous passages in which ordinary editions have further suffered the "improvements" of editors. For my own part, in writing this book I have created an imaginary edition based on Joseffy, Klindworth, and Mikuli as amended in view of Oxford and the specific comments of several modern writers. I am not aware of having made references that will be unclear to the possessor of any ordinary edition.

In quoting from Chopin's letters I have made my own translations from transcriptions that I have reason to consider accurate where the letters were originally in French, and from French translations likewise credibly accurate where the letters were originally in Polish. In a few cases I have been able to refer to photographs or photostats of the original holograph letters.

Quotations from George Sand and Delacroix have been made from reliable editions in French, except that in quoting from Delacroix's *Journal* I have arrived at my text by amending the Walter Pach translation in view of the original, thus preserving the most familiar English form while making the lines, it seems to me, more accurate.

H. W.

ACKNOWLEDGMENTS

MY INDEBTEDNESS to others who have written about Chopin is acknowledged in the Bibliography.

I am particularly grateful to Ernest Hutcheson for having given me two editions of Chopin's Seventeen Polish Songs; to Sam Morgenstern for reading the second half of this book in manuscript and giving me the benefit of detailed technical criticism and suggestion; to Gregor Piatigorsky for having discussed with me at length the Cello Sonata; to the staff of the 58th Street Music Library, New York, for many sorts of special assistance; to Wallace Brockway for invaluable aid in establishing the identity of obscure individuals mentioned in the text and index. My thanks go to Nicolas Slonimsky for lending me materials of particular value in reference to Chopin's family.

To Alfred A. Knopf and Blanche W. Knopf I am grateful for encouragement to write this book and several specific suggestions. To my mother, Edna Weinstock, Laurence R. Josephs, and William A. Koshland I give my thanks for having read all or part of the manuscript and made many detailed and useful criticisms. To Antoinette Leger I am grateful for having copied out many pages of French. Raymond A. Preston gave the entire manuscript the benefit of his unparalleled experience in copy-editing, as well as that of his rich store of general and musical information. My thanks go to Sidney R. Jacobs for his friendly and professional attention to all details of this book's design and manufacture.

To Ben Meiselman, finally, I am most deeply indebted for having permitted me to read this manuscript to him as it was written, rewritten, corrected, and retyped. I have turned to him for a thousand pieces of advice and help, and never once in vain. His expert assistance in preparing the indexes has been invaluable.

HERBERT WEINSTOCK

A NOTE ON

the Spelling of Polish Names in This Book

POLISH BELONGS to the group of Slavonic languages. Although it resembles Russian, it uses the Latin rather than the Cyrillic alphabet. For this reason many writers of books in English have assumed that the most useful form of Polish names was that of their originals, usually without some or all of the diacritical marks. How far this procedure deceives the ear of the unwary reader can be demonstrated by two examples. The name spelled Wągrowiec in Polish is pronounced approximately *Vongrovyets*, with the accent falling (as it always does in Polish) on the syllable before the last, and with *on* pronounced in the nasal French manner. Similarly, the name Jędrzejewicz is pronounced approximately *Yedzheyevich* or *Yindzheyevich,* with the *in* like that in Chopin.

I have therefore adopted the procedure of transliterating most Polish names and words exactly as though they were originally printed — as in effect they are — in an alphabet different from ours. In a few cases, of course, I have had to sacrifice consistency to long-established and familiar usage. Thus I have used *Warsaw* and not *Warszawa* or *Varshava; Kosciuszko* (it is actually *Kościuszko*) and not *Koshiushko.* I have not felt free to give a phonetic spelling to such well-known names as *Potocki* and *Radziwiłł* without presenting them, the first time they occur in my text, in their original spelling, followed that time with the transliteration used thereafter. In the less familiar names, however, I have introduced the transliteration immediately, giving the original spelling only in the index, where both spellings are given with cross-references.

My system of transliteration has been freely adapted from the one established by the Royal Geographical Society's book (1937) *Alphabets of Foreign Languages,* by Major-General Lord Edward Gleichen and John H. Reynolds. I do not pretend that it is either

i x

entirely accurate or entirely satisfactory. I have not, for example, found it possible to render the Polish *ł* as *w*, for it is actually "a hard l pronounced far back in the throat and consequently approaching w." All that I claim for my adaptation is that the reader of this book will have some conception of the actual sound of the Polish names used, a conception much more nearly accurate than he could have had if I had consistently used the Polish spelling with all its complex diacritical marks.[1]

The following table indicates the letter-values meant by their use in my transliterations:

a — as in *ah*	n — as in *net*
b — as in *boy*	o — ⎰ as in *go*
ch — as in *chore*	⎱ as in *horse*
d — as in *dot*	p — as in *pet*
e — as in *bed*	r — as in *red*
f — as in *fed*	s — as in *soy*
g — as in *go*	sh — as in *shame*
h — as in *hot*	t — as in *toy*
i — as in *hit*	u — as in *hussar*
k — as in *kill*	v — as in *very*
l — as in *let*	z — as in *zoo*
m — as in *met*	zh — as *z* in *azure*

The letter *y* followed by a vowel is semiconsonantal, approaching its sound in *yet* and *you*. When followed by a consonant, however, it has its sound in *my*. By *kh* I have indicated a sound that is close to the *ch* in the Scottish *loch* or the German *Reich,* but far from the *ch* in *Chicago* or that in *chance.*

H. W.

[1] None of the diacritical marks in Polish indicates accentuation of syllables. Thus *Sokołów* is pronounced halfway between *Sokoluf* and *Sokowuf,* accent on the middle syllable. The Polish *ó,* that is to say, differs from the Polish *o* (which varies between the short English *o* in *horse* and the long English *o* in *go*) in being nearer to the sound of *oo* in the English word *woof.*

CONTENTS

ILLUSTRATIONS

I

THE MAN

I

I N 1807 Napoleon met Alexander I, Tsar of Russia, on a raft
moored in the Memel River at the old town of Tilsit. The
arrangement worked out at their meeting was signed in July
of that year and came to be called after the town on the
riverbank. The Treaty of Tilsit added one more dizzying whorl to
the history of Poland, which only eleven years earlier had suffered its third partition. By its terms the Grand Duchy of Warsaw
was created from a small part of the once mighty Polish kingdom.
Over this emaciated territory was placed as Grand Duke Friedrich August I, King of Saxony, a longtime faithful friend to Napoleon, who in 1809 permitted the Grand Duchy to be enlarged by
half. Actual administration continued to be in French and Russian
hands.

When, on February 22, 1810, Frédéric-François [1] Chopin was
born near Warsaw to Nicolas Chopin, Frenchman, and his wife,
the Polish Tekla Justina Krzyżanowska (Yustina Kzhizhanovska),
he was thus technically a subject of the King of Saxony. Those
with a taste for the biographically curious may savor this fact.
For Friedrich August I, King, was a great-grandson of Friedrich
August I, Elector. And the most famous of the Elector's numerous
descendants — by way of his splendid illegitimate son, Maurice de
Saxe — was a great-granddaughter who was to enact a most important role in Chopin's life: George Sand.

When Chopin was born, in 1810,[2] however, Amandine-Aurore-

[1] This is the commonly used French form of names — Fryderyk Franciszek
— that are pronounced approximately Friderik Frantsishek.
[2] The date of Chopin's birth has never been established beyond question.
Josef Sikorski (1849), followed by Moritz Karasowski's biography in all its
editions through the English one of 1938, gave the date as March 1, 1809.
This was given the support of Chopin's friend Juljan (Yulyan) Fontana.
M. A. Szulc gave the date as March 2, 1809, Fétis as February 8, 1810,
Liszt merely as 1810. In 1893 the priest of Brochów (Brokhov), the parish
in which Chopin's birthplace was located, discovered and published both
the registry of the child's birth and his baptismal certificate, the former in

Lucile Dupin was little more than five and one half years old, two decades and more from her metamorphosis into that indomitable and tireless woman of letters, Mme Sand. In 1810 she was a mite tossed into life as the First French Republic merged into the First Empire, and no more interesting in her small self, no more remarkable in any way — except for her royal ancestry — than the tiny male child born at Zhelazova Vola, twenty-eight miles from Warsaw.

That the child Chopin was to enjoy early opportunities somewhat brighter than his father's worldly position alone could have supported was owing to the friendliness of the Skarbek family, owners of the village of Zhelazova Vola. The child's mother was a personal attendant on Countess Ludvika Skarbek, his father the tutor of the Countess's children. Frédéric-François's lifelong tendency to flower under the protection of nobility began with his birth: the young Countess Anna Skarbek (later Mme Vyesolovska) was his godmother; her brother Friderik, unable to attend the baptism, nevertheless allowed his name to be given to the child.[3]

Nicolas Chopin, having been born on April 15, 1771 (four months after Beethoven), was nearly thirty-nine when his wife gave birth to their only son. Because he himself was supposed to have been born near Nancy in Lorraine, it was long stated that he was partly of Polish descent. For in 1736 Stanislas Leszczyński (Leshchinski), a former King of Poland, had become Duke of Lorraine and Bar. Stanislas certainly had been trailed by Polish followers when, at fifty-nine, he settled down at Lunéville, near Nancy, to devote the final thirty years of his life to philosophy and science. One of his entourage, the tale ran, might have been a

---

Polish, the latter in Latin. These seem to have established that Chopin was born at six o'clock in the evening of February 22, 1810. It seems best, unless more definite evidence is found, to accept this date, though Chopin himself — in a letter dated January 16, 1833 — thanked the Polish Literary Society of Paris for honoring him with membership, and wrote at the bottom of the letter: "Born March 1, 1810, at the village of Żelazowa Wola [Zhelazova Vola], Palatinate of Mazovia." See documents transcribed in Appendix B, page 329.

[3] Chopin's actual godfather, substituting for the absent Count Friderik Skarbek, was Frantsishek Grebetski, a friend of the senior Skarbeks. Hence, perhaps, the names Friderik Frantsishek given to the boy.

Polish noble named Szop (the Polish spelling of Chopin is Szopen). And he might well have had a son or grandson named Nicolas. This romantic story was dear to writers and readers, Polish and foreign, who wanted to believe that Nicolas's great son was more than half Polish.

Unfortunately for the story, documentary evidence disproves it. Although Nicolas Chopin is not known ever to have spoken of the exact date and place of his birth, he once did write them down. Applying for retirement from his teaching post in Warsaw's Military School, he stated in writing to the Russian authorities (Napoleon was dead and Poland once more was Russian) that he had been born at the tiny village of Marainville, just north of Mirecourt in the department of Vosges, on April 17, 1770. When the records of vital statistics for Marainville were examined, it was found that his memory had deceived him by one year and two days: April 15, 1771 was his birthday, April 16 that of his baptism. The registers proved, furthermore, that the composer's paternal great-grandfather, another Nicolas Chopin, had lived in Marainville before Stanislas Leshchinski became Duke of Lorraine and Bar. That earlier Nicolas, his son, and the composer's father were French of the French. Frédéric-François's only Polish blood came to him from his mother.

The Marainville Chopins were humble in circumstances. The composer's grandfather, François, was a wheelwright who late in life abandoned his profession in favor of his father's, the cultivation of wine grapes. He was twice married. Nicolas was his son by his first wife, whose maiden name had been Marguérite Deflin. Nothing is known of Nicolas Chopin's childhood or of the exact date of his departure from the perhaps happy but certainly crabbed village of Marainville for the comparatively great city of Warsaw. The memoirs of his pupil, Count Friderik Skarbek, state that he arrived in Poland in 1787 — he would have been sixteen — to take up employment as cashier in a tobacco factory. According to this wholly credible story, Nicolas had been invited to Warsaw by a French friend who was making a good thing out of the increasing taste for snuff. Perhaps the most curious fact about Nicolas Chopin is that, so far as can be determined, he never returned to visit the village of his birth, never saw his family again, was unaware of the deaths of his parents, never mentioned his background at all. He became in effect a Pole without foreign or family ties.[4]

When Nicolas Chopin arrived in Warsaw, Poland was nominally independent under the kingship of Stanislas Poniatovski, ruling since 1764. But Frederick the Great and Catherine the Great, with assistance from Maria Theresa (the "Confederation of Bar"), had subjected the country to its first partition in 1772, taking from it about one quarter of its land, about one fifth of its people. In 1786, however, Frederick the Great had died, leaving Europe in a precarious unbalance of power. New wars were about to break out. Poland was not to be left in peace to enjoy its remarkable Constitution of 1775, which had begun to improve the quarreling, sordid, futile internal life of the nation. Nor was Nicolas Chopin to make a modest fortune peacefully in snuff. The tobacco factory closed. It was not long before he joined the Polish army.

In 1791, with Catherine the Great busy fighting the Turks, Stanislas Poniatovski persuaded the Polish Diet to accept a new constitution. This "Revolution of May 3" made the country a hereditary monarchy and gave it a parliamentary government of ministerial responsibility. It was stipulated that when Stanislas died the crown would revert to the family of the Elector of Saxony. Catherine and her advisers at once understood that this "Revolution" opened Poland's route toward the restoration of its former power, and for a time they fumed helplessly. Then, with the help of disaffected Polish nobles longing for their earlier unlimited privileges, the Tsarina selected a pretext for making war on Poland. When Stanislas Poniatovski asked Friedrich Wilhelm II of Prussia for the help guaranteed in a treaty of 1791, the German answered that he would not help to defend a constitution in which he had never concurred. This made it once more certain that Poland was doomed. Not even inspired patriots like Kollontai and Kosciuszko could save their country from the powerful armies of Russia. In 1793 Poland was partitioned for the second time (Prussia joined in at the kill), and found itself reduced to a population of about three and one half million.

[4] Frédéric-François appears to have ignored the existence of the Marainville Chopins, though two sisters of his father were living until 1845. It is at least possible that he had never heard of them.

6

The leading Polish nationalists fled to Leipzig. In 1794, by which time Nicolas Chopin had advanced to an army captaincy, Poland bred a mutiny that quickly became a full-fledged rebellion, with Kosciuszko, hero of the American Revolution and friend of George Washington, as its inflamed leader. The Polish cause prospered. Much territory was liberated. Warsaw and Vilna were taken. Kosciuszko was made dictator. But disagreements and frittering squabbles broke out among the Poles, and shortly it was the Russo-Prussian armies that were winning victories. On October 10, 1794 the Polish forces were routed at the Battle of Matsyezhovitse, where Kosciuszko was taken prisoner. Nicolas Chopin fought in that battle and fell back with the routed Poles to Praga, a Warsaw fortress-suburb. There, on November 4, they were blasted disastrously. Alexander Suvarov, the victorious Russian general, ordered the annihilation of the town, an order that resulted in the deaths of more than ten thousand soldiers and civilians. Polish resistance ceased, and in November 1795 Stanislas Poniatovski abdicated, clearing the way for the third partition, formalized in 1796. And on the horizon the squat, fateful figure of Napoleon Bonaparte was becoming clear.

Then (and not for the first time, it has been said) Nicolas Chopin decided to return to France. But he was ill, suffering from battle fatigue, perhaps complicated by wounds or a filth disease. He remained in a Warsaw momentarily again under Russian domination, a city from which many of his friends, both Polish and French, had temporarily fled or permanently emigrated. He began to give private lessons in the French language. For a time he tutored the four children of the Starostina Łączyńska (Lachinska) in their home at Cernajewo (Tsernayevo). There he met not only Napoleon's future mistress, Countess Marie Walewska (then one of his small charges), but also Countess Ludvika Skarbek, who persuaded him to become tutor to her sons at Zhelazova Vola.

On June 2, 1806 Nicolas Chopin married Tekla Yustina Kzhizhanovska, housekeeper and perhaps distant cousin to Countess Skarbek. She was a blonde with blue eyes, he a dark and not unhandsome man. Their first child, Ludvika,[5] was born on April 6,

---

[5] Ludvika Chopin, who had some literary talent, married in 1832 a professor of administrative jurisprudence, Józef Kalasanty Jędrzejewicz (Yedzheyevich), by whom she had three sons — Henrik, Anton, and Friderik — and one

1807, in Warsaw, whither the Skarbeks and Chopins had temporarily removed. Soon after her birth they returned to Zhelazova
Vola, where Nicolas and Yustina and their baby daughter lived
in an outbuilding on the Skarbek estate. It was in this narrow,
three-room, one-story building that, on February 22, 1810, Frédéric-François was born, his parents' only son.[6]

By 1810 Warsaw was the thriving center of the nominally independent, Bonaparte-created Grand Duchy. Thither, as the summer of 1810 merged into autumn, Nicolas Chopin again moved,
this time as the head of a family numbering four. He had accepted
a French professorship at the lyceum, the first of numerous teaching positions he was to fill.[7] With permission of the lyceum authorities, he and Yustina took six young boys [8] into their quarters for
private boarding-school training. Yustina had a better than elementary acquaintance with music, and she gave her husband's
pupils piano lessons, which they continued with a Czech named
Adalbert Żywny (Zhivny). She sang, and was addicted especially
to the *romances* of Jean-Jacques Rousseau. She also obliged at the
family grand piano for small entertainments and for the Italian
dancing-master's classes. Her husband could play both the flute
and the violin. It has been surmised that music-making first
brought them intimately together under the Skarbek roof. No remarkable musical talent has ever been claimed for either, but
both enjoyed music enough to be shocked when their infant son
wailed against its sounds.

daughter, also Ludvika, who married a man named Ciechomski (Tsyekhom-
ski). Ludvika Chopin died on October 29, 1855.

[6] In addition to Ludvika and Frédéric-François, the Chopins had two
younger children: Izabela, born July 9, 1811, and Emilya, born in 1813.
Emilya died in childhood, in 1827. Izabela married a school inspector, later
director of steam navigation on the Vistula River, named Anton Barcziński
(Bartsinski), and outlived everyone else in her family, not dying until 1881.

[7] At this period or somewhat later the Chopins occupied a small house in
Warsaw. I cannot trace the source of Ippolito Valetta's statement that, at
least at first, they lived in rooms in the so-called Saxon Palace, which housed
the lyceum, but I do not doubt it. They may have inhabited the palace rooms
first, their own modest dwelling later. The lyceum was transferred to the
Kasimirovski Palace early in 1817.

[8] The six included the three Wodziński (Vodzhinski) brothers, Feliks, Anton, and Kasimir. Chopin was later to fall in love with, and almost marry,
their sister Marya.

Away from the comforts of the Skarbek household, Nicolas
Chopin did not find the finances of married life easy, particularly
when the size of his family increased in 1811 and 1813. Again
Warsaw, all of Poland, was watching the countermarches of foreign armies. After the Napoleonic debacle before Moscow, the
armies of Alexander I occupied Warsaw on February 18, 1815. In
that year, too, the Congress of Vienna abased Poland in its fourth
partition. During all this ominous disquiet Nicolas Chopin struggled to increase his income. In 1812 he succeeded in obtaining the
French classes in the Military School and the School of Artillery
and Engineering. And in 1813 the lyceum promoted him to the
upper class in French literature.

During these years of struggle and alarm the Chopins made a
small discovery that delighted them. Not only was Ludvika musical and able to play the piano in a childlike way (she later composed mazurkas of minor charm), but they had been mistaken
about their son's reaction to music. He did not hate it or find it
painful. On the contrary, his little-boyish ears were so sensitive,
his musical reactions so keen, that he cried out of pleasure. No
sooner had Nicolas and Yustina learned this (which should, perhaps, have alarmed rather than pleased them), no sooner had the
little boy realized that there was something to be learned about
producing those enchanting sounds on the piano, than he began
to insist that his older sister teach it to him. And Ludvika, not
yet ten, became his first instructor in music. When she, in turn,
began to take piano lessons from Adalbert Zhivny, her tiny brother
begged to be allowed to join her. His parents granted his insistent
request in 1816, when he was six years old.

Zhivny, who had been born in Bohemia in 1756, had a fervent
admiration for Johann Sebastian Bach, then a most unusual taste.
Migrating to Warsaw, he had for some years been household pianist to a branch of the rich Sapieha family. Setting up as a private
piano instructor, he prospered, amassing something of a fortune
before his death in 1842. Originally a violinist, Zhivny never became more than an accomplished amateur at the piano. He was
a man of good taste, broad sympathies, and keen self-criticism.
Liszt, many of whose statements about Chopin's life have wilted
in the glare of scholarly examination, was probably correct in stating that Zhivny imparted a wholly classic Viennese education.

What he did not give, was incapable of giving, was a dependable foundation in the theoretical aspects of musical construction.

Frycek (Fritsek), as the boy was familiarly known, composed nonetheless, though he himself did not note down his first compositions. A Polonaise in G minor that he dedicated to Countess Victoire Skarbek in 1817 was actually published in that year.[9] More important than this first-mentioned of his juvenilia was the rapidly increasing excellence of his playing, which probably surpassed Zhivny's almost at once. News of the prodigy must have spread through aristocratic Warsaw. In *Memorial to a Good Mother*, published in 1819, Klementina Tanska-Hoffmann tells of hearing Chopin play at a soirée. She refers to him as "a child not yet eight years old who, in the opinion of connoisseurs of the art, is Mozart's heir."

In 1818, as part of a charity concert organized by the patriot and writer Ursin Niemcewicz (Nyemtsevich), little Fritsek was invited by Countess Zofia Zamoiska to perform in public for the first time. As she had been born into the Czartoryski (Chartoriski) family, this was notice from a level just below royalty. The other prodigious attraction of the event was to have been Zygmunt Krasiński aged six and already expected to become the fine poet he in truth became. But Krasinski did not appear, and the whole attention of a full salon of the highest Warsaw society was therefore focused on the fragile Chopin. It was his eighth birthday, February 22, 1818.

Although scarcely a match for Mozart or Handel, the boy who sat down at the pianoforte to play was a true prodigy. He was sensitive and intelligent; he dabbled in verse, specializing in birthday greetings to his parents; he drew and sketched with obvious talent. How proud Yustina Chopin, herself ill and unable to attend, must have been as father and son set out for the concert! How proud Nicolas must have been — and Zhivny, probably bedecked in the yellow coat and trousers he affected, and carrying a brilliant kerchief! Fritsek himself, dressed in knee-pants and velvet jacket, was at least as pleased by the special large collar he was permitted for the occasion as he was of his ability to play a concerto by Adalbert Gyrowetz.[10]

[9] See page 319.
[10] Gyrowetz (1763–1850), like Zhivny, was from Bohemia. When but

Did we know nothing of the effect that Chopin's mature playing was always to exercise under intimate circumstances, we
might suppose that the enthusiasm displayed by aristocratic Warsaw at his first public appearance was the effusiveness always
showered on a child doing anything besides act childish. It is
clear that the small blond Fritsek was attractive — though not
beautiful or even pretty — but what is clearer is that on his eighth
birthday his piano touch already bore the magic with which it was
to ensorcell close listeners all his life long. When the little boy was
taken home to his mother after the music, the applause, and the
imaginable flutterings, she asked him what the public had liked
most. His reply, according to a time-sanctioned tale that there is
no reason to doubt, was: "My collar, Mamma, my collar."

<hr/>

twenty-three, he had heard one of his symphonies led by Mozart. In later
years he had the dubious satisfaction of knowing that several of his compositions were being attributed to no less than Haydn. He was a prolific creator: his collected works included, among others, about thirty operas, nineteen Masses, sixty symphonies. As late as 1915 Alfred Einstein considered
Gyrowetz's autobiography worth republishing. Gyrowetz, in short, was one
of the minor composers now lost to listeners. His music might here and there
gratefully replace the hackneyed works of the great and familiar. And
Chopin (or Zhivny) had been stylish, not foolish or tasteless, in selecting a
Gyrowetz concerto for the debut.

II

AMAZED and delighted by the frail, dignified eight-year-old boy who performed so well at the piano, the nobility of Warsaw displayed its favor. The highest in rank to seek after and flatter Frédéric-François was Grand Duke Konstantin Pavlovich, actual ruler of Poland by virtue of his position as Commander-in-Chief of the Forces of the Kingdom (his brother, Alexander I, had declared himself King of Poland). Grandson of Catherine the Great, second son of the murdered Tsar Paul, Konstantin had been married when only seventeen to a woman who disliked him. In Warsaw, after a final attempt to persuade Juliana of Coburg to be his wife in fact as well as in name, he fell in love with a Polish lady named Yohanna Grudzińska. When it became possible, they were married; he renounced his claim to the Russian throne and she was given the courtesy title of Princess Lovitska. She joined her husband in favoring the boy Chopin. More than once the grand-ducal carriage, drawn by four Cossack-mounted horses, drew up before the Chopins' modest home to carry him off to the palace to perform. He became friendly with Princess Lovitska's son Paul and with Alexandrine de Moriolles, daughter of the boy's tutor.

Between Fritsek's eighth and fifteenth birthdays there could have been much more social preening, many more public performances than there were. But Nicolas and Yustina Chopin set themselves against any exploitation of their son's talent at the expense of his character, general and musical education, and health. Berlioz's remark that Chopin was dying all his life was not much truer of him than of the healthiest of men. Nor was Liszt justified in believing that the boy had been constantly unwell. He was delicate, however, and impressionably volatile, and naturally conscious of his talent. There can be no questioning of his parents' rightness in insisting that while he approached and then experienced adolescence he lead as average a boyish life as his musical

predilections would allow. That he was not considered average is
proved by the fact that when the Dowager Tsarina Marya Fyodo-
rovna, mother of the Tsar and of Konstantin Pavlovich, visited the
Warsaw Lyceum in 1818, he was selected to read French verses
of welcome to her. He was also permitted to present her with
two Polonaises of his own composition.[1]

In January 1820 the renowned Italian soprano Angelica Catalani gave a series of concerts in Warsaw (she had retired from
opera two years earlier). She was greatly successful. Frédéric-
François was presented to her, played for her, and won her affection. As a memento of the occasion, the dazzling lady gave him a
watch on which was engraved:

> *Mme Catalani*
> *à Frédéric Chopin,*
> *âgé*
> *de dix ans à Varsovie*
> *le 3 Janvier 1820*

Chopin kept this watch always; it descended through his sister
Ludvika to her son Anton. Liszt maintained that Chopin's only
knowledge of his own age was derived from its inscription —
though he was almost certainly not yet *"âgé de dix ans"* when
Mme Catalani presented it to him.[2]

Although Chopin had received little or no training in the theory
of musical composition, he continued to "compose." In 1820 he
dedicated a Military March to the Grand Duke. This was scored
for band and actually played for soldiers on parade. It was also
published, though without its youthful composer's name. No copy
of it is known to exist, and it is difficult to know how, if one came
to light, it could be identified with certainty, unless by dedica-

---

[1] These do not appear to survive, though one of them may be that dedicated to Countess Victoire Skarbek (see page 319).
[2] Catalani, who once earned £16,700 in a single opera season — which included some concerts — was one of the first female opera-managers. She
directed the Théâtre des Italiens in Paris from 1814 to 1817. When she
altogether gave up singing, she retired to Florence and there ran a singing-
school at which many students were given free instruction. She died, aged
sixty-nine, in Paris on June 12, 1849, four months before Chopin.

tion and date. Another of the probably numerous small pieces
that the boy turned out during these years may exist, but I have
been unable to identify it with complete assurance. He certainly
composed a Polonaise in A flat to honor Zhivny's 1821 birthday.
And James Gibbons Huneker, in his introduction to a Schirmer
edition of the Polonaises, wrote: "A facsimile reproduction of a
hitherto unpublished Polonaise in A flat was published in the
Warsaw 'Echo Musicale' to commemorate the fiftieth anniversary
of Chopin's death. Written at the age of eleven, this tiny dance
is a tentative groping after the form he later conquered so magnificently." Chopin was eleven in 1821, and the keys mentioned
are the same. The earliest of his pieces to be found in almost any
collected edition is the Polonaise in G-sharp minor, which probably dates from his twelfth year.[3] It is dull and wholly lacking
any touches of the imagination that enriches Chopin's compositions of a few years later.

By 1822 Nicolas and Yustina Chopin were ready to allow Fritsek's piano lessons with Zhivny to lapse. They were willing to
allow him to study composition, though they did not yet foresee
with certainty a composer's career for him. As his preceptor they
selected the best man in Warsaw, Joseph Elsner, a Silesian who
had become director of the newly opened Warsaw Conservatory
of Music in 1821. Elsner was a violinist and composer, and was
about fifty-four when Frédéric-François first went to him for
lessons in 1822 or 1823. He cultivated a liberal mind and enjoyed
such natural steadiness and humility that he encountered no difficulty in admitting to himself and to others that his young pupil
was soon, and in every way, his better as a musician. Chopin
naturally became deeply fond of Elsner; they communicated long
after Chopin had left Warsaw. Elsner lived to old age, outlasting
Chopin by five years, to die in 1854 at eighty-five.

From about the period of Chopin's first lessons with Elsner

[3] I should say here that Frederick Niecks, Huneker, and William Murdoch
agree in assigning the G-sharp minor Polonaise to a date after that of the
one in B-flat minor, known to have been composed in 1826. Although internal evidence is notably unreliable for judging Chopin's chronology, I agree
with Gerald Abraham, who finds in the G-sharp minor traces of Hummel
and Weber, but adds: ". . . actually there is little in the work that might
not have come from a very talented boy of twelve." Much of it certainly lies
on the keyboard like Weber at his least inspiring.

dates his intermittently lively, but banal Variations in E on a German National Air [*Der Schweizerbub*]. Although this piece was submitted to the Viennese publisher Haslinger before 1830, it was not published until 1851, two years after its composer's death, when it appeared to companion the Sonata in C minor, opus 4. As early as 1825 Chopin was able to have some of his works professionally published in Warsaw; it is my belief that he thus issued only compositions on which he had worked with Elsner or in the light of what he had learned from Elsner. Certainly his opus 1, the Rondo in C minor, is a more original piece than the Variations. Real insight into the theories and methods of composition had begun to free Chopin's genius for original creation. That is to say that Elsner was a first-rate teacher. Chopin's indebtedness to him, continually acknowledged, was genuine and important.

After a summer (1823) visit to Zhelazova Vola, Fritsek entered the lyceum, in which his father continued to teach. Despite having had no formal nonmusical education, but only that which he had been given at home, he was immediately placed in the fourth form, roughly equivalent to today's sophomore year of high school. During his first terms he was a star pupil. He took special delight in classes devoted to the study of Poland's past glories, literary and historical. The other classes were in Latin, Greek, mathematics, and natural history. In later terms his engrossment in music grew so passionate as to detract from other studies. Finally there was even some doubt about his being graduated.

Early in 1824 Fritsek and his eleven-year-old sister, Emilya, began to "publish" for the pupils of their father's boarding-school a hand-written *Literary Amusement Journal*. The charming and precocious Emilya had gleams of real literary talent. She had fallen in love with the stories of the Polish novelist Klementina Tanska-Hoffmann, and herself had written children's stories and translated into Polish — with her sister Izabela, two years her senior — a volume of German tales by Christian Gotthilf Salzmann. When Nicolas Chopin's birthday was celebrated in 1824, his family and a few intimates were regaled with the performance of a comedy by Fritsek and Emilya. *The Mistake, or the Pretended Rogue* was acted by a company that seems to have included all four of the Chopin children.

Fritsek's own literary effusions for 1824 did not end with his part in *The Mistake*. During the summer of that year he visited the country home of one of his schoolmates, Dominik Dzyevanovski. The place, in the district of Mazovia, was called Shafarnia. Instead of letters, Chopin sent his parents from there issues of a one-man hand-written journal he called the *Shafarnia Courier*. The editor's name was "Pichon," an obvious anagram of Chopin. Because government regulations required all periodicals to be censored, the *Shafarnia Courier* was "censored" too, by Dominik's sister, listed as Mme Dzyevanovska. Most of its contents are harmlessly amusing. There is talk of canters, of horseback races, of the fortunes and misfortunes of domestic animals. A cat had suffered fits. "A drake, sneaking from the poultry pen very early this morning, was drowned; to this moment no reason for this suicide has been established, and the family of the deceased will make no statement." M. Pichon had played the piano — a concerto by Friedrich Kalkbrenner.

Most of the *Shafarnia Courier* is gay, entertaining, adolescent. But it also preserves the earliest evidence of the unthinking anti-Semitism that remained — together with an overwrought sense of social hierarchy — Chopin's least attractive mental trait. Here it took a form no less cruel because so unconscious. "On August 29 a cartload of Jews came by. *Die ganze Familie* was made up of one old sow, three big Jews, two little Jews, and six head of Jew children. . . ." The mature Chopin never questioned or modified this inhumanity, though prejudice never kept him from social intercourse with a Mendelssohn, a Meyerbeer, or a Rothschild.

In September 1824 Frédéric-François was entered in the fifth form at the lyceum. Eight months later Alexander I officially opened a sitting of the Polish Diet in Warsaw. The Tsar remained in the Polish metropolis (it then had about 140,000 inhabitants) until June 13. His presence was celebrated appropriately. On May 27 and June 10 two large charity concerts were presented at the Conservatory under the direction of one of its teachers, Yozef Yavurek. At the second of these Chopin made his second public appearance.[4] At the concert of June 10, 1825 he played

---

[4] There can be little doubt that, in the years immediately succeeding his 1818 debut, he had played informally at many Warsaw homes, as well as at the grand-ducal palace.

one movement from Ignaz Moscheles's G-minor Piano Concerto, the long-popular piece with which, at the Leipzig Gewandhaus in 1832, the thirteen-year-old Clara Wieck was to make her debut. He also improvised on a hybrid instrument called the æolopantalon, invented by a Warsaw cabinet-maker. He does not appear to have performed any of his own compositions.

Reporting the June 10 concert, the Warsaw correspondent of the *Allgemeine musikalische Zeitung* (Leipzig) said nothing of the "Academist Chopin's" playing of the Moscheles, but concentrated on the æolopantalon improvisation, describing the instrument as a locally invented combination of the æolomelodicon and the pianoforte. The æolomelodicon was an immediate precursor of the harmonium, a free-reed instrument with a keyboard for releasing air pressure created by pedals. The æolopantalon somehow joined this proto-harmonium to the percussive action of the piano. It was at this instrumental mule that Chopin, says the *Zeitung*, "distinguished himself by his improvisatorial wealth of musical ideas." Further describing the boy as a "complete master" of this instrument, the writer added that with him at the keyboard it had "made a great impression."

Having been told about the æolomelodicon (also a Warsaw invention), the Tsar expressed a wish to hear it played. Accordingly, one was set up in the domed Protestant Church, the building possessing excellent acoustic properties. And Chopin again improvised. Alexander expressed his pleasure and thanked the fifteen-year-old æolomelodiconist by presenting him with a diamond ring. When, having shortly later officially closed the Diet, the Tsar left Warsaw, it was for the final time: during a journey undertaken partly for the Tsarina's health he died at Taganrog on the following December 1.

Three compositions certainly written by Chopin in 1825 continue in existence. Two Mazurkas, in G major and B-flat major, forecast the half-hundred (forty-one published during Chopin's lifetime) that make up one of the most satisfying among the groups of his works. The third 1825 piece is the Rondo in C minor, opus 1. In it are present for the first time through extended passages, and despite the feebleness of intervening measures, hints of the musical flavor now called Chopinesque. Nothing in the opening *allegro* section could surprise us as the work of another.

But in the *più lento* section that follows, the composer's profile begins to emerge in chromatic passagework, darkling harmonies, hints of sweet individual melancholy. And in the *tempo più moto* the profile has become unmistakable and clear:

This was something new under the sun. Frédéric-François Chopin was to compose music better realized in each detail; but no one else could have written even this. As the work of an adolescent it speaks with a voice all can agree to call genius. His vocation had become unmistakable. The Rondo was published in 1825 by Brzeżina (Bzhezhina) of Warsaw.[5]

During the summer vacation of 1825 Fritsek returned to Shafarnia and may also have visited Plotsk and Danzig, though the whimsical dating of his letters during this era leaves exact details impossible to establish. His final term at the Warsaw Lyceum began on September 22, 1825.[6] He had given up piano lessons with Zhivny several years earlier, but was still studying both regular school subjects and the finer points of composition. He was composing. He sometimes took the place of the organist on Sunday in the lyceum chapel. He had never been physically vigorous. Now he began to show signs of strain, of the weakness and intermittent illness that were to dog much of his later life. On February 12, 1826 he wrote Yan Bialoblotski: "They have put leeches on my throat because the glands have swollen. . . ."[7] The condition of his sister Emilya had become alarming to her parents by the spring of 1826, when she was thirteen. They determined that Yustina Chopin would take Emilya and Fritsek to Bad Reinerz, a spa in Prussian Silesia, for a summer cure, and that Ludvika, the eldest child, would accompany them. They set out from Warsaw late in July, traveling through Sokhachev, Breslau, and Glatz.

Just before going to Bad Reinerz, Chopin was graduated from the lyceum. By way of celebration he attended a singing of Rossini's delicious opera *La Gazza ladra* with his schoolmate Wilhelm Kolberg. As a souvenir of that event and of his departure he wrote a Polonaise in B-flat minor. In its first published form (Breitkopf & Härtel, 1872), its trio, in D-flat major, is headed: *"Au revoir!* After an air from *Gazza Ladra*," and there is a footnote stating that its original title was *Adieu à Guillaume Kolberg*. As the only piece known to survive from Chopin's sixteenth year, it should be included in collections of the Polonaises, from which it is now customarily omitted.

[5] In a November 1825 letter to his friend Yan Bialoblotski Chopin wrote: "I have done a new polonaise on the Barber [Rossini]." No trace of this Polonaise has been found.

[6] He was a "one-year student," which meant that the normal two years of the sixth form had for him been reduced to one.

[7] Twenty-three years later Chopin was to die of tuberculosis of the lungs and larynx.

The first of Fritsek's surviving letters from Bad Reinerz is to young Kolberg and is dated August 18. "I have been drinking whey and the local waters for two weeks," he wrote, "and they say that I am looking a little better. . . ." He describes the typical life of a spa, the walks back and forth to the wells at Brunn, the characters and types who momentarily inhabit the place. "But I have not yet been for the excursions that everyone takes," he adds, "because it's forbidden me. Near Reinerz there's a mountain with rocks known as the Heu-Scheuer, from which there's a wonderful view; but the air at the tip is not good for everyone, and unhappily I am one of the patients to whom it is not allowed." He had not been well, but he, at least, would recover most of his strength. Emilya was not to improve, and Yustina Chopin was already gravely worried over her condition.

In French the boy wrote to Elsner a letter that is a pleasant, if characteristically stiff, example of antique respect. "The fresh air and the whey that I very conscientiously take have so set me up that I am entirely changed from what I was in Warsaw. The magnificent views offered by lovely Silesia enchant and charm me; but one thing is lacking for which not all the beauties of Reinerz can compensate me — a good instrument. Imagine, Sir, that there is not one good piano, and all that I have seen are instruments that cause me more misery than pleasure."

While the Chopins remained at Bad Reinerz another of the guests died, leaving two small children orphans, unable to pay either the funeral costs or their own and an attendant's transportation home. Chopin volunteered or was asked to give a recital for their benefit. This he did on August 16 despite his probably justified depression over the local pianos. With the financial returns, however, he won the success that might have been expected, and he gave a second recital. The unfortunate deceased was buried. The servant was enabled to take the orphaned children back to whatever aunts or uncles may have been awaiting them.

On the return trip toward Warsaw, Fritsek stopped off at Stzhizhevo to be the guest of his godmother, Mme Vyesolovska, the former Countess Anna Skarbek. While there he became friendly with Prince Anton Radziwiłł (Radzivil), acting governor of the Grand Duchy of Posen. This member of a family of millionaires had married a Hohenzollern. He was an accomplished amateur cellist and composer, and took real interest in the sixteen-year-old boy of genius. In Liszt's curious *Life of Chopin,* a medley of observations on music and passages of irresponsible fiction, the statement appears that Prince Radzivil financially helped Chopin's parents to put the boy through the lyceum. This is almost certainly a misreading of one mote of evidence. Chopin's Trio in G minor for piano, violin, and cello is dedicated to Radzivil, who acknowledged this honor by sending the composer a letter and present by the hand of one Adam Kozhukhovski. This is the man whom Liszt calls the intermediary through whom the Prince "always paid his [Chopin's] pension from his first entrance into college, until the completion of his studies." Upon the publication of Liszt's book, the Chopin family formally denied this story. Aside from the fact that Radzivil had attended the charity concert at which Frédéric-François had played in 1825, nothing indicates that the two had met before the late summer of 1826, by which time Chopin's lyceum schooling was over. What is certain is that their friendship did not stop with that meeting, which occurred either at Stzhizhevo or at Radzivil's magnificent near-by estate, Antonin.

From his godmother's, Chopin proceeded to Sokolovo to visit the Bialoblotski family. Yan Bialoblotski had been one of his intimates for at least two years. The many letters written him by Chopin are models in small of letters the mature composer would continue to send several friends. They make strange reading for twentieth-century eyes and are liable to feverish misinterpretation. Their language, especially in English translation, is effusive; to us it must seem positively amorous. We cannot conceive of a modern fourteen-year-old boy writing to a school chum: "Give me a kiss and I'll forgive you." [8] Or the following phrases, all from letters of 1824, 1825, or 1826 to Yan Bialoblotski: "I kiss you heartily. . . . Give me a kiss! . . . Give your muzzle! I love you. . . . I press you to my lips. . . ." These phrases are embedded in texts alive with the ebullience of boyhood and adolescence. They indicate no more than that Fritsek had for his closest friends an emotion that was both less unusual and less suspect before Freud than it has been since.

[8] Chopin's letter of August 19, 1824, to Wilhelm Kolberg.

This is not to deny that Chopin as a youth displayed some of the recessive and almost neuter characteristics that were always to appear in his relations with women who had, or seemed to have, erotic feelings toward him. Everything known about him indicates that he wavered at the imaginary, arbitrary line that separates masculine from feminine. He was not vigorously male in emotion or in sexual appetite, however masculine much of his music proclaims his creative imagination to have been. That he was ever overtly conscious of any homosexual inclinations can be denied categorically in view of the surviving evidence, which is rich in both quantity and quality.

Home from Sokolovo, Fritsek bore a commission from Yan Bialoblotski's father: he was to order for the Bialoblotskis from the cabinet-maker Brunner a choraleon, an instrument resembling the æolopantalon. Writing to Yan on November 2, 1826, he said:

The commission or trust has been excellently fulfilled.[9] Now ask when I've had such *activitas*? A short answer — since Sokolovo. For really I got so fat, so lazy, that, in one word, I don't want to do anything, anything at all. Learn, my life, by these present lines. That I don't go to the lyceum. Really it would be stupid to sit still forcibly for six hours a day when both German and German-Polish doctors have ordered me to walk as much as I can; it would be stupid to listen twice over to the same things when one can be learning something new during this year. Meanwhile I go to Elsner for strict counterpoint, six hours a week; I hear [Kasimir] Brodziński, [Feliks] Bentkovski, and others on subjects in any way touching on music.[10]

Fritsek's claim to fatness may be discounted as playful, but there is valuable information in his other words. He was no longer attending the lyceum,[11] both because his health forbade it and

[9] As late as March 1827 the choraleon, complete by the preceding November, had not been forwarded to the Bialoblotskis: Brunner was considering the feasibility of sending it by Vistula boat.

[10] Kasimir Brodzinski (1791–1835) was a precursor of the Polish romantic master of poetry Adam Mickiewicz (Mitskyevich). A patriot, Brodzinski had been a member of the Polish Legion that aided Napoleon. His poetic output was small; his best poems are sympathetic pictures of peasant life in the Krakov area. Feliks Bentkovski (1781–1852) was a literary historian.

[11] Niecks's statement that Chopin's studies at the lyceum ended in 1827 could be made only because he was unaware of the existence of the boy's letters to Yan Bialoblotski.

because, as a "one-year student," he had already learned what was imparted more slowly to others. He was still studying theory with Elsner, and he was eagerly absorbing lectures on Polish literature and musical subjects. He had, in fact, been enrolled formally in the Principal Music School, a division of the Warsaw Conservatory of Music, shortly after his 1826 summer holiday.

Even more interesting is a passage in the same letter to Yan Bialoblotski. After saying that he may have to return to Bad Reinerz the following year for his health ("as a formality!"), Fritsek breaks out: "But it is a far cry to that; Paris would probably be better for me than the Bohemian frontier. Bartsinski is leaving before this year is over, and I — maybe in fifty years' time." In less than five years from the date of this letter Paris was to have become Chopin's permanent home.

Although Chopin published nothing during 1826, he was at work during that year on pieces that were completed or published in 1827. On January 8, 1827 he wrote to Yan Bialoblotski: "I also send you my mazurka, of which you have heard; perhaps you'll get another one later — it would be too much delight at once. They are already published; meanwhile I'm leaving my rondo, which I did want to have lithographed, smothering among my papers, though it's earlier and so has more right to travel. It's having the same luck as I'm having." The Mazurkas are probably the B-flat major and the G major composed in 1825.[12] The rondo is likely to have been the Rondo à la Mazurka, opus 5: it cannot have been the Rondo in C minor, opus 1, which had been published by Bzhezhina in 1825.

"We have illness in the house," Fritsek wrote to Yan on March 14, 1827. "Emilya has been in bed four weeks; she has a cough and has begun to spit blood, and Mamma is alarmed. Malch ordered bloodletting. They bled her once, twice. Leeches unnumbered, vesicatories, sinapisms, wolfsbane — horrors, horrors! — All this time she has eaten nothing. She has grown so thin that you wouldn't recognize her, and only now is beginning to be herself a little." But on April 10 Emilya died of tuberculosis of the lungs. Her death struck her brother with a more intimate, if scarcely a more profound, sorrow than news of Beethoven's death at Vienna

[12] I can find no record of these Mazurkas having been published by 1827, however. They appear to have been issued for the first time in 1902.

fifteen days before. The year was otherwise empty of significant
external incident for the youth devoting ever more of his fantasy,
energy, and time to composition. During the summer he returned
to Stzhizhevo to visit Mme Vyesolovska, and went on to Danzig to
be the guest for a short time of a brother to Rector Linde of the
Warsaw Lyceum.

The largest of the pieces that Chopin elaborated during 1827
was his first Sonata, the C minor, opus 4. It is the only one of his
completed and carefully worked-on compositions for which it is
impossible to feel any affection. So un-Chopinesque are these earnest pages that they appear unlikely from the hands of a young
man who had already composed the opus 1 Rondo, a fact that led
Gerald Abraham to suppose that many of them were actually
noted down long before 1827. Another piece almost certainly
composed in 1827 is the D-minor Polonaise, opus 71, no. 1, like
the Sonata a posthumous publication. In it, despite salon passagework reminiscent of the then popular Hummel and of Weber's
polonaises and *alla polaccas*, there are unmistakable premonitions
of Chopin's own masterworks in this form. There is also the Nocturne in E minor, opus 72, no. 1, which deserves better of critics
than it has received: it has some intrinsic charm and is apparently
the first of Chopin's essays in the genre of the night-piece.

Also from 1827 dates a brief piece that instantly outclassed all
that Chopin had composed earlier: the Mazurka in A minor, opus
68, no. 2, a completely realized miniature, punctual, precise, and
enchanting. Out of the simplest elements — triple time, a bass in-
clining toward the drone, displaced accents, and the filigree of
appoggiaturas and short trills — Chopin has created music wholly
his own and entirely satisfying. So familiar had he become with
the folk mazurka, heard probably at Zhelazova Vola, Stzhizhevo,
and Sokolovo, that he could re-form its characteristic elements
without the strain of self-consciousness. It has been customary to
place everything that Chopin composed at this period among his
juvenilia. But the A-minor Mazurka belongs with the best of his
numerous triumphs in this form. With a few other compositions
it entitles him to appear in the company of such young creative
prodigies as Handel, Mozart, and Mendelssohn.

More important for Chopin's reputation among his friends and
contemporaries was his opus 2, also composed or completed dur-

ing his eighteenth year. *"Là ci darem la mano,* varied for piano with orchestra accompaniment," dedicated to his most adored friend Tytus Woyciechowski (Voitsyekhovski) would be published in Vienna in 1830. Then it would win for its creator a ringing salute from the slightly younger paladin of musical romanticism, Robert Schumann. It was to make Chopin's a familiar name in the German states. Today it is all but forgotten. Between the extreme of Schumann's overpraise and today's neglect lies the fate the piece's inherent qualities justify. The music has, in addition to the irrepressible beauty of Mozart's duet, a plethora of surface charms. What it altogether lacks is original musical ideas.

III

O N February 22, 1828 Chopin celebrated his eighteenth birthday. The year that followed was to be of signal importance to him. It began the gradual process that would at last separate him from Poland and transform him into a Parisian. It gave him his first eager glimpses of life in the great cities beyond the Polish borders. It was not so rich in new compositions as 1827, partly because he still had burnishing to do on earlier pieces, partly because he spent considerable time in moving from place to place. But 1828 permitted him to hear music performed under optimum conditions that could not be duplicated in Warsaw despite the Polish capital's recognized musicality.

The early part of 1828 passed for the young Chopin in what had become average activities. He put the last touches on the Variations on *"Là ci darem la mano,"* and probably also began the C-major Rondo for two pianos, opus 73, and the Polonaise in B-flat major, opus 71, no. 2. When he had completed his second year as a Conservatory student, he again went to the country, visiting Sanniki, Stzhizhevo, and perhaps Danzig. Returned to Warsaw, he wrote Tytus Voitsyekhovski that he had begun to work at a trio (in G minor, opus 8, for piano, violin, and cello). "I expect this trio to have the same luck as my sonata and variations," he wrote. "They are already at Leipzig.[1] The first, as you know, is dedicated to Elsner; on the second — perhaps too boldly — I have put your name. My heart asked for it and our friendship allowed it, so don't be angry." He told Tytus of having heard two Rossini operas — *Il Barbiere di Siviglia* and *Otello* — and of being asked to contribute an article on the state of Polish music to François-Joseph Fétis's new Parisian *Revue musicale*. Naïvely he added: "I

[1] This is probably a mistake for Vienna, though it is possible that he approached a Leipzig publisher before sending the Sonata and Variations to Haslinger in Vienna.

have not yet judgment enough for a leading Parisian paper, which must publish only the truth." Within a few years the venality of the French press must have become a commonplace to him.

The exciting news in Fritsek's letter of September 9, 1828 to Tytus was that he was leaving for Berlin that same day. Professor Jarocki (Yarotski), a botanist or zoologist who taught at the University of Warsaw, was among the two hundred naturalists invited by Friedrich Wilhelm III to attend a congress at the University of Berlin under the presidency of Alexander von Humboldt. And Yarotski, a close friend of Nicolas Chopin, had suggested taking the young man with him. He was friendly with Martin Heinrich Carl Lichtenstein, explorer and zoologist, secretary of the congress, who was well acquainted with prominent musicians through the Berlin Singakademie, of which he was a member. These included its director, Carl Friedrich Zelter, friend of Goethe and teacher of Mendelssohn. During the congress, too, the great Spontini was to conduct one of his operas, either *Olimpia* or *Fernand Cortez*. Although Lichtenstein was not on friendly terms with Spontini, he might introduce Yarotski's youthful traveling companion to Mendelssohn and the fashionable pianists of the hour. It was small wonder that Fritsek wrote: "I'm writing now in a half-crazy state because I really don't know what's happening to me," or that he ended the letter in a flurry of kisses for Tytus.

The two travelers from Poland arrived in Berlin on Sunday, September 14, and put up at the Kronprinz Inn. Because they had to pay a courtesy call on Lichtenstein, Chopin could not go to a performance of *Das unterbrochene Opferfest,* an opera by the recently deceased but still enormously popular Peter von Winter. At Lichtenstein's quarters they were presented to the famous Humboldt, who might have told them thrilling anecdotes of his travels in Cuba, Mexico, and South America. Chopin, however, would certainly have preferred to hear Lichtenstein talk about his friend Carl Maria von Weber, who had died in London just two years before.

On September 15 the impatient Chopin suffered through a banquet held for members of the scientific congress. This stretched out so long that at last he had to abandon going to hear a recital by a nine-year-old violinist named Birnbaum. Writing to his

parents the following day, he announced that he had asked Yarotski to let him dine alone and thus be able to arrive on time for
the performance of *Fernand Cortez*. He added that he would have
preferred to spend the morning at Schlesinger's [2] music store
rather than wandering about the thirteen salons devoted to the
congress. He had visited two piano factories in vain, but the host
at the Kronprinz had a piano on which he could play. "Our inn-
keeper admires me every day when I go to visit him, or rather his
instrument."

By Saturday, September 20, Chopin was happier. He had heard
not only *Fernand Cortez*, but also Cimarosa's *Il Matrimonio se-
greto*, George Onslow's *Le Colporteur*,[3] and — "nearer to the ideal
I have formed of great music" — Handel's *Ode for St. Cecilia's
Day*. "Tomorrow," he added, "*Freischütz!*" Congress affairs prevented Lichtenstein from having time to introduce Yarotski's
young companion to the great and near great. Chopin therefore
had to glean what satisfaction he could from viewing at a distance
such celebrities as Spontini, Zelter, Mendelssohn, whose name he
constantly and variously misspelled, and the future Friedrich
Wilhelm IV. He was too shy to introduce himself to any of
them.

On September 27 the third and last of Fritsek's Saturday re-
ports from Berlin to his family announced that he would be home
on October 6 and that Yarotski and he would stop en route at
Posen for two days, having been invited to a dinner by its archbishop. As he had earlier remarked that Prince Anton Radzivil was
about to reach Berlin, this suggests that he had seen both Radzivil
and the archbishop, the leading prelate of Radzivil's territorial
estates. "My holiday is doing me good," Fritsek assured those at
home. "I do nothing but go to theater." In this letter he mentioned
only Winter's *Das unterbrochene Opferfest*, of which he expressed
no opinion. "Among the more important scenes of my trip I can
number my second dinner with the naturalists. . . . Every living
creature sang, and all who sat at the table drank and clinked

---

[2] Members of the Schlesinger family were later to be his publishers in both
Berlin and Paris.

[3] George Onslow was an Anglo-French composer whose somewhat saccharine chamber music had an intense brief vogue. On the death of Cherubini
in 1842, Onslow was elected to his place in the Institut.

glasses in time with the music. Zelter conducted. In front of him, on a crimson pedestal, stood a huge golden goblet, a mark of the highest musical status. We ate more than usual for the following reason: the naturalists, and especially the zoologists, have busied themselves chiefly with the improvement of meat, sauces, broth, and such things. So they have made great progress in eating during the few days of the session."

During the early morning of September 28 Yarotski and Chopin left Berlin by diligence for Posen. Their route ran through Frankfurt an der Oder. Beyond that town, at the post-station of Züllichau, they were distressed when the station-master reported that fresh horses were not immediately available, that they would have to wait for at least one hour. The indifferent attractions of the village were soon exhausted. Returning to the station, they found the diligence still horseless. Yarotski began to while away the time by eating and drinking, but Chopin, noticing that there was a piano in an adjacent room, sat down to try it out, improvising on a Polish folk tune. Finding the instrument in better condition than likely, he kept on. An audience slowly gathered: other diligence passengers, the postmaster and his wife and daughters — all soon were listening, quiet and attentive, to the charming improvisation.

Suddenly they were interrupted: "Gentlemen, the horses are ready!" Chopin leaped up from the piano, eager to get on to Posen. But now his audience did not want him to stop playing, and after some cajoling (in later years he remembered the postmaster's daughter as pretty), he consented to play a little longer. He finished improvising — on one of the melodies used in his Grand Fantasy on Polish Airs, opus 13 — whereupon the postmaster treated the assemblage to wine, himself toasting the pianist as the "favored of Polyhymnia." One village elder, saying that he himself when young had played the piano, remarked: "If Mozart had heard you, he would have taken your hand and shouted 'Bravo!'" In response to this sincere praise Chopin gracefully reseated himself at the keyboard and kept horses and willing passengers waiting the time it took him to perform a mazurka. Then the delighted postmaster carried him as though in triumph to the steps of the diligence.

During the two days Chopin passed as a guest of Archbishop

Wolicki (Volitski) he saw a good deal of Prince Radzivil. It is likely that he played through, or at least talked over, his unfinished Trio, for the Prince was a chamber-music enthusiast. Although Radzivil certainly did not, as Liszt stated, pay for Chopin's "complete education" (a thing Chopin never had), the youth felt toward him sufficient friendship to dedicate the Trio to him when it was finally published, by Probst-Kistner of Leipzig, in March 1833, as his opus 8. It was this Trio, among other compositions, that Chopin began to complete after reaching Warsaw on October 6. Realizing the potential importance of his composing, his parents had set aside a small room as his studio. It was there, during the last months of 1828 and the first of 1829 that he labored over the Trio; the Grand Fantasy on Polish Airs, opus 13; the Krakoviak, opus 14, and several small pieces for piano alone.[4]

The compositions that Chopin worked over in 1828–9 show that he had begun to plan a career as a pianist. He was now concentrating his energies chiefly on the production of concert pieces, longer compositions with orchestral accompaniment. These were to be the vehicles of his own public appearances. Such are the Grand Fantasy and the Krakoviak: he was not yet ready to attempt a full-fledged concerto. Both are wide steps ahead of the Variations on "*Là ci darem la mano*"; both are difficult and ostentatious, elaborated to display the performer's technique. In plan, in pattern, they are preliminary, weak, and finally frustrating. But in melody they are earnests of Chopin's exhaustless store, while in harmonic and rhythmic variety they are his most accomplished creations up to the date of their completion. They should be restored to concert life if, in the attempt to bring their sparse, inept orchestration up to parity with the volume of a modern concert grand piano and a modern concert hall, conductors and orchestrators could be persuaded not to deprive them of their essential, and now antique, delicacy.

Writing to Tytus Voitsyekhovski on December 27, 1828, Fritsek

---

[4] These included the F-minor Polonaise, opus 71, no. 3; the Waltzes in B minor, opus 69, no. 2, in D-flat major, opus 70, no. 3, and in E major, no opus, published in 1872; the D-major Mazurka, no opus, rewritten in 1832, published in both versions in 1851 and republished in 1902; and the Funeral March, opus 72, no. 2.

rambled and gossiped. A governess had become pregnant. "The best part of that is that they at first thought that I must have been the seducer because during more than a month at Sanniki I had continually walked in the garden with the governess. But I walked, and that was all. She is unattractive. Poor me — I have no appetite for such good luck for myself." He was scoring the Krakoviak; the Trio remained incomplete. He wrote of a Rondo for two pantaleons, describing it as "orphaned." [5] "You don't like to be kissed," Fritsek added below his signature. "But let me do it today." His spirits had risen to overflowing. This is the letter of a happy scatterbrain.

There were more than Tytus that Frédéric-François Chopin longed to kiss. One of his fellow pupils at the Warsaw Conservatory was Konstantsya Gladkovska. Toward her fresh charm he began, late in April 1829, to direct his previously unfocused ardors, his artistic idealism, his unformulated, indefinite sexual yearnings. He was a delicate and sensitive youth, too shy, too unforceful, too mentally exalted, to attempt seduction, caresses, flirtation, or, for that matter, even speech with the girl who soon meant to him poetry, music, passion, and the weaving of dreams. It is clear that his masculine component responded to Konstantsya Gladkovska in exact parallel to the passionate but inactive response of his feminine component to the independent, masculine, friendly, but indifferent Tytus. This ambiguity in Chopin's reaction to all women and some men is important to us because its complex counterpart exists in his music. It was important to him for its immediate sensations and because it strongly influenced the course of his mature life.

Early in 1829 Chopin heard in Warsaw two of the foremost virtuosos of the time, the pianist Hummel and the legendary violinist Paganini. With Hummel he became friendly, but his contact with Paganini was cursory. The violinist's pyrotechnic playing and dazzling talent for composing music to display that playing suggested to Chopin, as they did even more forcefully to Liszt, the possibility of applying them to the piano, though Chopin soon

---

[5] I have been unable to trace or identify this composition. It is probably not the C-major Rondo for two pianos, opus 73, which Chopin mentions in the same letter as having been rewritten on September 9.

discarded the suggestion. The brilliance of the Études, of which the earliest date from 1829, is of another nature.[6]

Johann Nepomuk Hummel, noted for the imperial elegance of his playing, the suavity of his compositions, and his Beethoven-rivaling improvisations, influenced Chopin more lastingly. The orderly Hummel had, in 1828, published a *School of the Piano* notable, among other qualities, for its advocacy of a practical method of fingering. To this important detail the maturing Chopin was to pay the closest attention. Although no particular fingering will prove suitable for all hands, the indications that Chopin wrote into his pieces are of almost as much importance in determining procedure for a proper performance as is study of his agogic signposts. Nor is this the only department in which Hummel's influence may be discerned in Chopin's music: very often Chopin's figurations and simpler harmonic motions are those of a composer who could scarcely have composed exactly that way if he had remained unacquainted with Hummel's music.

In July 1829 Chopin passed his final examinations at the Warsaw Conservatory. Elsner's report on his pupil's standing in composition classes reads as follows: "Lessons in musical composition: Chopin, Frideric, third-year student, amazing capabilities, musical genius." It was never Chopin's unhappy lot to be unappreciated or misdirected by his teachers, musical equals, or musical superiors. His problem was always the full and wise cultivation of abilities admitted and genius praised. That he never became overbearing or unpleasantly egotistical testifies to mental balance and innate sweetness of disposition. A snob and a bigot he could, at times, show himself to be; an egomaniac or megalomaniac he never became.

On at least one occasion the Polish Ministry of Public Education had granted a fellowship for foreign travel and study to an especially promising graduate of the Conservatory. With this in mind, in April 1829 Nicolas Chopin applied to the proper minister for such a grant to Frédéric-François, adducing the enthusiasm of royal personages — the late Alexander I and Grand Duke Konstantin Pavlovich — and of connoisseurs as proof of the young man's talent. The minister endorsed the application, but in June

[6] The A-major Variations, entitled *Souvenir de Paganini,* first published in 1881, probably reflected Chopin's bedazzlement.

the final authorities, their treasury perhaps depleted by the expenses of the recent coronation of Nicholas I as King of Poland, rejected the application out of hand. Nicolas Chopin had asked funds for a three-year trip to France, Italy, and Germany. The official reply was almost brutal: "State funds cannot be wasted [crossed out] applied to the support of this class of artists." The nature of the talents displayed by the young Chopin as a pianist and as a composer exclusively for piano very probably weighted this decision. One of his classmates who had won such a government subsidy was recognized chiefly as the composer of a large-scale Mass.

By July 20, the date of Elsner's report, Chopin was off on his second long journey abroad. He had set out from Warsaw with at least three other youths, Celiński (Tselinski), Hube, and Franciszek Maciejowski (Frantsishek Matsyeyovski), the last a nephew of Nicolas Chopin's friend Waclaw (Vatslav) Alexander Matsyeyovski, a professor of jurisprudence at the University of Warsaw. The friends went first to Poland's magnificent ancient capital, Krakov. Thence, after midday dinner on a Saturday, probably July 24, they set out in a privately hired carriage for Ojców (Oitsov), heart of the region foolishly called "the Polish Switzerland." This country had been lovingly described by Klementina Tanska-Hoffmann, the writer so much admired by Chopin's dead sister Emilya. The young men were looking for a man named Indik who put up travelers for the night in a house where the novelist had stayed. Their peasant driver got them to Oitsov, where they learned that Indik's house lay about five miles out of town. Soon they had become lost, and at last they found themselves stuck between boulders in the shallow Pradnik River. Out of the carriage, they wandered about helplessly until they were rescued at nine o'clock that evening by passers-by who guided them along the two-and-one-half-mile walk to Indik's place.

Chopin and his friends at last reached their goal in complete darkness. Their astonished host gave them one room in a travelers' hut built under an overhanging cliff. Although Fritsek was excited to know that he was in the very room in which Mme Tanska-Hoffmann had slept, he found that room not very comfortable. He and his companions had arrived drenched. The others were drying their clothing by the fire, but he hesitated to undress.

33

Then, watching Indik's daughter fetch bedding from a cupboard, he spied a pile of the double woolen caps characteristic of the Krakov district. Having persuaded the girl to sell him one of these, he tore it into two pieces, wrapped one piece about each of his wet, cold feet, and felt that he had saved himself from a chill. Then he sat by the cheering fire with his friends, drank a little wine, and went contentedly to sleep on one of the beds Indik had made up for them on the floor. He described this incident in detail when writing from Vienna to his family one week later.

From the neighborhood of Oitsov, the group traveled on through Byelsk to Upper Silesia and Moravia — modern Czechoslovakia. Thence they went into Austria proper and arrived at Vienna on the evening of July 31, 1829.

IV

VIENNA was the first foreign city in which Chopin was to offer his talents as composer pianist to a metropolitan audience acquainted intimately with performances by the leading composer virtuosos of the day. Beethoven had died there only twenty-eight months before Chopin's arrival, Schubert but eight and one half months. It was because the lovely Austrian city shared with Paris the musical captaincy of the Western World that Fritsek had been able to persuade his father to the expenditure that permitted him to accompany his friends. In Vienna, also, was the publisher Tobias Haslinger, to whom, two years earlier, he had sent for publication his C-minor Sonata, Variations on a German National Air, and Variations on *"Là ci darem la mano."*

"Thanks to Elsner's letter," Fritsek wrote to his parents from Vienna on August 8, "Haslinger doesn't know what to do with me. He told his son to play to me, showed me everything of musical interest that he has, and apologized for not introducing me to his wife because she is away from home. With all that he still has not printed my things. I didn't ask him about them, but while showing me his finest editions he told me that my Variations [on *"Là ci darem la mano"*] will probably come out in one week in the *Odeon*. I didn't expect that." He must have found it interesting to discuss music with this man, who had known Beethoven well. But he was correct in not expecting his Variations to appear so soon: they were actually issued about seven months later, probably in March 1830. As for the other Variations and the stiff C-minor Sonata, it was not until three years after Tobias Haslinger's death that his son — the boy Karl, whose accomplishments at the keyboard had been displayed to Chopin in 1829 — sent proofs of them to the composer in Paris. Not until Chopin himself had been dead two years did Karl Haslinger, in 1851, get around to issuing the stillborn, unattractive pieces.

Fritsek's August 8th letter home is dotted with the names of musically important individuals whom he had either met or heard in performance. Ignaz Schuppanzigh, onetime teacher and long-time friend of Beethoven (he had led Razumovsky's quartet), had told him that though he was not giving recitals at the time, he would try to arrange one during the young man's Vienna stay. Having played informally at the home of Count Hussarzewski (Hussazhevski), an old Polish nobleman whom he had met in Warsaw, Chopin was urged to present a public concert. Two piano-manufacturers, Stein and Graff ("who, by the way, makes better instruments"), had offered to send pianos to his lodgings and to any concert he might give. Among those urging the concert upon him were Wenzel W. Würfel, a conductor and pianist whom he knew from Warsaw, and the journalist Blahetka. He had been pre-sented to the fabulous Count Wenzel Robert von Gallenberg, whose wife was Beethoven's Giulietta Guicciardi, and who had been a friend and colleague of Domenico Barbaja, the itinerant impresario whose mistress had become Rossini's first wife. "He is director of the theater where I have already heard several bad concerts. . . . Only Czerny I have not yet met, but Haslinger promises to introduce me to him."

Among the musical performances that Chopin had attended during his first week in Vienna were three operas: one called *Kosciuszko,* Boïeldieu's *La Dame blanche,* and Meyerbeer's *Il Crociato in Egitto.* He had twice heard solos played by Joseph Mayseder, another member of Schuppanzigh's quartet. He was about to hear an opera he calls "Joseph in Egypt," possibly Méhul's *Joseph* or Rossini's *Mosè in Egitto.* His August 8th letter ends with a postscript in which he announces his decision to give the concert so universally being urged upon him.

Blahetka says that I shall make a furor, that I'm a virtuoso of the first class, that I rank with Moscheles, Herz, and Kalkbrenner. Würfel today introduced me to Count Gallenberg, Kapellmeister Seyfried,[1] and everyone else he encountered, as a young man he was persuading to give a concert (*nota bene,* without remuneration), which greatly

---

[1] Ignaz Xaver, Count von Seyfried, who had studied the piano with Mozart, composition with Haydn and Winter, had conducted for Emanuel Schikane-der (producer of *Die Zauberflöte*), and had been close to Mozart. His hun-dreds of compositions are now unheard.

pleased Count Gallenberg, as it is a question of his purse. The journalists
all stare at me with round eyes; the members of the orchestra bow
deeply because the director of the Italian Opera, which no longer exists, walks arm in arm with me. Würfel makes everything simple for
me; he will himself attend the rehearsal, and is really taking pains over
my debut. . . . I hope the Lord will help me. Don't worry!

Frédéric-François Chopin's first Vienna concert was announced
for Tuesday, August 11, 1829, at the Kärntnertortheater. He originally intended to present the following program:

1. Overture to *Die Geschöpfe des Prometheus* — Beethoven
2. Variations on *"Là ci darem la mano"* — Chopin, with the composer at the piano
3. Songs — Vaccai and Rossini, sung by Mme Charlotte Veltheim
4. Krakoviak, Grand Concert Rondo — Chopin, with the composer
   at the piano
5. More songs, sung by Mme Charlotte Veltheim
6. A short ballet

At the first rehearsals, however, it was discovered that the men
of the orchestra had excessive trouble with the parts for the
Krakoviak, which may well have been badly copied. Chopin
agreed to replace it with solo improvisations, which turned out to
be on a drinking song called *"Khmyel"* ("The Hop Plant") and
on a theme or themes from *La Dame blanche*.

Reporting to his parents and sisters on August 12, Chopin wrote:

So yesterday, that is, Tuesday evening at 7, in the Imperial-and-Royal
Opera House I made my entry into the world! . . . As soon as I appeared on the stage the bravos began; after each variation the applause was so loud that I couldn't hear the orchestra's tutti. When I
finished, they clapped so much that I had to go out to bow a second
time. The *Freie Phantasie* [i.e., the solo improvisations] didn't go off
quite so well, but there was a lot of clapping and bravos, and I had
to go out again. . . . My friends and colleagues spread themselves
through the hall to listen to opinions and criticisms. Tselinski can tell
you how little fault-finding there was; only Hube overheard more.
Some lady said: "Too bad the young man is so poorly dressed." If
that is all the fault anybody found — and otherwise they assure me
that they heard only compliments and that they themselves never
started the bravos— then I don't have to worry!

In the same letter Chopin discusses a subject that was to be bruited whenever and wherever he played the piano in public. "All the same, it is being said everywhere that I played too softly, or, rather, too delicately, for people used to the piano-pounding of the artists here. I expect to find this reproach in the paper, especially as the editor's daughter [Leopoldine Blahetka] thumps frightfully. It doesn't matter, there must always be a *but* somewhere, and I should prefer this one to having people say that I played too loudly." Chopin's touch, though capable of great volume when he desired to produce it, always remained too soft and delicate for the taste of audiences in the larger concert halls. He was at his best in a smaller salon, and in a big one never electrified listeners as did the more resplendent and voluminous touches of Thalberg, Liszt, and Kalkbrenner.

Between Fritsek's August 8th and August 12th letters to Warsaw he met more of the locally prominent musicians. Among them were Adalbert Gyrowetz, whose concerto he had played in Warsaw on his eighth birthday; Schubert's friend Franz Lachner; Mayseder; and the composer Conradin Kreutzer, then *Kapellmeister* at the Kärntnertortheater. After the news he ended his August 12th letter with the following high jinks: "Today I am wiser and more experienced by about four years. Ah! You must have been surprised that my last letter was sealed with 'Madeira.' I was so distracted that I picked up the seal nearest my hand — it was the waiter's — and sealed my letter in a hurry."

For the elegance of his playing Chopin was fawned on by such representatives of high Vienna society as the Schwarzenbergs, the Wrbnas, and the Dietrichstein whom Francis II had sent to watch over the son of Napoleon and Marie-Louise. The constantly attentive Würfel presented him to Count Moritz Lichnowsky, the friend and patron to whom Beethoven had dedicated both the E-minor Sonata, opus 90, and the magnificent "*Eroica*" Variations. The sonata was rumored to depict Lichnowsky's infatuation for a singer, Fräulein Stammler, the lady whom Chopin now met as Countess Lichnowska. "Countess Lichnowska and her daughter, who came onto the stage, are greatly delighted that I am to give a second concert next Tuesday," he wrote on August 13. "She told me that if I go to Paris by way of Vienna I should not forget to call on them, and that they will give me a letter to some *com-*

tesse, Lichnowsky's sister." He had also met Czerny, who smothered him in compliments; they had played two-piano music together. His decision to give a second concert was definite.

"I shan't give a third concert, and wouldn't even give a second except that they insist on it. Besides, it occurred to me that people in Warsaw might say: 'What's this? He gave only one concert and then left? Perhaps it was a failure.' I am promised good reviews. Today I called on a journalist; luckily he likes me. . . . This time I shall again play for nothing, but that is to please the Count [Gallenberg], whose purse is emaciated. But this is a secret. I shall play the Rondo [Krakoviak] and improvise." Incorrectly deducing that the smallness of Chopin's tone at the first concert had been the fault of the Graff piano used, Count Lichnowsky offered his own piano for the second. Writing to Tytus about this in September, Chopin made clear the consciousness with which he had imposed limitations upon himself: "Lichnowsky, Beethoven's protector, wanted to give me his pianoforte for the concert — that's a good deal to offer. He thought that mine was too weak in tone. But that is my way of playing, which, again, delights the ladies, and especially Blahetka's daughter, the leading pianist of Vienna."

At the Kärntnertortheater, on Tuesday, August 18, Chopin gave his second Viennese concert. It seems to have concluded, like the first, with a short ballet. It also contained the Overture to Peter Joseph von Lindpaintner's *Der Bergkönig;* a Mayseder Polonaise for violin, played by a prodigy named Joseph Khayl, and Chopin's Krakoviak and Variations on *"Là ci darem la mano,"* the latter repeated by request. This time one of the composer's Polish friends, Tomas Nidetski, had generously undertaken to correct the orchestral parts of the Krakoviak, and the orchestra was able to perform them without difficulty.

Writing to his parents on the day following the concert, their Fritsek was exuberantly satisfied:

If I was well received the first time, it was still better yesterday. The moment I appeared on the stage there were bravos, three times repeated, and the audience was larger. Baron —— I don't know his name, the manager of the theater, thanked me for the take, saying: "If such a crowd has come, it is surely not for the ballet, which everybody knows well." All the professional musicians are captivated by my Rondo. Beginning with Kapellmeister Lachner and ending with the pianoforte-tuner, they are surprised by the beauty of the composition. I know that both ladies and artists liked me. Gyrowetz, standing near Tselinski, clapped and shouted "Bravo!" I only don't know whether I pleased the petrified Germans. . . . I have played twice, and the second success was greater than the first. It goes crescendo. That's what I like.

Blahetka, with whose pianist daughter Chopin had indulged in a mild flirtation, expressed astonishment that so much of the art of music could be learned in Warsaw. "I answered that under Zhivny and Elsner the greatest donkey could learn." Schuppanzigh, to whose insistence that he soon return to Vienna Chopin replied that he would come back to learn, remarked testily: "Then you have nothing to come for." Czerny, whom Chopin later described to Tytus as "a good fellow, but nothing more," and whom he also characterized for his parents as "more sensitive than any of his compositions," was one of many Viennese unashamed to show their sadness over the young Chopin's departure. Blahetka, his daughter, Schuppanzigh, Gyrowetz, Lachner, Kreutzer, and Seyfried had been deeply impressed by the winning personality and mercurial genius of the slender, blond young man from Warsaw. The son of Stein the piano-manufacturer actually wept while saying good-by to him. This response flattered Chopin, who again and again made clear his pleasure over having "captured both the learned and the emotional folk." His only expressed regret at leaving Vienna was that he was leaving too soon to see the press reviews of his concerts. At nine o'clock on the evening of Wednesday, August 19, he and one or two of the friends with whom he had left Warsaw (Hube, at least, lingered in Vienna) climbed into the Prague *Eilwagen*. Nidetski and some other Vienna Poles rode out with them for half an hour and then returned to the city. Chopin and his companions arrived in Prague at noon on Friday, August 21.

When reviews of Chopin's compositions and playing did appear in the Vienna press, they were preponderantly enthusiastic. Of the first concert the *Wiener Theaterzeitung* said in part (August 20, 1829):

His playing, like his compositions — of which on this occasion we heard only variations — has a certain modest character that seems to indicate that to shine is not the aim of this young man, though his execution conquered difficulties the overcoming of which could not fail to astonish even here, in the home of pianoforte virtuosos. Nay, with almost ironical naïveté he takes it into his head to entertain a large audience with music as music. And lo, he succeeded in this. . . . His touch, though neat and certain, has little of that brilliance by which our virtuosos announce themselves as such in the first bars. . . . He plays very quietly, without the daring élan that generally distinguishes the artist from the amateur immediately. . . . As in his playing he was like a beautiful young tree that stands free and full of fragrant blossoms and ripening fruit, so he showed as much estimable individuality in his compositions. . . .

Of the second concert the same paper (September 1, 1829) said:

He is a young man who goes his own way and knows how to please in that way, though his style of playing and composing differs greatly from that of other virtuosos; and, indeed, chiefly in this, that the desire to make good music in his case notably dominates the desire to please.[2]

The *Wiener Zeitschrift für Kunst, Literatur, Theater und Mode* likewise reviewed both concerts, and generally was full of praise. In the second notice, however, the critic could not refrain from saying: "A longer stay in Vienna might be to the advantage of his touch as well as of his ensemble playing with the orchestra." But the most important criticism of Chopin's trial flights in Vienna appeared on November 18, 1829, when a writer in the *Allgemeine musikalische Zeitung* (Niecks thought that it was the paper's former editor, Friedrich August Kanne), after wrongly calling Chopin a pupil of Würfel, went on:

The exquisite delicacy of his touch, his indescribable mechanical dexterity, his finished shading and portamento, which reflect the deepest feeling; the lucidity of his interpretation, and his compositions, which bear the mark of great genius — *variazioni di bravura,* rondo, free fantasia — reveal a virtuoso most generously endowed by nature, who, without previous trumpet blasts, appears on the horizon like one of the most brilliant meteors.

[2] Chopin was rightly infuriated to discover later that a Warsaw paper had mistranslated the last clause, making it read: ". . . that the desire to make good music in his case is notably dominated by the desire to please." He suspected this misinterpretation as a conscious attempt to make him appear ridiculous.

Kanne — if it was he — had well spoken of Chopin as a meteor. But it was not as a virtuoso that he was to blaze meteorlike. As Frédéric-François's life progressed, it became clear that the most important result of his Vienna visit was Haslinger's promise, made just before Chopin left for Prague, to publish his Variations on *"Là ci darem la mano"* within five weeks. Although this promise was not kept to the letter, it was kept — within seven months. And that piece of published music was to win for Chopin his first enthusiastic salute from one of his peers.

Arrived in Prague, the Polish friends had dinner and went to visit the Cathedral. As Matsyeyovski had a letter of introduction to Vatslav Hanka, philologist and librarian of the National Museum, they then called on him, but found him out. When they finally met Hanka, he was pleased to have from Chopin news of his friends the Skarbeks. He asked the young men to inscribe their names in the museum's book of visitors. As Chopin wrote his parents, "Sveikovski [3] wrote a long speech. What was a poor musician to do? Luckily, Matsyeyovski hit upon the idea of writing a four-verse mazurka, so I added music to it and inscribed myself together with the poet as originally as possible. Hanka was pleased: it was a *mazur* for him, celebrating his services to the Slavonic world."

Later in the same letter (dated at Dresden on August 26), Chopin added that a letter from Blahetka and Würfel had won him a kind reception from the renowned violinist and conductor Friedrich Wilhelm Pixis (the younger). Würfel had also given him an introduction to the organist of the Saxon court, August Alexander Klengel, pupil and friend of Muzio Clementi. Chopin had expected to deliver this in Dresden. While calling on Pixis in Prague, however, he saw Klengel's calling-card on a table. When Pixis learned that his young guest had been hoping to meet the distinguished organist in Dresden, he instantly invited him to dine with Klengel and himself that evening. Klengel played his own fugues for two hours. "I didn't play," Fritsek told his family, "because they didn't ask me to do so. He plays well, but I should have liked him to play better (hush)." Klengel maintained the chain

---

[3] It is possible that this man had accompanied Chopin and his other friends from Warsaw. He is not mentioned earlier in Chopin's letters, however, and may therefore have joined them in Vienna.

of introductions by giving Chopin a letter, to be presented in Dresden, to the Royal Saxon *Kapellmeister,* Weber's onetime stumbling-block, Francesco Morlacchi.

Chopin held to a decision not to play publicly in Prague, adducing as one reason that Paganini had been poorly received there. But in Teplitz, whither he and his friends went after three days in the Bohemian capital, he did perform privately under the highest social auspices. The trip from Prague to Teplitz took from noon to evening by *Separatwagen.* The next morning Chopin encountered a Polish acquaintance named Ludvik Lempitski, who invited him to spend the evening at the home of Prince Clary. Having accepted, Chopin set out for a day of sightseeing with his friends. "In the evening, instead of going to theater, I dressed, put on the white gloves of my second Viennese concert, and at eight thirty went with Lempitski to the Prince's." He enumerated the assembled company as "some Austrian prince, some general — I've forgotten their names — an English sea-captain, several fashionable young men — probably also Austrian princes — and a Saxon general named Leiser, covered with orders and with a scar on his face."

When he was invited to play, Chopin asked for a theme on which to improvise. After some discussion the tutor to Clary's son was summoned. He suggested a melody from Rossini's *Mosè in Egitto.* The improvisation apparently pleased, as the pianist was bidden back to the keyboard thrice during the evening. Learning that Chopin was en route to Dresden, General Leiser wrote a combination French-German letter recommending him to Baron von Friesen, master of ceremonies to the King of Saxony. Then Lempitski offered to take Chopin to Dresden with him if the traveler would remain in Teplitz for another dinner to which the Clarys had invited him. Chopin declined. Instead, at five o'clock in the morning of August 26 he set off with Sveikovski and Matsyeyovski in a hackney-coach, by which means they arrived at Dresden by four that afternoon.

On his first day in the Saxon metropolis Chopin called on Baron von Friesen, walked through a picture gallery, visited a produce exhibition, looked at the principal gardens, and stood in line outside a theater from four thirty until six o'clock to get into a performance of Ludwig Tieck's adaptation of the first part of *Faust*

43

(it was Goethe's eightieth birthday) that lasted from six to eleven. Karl Devrient, the foremost German actor of the period, was Faust, and between the acts selections from Spohr's operatic setting of the play were performed. On another day Francesco Morlacchi called (Chopin recognized this as an honor) and took him to visit Mme Pesadori, *née* Pechwell, a pupil of Klengel, who had told Chopin that she was Dresden's best pianist. To Tytus, Chopin later reported: "She plays well." He regretted having to depart from Dresden the very day of a singing of Meyerbeer's *Il Crociato in Egitto*, which he had already heard in Vienna.

From Dresden Chopin and his friends proceeded through part of Saxon Switzerland. Thence, via Breslau, they returned to Warsaw, arriving before September 10. When Fritsek greeted his parents and his sisters he had been away not quite two months.

V

ON October 3, 1829 Chopin, having written Tytus that he felt the necessity of another visit to Vienna, went on to insist that his thoughts were not drawn back to the Austrian metropolis by any infatuation with Leopoldine Blahetka. "She is young, pretty, and a pianist, but I, perhaps unfortunately, have my own ideal, which I have served faithfully, though silently, for half a year; of which I dream, to thoughts of which the adagio of my concerto [F minor, opus 21] belongs, and which this morning inspired the little waltz [opus 70, no. 3] I am sending you."

Chopin's "ideal" was the young soprano Konstantsya Gladkovska. If his statement was accurate, he had been infatuated with this girl since April. She was young, pretty, and unspoiled, and both he and others thought her musically talented. For another two years he would think of Konstantsya with varying sentimental intensity, always without declaring his passion to her or permitting it to interrupt his progress as a composer. Marriage is never mentioned in the letters, to Tytus and others, in which he occasionally poured out his exalted tenderness for Konstantsya. He was no seducer, and there is no proof that his desire for her was ever formulated in his own conscious mind as specifically physical. He mooned over her image, glorified her singing, considered himself to be in the grasp of hopeless love. But it was the calf-love of any immature, indecisive, and idealistic young man. That the actual Konstantsya knew of Chopin's feelings at the time is doubtful: he was too timid and too inexperienced to have been able to phrase them to her, however he could poeticize and inflame them to Tytus and to himself.

Despite the presence of Konstantsya, despite freedom and time for composing, Chopin was becoming restive in Warsaw. In the letter to Tytus quoted from above he said: "You wouldn't believe how dreary I now find Warsaw. If it weren't for my family's mak-

ing it a little more cheerful, I shouldn't stay." Partly this was longing for Tytus, for a friend "to go to in the morning to share one's
griefs and joys"; partly it was his sensation of helplessness in the
face of his feelings for Konstantsya. But partly, too, it was genuine dissatisfaction with the life of a city he was now equipped to
compare with Berlin and Vienna and find seriously wanting. From
the time of his return in September 1829 until his final departure
in November 1830 he constantly planned to depart, postponed his
departure for one reason or another, and then made new plans for
escape into the wider world. He behaved, that is to say, like the
typical romantic young poet or musician of the era. The difference
between Frédéric-François Chopin and most such young men as
portrayed in the letters and memoirs of the time was that he was
unceasingly active and that his activity produced results of genuine importance.

During this period of waiting, Chopin began, worked at, or
completed the Trio, opus 8; the Waltzes in D-flat major, opus 70,
no. 3, and B minor, opus 69, no. 2; the Concerto no. 2, F minor,
opus 21; the Polonaise in F minor, opus 71, no. 3; the Introduction
and Polonaise brillante for cello and piano, opus 3; Mazurkas in
D major and A minor, no opus; the Concerto no. 1, E minor,
opus 11; the Études, opus 10, and the Écossaises, opus 72, no. 3.
This is not the record of a youth rendered artistically impotent by
accesses of unfulfilled emotion. It is exactly the opposite, the
record of a young man whose creative enterprise is spurred on by
dissatisfaction, who pours into his art (or believes that he pours
into his art) the very sublimation of his amorphous yearning and
unfulfilled desire. "Sublimation of emotion" is a phrase whose scientific accuracy may be questioned, but whose brilliance as a
figure of speech may not. But it is never the whole story. In
Chopin's case, at least during his twentieth and twenty-first years,
music itself was a passion. He might not have composed what he
did had he possessed easy means for indulging otherwise the emotions, impulses, and desires that throb and waver unfulfilled
through his letters. Of him at that time it was true that music
was his only mistress.

On October 20, 1829 Chopin left Warsaw by diligence to visit
the Vyesolovskis and Prince Anton Radzivil. Earlier there had
been some tentative, and perhaps politely insincere, discussion

about his going to Berlin to live in Radzivil's palace there. Nicolas
Chopin had accepted this talk in all earnestness, and Fritsek —
who neither believed in it nor desired to return to Berlin — went
to seek out the truth in order to satisfy his father. The week before
his departure he had heard music at the home of Joseph Christoph Kessler, the German composer pianist, who was sojourning
briefly in Warsaw. Among the works played were Hummel's Trio
in E major, a quartet by Prince Ludwig Ferdinand of Prussia,
Ferdinand Ries's Concerto in C-sharp minor, and Beethoven's
"Archduke" Trio, opus 97. Of the last, on the very day of his setting out, Chopin wrote Tytus: "I haven't heard anything so great
for a long time. Beethoven snaps his fingers at the whole world."
This letter also mentions work on two movements of a piano concerto, evidently the E minor, opus 11.

Chopin spent an entire week at Antonin and then was loath to
leave the Radzivils' warm hospitality. The Princess was attractive.
In the Prince's music for *Faust* Chopin found "much ingenuity,
even genius," and he was delighted by Radzivil's admiration for
Gluck. Then there were two young Radzivil princesses, of whom
one — Vanda — he described to Tytus as "quite young: 17, and
pretty." Largely for her he had composed the Polonaise brillante
for cello and piano, in which her father undoubtedly tried the
cello part (the Introduction was a delayed afterthought). The
other young Princess, Eliza — who died a few years later — was
captivated by the Polonaise in F minor, opus 71, no. 3, and Chopin
had promised to make her a copy of it: in a letter written at Warsaw on November 14 he would beg Tytus to return it to him so
that it could be forwarded to Antonin. His plans, as customary,
were vague: "Princess Radzivil wants me to go to Berlin in May,
so there is nothing to prevent my spending the winter in Vienna.
I don't think that I shall leave here until December." Nothing of
all this scheme came to pass. Near the end of the letter he had
written: "I have composed a few exercises; I could play them to
you well." On October 20, further, he had told Tytus: "I have done
a big *exercise en forme* in a manner of my own; I shall show it to
you when we meet." These are references to first drafts of some
of the Twelve Grand Études to be published in July 1833 as Chopin's opus 10.

On February 22, 1830 Chopin was twenty years old. Twenty-three days later, having finally completed his F-minor Concerto,[1] he gave his first public concert in Warsaw. It had been announced for the National Theater for March 17, and no reserved seats could be bought by March 14. The program was as follows:

1. Overture to the opera *Leshek Biali* — Elsner
2. Allegro (maestoso) movement of Concerto in F minor — Chopin, with the composer at the piano
3. Divertissement for French horn — Görner, played by the composer
4. Adagio (larghetto) and Rondo (allegro vivace) movements of Concerto in F minor — Chopin, with the composer at the piano

INTERMISSION

5. Overture to the opera *Tsetsilia Piasechinska* — Karl Kasimir Kurpiński
6. Variations — Paër, sung by Mme Meier
7. Grand Fantasy on Polish Airs — Chopin, with the composer at the piano

The results of this first concert were disappointing to Chopin. At once he announced a second for the following week. It was as though he was certain that he could win the second time a public he had failed to win the first. Some of the complaints he had heard or been told had dwelt, as always, on the diminutiveness of his tone. He had used his own piano on March 14; for March 22 he would borrow a Viennese piano. The program announced for the second concert was:

1. Symphony — Yozef Novakovski
2. Allegro (maestoso) movement of Concerto in F minor — Chopin, with the composer at the piano
3. Air varié for violin — Charles de Bériot, played by Yozef Byelavski
4. Adagio (larghetto) and Rondo (allegro vivace) movements of Concerto in F minor — Chopin, with the composer at the piano

[1] He had rehearsed it with orchestra early in February and had repeated it, in a sort of dress rehearsal, on March 3. On the latter occasion it was part of a musicale with orchestra given at the Chopin home.

5. Krakoviak — Chopin, with the composer at the piano
6. Aria from the opera *Elena e Malvino* — Carlo Evasio Soliva, sung by Mme Meier
7. Improvisation — Chopin [on a Polish folksong, "There are strange customs in the town"]

On March 27, the Saturday after the second concert, Fritsek described both his Warsaw appearances in a letter to "My Dearest Life" — Tytus:

About the first concert: the hall was full, and both boxes and stalls were sold out three days beforehand, but it did not make the impression I expected on the mass of the audience. The first Allegro [of the F-minor Concerto] is accessible only to the few; there were some bravos, but I think only because they were puzzled: — What's this? — and had to pose as connoisseurs! The Adagio and Rondo produced more effect; one heard some spontaneous shouts; but as for the potpourri on Polish themes, in my opinion it failed to come off. They applauded in the spirit of: let him go away knowing that we weren't bored. Kurpinski found new beauties in my concerto that evening, but Viman still admitted that he can't see what people find in my Allegro. Ernemann was entirely satisfied; Elsner complained that my pianoforte was dull, and that he couldn't hear the bass passages. That evening the "gods" and the people sitting in the orchestra were entirely content; on the other hand, the pit complained that I played too softly; they would have preferred to be at Koptsyushek's [an artists' café] hearing the discussions that seem to have centered on my person. Therefore Mokhnatski, praising me to the skies in the Polish Courier — especially for the Adagio — ended by counseling more energy. I guessed where that energy lies, so at the next concert I played on a Viennese piano instead of my own. Diakov, the Russian general, was kind enough to lend me his own instrument, which is better than Hummel's; and consequently the audience, an even larger one than before, was pleased. Applause, exclamations that I had played better the second time than the first, that every note was like a pearl, and so forth; calling me back, yelling for a third concert. The Krakoviak Rondo produced a tremendous effect, the applause breaking out again four times. Kurpinski regretted that I had not played the Fantasy on the Viennese piano, as did Grzymala [Gzhimala] in the Polish Courier the next morning. Elsner says that it's only after this second concert that people can judge me; but I sincerely prefer to play on my piano. However, the unanimous verdict is that the other instrument fits the place better. . . . Finally I improvised, which greatly pleased the first-tier boxes. To tell you the truth, I didn't improvise as I should have liked; that would not have been for that public. Nevertheless, I am surprised that the Adagio was so generally admired; wherever I turn, I hear only about the Adagio. You undoubtedly have all the newspapers, or at least the most important ones, so you will see that they were pleased. . . . Last week they wanted me to give one more concert; but I won't.[2] You can't imagine what misery the last three days before a concert are. For the rest, I shall finish the opening Allegro of the second concerto [3] before the holidays, and then wait with my third concert until after the holidays; though I realize that I might have a larger audience now because all the fashionable world wants to hear me again. . . . From the two concerts, after paying expenses, I had less than 5,000 florins [approximately $600], though Dmushevski said that they never had so large an audience for a piano concert as for the first one, and the second was still larger. . . .

Praise — justified, welcome, and preposterous in about equal parts — was lavishly bestowed on the overslender, pale young man with the aquiline nose, blond hair, and rather haughty manner who was fast becoming a civic and national hero. His childhood friend Alexandrine de Moriolles sent him a wreath of laurel. The publisher Bzhezhina requested a portrait, but Chopin refused the request, remarking wryly that another musician's portrait had been used for wrapping butter. The *Polish Courier* and the *Official Bulletin* obliged with a sonnet and with maudlin panegyric. Anton Orlovski, a violinist composer, indited a set of waltzes and mazurkas on themes from the F-minor Concerto; these — against Chopin's expressed wish — were published, to his great annoyance. All this hubbub made the young composer fear that he might be made to appear ridiculous, particularly when the writer in the *Official Bulletin* said that one day the Poles would be as proud of Chopin as the Germans were of Mozart.

Chopin turned from the excitements of public appearance to the completion of his E-minor Concerto. The first two movements were finished by May 1830, the concluding Rondo by August. This was for him a period of nervous unhappiness. Writing to

[2] On October 11, however, he did.

[3] The E-minor Concerto, opus 11, though now called the "first," was thus actually composed later than the "second," F-minor Concerto, opus 21.

Tytus on April 17, he said: "I wish that I could throw off the thoughts that poison my happiness, and yet I love to indulge them; I don't myself know what's wrong with me; perhaps I shall be more tranquil after this letter; you know how I love writing to you." Then, after reporting that concerts by Henrietta Sontag had been scheduled for the time of the sitting of the Diet, and having retailed considerable local gossip, he closed: "If you come to Warsaw while the diet is sitting, you will certainly be here for my concert [Chopin had changed his mind again] — I have a sort of premonition — I shall believe in it implicitly however it turns out, for I often dream of you. How often I mistake night for day and day for night; how often I live in my dreams and sleep in the daytime — worse than sleep, because I feel just the same; and instead of recuperating in that numb state, as one does while sleeping, I grow weaker and more weary than ever; love me, please."

Writing to Tytus again on May 15, Chopin sent definite word of Sontag's impending arrival. There was a possibility of Pasta too, though he was inclined to doubt her coming.[4] "There is more likelihood of the famous though rather *passée* singer Frau Milder Hauptmann." A letter of June 5 is a hymn in praise of Sontag, conquering both by the luminous charm of her personality and by the perfection of her singing. "It seems that she breathes some perfume from the freshest flowers into the hall; she caresses, she strokes, she enraptures, but she seldom moves to tears. Although Radzivil told me that she acts and sings Desdemona's last scene with Othello [Rossini] so that nobody can refrain from weeping." In Sontag's rooms Chopin met the idealized Konstantsya Gladkovska, perhaps for the first time, and the famous singer's helpfulness to the girl raised them both in Chopin's infatuated estimation.

Despite Fritsek's repeated beseechings, Tytus did not get to Warsaw for the festivities that accompanied Nicholas I's visit and the opening session of the Diet. Chopin himself played no brilliant part in the musical events of the hour, though when copies

---

[4] Also appearing in Warsaw during these weeks were a sixteen-year-old pianist named Worlitzer, already pianist by appointment to the King of Prussia; Karl Yozef Lipiński, the Polish violinist who had twice shared public programs in Italy with Paganini, and Anna Caroline de Belleville (later Mme Oury), a young pianist of great brilliance.

of his Variations on *"Là ci darem la mano"* arrived in published form from Haslinger in Vienna, he performed them as part of a concert given on July 8 by Mme Meier. This was after the Tsar's departure, and shortly later Fritsek went to Poturzhin to visit Tytus. Thence he proceeded to join his family as guests of the Skarbeks at Zhelazova Vola, and returned to Warsaw in time to hear Konstantsya Gladkovska's debut in the title role of Paër's *Agnese* on July 24. Refreshed by having shared his thoughts and dreams with Tytus in the country air, he was somewhat calmer. But he still made rapidly broken plans to leave for western Europe, intending to pass two months in Vienna, the rest of the autumn and winter in Milan.

By August 21 Chopin had completed his E-minor Concerto.[5] He confessed that a rehearsal of the G-minor Trio left him "rather pleased." But his letters became feverish with discontent, meandering from triviality to nonsense only to insist again and again on his pervading malaise. Having, at Elsner's suggestion, rehearsed the piano part of the E-minor Concerto with a string quartet, he finally set October 11 as the date of the concert he would use to bid farewell to Warsaw. He invited Konstantsya Gladkovska and Mlle Volkov, another budding singer, to assist him. On September 23 the dress rehearsal of the Concerto, this time with orchestra — and in the Chopins' home — brought together most of Warsaw's musical leaders. It was reviewed by several periodicals as though it had been a public concert. They were no more than polite to the Concerto, their thin praise going chiefly to its final Rondo.

Chopin's plans for his journey were again shot through with doubt by news of political disturbances in Austria, the German states, and Italy. Passports were being refused outright, but he believed that he could obtain one for Prussia and Austria — he was still planning to go to Vienna by way of Krakov. On October 5, writing to Tytus, he could announce both settled plans for the October 11th concert and (he believed) certain news that he

[5] The E-minor Concerto was published in 1833 as Chopin's "First," opus 11. The F-minor, composed earlier, was not issued until 1836, when it was labeled the "Second," opus 21. The reason for the delay in publishing the earlier Concerto was that Chopin mislaid the orchestra parts en route to Paris and dallied over redoing a task that he found uncongenial.

would have quit Warsaw a week after it. "My traveling trunk is
bought, my whole outfit is ready; my scores are corrected, my
pocket handkerchiefs are hemmed, my trousers are made. Only to
say good-by, and that's the worst." This letter closes on one of the
most shadowed glimpses into his ambivalent emotions: "Give me
a kiss, dearest beloved. I know that you still care for me, but I'm
always so afraid of you — as if you were some sort of tyrant over
me; I don't know why, but I'm afraid of you. God knows, it's only
you that have power over me, you and — no one else. Perhaps this
is the last letter I shall write you.[6] Till death, your F. Chopin."

The program of Chopin's last concert in Warsaw was:

1. Symphony — Görner
2. Allegro (maestoso) movement of Concerto in E minor — Chopin, with the composer at the piano
3. Aria — Soliva, sung by Mlle Volkov with chorus
4. Adagio (romanze — larghetto) and Rondo (vivace) movements
   of Concerto in E minor — Chopin, with the composer at the
   piano

                        INTERMISSION

5. Overture to *Guillaume Tell* — Rossini
6. Cavatina from *La Donna del Lago* — Rossini, sung by Konstantsya Gladkovska
7. Grand Fantasy on Polish Airs — Chopin, with the composer at
   the piano

The next day Fritsek broke his half-resolve not to write to
Tytus again, pouring out his impressions of the concert in a spirit
significantly undarkened by the complaints and whining uncertainties of the preceding months:

                                    Tuesday, 12 October 1830
My dearest Life!

Yesterday's concert was a success; I hasten to let you know. I inform
your Lordship that I was not a bit, not a bit nervous, and played as I
play when I'm alone. It went well. Full hall. First, Görner's Symphony.
Then my noble self's E-minor Allegro, which I just reeled off — one
can do that on a Streicher piano.[7] Furious applause. Soliva was de-

---

[6] Tytus was to join him en route to Vienna.

[7] Johann Andreas Streicher, a school friend of Schiller, helped to found the
piano-manufacturing firm of Streicher & Sohn. He improved the mechanical
proficiency of the "Viennese" piano, first developed by his father-in-law,
Johann Andreas Stein.

lighted; he conducted because of his aria with chorus, beautifully sung by Mlle Volkov, who was dressed in sky blue like a cherub. After the aria came the Adagio and Rondo; then the pause between the first and second parts. When they returned from the buffet and left the stage, which they had mounted to produce an effect favorable to me, the second part began with the Overture to Guillaume Tell. Soliva conducted well, and it made a great impression. Really, the Italian has showed me so much kindness this time that it's difficult to thank him enough. He then conducted the aria for Mlle Gladkovska (dressed just right for her face, in white, with roses on her head) — she sang the cavatina from La Donna del Lago, with the recitative, as she has sung nothing yet except the aria in Agnese. You know — "Oh quante lagrime per te versai." She took "tutto detesto" down on the low B in such a way that Zyelinski said the B was worth a thousand ducats. You must understand that the aria was transposed for her voice, which greatly profited by the change. After Mlle Gladkovska had been escorted from the stage, we started the potpourri on "The moon has set, etc." This time I was all right and the orchestra was all right and the pit understood. This time the final mazurka [8] elicited big applause, after which — the usual farce — I was called up. No one hissed and I had to bow four times — but properly now, because Brandt has taught me how to do it. I don't know how things would have gone yesterday if Soliva had not taken my scores home with him, read them, and conducted so that I couldn't rush as though to break my neck. But he managed so well to hold us back that, I assure you, I never succeeded in playing so comfortably with the orchestra. The piano, it seems, was much liked; Mlle Volkov still more — she shows up well on the stage. . . . I think now of nothing but packing; either on Saturday or next Wednesday I start, going via Krakov. . . .

The rest of the October 12th letter is equally gay. The response to his third Warsaw concert, the imminence of his departure, and the happy prevision of a meeting with Tytus had combined to banish Chopin's mental unease and emotional gnawings. But it was not until Monday, November 1, 1830, that Chopin bade farewell to his parents and his sisters.[9] Then, accompanied by Elsner and a few schoolmates and close friends, he set out from Warsaw.

[8] In the score it is called a kujawiak (kuyaviak), a dance (from the district of Kuyavia) resembling the mazurka (from the district of Mazovia).
[9] Chopin never again saw his sister Izabela, of whom, indeed, there is no sign that he was particularly fond.

Arriving at suburban Vola, he discovered that a group of male Conservatory students was prepared to honor him by singing a cantata with guitar accompaniment that Elsner had composed expressly for this occasion. After it was over, everyone sat down to a banquet, near the close of which someone made the valedictory speech, which rose to this peroration:

May you, wherever you wander or linger, never forget your homeland or cease to love it with a warm and faithful heart! Think of Poland, think of your friends, who are proud to call you their fellow countryman, who expect great things of you, whose good wishes and prayers accompany you!

Final farewells were exchanged in a mist of tearful emotion. Chopin had several times expressed the belief that once he left Poland more than briefly, he would never return. The moment of departure was at hand, and sadness is the climate of partings. Ahead for the twenty-year-old traveler lay Kalish, the village at which Tytus would join him. Ahead lay Vienna. Ahead — and Frédéric-François Chopin was the sort of young man to realize it — lay the whole world.

VI

CHOPIN and Tytus Voitsyekhovski arrived at Breslau shortly after six o'clock in the evening on Saturday, November 6, 1830, putting up at the Golden Goose. Established there, they at once ran off to hear a singing of *Der Alpenkönig*, an opera by Roser von Reiter. "The pit admired the new scenery," Chopin wrote to his family three days later, "but we found nothing to make a fuss over." On their second day in Breslau the opera was Auber's *Le Maçon*, given badly. And as Fritsek finished writing to Warsaw on the fourth day of the Breslau visit, he and Tytus were getting ready to go to the opera again, this time to hear *Das unterbrochene Opferfest*, the Peter von Winter work that he had heard in Berlin in 1828. "I am curious to see how it goes. They have no very good singers; but the theater is very cheap; a stall seat costs two zls. I like Breslau better this time."

Of the five days that Tytus and Fritsek dallied in Breslau, the third was the most interesting. In the morning on that Monday they attended a rehearsal for one of the thrice-weekly concerts given on a semiprofessional basis at the Resource under the direction of Joseph Ignaz Schnabel, a *Kapellmeister* whom Chopin had first met five years before. One of the Society's members, an amateur pianist named Hellwig, was preparing to rehearse Moscheles's E-flat major Concerto. But Schnabel insisted instead that Chopin sit down at the piano at once and play for those present. Because of Schnabel's friendship for Elsner, Chopin acquiesced, turning off part of the Variations on *"Là ci darem la mano."* Then the *Kapellmeister*, insensitively disregarding Hellwig's feelings, insisted that Chopin become that evening's soloist. The score of his E-minor Concerto was fetched from the Golden Goose, and he played through the Romanze and Rondo movements to Schnabel's satisfaction. Tytus heard one man's comment: "He can play, but he can't compose."

A kind acquaintance had obtained guest tickets to this very

Resource concert for Chopin and Tytus, and the former was
highly amused on thinking of the surprise the man must have felt
on seeing him as soloist. Besides playing the two movements of
the E-minor Concerto, he improvised on themes from Auber's *La
Muette de Portici*. Poor Hellwig, seemingly more versatile than
talented, had to content himself with singing an aria from *Il Barbiere di Siviglia* ("badly," Fritsek informed his parents). There
was an overture, and then there was dancing. Schnabel was all
amiability. "He kept taking me under the chin and caressing me
every moment." At last he offered Chopin and Tytus supper and
a carriage home. Chopin accepted some broth, but declined the
carriage, and after the amenities the friends returned to the
Golden Goose at nine o'clock. They were departing from Breslau
the following afternoon at two.

Dresden followed Breslau on their route. By Sunday, November
14, Fritsek was sending his family a letter from Dresden brim-
ming with activity and effervescence. He had called at once to re-
new his acquaintance with the pianist Antoinette Pechwell. She
had invited him to a meeting of the local Resource, at which she
was to play that evening. He would have preferred to go to the
opera with Tytus to hear *La Muette de Portici*, but politeness won
out. Donning his finest clothes, Chopin ordered a sedan chair,
which he called "this queer box," adding: "I laughed at myself on
the way, being carried by those bearers in livery; I was greatly
tempted to stamp out the bottom, but restrained myself." He is at
his epistolary best in describing the scene that greeted him after
he had descended from the sedan chair onto the steps of Herr
Kreissig's house, where the Resource was meeting:

The master of the house came out with bows and scrapes and many
compliments, and conducted me into the hall, where I found, along
the two sides, eight huge tables at which sat a crowd of ladies. Their
adornments, consisting less of diamonds than of knitting-needles,
flashed in my eyes. Joking aside, the number of ladies and needles was
so great that one might have feared some revolt against men, which
only their baldness and their spectacles could combat; there was a
large display of glasses and there were a good many shiny heads.

The chattering of needles and teacups was at last broken when,
from another salon, came the sounds of an orchestra launching

into the Overture to Auber's *Fra Diavolo*. Then "the best local woman singer" sang ("not bad") and Fräulein Pechwell played (no comment). As soon as his politeness had been demonstrated, Chopin edged his way out of the Kreissig mansion and rushed to the opera to hear the last part of *La Muette*. Meanwhile he had met a brother of the great tenor Giovanni Battista Rubini, who was then in Italy and to whom the brother promised him a letter of introduction. He had also been invited to attend a rehearsal of a Vespers by Morlacchi.[1] His real interest in Dresden continued, however, to be Italian opera, still — fourteen years after Weber's attempt to raise German opera to the level of Morlacchi's Italian opera — the rage of the town. On November 14 he heard a poor singing of Rossini's *Tancredi;* on the 15th he heard *La Muette* through. He renewed his personal contacts with Morlacchi and Klengel, but refused the latter's persistent request that he give a concert in Dresden. "I have no time to lose, and Dresden will give me neither fame nor money. . . . Except my Klengel . . . there is nothing here worth noticing." Klengel listened with open admiration as Chopin played through the E-minor Concerto, and then praised the young Pole as both composer and virtuoso, comparing him to John Field.

Dresden had a colony of wealthy Polish exiles. Its members showered their talented countryman with social favors. He met Princess Augusta, daughter of the recently deceased King Friedrich August I, and Carlotta of Lucca, the wife of King Anton's brother Maximilian. These princesses sent round to Chopin's inn letters of introduction to the Queen of the Two Sicilies, then in Naples, and to a Saxon-born Princess Ulasino, in Rome. They promised to forward to Vienna introductions to the reigning Princess of Lucca and to Maria, Grand Duchess of Tuscany, wife of the Viceroy, at Milan. Among the Poles whom Chopin may have met while in Dresden was Countess Delphine Potocka (Pototska), a beautiful and talented young woman whom he was to know intimately later on.

Between Dresden and Vienna Fritsek and Tytus probably stopped briefly at Prague, but no record of their activities there

---

[1] It is interesting to note that this Vespers — in Germany, as late as 1830 — was sung by two Neapolitan *castrati*, Sassaroli and Tarquinio. On their voices Chopin unfortunately made no comment.

has survived. They reached Vienna at nine o'clock on the morning of Tuesday, November 23, putting up first at a hotel called the City of London. This they immediately realized to be beyond the capacity of their purses. Next they installed themselves at the Golden Lamb until an English admiral should vacate the private quarters they had engaged in the Kohlmarkt. Chopin undoubtedly looked forward to quiet composing and perhaps to a public concert or two, his need for companionship perfectly answered by the constant presence of Tytus. But politics abruptly interfered. In Warsaw on November 28, as the culmination of rising discontent against the Russians, a group of astonishingly ill-informed conspirators attempted to kidnap Grand Duke Konstantin Pavlovich. Not knowing even that the Tsar's brother had already left the city at the head of an army, they apparently intended to hold him as a hostage to reforms. They succeeded only in murdering a group of loyalists, including the Polish-born Minister of War, Hauke.

The wave of revolutionary disturbances that had almost kept Chopin in Warsaw had culminated in France with the overthrow of Charles X and the accession of Louis-Phillipe. Belgium had separated itself from Holland. The Polish uprising, in fact, was set off partly by gossip that the Russians planned to use a Polish army to force the Belgians back into the confining arms of the House of Oranje-Nassau, and partly by a belief that Konstantin Pavlovich, long at loggerheads with Nicholas I, could be persuaded to hear the Polish forces of rebellion. In reality, the Grand Duke behaved like the wavering and indecisive tyrant that he was, failing his duty as Viceroy by allowing the rebellion to get out of control, and then cheering Polish victories because he himself had trained the Polish forces. Having fled Poland altogether, he died at Vitebsk of cholera on June 27, 1831, about three months before his brother's armies succeeded in annihilating the Polish rebellion.

News of the first outbreak in Warsaw reached Chopin and Tytus very quickly. Waiting only one day, Tytus set off from Vienna to join the rebels. Chopin, indecisive as Konstantin Pavlovich and ambiguous as always in a nonmusical crisis, waited one day more and then departed too, using post-horses in the hope of overtaking Tytus. Before leaving Vienna, however, he had received from his parents word urging him to remain in Austria and, because of his uncertain health, not attempt to return to Warsaw. After racing two or three stages, he realized that he could not overtake Tytus; then he posted back to Vienna in low spirits, which would have been abysmal had he known that in eighteen more years of life he would never see his beloved friend again.

It is impossible not to deduce from the evidence that Chopin, however much he loved Poland, and even however much he loved Tytus Voitsyekhovski, had no very powerful urge to return to Warsaw and join the rebelling troops. The army was a career for which he had not one qualification. As always in his life, too, all other attachments were superficial when placed in contest with that to himself as a musician. No loyalty to any person or any idea could infringe upon his deep, unconscious loyalty to his own musical self. The top of his consciousness wanted him to rejoin Tytus and fight the Russians for Polish independence; the base of his consciousness insisted that he accept his parents' orders and return to Vienna, where in comparative safety he could compose. Yet his mind was thus divided, and the period of this stay in Vienna, which lasted until July 1831, was one of his least productive.

Chopin in Vienna composed a few small pieces, twice played in public, probably heard Thalberg,[2] indulged in a spate of frivolous activities, moped, and gave way to his increasing neurotic habit of longing for every place he was not and every person and thing he had not. He worried about family and friends caught in the swirl of the Polish rebellion. His entire mental climate was unfavorable to creation; local circumstances were no better. Of his earlier Viennese friends, some were dead or ill, others out of the city. The Blahetkas were in Stuttgart; Schuppanzigh had died. The perhaps deceitful Haslinger had not published anything of Chopin's after issuing the Variations on *"Là ci darem la mano."* There was a cholera scare. Poles were unpopular. The King of Naples had died, and the Austrian court was consequently in mourning. Not for long could Chopin continue to tell himself that he was still in love with Konstantsya Gladkovska, but neither

[2] Thalberg presented one of his own concertos at a concert of the Gesellschaft der Musikfreunde on March 20, 1831.

could he banish her from his thoughts or stop reacting somewhat hysterically to memories of her, any mention of her name, or even a new acquaintance whose name happened to resemble hers. By the beginning of the summer of 1831 he was summing up his depression in a notebook:

Today it was lovely on the Prater. Crowds of people with whom I have no connection. I admired the foliage; the spring odor and the innocence of nature brought back a feeling from my childhood. A storm was brewing, so I went inside, but there was no storm. Only I was melancholy — why? I don't care even for music today. It is late, but I am not sleepy. I don't know what is wrong with me. And I've begun my third decade! The papers and posters have announced my concert.[3] It is to be in two days' time, and it's as though there were no such thing. It seems to have nothing to do with me. I don't listen to compliments; they seem more and more stupid to me. I wish that I were dead, yet I should like to see my parents. Her [Konstantsya Gladkovska's?] image appears before me: I don't think that I love her any longer, but I cannot get her out of my head. Everything I have seen abroad up to now seems to me old and hateful, and just makes me sigh for home, for those blessed moments I didn't know how to value. What used to seem great now seems common; what I used to consider common now seems incomparable, too great, too lofty. The people here are not my people; they are kind, but kind by habit. They do everything too respectably, flatly, moderately. I don't want even to think about moderation. I'm puzzled, I'm melancholy, I don't know what to do with myself; I wish that I weren't alone! —

Some of this sickly indecision arose from lonely eroticism, felt but unexpressed. Some of it was sexual — but more of it was Frédéric-François Chopin's need for a guiding hand, if not that of Tytus, whom he had now lost, then that of George Sand, whom he was to find within a few years. A sure hand was his need, a guide to onward movement in the multiple and pathless realm that living in the everyday world otherwise appeared to him to be. Once concentrated, once set out upon creative work, he was as fierce as a monomaniac in accomplishment, but until that new embarkation he was a fritterer, a whiner, a frail and faulty vessel becalmed or blown directionlessly about. During eight months in Vienna he alternated between calms and pointless sorties. Not un-

[3] The date of this concert is unknown.

til he reached Paris in September 1831 was he to recover direction and get along on his creative voyage.

The first wave of the waltz craze had risen in Vienna, which only a few years before had honored Haydn and Beethoven, where Schubert was dead little more than two years. Chopin's bitter letters make it clear that the music most heard and most published was the waltzes, *Ländler,* quadrilles, polkas, galops, and marches of Joseph Franz Karl Lanner, just thirty, and Johann Strauss, Sr., three years younger, but already father of a five-year-old boy who would become world-renowned as "the" Waltz King. Lanner and Strauss were, in sober fact, the finest living Austrian composers, for music of more serious demeanor was, in 1831, wholly the work of second-rate men. Performance remained on a higher level with such pianists as Czerny, Thalberg, and Alois Schmitt, such a cellist as Joseph Merk or violinist as Joseph Slavik, and such singers as Sabine Heinefetter and Franz Wild. The Opera still gave performances in which the Polish visitor could find pleasure. But Vienna's primacy in musical creation was just over, having passed to Paris and the cities of the Rhineland.

Although in Vienna as elsewhere Chopin spent much time in the company of other Poles, the most important of his new friends there was Dr. Malfatti, physician-in-ordinary to the Emperor, Francis II. This artistically inclined and broadly educated man had known Beethoven well. The sudden infatuation of Beethoven with Malfatti's daughter Therese had, indeed, precipitated one of the crises in his stormy life. Malfatti had been among the committee of physicians that attended Beethoven during his final illness. Now he lived in splendor in a hillside villa overlooking the city. The court paid him an annual official visit. He liked to entertain musicians and intellectuals, and in his villa Chopin became a familiar, enjoying the company, the stimulation of Malfatti's wonderful conversation, and the Polish foods that the thoughtful doctor served whenever his young Polish friend was present. Malfatti also gave Chopin letters of introduction to be presented in Paris to several musicians, including Paër.

In his letters home Chopin mentioned meeting Anton Diabelli, music-publisher and creator of the banal melody on which Beethoven had constructed his colossal "Diabelli" Variations; Czerny, whom he knew but perfunctorily; Sigismond Thalberg, love-child of a prince and a baroness, one of the most feted pianists of the era. "Younger than me, pleases the ladies, makes potpourris from the Dumb Girl,[4] gets his *piano* by pedal not by hand, takes tenths as easily as I octaves — has diamond shirt-studs": such was Fritsek's description of a man he could not like and eventually came to detest.

Chopin had lost none of his love for opera, particularly Italian opera, the love so many times reflected in the contours, recitative-like passages, and vocalizing tendency of his own melodies. He naturally came to know the luminaries who were managing to keep the Opera alight, Franz Wild and Sabine Heinefetter. His letters often mentioned operatic enjoyments. In November 1830 it is Heinefetter looking lovely and singing beautifully in Rossini's *Otello;* in December, Auber's *Fra Diavolo,* Mozart's *La Clemenza di Tito,* and Rossini's *Guillaume Tell.* Later the same month it is Heinefetter again, "lovely" in Meyerbeer's *Il Crociato in Egitto* and announced to sing in Rossini's *La Gazza ladra.* Finally, in July 1831, just before Chopin left for Paris, he mentioned Rossini's French opera *Le Siège de Corinthe:* "Very good. I am happy that I remained for this opera. Wild, Heinefetter, Binder, [Anton] Forti; in a word, all the best that Vienna has took part, and beautifully." In the midst of this constant musical activity Chopin must have realized bitterly the accusation of his own failure to act.

Writing just after Christmas 1830 to Yan Matuszyński (Matushinski), Fritsek condensed his loneliness with a literary self-consciousness unusual for him. Saying that he had just visited Slavik ("a famous violinist with whom I have made friends — since Paganini I have not heard anything like him: he can take ninety-six notes staccato on one bow, and so forth"), he told of his peregrinations on Christmas Eve:

I strolled along slowly all alone, and at midnight went into St. Stephen's. When I entered no one was there. Not to hear the Mass, but just to look at the huge building at that hour. I got into the darkest corner at the foot of a Gothic pillar. I can't describe the grandeur, the magnificence of those huge arches. It was quiet; now and again the footsteps of a sacristan lighting candles at the rear of the sanctuary would break in on my lethargy. A coffin behind me, a coffin beneath

4 Auber's *La Muette de Portici,* also called *Masaniello.*

me — only the coffin above me was lacking. A mournful harmony all around — I never felt my loneliness so clearly; I loved drinking in this great sight, until people and lights began to appear. Then, turning up the collar of my cloak as I once did — do you recall? — along the Krakov Suburb, I went to hear the music in the Imperial Chapel. On the way there, I passed through Vienna's finest streets, not alone now, but in the company of a cheerful throng, and reached the Palace, where I heard three numbers of a mediocre Mass sleepily sung, and then, at one in the morning, went home to bed. I dreamed of you, of all of you, of them, of my dear children.

Some justification existed for Chopin's failure to give a concert in Vienna. It lay first in the general condition of the musical scene and then, as 1831 advanced into spring, in the lateless of the season. He more than once expressed regret over what he was costing his father, whose admirable patience at last began to fray. Late in February or early in March 1831 a mild remonstration went from Warsaw to Vienna. On April 2 the *Theaterzeitung* announced that Mme Garzia-Vestris, a singer, would give a morning concert in the Redoutensaal two days later. Of the ten assisting artists promised,[5] only one had to be identified for the Viennese: Chopin. This "pianoforte-player" performed a solo version of his E-minor Concerto, which was mentioned in the *Allgemeine musikalische Zeitung* for September 21, 1831, as a serious composition that gave Vienna no cause for reversing the high opinion Chopin had earned from the city in 1830.

Many writers have stated that still later in the spring, with Vienna's population diminished by cholera scare and country holidays, Chopin himself gave the concert spoken of in his notebook. The date and location of this concert have never been determined, however. None of Chopin's surviving letters mentions either his

[5] They are an interesting group because of the wide scope of their connections. Sabine and Clara Heinefetter were but two of the six singing Heinefetters; Clara was only fifteen years old at the time. Franz Wild was the tenor so admired by Chopin. Joseph Böhm was a violinist composer who was to number Joseph Joachim among his pupils, with Leopold Auer and Eduard Reményi. Georg Hellmesberger, like Böhm, his teacher, taught at the Vienna Conservatory, and was to instruct both Joachim and Auer. He also founded a violinistic dynasty that endured at least until 1907. Chopin's other colleagues on this occasion were the cellist composer Joseph Merk and two horn-playing brothers named Levy.

appearance with Mme Garzia-Vestris or any concert of his own. His sojourn of nearly eight months in Austria served not at all to increase his fame or advance his career.

Nor was any creative enlargement signified by most of the compositions that can now be dated with any likelihood from Chopin's last visit to Vienna. They include the Mazurkas in C major and F major, opus 68, nos. 1 and 3; possibly the three trifling Écossaises, opus 72 (though these had been begun earlier); possibly the Andante spianato and Grande Polonaise brillante, opus 22, and the Allegro de concert, opus 46, though the last was probably a reworking of materials originally designed for use in a concerto for two pianos and orchestra. Better than any of these pieces would be several of the Études, opus 10, but it is now impossible to date all of the individual Études, which were composed in 1829, 1830, and 1831.

With strife continuing in Poland, conditions unsettled elsewhere in Europe, cholera both feared and actual in Vienna, and his own career threatened with withering in inanition, Chopin finally felt an acute need for new scenes. He had difficulty in obtaining a passport, but by August 1831 (and possibly earlier) he was able to leave Vienna, setting out with a Polish friend named Norbert Alfons Kumelski for Linz, Salzburg, Munich, Stuttgart, and Paris. He was never to revisit Austria. His passport stated that he was en route to London, probably because that was the only sort of passport he had been able to obtain.

Reaching Munich, Chopin found his journey necessarily interrupted: additional funds he had requested from his father had not arrived from Warsaw. On August 28 he gave a morning concert in the hall of the Munich Philharmonic Society, being assisted by four singers, a clarinettist, and a *Kapellmeister* (who may simply have accompanied him at a second piano). He played his E-minor Concerto and Grand Fantasy on Polish Airs. A reviewer in the local *Flora*, August 30, 1831, was lavish with inflamed adjectives and stated that the composer pianist won "unanimous applause." When the much-needed money arrived from Warsaw, Fritsek moved on to Stuttgart. There he learned with consternation and terror for many he loved that the Russians had occupied Warsaw on September 8. Feelings of guilt (he was a Pole — why was he safely in Germany instead of fighting for his country and

to protect his loved ones?) and frenzy assailed him. He poured
them out in a notebook: [6]

The suburbs have been demolished, burned down. Yas [Yan Matu-
shinski], Vilus [Kolberg] probably have died on the barricades. I see
Marcel [Tselinski?] a prisoner! The brave Sovinski in the hands of
those villains. Paskyevich, one of the Mohilev dogs, occupies the seat of
the first monarchs of Europe. Moscow rules the world! O God, do You
exist? You do, and yet You don't avenge. Have You not had enough of
Moscow's crimes — or — or are You Yourself a Russian too? My poor
father! That dear old man, is he starving, and my mother unable to
buy bread? Perhaps my sisters have fallen to the rapacity of Musco-
vite soldiery on the rampage. Oh, Father, what comfort in your old
age! Mother, poor suffering Mother, have you borne a daughter only
to see a Russian violate her to the bone? Mockery! Has even her
[Emilya's] grave been respected? Trampled. Thousands more corpses
cover the grave. What has happened to her [Konstantsya Gladkovska]?
Where is she? Poor girl, perhaps in some Russian's grasp — a Russian
strangling, killing, murdering her! Oh, my Life [Tytus?], here I am,
alone; come to me and I'll wipe away your tears, heal the wounds of
the present, recall the past to you — the time when there were no
Russians, the days when the only Russians were some eager to entertain you, and you laughed at them because I was there. Has your
mother survived? Such a cruel mother, and mine is so gentle. But perhaps I have no mother, perhaps some Russian has killed her, murdered
— My sisters, screaming, resist — Father in despair can do nothing — I
here, useless! And I here empty-handed. At times I can only groan,
suffer, and pour out my despair at my piano! God, shake the earth, let
it swallow up the men of this time, let the most severe punishments
fall on France, which refused to come to our aid —
    — The bed I go to — perhaps dead bodies have rested on it, rested
a long time — yet today that does not nauseate me. Is a corpse any
worse than I am? A corpse knows nothing about father, mother, sisters,
Tytus; a corpse has no beloved one, its tongue cannot carry on conversation with those around it — a corpse is as colorless as I am, as
cold as now I am cold to everything —
    Stuttgart's clocktowers strike the night hours. How many new
corpses is this minute making in the world? Mothers losing children,
children losing mothers — So much grief over the dead — and so much

[6] In reply to doubts cast on the authenticity of these notebook entries,
Arthus Hedley, in his *Chopin*, succinctly states: "I have read them in Chopin's album myself." The translation is somewhat abridged.

glee! A vile corpse and a decent one — virtues and vice are all one, when they are corpses they are sisters. Death, then, is evidently man's best act. And what is his worst? Birth. It is directly opposite to his best. I am right to be angry that I came into the world. Of what use is my life to anyone? I am unfit for human beings, for I have neither a snout nor calves on my legs — and does a corpse have them? A corpse has no calves either, and so lacks nothing of a mathematical closeness to death. Did she love me, or was she only making believe? That's a knotty point to settle — yes, no, yes, no, no, yes — finger by finger — "She loves me?" Certainly she loves me — let her do what she likes —

Father! Mother! Where are you? Are you corpses? Perhaps some Russian has made sport — oh, wait, wait. But tears — they have not flowed for so long, oh, so long, so long that I could not cry. How glad — how miserable — glad and miserable. If I'm miserable I can't be glad, and yet it is sweet — This is a curious state, but that is the way it is with a corpse — it is well and sick at the same moment. It has been transported to a happier life, and is glad. It regrets the life it leaves behind, and is sad. It must feel as I felt when I stopped crying. It was like a temporary death of all feeling; for a moment I died in my own heart — no, my heart momentarily died in me. And why not forever! Perhaps then it would be more endurable. Alone! Alone! There are no words for my wretchedness — how can I bear this feeling —

There is an unprovable story, which may be true, that Chopin drained himself of this frenetic agitation, this sincere, melodramatic, and ambivalent self-castigation, by sitting down and in a gust of passion composing the C-minor Étude, opus 10, no. 12, the eternally stirring "Revolutionary." [7] There is no record of his having performed while in Stuttgart; unless he did, his August 28th concert in Munich was his last performance on German soil, though he revisited the German states several times in later years.

Chopin's reputation in Germany received a strong impetus in 1831. It was then that the customarily staid and sober *Allgemeine musikalische Zeitung* published a review of the Variations on "*Là ci darem la mano*," a prescient but overwrought pæan that has become famous for its salutation: "Hats off, gentlemen, a genius!" This review, which today makes uncomfortable reading, helped

[7] No one who heard this piece broadcast and rebroadcast from Warsaw during the German bombardment of that city in September 1939 is likely ever to forget the music or its occasion.

to establish Chopin's reputation with the friends and admirers of its twenty-one-year-old author, Robert Schumann.[8] But it had more immediate repercussions, of a less pleasant sort, on its perpetrator. Angry subscribers to the *Zeitung* protested against rhapsodies so lavish over music so "revolutionary" in nature. It is possible that these good people believed that everything Polish was necessarily revolutionary. The paper printed a second, anonymous review, signed by "an old musician." Cool and censorious, this was unquestionably criticism of a higher order than Schumann's. When Schumann's connection with the *Zeitung* was summarily terminated, his future father-in-law, Friedrich Wieck, seems to have tried to answer the anonymous "old musician" with a review less flowery but no less enthusiastic than the first. This the *Zeitung* refused to print, and Wieck finally published it in a journal called *Cæcilia*. More important, partly at Schumann's suggestion, Wieck persuaded his daughter Clara to play Chopin's Variations at Leipzig in July 1832, the first occasion recorded of a famous pianist's performing his music in public. There can be little doubt that it was these events that led the Leipzig publisher Probst-Kistner to begin issuing Chopin's compositions in December 1832.

During the third week of September 1831 Frédéric-François Chopin arrived in Paris, where he was all but unknown. The overture to his creative life, some of it music of a lofty sort, some of it the merest inescapable marking of time, had been concluded on a stormy strain. There was a lull. The curtains were about to part and rise, revealing the scenes against which his mature activities would, for the most rart, be played out. He had found his second and final home.

[8] The review also marked the first appearance in print of the pseudonymous members of Schumann's *Davidsbund:* Florestan, Master Raro, Eusebius.

VII

FOURTEEN months before Chopin's arrival in Paris, Charles X — last of Louis XV's three grandsons to rule — had been forced to abdicate the unsteady throne he had occupied for six years. This septuagenarian autocrat, in whom the Bourbon philosophy of statecraft was essentialized too late, had attempted to pass on the crown to his own grandson. But just when it had seemed that he might succeed, the aged Lafayette had thrown his support to the supposedly liberal Louis-Philippe, not a true Bourbon, but a Bourbon-Orléans, being descended not from Louis XIV, but from *le Roi Soleil's* younger brother. An Orléans king meant that the *ancien régime*, several times killed, was dead at last. Louis-Philippe was a "citizen-king," the Orléanist monarchy bourgeois. It was near the beginning of the eighteen-year reign of Louis-Philippe that Chopin, a blond twenty-one-year-old composer pianist with a frail body and a dandified aristocratic bearing arrived in the French capital to try his fortune. There he was to live out Louis-Philippe's reign and witness the inception of the Bonapartist return.

In 1831 Paris was an exciting arena for a young man of genius with artistic predilections. The Conservatoire was presided over by Cherubini, who at seventy powerfully frowned on innovation. But Hector Berlioz (temporarily absent at Rome) was already a Parisian, and at twenty-seven was ready to compose some of the greatest music of the nineteenth century. It was the year of Hérold's *Zampa* at the Opéra-Comique. Auber, already forty-nine, had composed *La Muette de Portici*, and the year before Chopin's advent had presented *Fra Diavolo*. At the Opéra it was the year of Giacomo Meyerbeer's first stupendous and flashy French opera, *Robert le diable*. The handsome Franz Liszt, one year Chopin's junior, was a Parisian too, a pianist of dazzling glitter, a romantic young man of Byronic moods. Rossini, whose *Guillaume Tell* (1829) was as essential to the foundation of French spectacle grand opera as *La Muette de Portici* and *Robert le diable,* had retired from the field, but his name was the foremost in musical Paris, Cherubini's alone challenging it.

At the Opéra-Comique, the year of Chopin's arrival at Paris, an opera called *La Marquise de Brinvilliers* was given its first performance. Its two librettists and nine composers summed up much of the qualities and the struggle of opposites then characteristic of the Parisian scene. The libretto was in part the work of Augustin-Eugène Scribe, the seventy-six volumes of whose complete works include the best texts used by Auber and Meyerbeer, and even one — *Les Vêpres siciliennes* — used by Verdi. His collaborator on the communally produced *La Marquise de Brinvilliers* was the music critic of the influential *Journal des débats,* a confused and mediocre writer known as Castil-Blaze (his real name was François-Henri-Joseph Blaze). He it was who, in 1824, had produced the monstrous French adaptation of *Der Freischütz* that became the rage of Paris as *Robin des bois* and won the uncritical enthusiasm of Victor Hugo, though it later rendered Berlioz almost incoherent with fury.

The composers of *La Marquise de Brinvilliers,* nine strong, supplied a cross-section of current Parisian music. Almost forgotten now are Désiré-Alexandre Batton, an unsuccessful fashioner of operas; Henri-Montan Berton, a violinist, theorist, and conductor whose father had tried to mediate the Piccinni-Gluck "war," and who himself composed nearly fifty operas; an itinerant Italian named Giuseppe Marco Maria Felice Blangini; and another Italian called Michele Enrico Carafa di Colobrano. More important were the other five composers, great figures all: Auber, Cherubini, Hérold, Boïeldieu (whose *La Dame blanche* dated from 1825), and Ferdinando Paër, the greatly talented sixty-year-old Parmesan to whom Dr. Malfatti in Vienna had given Chopin a letter. In the hands of these men, with a few others, lay the immediate future of Parisian musical entertainment.

In literature and painting, as in music — and, for that matter, politics — France was seeing the citadels of classicism constantly challenged by the romantics. In 1831, the year after the scandal attending the first performance of *Hernani,* Victor Hugo, not yet thirty, published *Notre-Dame de Paris.* Mme de Staël was dead, but the Vicomte de Chateaubriand, who three decades before had prefigured the romantics in *Atala,* was still a dominant voice at past sixty. Honoré de Balzac, having published *Le Dernier Chouan,* his first salute to Scott, in 1829, was already embarked on the superhuman voyage of his masterworks, and in 1831 published *La Peau de chagrin.* Prosper Mérimée was the author of admired novels. Alexandre Dumas *père* was a prominent dramatist and the father of a seven-year-old boy who one day would write *La Dame aux camélias.* New sorts of poetry were being published by Théophile Gautier, Alfred de Vigny, and Alfred de Musset. It was the year of *Le Rouge et le noir,* the earlier of two great novels by a middle-aged man named Beyle, known as Stendhal, who had already published biographical studies of Haydn and Rossini. It was the year, too, of *Rose et Blanche,* a collaboration by Jules Sandeau and a pseudonymous writer soon to be called George Sand. Arriving on the Parisian scene as Chopin did was Heinrich Heine.

The ordered pictorial classicism of the recently dead Jacques-Louis David was being continued on canvas by his great pupil, Ingres. Painting, easier to control and codify in the best French manner than either literature or music, was rapidly becoming a war, with Ingres holding the fortress of the past against the insistent attacks of Delacroix, who reappeared in the salon of 1831, asserting once more the liberties earned earlier by Géricault and thus beginning the enlistment of the most vital younger painters into the ranks of rebellion. Hippolyte-Paul Delaroche was vainly trying to make the best of both worlds. Paris was the capital of painting as it was the capital of music. In that world metropolis, Frédéric-François Chopin established himself at 27 boulevard Poissonière.[1]

Among the new friends and acquaintances whom Chopin made during his first years in Paris were Liszt, Ferdinand Hiller, Berlioz, Paër, Kalkbrenner, Rossini, Bellini, Mendelssohn, Cherubini, Heine, and the cellist Auguste-Joseph Franchomme. He also frequented the aristocratic and wealthy Polish colony. Very shortly after his advent on the French scene he was persuaded to give a

---

[1] Within a short time Chopin twice moved, first to 4 cité Bergère, then to 5 rue de la Chausée d'Antin; the latter, a considerably more elegant apartment than the first two, he shared for a time with his friend Yan Matushinski, who taught medicine.

concert, first scheduled for Christmas Day, 1831. A concert then still meant the concurrence of other instrumentalists and, usually, singers. Chopin encountered no difficulty in enlisting prominent instrumentalists to assist him, but the requisite singers proved harder to provide, and the concert was put over to January 15, 1832.

Next, Kalkbrenner, one of the chief promised attractions of Chopin's concert, fell ill. The *"salons de MM. Pleyel et Cie.,"* the piano-manufacturers, located at 9 rue Cadet, were not the scene of Chopin's Paris debut until February 26. What was then offered to the public at ten francs per ticket was billed as a "Grand Vocal and Instrumental Concert, given by M. Frédéric Chopin, of Warsaw," and it would inevitably strike today's audiences as a monstrous hash. The performers included a string quartet, two lady singers, an oboe soloist, and five well-known pianists in addition to Chopin himself. The program as announced for January 15 was:

1. Quintet [C major, opus 29] — Beethoven, performed by Messrs. Baillot, Vidal, Urhan, Tilmant, and Norblin
2. Duet — Mlles Toméoni and Isambert
3. Concerto for piano [F minor, opus 21] — Chopin, performed by the composer
4. Aria — Mlle Toméoni

INTERMISSION

5. Grand Polonaise, preceded by an Introduction and a March, composed for six pianos — Kalkbrenner, played by Messrs. Kalkbrenner, Mendelsohn-Bartholdy [*sic*], Hiller, Osborne, Sowinski, and Chopin [2]
6. Aria — Mlle Isambert
7. Oboe solo — played by M. Brod
8. Variations on *"Là ci darem la mano"* — Chopin, with the composer performing

Several of Chopin's assisting artists were musicians of high rank. Chrétien Urhan, Pierre-Marie-François de Sales Baillot, Jean-Jacques Vidal, and Alexandre Tilmant were all prominent string-

[2] At the actual performance on February 26, Mendelssohn's place was taken by Camille-Marie Stamaty, a Greek pupil of Kalkbrenner and later the teacher of both Saint-Saëns and the fantastic American Louis Moreau Gottschalk.

players, despite which the Beethoven was described, in the old-fashioned way, as a "quintet for violin." Henri Brod was the foremost oboist of the period. Kalkbrenner and Hiller were both considered great pianists. Adalbert Sovinski was a noted Polish pianist, and George Alexander Osborne was an Irish pupil of Kalk-brenner. As no orchestra or conductor is mentioned, it is likely that Chopin played both his Concerto and his Variations as piano solos without accompaniment.

Following the garbled account of this concert given by Frederick Niecks, many writers have stated that it was a failure financially, that only the Poles present paid for their tickets, while the French auditors were admitted gratis, and that the box-office take did not cover the expenses. This story was based on three misconceptions: that Chopin paid for use of the Salle Pleyel, that he paid all of the assisting artists, and that he was accompanied in the Concerto and the Variations by an orchestra. In fact, the hall was his for nothing, he certainly paid either none of the assisting performers or but two or three of the least well known, and he performed his own compositions either as piano solos or accompanied at a second piano by one of his colleagues. Tickets were ten francs each, and the hall was well filled. The financial returns must have been pleasant, but they were admittedly less important than the fact that Liszt and Mendelssohn applauded vociferously with the others. At a bound the concert established Chopin among the foremost musicians of Paris.

François-Joseph Fétis, the Belgian music historian, had founded the *Revue musicale* in 1827; by the time of Chopin's Parisian advent he was the most respected critic in the French capital. His criticism of the young Pole's maiden concert, printed in the *Revue musicale*, is a far cry from the dithyrambs of Schumann: it is creative criticism and it is full of information. It reads:

Today to say of a pianist that he has a bountiful talent or even, if one will, a great talent, is to give the impression that he emulates or rivals first-rank artists whose names at once come to mind; to add that his music is excellent leads to the supposition that its merit is like that of Hummel's works and that of the works of a few renowned composers; but by these eulogies it is difficult to convey any conception of novelty or originality because, except for certain shadings of style and workmanlike ability, pianists' music is generally written in conventional forms that can be considered basic, forms that have been constantly reproduced for more than thirty years. The flaw is stylistic, and our cleverest artists have been unable to rid their works of it. But here is a young man who, giving way to his natural leanings and taking no model, has found, if not a way of reviving piano music completely, at least some of what has so long been vainly sought, that is to say an abundance of original ideas of which the type is nowhere to be discovered. That is not to say that M. Chopin is gifted with the power of a Beethoven, or that one finds in his music the vitality of conception that is so remarkable in that great man. Beethoven has composed music for the piano, but here I am speaking of music for pianists, and in this realm I find, in the inspirations of M. Chopin, indications of a change of form that may in the future exercise considerable influence on this branch of art.[3]

At the concert that he presented on the 26th of this month in the salons of MM. Pleyel & Cie., M. Chopin played a Concerto that astonished as much as it delighted his audience, both by the novelty of the melodic ideas and by the patterns, the modulations, and the general arrangement of the movements. There is soul in his melodies, fantasy in his figuration, and originality in everything. Too much richness of modulation, a lack of order in the sequence of phrases, so that at times one seems to be hearing improvisation rather than written music — these are the defects that mingle with the qualities already mentioned. But these defects are owing to the artist's youth; they will disappear when he gains experience. If M. Chopin's later works fulfill the promise of his debut, one cannot doubt that he will win a brilliant and well-merited reputation.

As a performer this young artist also deserves praise. His playing is elegant, facile, graceful, and has brilliance and clarity. He brings little tone out of the instrument, and in this resembles most German pianists. But the study that he is making of this department of his art with M. Kalkbrenner cannot fail to give him an important quality on which the finesse of execution depends, and without which the voice of the instrument cannot be modified.

As early as September 18, 1831 Chopin had written to his friend Kumelski that Kalkbrenner was "the first pianist of Europe. . . . He is one whose shoelace I am not worthy to untie." To Tytus Voitsyekhovski, two months later, he was even more en-

[3] Had Fétis lived to hear the piano music of Skryabin, Debussy, Ravel, and Prokofiev, to mention only four composers, he would have been confirmed in his beliefs as a prophet.

thusiastic: "You know how curious I was about Herz, Liszt, Hiller, etc. — They are all zero beside Kalkbrenner. I confess that I have played like Herz, but would wish to play like Kalkbrenner. If Paganini is perfection, Kalkbrenner is his equal, but in an entirely different style. It is difficult to tell you of his calm, his enchanting touch, his incomparable evenness, and the mastery that he displays in every note; he is a giant walking over Herz and Czerny and all — and over me." Later in the same letter he told Tytus that Kalkbrenner had offered to teach him for three years, guaranteeing to "make something really — really out of me." He consulted his parents; with some fear of hurting feelings, he consulted Elsner. And the final decision was that he had better be Frédéric-François Chopin than a replica of the style and theories of Kalkbrenner. From the German he may have had a few hints, but no more.

In the letter to Tytus mentioned above, Chopin went on for hundreds of tumbling words about the wonders he had been hearing in opera. He listed the great singers of the hour: Rubini, Malibran, Lablache, Pasta, Schröder-Devrient, Cinti-Damoreau, Nourrit, and Chollet.[4] The operas he had most enjoyed were *Il Barbiere di Siviglia, L'Italiana in Algeri,* the extravagantly produced *Robert le diable, Fra Diavolo, La Fiancée* (Auber), and *Zampa.* He also sent Tytus the description of an incident that is so lively as to deserve quotation in his own words:

I can't refrain from telling you about my incident with [Johann Peter] Pixis [the well-known German pedagogue, pianist, and composer, then forty-three]. Imagine this — he has a very pretty fifteen-year-old girl [Francilla Pixis, later an admired mezzo-soprano] living with him, whom he is said to consider marrying, and whom I met when I called on him in Stuttgart. Pixis, on his arrival here, invited me to call, but failed to say that the girl, whom I had forgotten, had come with him. (I might have called sooner if I had known.) He asked me to call, so a week later I went. On the stairs I was pleased to meet the young pupil; she invited me in, saying that Herr Pixis was out, but that did not matter, come in and rest, he will soon return, etc. We both feel a

---

[4] He mentions a performance of Rossini's *Otello* in which Malibran, "blacked up and playing the role none too well," was Othello, while Schröder-Devrient was Desdemona! "Malibran is small, the German woman tremendous; it looked as though Desdemona would smother Othello."

little tremulous. Knowing how jealous the old man is, I excuse myself; I shall return, and so forth. Meanwhile, as we stand prettily talking on the stairs in the innocence of our hearts, up comes little Pixis, stares (in Soliva's manner) through large glasses to see who is on the stairs talking to his belle, and then, rushing upstairs, poor fellow, stops before me and brusquely says "Good day," and to her "What are you doing here?" — and a great jeremiad of German devils at her for daring to receive a young man during his absence. I too (smiling and ignoring everything) uphold Pixis, scolding her for coming out so lightly clad, just in her cloth dress, and so forth. At last the old man realized; swallowed, grasped me by the arm, led me into the salon, didn't know where to have me sit, he was so afraid that I might become offended and play some trick on him in his absence, or else murder his pupil. Later he went downstairs with me, and noticing that I was still laughing — (I could not conceal my amusement at the joke of anyone's considering me capable of that sort of thing) — he went straight to the concierge to learn when and by what means I got onto the stairs, and so forth. Since that day Pixis can't say enough in praise of my talent to all the publishers, and especially to Schlesinger, who has hired me to write something on themes from Robert, which he has bought from Meyerbeer for 24,000 francs.[5] How do you like this — me as a seducer?

On December 25, 1831 Chopin again wrote to Tytus, sending, as he put it, "your name-day wishes from beyond ten frontiers." In the midst of a rambling, disorganized letter he suddenly said:

I have received your letter from Lvov; we shan't meet, then, until later, and perhaps never, for, seriously, my health is poor. On the outside I am gay, especially among my own (I count Poles as my own), but inside me something gnaws, some presentiment, anxiety, dreams — or sleeplessness — melancholy, indifference — desire for life and the next moment desire for death: for some sweet sort of peace, some kind of numbness, lack of consciousness; and sometimes definite memories taunt me. My mind is sour, bitter, salt; some horrible mixture of sensations shakes me.

"My health is poor" may well be taken as the first certain indication that Chopin was suffering pangs of the tuberculosis that would kill him within eighteen years. He was never for long to be entirely well, though the disease did not make a total invalid of

---

[5] Chopin and Franchomme together did compose a Grand Duo for cello and piano on themes from *Robert le diable*.

him, except for very short periods, until nearly the end. Almost certainly he did not himself name his condition until much later; he believed that his bad health was brought on by loneliness and a nostalgia for what and for whom he had not.

Some part of Chopin's melancholy in December 1831 may have been brought on by the news, sent him by his sister Izabela, that Konstantsya Gladovska had married one Yosef Grabovski. Izabela had felt it necessary to castigate the girl as heartless, and to suggest that she had married the well-to-do Grabovski because he owned a handsome château. "She had feeling only in her singing," she commented. That Chopin, who had never indicated that he himself either planned or desired to marry Konstantsya, was very deeply hurt by the news cannot be asserted on the evidence of his only surviving mention of her marriage. In the December 12, 1831 letter to Tytus already quoted in part, he said in passing: "Mlle Gladkovska has married Grabovski, but that does not preclude platonic sentiments." He seems never to have mentioned his adolescent infatuation again.[6]

Chopin's second public appearance in Paris occurred on May 20, 1832, at a charity concert sponsored in the great hall of the Conservatoire by the Princesse de la Moskowa (widow of Marshal Ney), and graced also by a Mass composed by her son Joseph-Napoléon. The first movement of the F-minor Concerto was received with diminished enthusiasm, for which Fétis's *Revue musicale* blamed the thin tone of the piano used and "the small amount of sound that M. Chopin draws from the piano." The stellar place at the concert was held by Henri Brod, the oboist who had played a solo at Chopin's first Paris concert.

The meager, unsatisfactory issue of his second appearance in Paris was a blow dealt Chopin on top of loneliness, melancholy, and a flat purse. Perhaps, he fell to thinking, Paris was not the place for him. Perhaps the public there had been surfeited by heaven-storming virtuosos who could — and would — drown out

[6] According to Count Vodzhinski, whose *Les Trois Romans de Frédéric Chopin* has supplied large amounts of fiction to unsuspecting biographers, Konstantsya later became blind. Writing before 1886, Vodzhinski said: "Someone who knew her during the last part of her life assured me that, from her poor eyes, left clear in their blindness, huge tears fell drop by drop." She died in 1889.

the delicate tone he preferred to draw from his piano. He would leave France, go elsewhere. To England? It has often been stated that he considered the United States, though this is without proof. Whatever his half-formed plans, he offhandedly retailed them to one of his wealthy Polish friends, Prince Valentin Radzivil. The Prince then displayed his intelligence by persuading Chopin to go with him to a soirée at the home of one of the Rothschilds. And there, in a resplendent candlelit salon, surrounded by titled ladies and suave gentlemen, Chopin conquered the part of Paris that was always to matter to him. This was his milieu. Here the intimacy of his playing was exactly right. His hearers were wrapped in a spell. Soon the financial element would be removed from his difficulties by pupils willing to pay twenty francs per lesson.

That Chopin had the manners of a gentleman was of utmost importance to his career in Paris. It was good, in fact, that he was something of a dandy. He always wore white gloves; he kept a carriage even when he could scarcely pay for it. His social position was high in a day when most musicians — including a ubiquitously popular composer like Rossini or a concert-hall darling like Lizst — were tolerated in snobbish society only as a superior sort of entertaining servants. That attitude toward himself Chopin would certainly have refused to bear. He was himself a social snob, and his blond, attenuated, aquiline appearance, with its connotation of spiritual refinement and controlled sensuality, made it easy for duchesses, princes, and the families of millionaires to accept him almost as one of their own. He conveyed, rather than accepted, distinction by appearing at a soirée to play the most insinuating and least vigorous of his pieces.

Chopin himself was entirely aware of his good fortune. Writing to his boyhood friend Dominik Dzyevanovski early in 1833, he said:

I have got into the highest society; I sit with ambassadors, princes, ministers, and I don't even know how it came about because I didn't aim at it. It is an essential thing for me because good taste is supposed to depend on it. Your talent is bigger immediately you have been heard at the English or Austrian embassy; you play better if Princess Vaudemont (last of the old Montmorency family) was your protector — I can't say "is" because the old woman died last week.

Expanding, Chopin told Dominik of his relations with other leading artists on the Paris scene:

Although this is only my first year among the artists here, I have their friendship and respect. One proof of the respect is that even people with enormous reputations dedicate compositions to me before I do to them: Pixis has inscribed his latest variations for military band to me; people also compose variations on my themes. Kalkbrenner has used a mazurka of mine in this way; the pupils of the Conservatoire, Moscheles's students, those of Herz and Kalkbrenner — in a word, finished artists, take lessons from me and couple my name with that of Field. In short, if I were even more stupid than I am, I should think myself at the peak of my career. Yet I realize how much I still fall short of reaching perfection; I see it more clearly now that I am living only among first-rank artists and know what each one of them lacks.

He closes on a social note:

I have five lessons to give today; do you think that I am making a fortune? Carriages and white gloves cost more, and without them one would not be in good taste. I love the Carlists, I can't endure the Philippists, I myself am a revolutionist; also I care nothing for money, only for friendship, for which I beg and beseech you.

It was not only Paris that was beginning to know Chopin. In Leipzig, Clara Wieck had drawn attention to him in July 1832 by playing his Variations on *"Là ci darem la mano."* Five months later the Leipzig publishing house of Probst-Kistner issued the nine Mazurkas that make up Chopin's opus 6 and opus 7. The latter is dedicated to a plebeian "Mr. Johns of New Orleans," but opus 6 bears the name of "Mlle la comtesse Pauline Plater," one of Chopin's noble pupils. Reviewing the opus 7, Ludwig Rellstab, the volcanic Berlin critic who once went to prison for libeling Henriette Sontag, spewed scoriae: "If Herr Chopin had showed this work to a master, the latter would, it is to be hoped, have torn it up and thrown it at his feet, which we herewith symbolically do." Others than Rellstab (who had his reasons) were irritated by the strange harmonies and unprecedented resolutions of Chopin's most Slavic manner. The Mazurkas nonetheless made their way, the B-flat major of opus 7 shortly becoming a favorite home and concert piece. A public demand for Chopin is indicated by the publication during 1833 of the Trio, opus 8; the Introduction and Polonaise brillante for cello and piano, opus 3; the Études, opus 10; [7] the E-minor Concerto, opus 11; the Nocturnes, opus 9; the Grand Duo for piano and cello on themes from *Robert le diable* (composed with Franchomme), no opus number; and the Variations brillantes on a theme from *Ludovic,* opus 12. [8] Mostly these were issued in Leipzig by Probst-Kistner and in Paris by Maurice Schlesinger, publisher of the *Gazette musicale*.

At least three times during 1833 Chopin appeared in public performance with Liszt. Berlioz's *idée fixe*, the Irish actress Henrietta Smithson, fell from a carriage and broke her leg. The frantically infatuated Berlioz then enlisted Chopin and Liszt to play during a theatrical benefit performance for — and partly by — her on April 2. Each of them performed a piano solo in an entr'acte. The following day Liszt and Chopin were assisting artists at a concert given by Henri Herz and his brother Jacques. On this occasion the four men played one or more pieces for eight hands at two pianos. And on December 15 Chopin and Liszt appeared at a Conservatoire concert given by their friend Hiller, this time taking part in at least one movement of a Bach concerto for three pianos.

Early in 1834 Chopin accepted one invitation and refused another. The latter was from the Vodzhinski family, three of whose sons had been his schoolmates; he had also given primary piano lessons to their small sister, Marya. Having fled from the disturbances in Poland, the Vodzhinskis were residing in Geneva, whither they invited Chopin. He declined, which he would almost certainly not have done had he then felt toward Marya the love he was to have for her later. The other invitation, from Hiller, bade him to the Lower Rhine Music Festival at Aachen in late May, and this he accepted.

Arrived at Aachen, Chopin went to a rehearsal of Handel's

[7] The embarrassing Rellstab — who was later to recant with respect to Chopin — was not less violent about the Études than about the Mazurkas: "Those who have twisted fingers may cure them by practicing these Études, but those who have not should not play them, at least not unless they have a surgeon handy."

[8] *Ludovic,* an opera left unfinished by Hérold on his death in January 1833, was completed by Halévy and produced on May 16 of that year.

CHOPIN
a painting by Anton Kolberg

CHOPIN
after a painting by Ary Scheffer

MARYA VODZHINSKA
as Chopin knew her

Deborah and there met Mendelssohn. Writing to his mother on May 23, Mendelssohn reported the incident as follows:

Now I had my full share of pleasure in the Music Festival, for the three of us lived together and took a private box in the theater (where the oratorio is sung), and of course next morning we betook ourselves to the piano, where I had the greatest delight. They have both improved greatly in execution, and Chopin as a pianist is now one of the very first of all. He produces new effects as Paganini does on the violin, and achieves wonderful passages such as no one could have thought possible earlier. . . . After the festival we traveled together to Düsseldorf and spent a most agreeable day there playing and talking about music; then I accompanied them to Cologne yesterday. Early this morning they went off to Coblenz by steamer — I in the opposite direction — and the pleasant episode was over. . . .

The year 1834 marked the apogee of Chopin's brief, intense friendship with Vincenzo Bellini, the sparkling young composer of *La Sonnambula* and *Norma,* who was to die the following year after the brilliantly successful *première* of his *I Puritani.* Critics divide sharply over the extent of Bellini's influence on the undoubtedly Italianate profile of many of Chopin's melodies. While it is more reasonable to suppose that Bellini and Chopin were both persuaded by the same earlier Italian music (certain of Rossini's operas especially), those who favor Bellini's direct bearing on the melodies of his Polish friend have perhaps their best argument in a piece composed in 1834. This, the Fantaisie-Impromptu, has a very Bellinian melody indeed [9] as its middle section. It would not appear out of place in *Norma.* The point about this particular melodic line is that it could not be Rossini's, whatever its remote origins in folk melody may have been.

It was during 1834, too, that old Elsner, in a letter dated September 14, wrote his former pupil to congratulate him on several successes, but added: "What you have done thus far I do not consider enough." Elsner was not satisfied with Chopin the composer for piano, but desired him to compose an opera. Karasowski is the source of the statement that Elsner's letter shook Chopin considerably, even led him to ask Stanislas Kozmian for a libretto

[9] This was, of course, the basis of the once epidemically popular American song "I'm Always Chasing Rainbows."

based on Polish history. But this may be fiction. What is certain
is that Chopin never undertook to compose an opera. He never,
in fact, wrote a piece in which there was not a piano part,[10] never
— except for the few pieces composed for cello-playing friends —
a single instrumental piece in which the piano did not hold the
leading role. He had made a choice of necessity and genius combined, and the feeble, tentative orchestrations washed in behind
the piano in some of his concert pieces do not invalidate the
statement that he was a composer for the piano and for nothing
else.

At the Conservatoire on December 7, 1834 Berlioz conducted a
program of his own music, including the third performance of his
recent *Harold en Italie*, the *Roi Lear Overture*, and the Overture
to *Les Francs-Juges*. And somewhere in this overpowering blaze
of orchestral color the slender Chopin sat at a piano to play the
larghetto middle movement of his F-minor Concerto. Both its
orchestration and Chopin's piano tone were notoriously thin;
they utterly lacked brightness among Berlioz's richly capari-
soned pieces — and the larghetto quite naturally produced little
effect. This event severely discouraged Chopin, who still had no
desire to approach the piano like a Kalkbrenner, a Herz, or a
Liszt and who would have omitted altogether to play in public if
he could have followed his own inclinations. To play and be
badly received was therefore doubly discouraging.

On Christmas Day, nevertheless, Chopin had to return to the
Pleyel rooms in which he had first wooed a Parisian public. This
time he was assisting at a very goulash of a concert organized by
Dr. Franz Stöpel, an itinerant musical theorist and pedagogue.
The others supporting Stöpel included Liszt, the famous violinist
Heinrich Wilhelm Ernst, and Sabine Heinefetter — not to mention a grandniece of Jean-Jacques Rousseau, a Mme de la Haye
who improvised on a harmonium. Liszt and Chopin led off with a
Moscheles duet (or two-piano piece) in a way that the critic for
the *Gazette musicale* viewed with ecstasy. Encoring this, the
two friends "electrified" the audience with a Liszt two-piano
piece, apparently a lost set of variations on a theme by Mendelssohn.

By the end of 1834 Chopin had published in one year seven of

[10] For a possible exception, see page 326.

the sixty-five works that were to be issued with opus numbers during his lifetime. That year's harvest included the Grand Fantasy on Polish Airs, opus 13; the Krakoviak, opus 14; the Nocturnes, opus 15; the Rondo in E-flat major, opus 16; the Mazurkas, opus 17; the Grande Valse brillante, opus 18; and the Boléro, opus 19. He was gradually clearing from his desk those pieces which he had composed in Warsaw and still desired to preserve. During 1835, in fact, only two opus numbers were to be added. The year was to be scarcely more rich in newly composed pieces.

The reason for Chopin's comparative lack of creative activity in 1835 is biographical. The year began badly for him, included considerable travel, saw the inception of an infatuation more mature and more shattering in its outcome than the one for Konstantsya Gladkovska, and ended in a spell of sickness so confining that Paris heard more than one report that the young Polish émigré of musical genius had died.

VIII

A<small>T</small> the Italian Opera on April 4, 1835 François-Antoine Habeneck, the conductor who had introduced Beethoven's symphonies to Paris in superb fashion, led a gala concert for the benefit of the numerous all-but-penniless Polish refugees. Among those who contributed their prestige and services were the dazzling dramatic soprano Marie-Cornélie Falcon, the tenor Adolphe Nourrit (who had created the role of Eléazar in *La Juive* less than two months before), the violinist Ernst, Hiller, Liszt, and Chopin. The program included the overtures to *Guillaume Tell* and *Oberon;* Chopin's E-minor Concerto, with the composer as soloist; a duet from *Guillaume Tell,* sung by Falcon and Nourrit; Schubert songs, sung by Nourrit, with Liszt at the piano; and a two-piano piece, played by Hiller and Liszt. Many of these selections must have aroused thundering enthusiasm. But when the Chopin Concerto had ended, according to a writer in the *Grand Dictionnaire* of Larousse, "The bravos of his [Chopin's] friends and a few connoisseurs alone challenged the chilly and somewhat bewildered attitude of the larger part of the audience." It had been proved once more, if it still required proof, that neither Chopin the concerto-composer, with his lackadaisical orchestration, nor Chopin the pianist of highly graded nuances would conquer the largest audiences in the largest of the Parisian halls.

More enthusiasm was aroused by Chopin's appearance, three weeks later, at one of the notable Habeneck concerts of the Société des Concerts du Conservatoire. As one incident of an enormous program that represented Beethoven by his Sixth Symphony, the scherzo from the Ninth Symphony, and the finale from the Fifth, Chopin played the solo part of his Andante spianato and Grande Polonaise in E-flat major, opus 22 — the only time he ever performed it publicly with its perfunctory orchestral accompaniment. He won something resembling a popular success on that April 26, but the victory did not swerve him from his dislike of acting the virtuoso in competition with the keyboard thunderers who could always overwhelm him. Except for Liszt's "farewell" concert of April 9, 1836, during which Chopin and Liszt played one duet, Chopin never again appeared in Paris at a large public concert. His few semipublic appearances in later years were at small musicales that partook not at all of the nature of large commercial concerts. From 1835 on, Chopin was a composer who sometimes played the piano for his friends and his own small public. Under intimate conditions of that sort he was not so much a pianist as a sorcerer, as is proved by the abundant testimony of those who heard him.[1]

During the midsummer of 1835 Nicolas and Yustina Chopin journeyed from Warsaw to Karlsbad, probably so that Nicolas could take the cure there. At four o'clock in the morning after their arrival they were awakened by news that their son had reached Karlsbad and was looking for them everywhere. The reunion after nearly five years was a happy one. The three of them wrote a joint letter to Ludvika and Izabela on August 16, and Fritsek's postscript to it was positively breathless:

Well, my children, I embrace you; and forgive me for not being able to collect my thoughts or write about anything more than that we are happy at this moment, that I had only hope and now have the realization, and am happy, happy, happy. I could hug you and my brothers-in-law to death — my dearest in the world.

When the Chopins left Karlsbad three weeks later, it was to go to Teschen to visit the Thun-Hohenstein family.[2] From Teschen the elder Chopins started for Warsaw. They and their famous son were never to meet again.

Chopin traveled from to Teschen to Dresden after the middle

---

[1] Earlier in 1835 Chopin had twice played at public or semipublic concerts. On February 25, at the Salle Érard, he had played a Hiller two-piano piece with the composer. And in March, in the Salle Pleyel, he had joined Herz, Osborne, Hiller, Stamaty, and Anton Reicha in what the *Ménestrel* for March 22 called "various pieces." William Murdoch reasonably guessed that one of the pieces was Kalkbrenner's monstrous work for six pianos, which had appeared on the program of Chopin's first Paris concert.

[2] Chopin's Waltz in A-flat major, opus 34, no. 1, composed on September 15, 1835, is dedicated to a Mlle de Thun-Hohenstein.

of September. The Vodzhinskis, who had been living out the Polish troubles in Switzerland (except for Anton, who had been in Paris, where Chopin had enjoyed his company), were traveling back to Warsaw and had invited him to visit them en route at Dresden. They were exactly the sort of people he liked most, being rich and of noble blood.[3] He no doubt looked forward to renewing his acquaintance with the Countess — with whom he had been corresponding — the other two sons, and little Marya. Reaching the Saxon capital, he put up at the Stadt Gotha Inn.

Marya Vodzhinska was nineteen years old, not beautiful or even pretty, but vivacious and attractive — her dark skin and black hair perhaps particularly winning to the pale, blond Chopin. She was a young lady of the world and a budding flirt. Among the men whom she had already attracted were Yulius Slovatski, a Byronic Polish poet whom Chopin would later meet in George Sand's salon, and Louis-Napoleon Bonaparte, future Emperor of the French. Nothing recorded of Marya suggests that she possessed the ardor or the breadth of comprehension that might have led a different girl to step down from her social class to the level of a poor musician, however famous and however well-mannered and aristocratic in bearing. It was this girl with whom Chopin allowed himself to fall rapidly and at last completely in love.

The Countess, Marya's mother, was at first inclined to regard Chopin's undeclared suit for her daughter's hand with indulgence. Nor was it visibly frowned upon by the girl's uncle, the elderly Palatine Vodzhinski, at whose Dresden refuge the family was staying. For Marya the young man composed the A-flat major Waltz, posthumously published as opus 69, no. 1. To her he gave a card containing the words *"Soyez heureuse"* and the opening line of his E-flat major Nocturne, opus 9, no. 2. Just before he left Dresden, on September 26 — the parting messages have often been imagined, but can never be known — Marya took one bloom from a bouquet of roses and presented it to him.

Going on to Leipzig, Chopin put up at the Hotel de Saxe. His chief reason for visiting the city was a hope of hearing Clara Wieck play the piano. Instead of going immediately to her father,

[3] They were descended both from the Sforzas and from the Polish-Lithuanian dynasty of Jagiello.

the irascible and mandatory Friedrich Wieck, he passed several days in Leipzig — seeking out Henrietta Voigt, a musical friend of Mendelssohn and Schumann — before presenting himself at the Wieck home. This infuriated Clara's father, who retired into an inner section of the house as soon as Chopin finally did call, and refused to come forth again until the guest had left. It was Mendelssohn who had at last taken Chopin to meet Clara; he is said to have entered the room in which were Clara, her mother, her aunt, Schumann, and three of Wieck's pupils, with the words: "This is Chopin" — having said which, he went on to another engagement. Then there was music-making. Clara played Schumann's newly completed Sonata in F-sharp minor, opus 11, as well as two of Chopin's Études and a movement from one of his Concertos. The finicky guest, finding the Wieck piano too massive for his taste and touch, responded only with his recently composed E-flat Nocturne. Clara thought Chopin's playing too whimsical. Perhaps his famous rubato annoyed her methodical German mind. Chopin referred to her flatly as "the only woman in Germany who can play my music."

From Leipzig Chopin moved on to Heidelberg for a short visit with the parents of his sixteen-year-old wonder pupil, the physically luxuriant Adolf Gutmann. Thence he returned to Paris, arriving in mid-October after being gone about two and one half months. He had met Schumann and Clara Wieck, had renewed his pleasant friendship with Mendelssohn. He had spent happy days with his parents. He had seen the Vodzhinskis. He was in love.

The winter of 1835–6 was a bad one both for Chopin's health and for his reputation as a concert artist. For a considerable period he was very ill. His ailment was described as "influenza" — a vague term, especially as applied more than a century ago — but it is actually almost certain that what he underwent was a preliminary, but fierce assault of the tuberculosis that was to become unmistakable in Majorca just two years later. He was not seen in public. He was not heard of at all, except occasionally as the composer of pieces performed by other pianists. In January 1836 a Warsaw newspaper contradicted rumors that he had died. His illness had been so severe that he had been unable to write to his parents. Count Vodzhinski, asserting that he was awaiting

Fritsek's news of his son Anton — also in Paris — remained in Warsaw until Chopin's first letter finally arrived and put a definite end to the belief that he might be dead. Up to this time the Count may or may not have looked with approving eyes on the young musician's courtship of his daughter. Any opposition he may have entertained to the prospect of Marya's becoming the wife of a composer was unquestionably stiffened by knowledge of Chopin's bad health.

The sensation of the Paris concert halls, meanwhile, was the brilliant love-child of Prince Moritz von Dietrichstein and Baroness Wetzler, Sigismond Thalberg. Chopin had heard Thalberg, a youth of eighteen, in Vienna in 1830, and had found in him little to admire or emulate. Now a dandified young man of twenty-three, the aristocratic Thalberg burst onto the Paris scene as both pianist and composer. His assistants at the concert included such leading musical personalities as the great tenor Gilbert-Louis Duprez, Pauline García, and the renowned Belgian violinist Charles-Auguste de Bériot, who was shortly to marry García's more famous sister, Maria Malibran. Thalberg was at once hailed as the foremost pianist of the time, while his vapid compositions were warmly praised. Kalkbrenner was a cold formalist by comparison; Moscheles was living in England; Liszt, in Switzerland with Countess Marie d'Agoult, who had just borne him an illegitimate daughter, was far from the Parisian scene. For a time Thalberg, another technical wizard, bowled along over all opposition. In the midst of this clamor the ailing, soft-spoken Chopin cut no figure at all. More and more he was turned in upon himself and upon the small, pathetically select circle of those who had the rare opportunity to admire him as he played and improvised in the flower-and-cosmetic atmosphere of private salons.

With Hector Berlioz, recently become critic of the highly respected pro-regime *Journal des débats* — and on the verge of composing his magnificent Requiem — Chopin maintained his casual friendship. In January 1836, in fact, he assisted Berlioz — never well disposed toward the piano — to arrange for two pianos his overture to the unfortunate opera *Les Francs-Juges*. The record of Chopin's own composing and publishing for 1835 was meager. Published were only the B-minor Scherzo, opus 20, and the Mazurkas of opus 24, while only three or four Waltzes and a like number of Mazurkas can be assigned 1835 as their year of composition.

With spring and warmer weather Chopin's health improved. About April 1 he refused Mendelssohn's invitation to join him at Düsseldorf during the summer for the Lower Rhine Festival, where he was to conduct the *première* of *St. Paul.* Perhaps Chopin refused because he still felt too weak to contemplate the trip, perhaps because he was already planning another visit to the Vodzhinskis, this time in Marienbad. All positive statements of his exact feelings for Marya at this time are fiction, but it is easy to deduce that he had managed to concentrate on her unlikely person — as earlier he had on Konstantsya Gladkovska — all his romantic yearnings. There is indication, too, that Countess Vodzhinska definitely favored the prospect of Marya's accepting him, and therefore abetted, or even instigated, his plan to see the girl again.

Chopin arrived at the Vodzhinskis' rented Marienbad villa late in July 1836. During August Marya sketched his portrait. They went on to Dresden with her family; there, on September 9, Chopin asked Marya to marry him and she accepted his proposal. He then placed it before her mother, who consented, but extracted a promise that the engagement would be kept entirely secret until such time as she herself should be able to convince Marya's father to add his consent. Two days later, perhaps in the rosy glow of belief that Marya shortly would be his, Chopin went to Leipzig. He had promised to guard his health.

Chopin and Marya Vodzhinska never met again. Although the Count and Countess, visiting Warsaw, called on Chopin's parents and gave them a copy of the portrait Marya had made of Fritsek, his relations even with the Countess shortly began to taper off coolly. Another attack of serious illness in the winter of 1836–7 may have accounted for Count Vodzhinski's refusal to sanction the marriage — or he may have been resolute against it from the beginning. The unannounced bethrothal could not be broken publicly, and it was consequently permitted to die unborn. Chopin continued to correspond with various members of the Vodzhinski family for two or three years, and his friendship with Marya's brother Anton was close as late 1845. But it was only a short while until the remaining story of his love was enclosed in a small packet of letters containing the rose Marya had given him in 1835. This packet was found among Chopin's effects after his death. It was labeled in his handwriting: *"Moja bieda"* — my misery.[4]

On September 14, 1836 Robert Schumann wrote a letter to his former teacher Heinrich Dorn, then conductor of the Riga Opera. In part he said:

Day before yesterday, just when I had received your letter and was about to reply to it, who should come in? — Chopin. This was a great pleasure for me. We had a very happy day together, and yesterday we held a post-celebration. . . . I have Chopin's new Ballade.[5] It seems to me to be the piece that shows most genius, and I told him that I liked it most of all his works. After thinking a long time he said with great feeling, "I'm glad of that because it's the one I prefer too." He also played for me some new études, nocturnes, and mazurkas, all of them incomparable. You would like him enormously.

It would be interesting to know if Schumann let his guest hear the *Carnaval,* completed in 1835: its twelfth section, headed "Chopin," is a wonderfully poetic evocation of the more lyric aspects of Chopin's creation. The two young men — Schumann was Chopin's elder by only four months — were on the best of terms. While in Leipzig, Chopin also called on Henrietta Voigt and her husband, playing for them a full hour. Henrietta, herself an accomplished pianist, described his playing as marvelous, saying that it made her hold her breath. In her diary she wrote: "He transported me in a manner unknown to me before. It was his childlike directness and simplicity of manner while playing that chiefly delighted me."

From Leipzig, after again paying a short visit to the Gutmann family in Heidelberg, Chopin returned to Paris. There he soon learned that Liszt and Countess Marie d'Agoult had returned from Switzerland and were openly living together at the Hôtel de France with their infant daughter Blandine. However the

[4] In 1841 Marya Vodzhinska married Count Yozef Skarbek, a son of Chopin's godfather. This marriage was annulled, and she later married a man named Orpishevski. She died a widow, in 1896. The Count Anton Vodzhinski (1852–?) who wrote the notorious novel *Les Trois Romans de Frédéric Chopin* was her nephew.

[5] The G-minor Ballade, opus 23, was published in June 1836.

strictest Parisian society may have disapproved of the manner in which they flaunted their liaison — particularly as the Countess was estranged but not divorced from her husband — few cared to refuse invitations to the soirées by means of which the attractive couple began to enliven the scene. It was at one of these musical and artistic evenings that, late in 1836, Chopin was introduced to the most famous Frenchwoman of the day, George Sand.

Still infatuated with Marya Vodzhinska, still looking forward to an early marriage, Chopin was naturally not attracted to the somewhat formidable writer, five and one half years his senior, not physically seductive in any superficial way, and already the notorious heroine of dramatic *affaires du coeur* with Jules Sandeau and Alfred de Musset. He is likely to have regarded her with much of the interest she aroused in all her contemporaries, though he was not sufficiently literary by nature to appreciate her as a creative writer. At a small evening party of his own on December 13, Chopin entertained Liszt (who played), Nourrit (who sang), and George Sand. Another of the guests, Yozef Bzhovski, described the soirée in his Mémoires — a passage quoted by Ferdinand Hoesick in his great Polish biography of Chopin. Bzhovski described George Sand, dark, dignified, and cold, as continually blowing out clouds of cigar-smoke. She wore a white dress with a scarlet sash and had her hair arranged in clusters of curls at the sides of her face. Bzhovski further made a special point of saying that she gravely entered into the conversation of the men. Although Countess d'Agoult and Heinrich Heine were also present, he made no mention of them.

As 1836 drew to a close, then, Chopin had met the woman who was to be the most important person in his life for more than ten years. The twelve months then just past had been richer in his publications than 1835, for it had seen the issuance of the delayed "Second" Concerto, in F minor, opus 21; the Andante spianato and Grande Polonaise brillante, opus 22; the G-minor Ballade, opus 23; the Polonaises of opus 26; and the Nocturnes of opus 27. He had completed the magnificent set of Études, begun about four years earlier, and to be published as his opus 25 in 1837.

Chopin's illness recurred during the winter of 1836–7. He continued to correspond sporadically with Countess Vodzhinska, giving her what news he had of her son Anton, who was with the Polish Legion in Spain, which unhappy country was then suffering from the Carlist War. On August 14, 1837 he told her that he had himself spent the preceding month "dawdling about London." He had been persuaded to his first visit to England by Camille Pleyel, whom he accompanied. Not many details of this visit are known. Mendelssohn, writing from London on September 1, told Hiller:

It seems that Chopin came over here quite suddenly a fortnight ago (!), paid no visits, and saw nobody, played very beautifully at Broadwood's one evening, and then took himself off again. They say that he is still very sick and unhappy.

Stanislas Kozmian, a Pole whom Chopin and Pleyel met in London, wrote thus to his family about their times together:

Chopin has been here incognito for a fortnight. He knows nobody and doesn't want to know anybody but me. I spend the whole day with him, and sometimes — as yesterday — the whole night. He is here with Pleyel, well known for his pianos and for his wife's adventures.[6] They have come to "do" London. They are at one of the best hotels, they have a carriage, and in brief they are simply looking for the opportunity to spend money. So one day we went to Windsor, another to Blackwall, and tomorrow are off to Richmond.

Kozmian further reported that he had not been able to attend a performance of Marliani's *Ildegonda* because Chopin refused to be bored by it, and that at a concert unsuccessfully given to raise funds for the Beethoven Memorial at Bonn, Chopin had heard Moscheles play a long concerto — probably of his own composing — in what he described as a "fearfully baroque way." Chopin's appearance at Broadwood's, mentioned by Mendelssohn, was at the home of James Shudi Broadwood, the piano-manufac-

[6] This was the Marie-Félicité-Denise Moke with whom Berlioz had once been infatuated, but who had jilted him for Pleyel. She was a nymphomaniac as well as a first-rate pianist. She later had an affair of sorts with Liszt, which led to the end of the Liszt-Chopin friendship. The exceedingly straitlaced Chopin learned that Liszt had borrowed his rooms for the purpose of an assignation with Mme Pleyel — and the friendship suffered permanently.

turer, where he is said to have been introduced simply as "Monsieur Fritz." The legend has it that the Broadwoods recognized him as Chopin the moment he began to play the piano, but no mention is made of where they might have heard him earlier.

Chopin's excursion to England may well have followed his final realization that Marya Vodzhinska would never be his wife. This sad recognition, plus his intermittently bad health, plus his inability to make a big place for himself in the Parisian world of concerts — these blows conditioned him for receptivity to George Sand. After her return from her summer 1837 visit to her château at Nohant, he saw more and more of her. He was lonely, he was feverishly sensitive. Everything feminine and recessive in his character appealed powerfully to everything that was motherly, dominating, and to some extent masculine in George Sand. She was a woman quite capable of making the first overt gesture toward a man who appealed to her most deep-seated instincts as Chopin did. To him, as the months passed, she seemed to promise simultaneously a mistress's love, a mother's care, surcease from worry, and mental stimulation.

All that stood in the way of a love affair was Chopin's overweening sense of propriety. But he was twenty-seven, and his senses and emotions — both perhaps exacerbated by the tuberculosis already attacking his body — had been denied too long. He and George Sand soon were lovers. Partly of his own volition, partly as the neuter pawn of forces he could not control, partly as a child of his romantic times, Chopin had made the most fateful step of his life. He had embarked on his first major — and, as it turned out, his last — attempt to reach out with eager hands toward a fulfillment apart from music.

Here it must be said that some French writers on Chopin — and particularly Édouard Ganche in a curious book called *Souffrances de Frédéric Chopin: Essai de médecine et de psychologie* — continue to express the belief that the Sand-Chopin relationship was passionate but chaste. In some cases this reading of the documents is a result of taking Sand's own proclamations and statements at face value. In others it derives directly from a belief that Chopin was incapable of having sexual relations, either out of fastidiousness and prudery or — as Ganche would have it — out of physical inability. Ganche believes that Chopin, suffering from a complication of ailments including lifelong anemia, was impotent, and from that wholly unprovable premise builds the portrait of a natural eunuch who could not conceivably have composed a dozen of Chopin's greatest pieces. All the ancillary evidence (there is no other kind) contradicts this to indicate a sexually recessive and perhaps sexually feeble man whose lack of aggressiveness was exactly one of the qualities that attracted Sand to him. That he could not or would not respond to aggressive overtures on her part there is not one word of reliable evidence to suggest. Sand herself, protesting that the relationship was chaste, stated that she had kept it so against Chopin's desires!

IX

BORN Amandine-Aurore-Lucile Dupin on July 1, 1804, George Sand was the daughter — legitimate by one month — of Maurice Dupin and Sophie-Victoire-Antoine Delaborde. The amount of bastardy in her immediate ancestry was so great that her family tree shimmers with wavy lines. Her mother was the daughter of one Antoine Delaborde, dealer in live birds and operator of a billiard salon. Her father was the legitimate son of an illegitimate daughter of an illegitimate son of Friedrich August I, Elector of Saxony.[1] She herself was married, when eighteen, to Casimir Dudevant, bastard of Baron Jean-François Dudevant. The marriage was a failure from its first night, and ended nine years afterward in a separation that was at last made legal. By her husband, at a period when as a solace to her unhappiness she had begun to write a novel, Amandine-Aurore had a son, born June 30, 1823, and named Maurice. Her only other child, a daughter called Solange, was born on September 14, 1828.[2] Early in 1831, recognizing her marriage as finished, Baroness Dudevant (for Casimir had succeeded to his father's title) went from the family estate at Nohant to Paris.

Baroness Dudevant, aged not quite twenty-seven, was an in-

---

[1] Friedrich August I, by Countess Aurore Königsmark, had an illegitimate son who became the famous Marshal Maurice de Saxe. By an actress, Marie Rinteau (sometimes known as Victoire de Verrières), Saxe had an illegitimate daughter who was eventually recognized and allowed to style herself Marie-Aurore de Saxe. This girl, after a brief, unhappy marriage to Count Antoine de Horn, a bastard of Louis XV, married Claude Dupin de Francueil, writer, painter, master of the embroiderer's needle, philosopher, and musician, who had assisted Jean-Jacques Rousseau with his opera *Le Devin du village*. Their son was Maurice Dupin, father of the future George Sand.
[2] Solange does not seem to have been legitimate. It is likely that her father was Stéphane de Grandsaigne, a handsome medical student with whom her mother had been on intimate terms late in 1827 and early in 1828.

tellectual. Her Parisian friends belonged among the ardent admirers of Victor Hugo, among painters, musicians, and wealthy dilettantes. One of them was a weak and beautiful young man by the name of Jules Sandeau, twenty years old and in the process of abandoning a legal career for a fling at literature. Soon this ill-matched pair was living and writing together, contributing articles to *Figaro* and the *Revue de Paris*. They became a familiar sight in artistic circles — the somewhat masculine Baroness in her unconventional trousers, the effete Sandeau with his blond hair worn long. She began to publish stories and novelettes. Together they planned and wrote a novel subtitled *L'Actrice et la nonne,* but known by the names of its chief female characters as *Rose et Blanche.* This was published as the work of "Jules Sand," and it was a success. Its publisher asked for more, and the female half of Jules Sand took from her trunk *Indiana,* a novel that she had written at Nohant. This was issued as the work of "George Sand." [3]

The publication of *Indiana* on May 9, 1832 quickly made George Sand a familiar name to thousands of readers. It launched the Baroness on a literary career that was to be long-enduring and prolific. It also shortly made inevitable the end of her liaison with the less successful Sandeau. By the summer of 1833, when she returned to Nohant for a visit, he had begun to seek relief from her fame and dominating spirit in the arms of other women. George Sand, too, was bored with Jules Sandeau: his almost feminine delicacy and etherealized ardors had not proved, as she had hoped, the satisfaction she had never received from the coarse and thoroughly masculine Dudevant. She continued to write and to publish — her second novel, *Valentine,* appeared in 1832, the more renowned *Lélia,* in 1833. And on June 20, 1833 she had been introduced to the passionate and dazzlingly handsome author of *Contes d'Espagne et d'Italie* and *Un Spectacle dans un fauteuil,* Alfred de Musset. He was twenty-three when they met; eleven days after that event she became twenty-nine.

By the end of 1833 George Sand had convinced Alfred de Mus-

---

[3] The selection of George as the first name seems to have been accidental. Any masculine name would have served. The purpose was to hide the then incredible fact that this full-blooded story had actually been written by a woman.

set's mother that a trip to Italy with her was just what he needed. In January 1834 the two were established in Venice. There George divided her time between love-making, endless discussions of art, marriage, poetry, free love, and politics, and eight daily hours of working at a new novel. After a brief interval all this naturally began to oppress the mercurial Musset, who took to drink and secret debaucheries. Shortly he began to suffer attacks of delirium tremens; then he had a nervous collapse. Momentarily putting her eternal writing aside, George nursed her lover under the direction of Pietro Pagello, a Venetian physician. What was inevitable with her happened — George Sand and the vigorous and handsome young doctor were soon lovers. As quickly as Musset became well enough to be left, George left him, going off to Paris with the bewildered Pagello. There were some later flare-ups of her love for Musset, but the liaison was never wholly re-established, and before long it altogether ended.[4]

Pietro Pagello did not hold George Sand's attentions for long. There were other men, including a lawyer named Michel de Bourges, who during a brief reign intensified her interest in socialism and succeeded in finalizing her divorce from Dudevant. The Baron was awarded forty thousand francs from her personal fortune, in return for which he released the two children, Maurice and Solange, into their mother's custody. On August 28, 1836 George Sand, with the children and a maid, left Nohant for Geneva, whither she had been pressingly invited by her friends Marie d'Agoult and Franz Liszt. At that moment, having broken with Michel de Bourges, she had no lover, for the intimate position then or shortly later occupied by little Maurice's tutor, Félicien Malefille, scarcely justified that eminence. It was freshly returned from Switzerland late in 1836 that George for the first time met Liszt's Polish friend, Frédéric-François Chopin.

George Sand has been called a nymphomaniac, a female Don

[4] Musset's view of the whole affair was put into his novel *La Confession d'un enfant du siècle*, published in 1836. Although George Sand used her view as copy in various writings, her most complete expression of it was the novel entitled *Elle et lui*, not published until after Musset's death. To this, Musset's brother Paul replied in a fatuous novel entitled *Lui et elle*, which in turn called forth from Louise Colet — mistress of both Musset and Flaubert — an even feebler *roman à clef* starkly called *Lui*.

Juan, an unconscious Lesbian, and a woman ridden by love for
her son. Any description of that trouser-wearing, cigar-smoking,
many-lovered woman can be documented and with identical
facts differently viewed. Certainly she was a woman of powerful
intelligence and powerful appetites, who always demanded from
life more than it could give her. She was fearless and shameless,
a caressing and foolish mother, a fickle and foolish mistress. Writing — which, be it said, she did superbly well — was for her a
passion and an immediate necessity. For it she constantly sought
illumination, wisdom, and inspiration. From the abruptly male
man to whom she had been married she had received none of the
tenderness she later sought from ephebic types like Musset and
Chopin. These she tried to mother while charging their femininity
with her own masculine energies. But by the very nature that attracted her in them they were incapable of satisfying her as a female. And so she tried one after another, not solely out of inflamed sexual hunger, but as much out of her complex need for
reciprocal companionship. Often a figure of fun, George Sand was
also a tragic woman of genius. In Chopin she met a man who was
no match for her vigor, but who was her equal in the tortuousness
of his make-up. The results of their love were certain to be fevered
and damaging. When they became lovers she was a bitterly experienced woman of thirty-three or thirty-four, he a loftily romantic (and almost certainly a virgin) young man of twenty-
seven or twenty-eight.

   During the summer of 1838 George Sand was, as usual, at Nohant. She made several forays into Paris incognito, however, and
it was probably during one of them that Chopin, a petted child
and awkward lover, first lay in her arms. Earlier that year he had
made two semipublic appearances. On March 2 the prodigious
pianist composer Charles-Henri-Valentin Alkan had enlisted the
assistance of Chopin and Adolf Gutmann for a concert. The three
of them were joined by Alkan's teacher, Pierre Zimmermann, in a
performance at two pianos of parts of Alkan's eight-hand arrangement of Beethoven's Seventh Symphony. During March also Chopin had traveled to Rouen at the invitation of Anton Orlovski, a
Polish friend who had irritated him eight years earlier by publishing a series of mazurkas and waltzes on themes from the F-minor
Concerto. Orlovski was giving a concert in Rouen, and Chopin

had agreed to perform the E-minor Concerto, which he did to everyone's satisfaction. The concert was held in a small salon in the Rouen Hôtel de Ville, and the audience numbered only five hundred. Reporting the event for the Paris *Gazette musicale*, Ernest Legouvé, after lines of rapture, besought Chopin to give up playing "for five or six persons" and unselfishly give his marvelous talent to all. "And when it shall be asked who is the first pianist of Europe, Liszt or Thalberg, let all the world answer, as do those who have heard you — 'It is Chopin.'" [5]

But Chopin's disease was again demonstrating its presence. He was in a condition of constant depression in the spring of 1838. When George Sand, weary of Malefille, infatuated with her new Pole, worried over the rheumatism from which her son, Maurice, suffered, and generally at loose ends, suggested that he accompany her and her children to Majorca, he agreed. His physician had ordered him to spend some recuperative months in the south, and well-meaning friends had assured her that the Balearic island had a clement climate. It was off the beaten roads of travel. By sound it was suitably romantic. There George could nurture their love and hope to re-establish the health of both Chopin and little Maurice.

Chopin must have been desperately in love with his Egeria, for it was unlike him to rupture convention so openly. He told only two or three friends where and with whom he was going, but he knew that it was impossible to associate with Sand in secret. The party did not set off as a unit. George, Maurice, Solange, and a nursemaid left Paris on October 18, going via Lyon, Avignon, and Arles to Perpignan, the appointed meeting-place. Chopin, meanwhile, in order to raise funds for the trip, had been forced to sell an incomplete work. He had for more than two years been adding off and on to a proposed group of twenty-four Préludes, one in each major and minor key. Now he sold the series, of which two or three Préludes were uncomposed and more incomplete, to his friend Camille Pleyel for two thousand francs, of which he took five hundred as an advance. With the Pleyel contract as collateral, he then borrowed an additional thousand

[5] Some time early in 1838, probably on February 24, Chopin also appeared by command at Louis-Philippe's court, where his improvisations were the center of astonished admiration.

francs from a Jewish banker, Auguste Léo. With fifteen hundred
francs in hand, he was able to meet the others at Perpignan just
before November 1. His mistress said that he bore his four nights
in a mail coach heroically and arrived looking "fresh as a rose and
rosy as a turnip."

From Perpignan the little party went to Port-Vendres, whence
a small steamer bore them around the northeast hump of Spain
to Barcelona. On the night of November 7, after a brief look at
the Catalan city, they boarded the S.S. *El Mallorquín* for Palma
de Majorca. They passed eastward through a clear, calm night,
enjoying the continuous chant of the steersman, who sang to keep
himself awake. On the morning of November 8 they debarked
at Palma. At first it seemed the promised land. The summery
weather was most welcome after a wintery France. But accommodations giving even primitive comforts were unobtainable, and
the highly seasoned Majorcan food was distasteful to them. In a
few days, however, they rented a near-by country house, the
Villa Son-Vent. Sand described it as "a pretty furnished house
with a garden and a magnificent view, for fifty francs a month,"
and added that she had besides leased three rooms "and a garden
full of oranges and lemons" in the huge Valdemosa monastery
"for thirty-five francs *a year.*"

Chopin was enchanted. On November 19 he wrote to his Polish
friend Yulyan Fontana in Paris:

My dear:
I am in Palma among palms, cedars, cacti, olives, pomegranates, etc.
Everything the Jardin des Plantes has in its greenhouses. A sky like
turquoise, a sea like lapis lazuli, mountains like emerald, air like
heaven. Sun all day, and hot. Everybody in summer clothes. At night
for hours guitars and singing. Huge balconies with grapevines over-
head; Moorish walls. Everything faces toward Africa as the town does.
In short, a glorious life! Love me. Go to Pleyel, the piano has not arrived yet. How was it sent? You will soon receive some preludes. I
shall probably live in a wonderful monastery, the most beautiful location in the world: sea, mountains, palms, a cemetery, a crusaders'
church, ruined mosques, ancient trees, olives a thousand years old. Ah,
my dear, I am coming to life a little — I am close to what is most beautiful. I am better. Give Gzhimala my parents' letters and anything you
have to send me — he knows the safest address. Embrace Yasio. How

well he would recover here! Tell Pl[eyel] that he will soon get his manuscript. Don't discuss me much with people I know. I'll write you many things later — say that I'm returning after the winter. The post leaves here once a week. I write through the local consulate. Send my letter to my parents just as it is — post it yourself.

Your

I'll write to Yasio later.[6]

Ch.

Enjoying, as so many northern men enjoy them, the beauties of the semitropics, Chopin went on short walking expeditions, believing that the exercise and fresh, balmy air would help him to regain some of his lost energy and strength. Once several members of the group went to visit a hermitage three miles distant. As they returned, a storm broke about them. A violent wind swept rain against them, at times in gusts severe enough to make Chopin lose his uncertain footing and fall. Cobbled roadways had already tortured his feet, and by the time the party reached the Villa Son-Vent he was chilled and wet. In a few hours his exhaustion developed into an attack diagnosed as acute bronchitis. In a day or two it was clear that he was seriously ill. He had not been dying all his life, but it is reasonable to say that after the visit to Majorca he died slowly for eleven years.

For a long period no letters or other news arrived from Paris. On December 14 Chopin heard that the piano Pleyel had promised had been embarked at Marseille only on December 1. The weather shifted to constant rain and dampness, a dampness caught and held by the villa's uncovered plaster walls. The only heat was from open fires; these smoked, thus irritating Chopin's cough. Alarmed, George Sand summoned three local medicos. On December 3 Chopin wrote to Fontana:

One sniffed at what I spewed up, the second tapped the place from where I spat it, and the third poked around and listened while I spat it. The first said that I had already croaked, the second that I am dying, the third that I shall die. And today I'm the same as always — only I can't forgive Yasio for not giving me the examination when I had an acute attack of bronchitis, which can always be looked forward to with me. I could scarcely prevent them from bleeding me, and they put no setons or vesicants. But all this has delayed the preludes, and

[6] The piano sent by Pleyel did not arrive until January 1839. "Yasio" was Yan Matushinski.

God knows when you will receive them. I shall remain a few days in the most beautiful region of the world: sea, mountains, everything you desire. I shall lodge in a huge old ruined Carthusian monastery that Mendizabal [7] cleared of monks as if especially for me.

At the end of this letter Chopin added: "Don't tell people that I've been ill, or they'll make up a story." He did not desire to be reported dead again, and was probably also afraid that Pleyel might start to worry about the five-hundred-franc advance, Léo about the thousand-franc loan. Also, gossip about his ailment was already causing serious difficulties nearer at hand. The three local doctors had carelessly let descriptions of his symptoms be bruited about, and it was assumed in the neighborhood that he was tubercular. The Majorcans had a special fear of the disease. Chopin, Sand, and their party became objects of hostile fear. The owner of the Villa Son-Vent abruptly ordered them to get out, further insisting that the house must be cleaned out and rewhitewashed at their expense. This forced them to remove to the Valdemosa monastery, to the "cells" that Sand seems to have intended as no more than a supplementary retreat for writing and composition.

Mid-December arrived. On the 14th Chopin again addressed Fontana:

Not a word from you yet, and this is my third letter, if not the fourth. Perhaps my family has not written? Perhaps some calamity has befallen them? Or are you lazy? No, you're not, you're a good fellow. Undoubtedly you have forwarded my two letters to my family (both from Palma) and have written to me, and the post here, the most irregular on earth, has not delivered the letters — only today I heard that the piano was put on a freighter in Marseille on December 1. The letter took fourteen days from Marseille. So I can hope that the piano will pass the winter in the dock or at anchor (for here nothing moves except the rain) and that I shall get it when I start back — which will be a great consolation because, in addition to a duty of five hundred francs, I'll have the pleasure of dispatching it back again. Meanwhile my manuscripts sleep and I can't. I only cough and, covered for a long time now with poultices, await the spring or something else — tomorrow I go to that wonderful monastery of Valdemosa to compose in

[7] Juan Álvarez y Mendizabal, the Spanish politician who pushed through the secularization of monasteries, was a friend of George Sand.

some old monk's cell, some monk who perhaps had more fire in his soul than I have, but stifled it, stifled and extinguished it because he had it in vain. I think that I'll shortly send you my preludes and a ballade. Go to Léo. Don't say that I'm ill; he'd get scared about his thousand francs. Or to Pleyel.

By mid-December, then, Chopin had all but completed the last of the twenty-four Préludes, opus 28. The Ballade is the second, in F major, opus 38. It was only his ability to accomplish this polishing that allowed him to keep up his spirits at all. (The Ballade had been begun two years before, and of the Préludes only two were certainly composed in Majorca, as was the Mazurka in E minor, opus 41, no. 2.) The unconquerable and untiring George Sand was, of course, busily writing, this time at her novel *Spiridion*. On the day following the above-quoted letter to Fontana, she, the two children, their nurse, and Chopin established themselves at Valdemosa. On December 28 Chopin dated a letter to Fontana from Palma, and then added:

or rather Valdemosa, a few miles away. Built between the rocks and the sea, it's an enormous Carthusian monastery where you may picture me, with no white gloves and with my hair uncurled, as pale as always, in a cell with doors larger than Parisian gates. The cell is the shape of a tall coffin, the enormous vaulting is covered with dust, the window tiny; outside the window there are orange trees, palms, and cypresses, opposite the window my bed on thongs under a Moorish filigree rosette. Near the bed is a square rickety writing-desk that I can scarcely use; on it (this is a great luxury) a candle in a leaden candlestick. Bach,[8] my scrawls, old papers (not mine) — silence — you could yell — still silence. In short, I write you from a strange place. . . . You write that you have sent on a letter from my family; I never saw it, never received it. And I do need it so much! Did you stamp it? How did you address it? Your letter is the only one I have received up to now, and it was so badly addressed. . . . The piano has been standing at the port for eight days according to the customhouse, which wants a mountain of gold for the swinish thing. Nature here is benevolent, but the people are thieves. They never see foreigners, so they don't know how much to ask. Oranges can be had for nothing, but a fabulous amount is asked for a trouser-button. But all that is a mere grain of sand when one has this sky, the poetry

[8] Chopin had brought with him from Paris several volumes of Bach's music.

breathed here by everything, and the color of this magnificent scenery still not robbed of its color by the eyes of men. Few have yet frightened the eagles that daily soar above our heads. For Heaven's sake, write, always stamping your letters and adding: "Palma de Mallorca."

When the upright Pleyel piano was at last safely installed in his cell in mid-January, replacing a poor instrument rented locally, Chopin set about satisfying himself with the final form of his Préludes. In the letter with which he forwarded them to Yulyan Fontana, he asked his friend to settle his most pressing financial affairs with the payment due and suggested that Fontana try to close his Paris apartment and store part of the furniture with Yan Matushinski and part with Voitsyekh Gzhimala. In a few weeks, he said, Fontana would be receiving other manuscripts from him — a ballade, a polonaise, and a scherzo. Things were a little more bearable in the monastery cells than they had been at the Villa Son-Vent, though Chopin's health did not materially improve. George Sand seems to have been eternally cheerful, though she too had been forced to borrow against future payments from her publishers.

With a good piano at hand, Chopin set to work. He completed the second of the two Polonaises of opus 40, in C minor (the first, the "Military," in A major, had been composed before his departure from Paris), and began the Scherzo in C-sharp minor, opus 39. The two Polonaises and the Ballade in F major, opus 38, were sent off to Paris. Sand, too, was working. But both of them, despite the satisfactions of their relationship (and her pleasure in little Maurice, Chopin's in Solange), felt their isolation in this remote and not friendly place. To terror of Chopin's illness the neighboring peasants added that the whole party was irreligious; this was enough to ostracize them from any but the most casual contacts. They could not keep a servant. Sand herself had to prepare Chopin's food — he could not eat the native dishes drenched in spices and garlic.

On January 22 Chopin wrote Camille Pleyel a letter so full of contractual arrangements that he added in a postscript: "I see that I have not thanked you for the piano — and that I have discussed nothing but money. I am positively a businessman." From this letter we learn that he had sold the Préludes to Breitkopf &

Härtel for 1,000 francs, this in addition to what he would receive for the French and English editions. He added that other manuscripts were awaiting Pleyel's orders: the Ballade, opus 38, for which he believed the French and English rights to be worth 1,000 francs; the Polonaises, opus 40, with world rights valued at 1,500 francs; and the Scherzo, opus 39, worth 1,500 francs for all-Europe rights. As long as he could continue to compose and to demand and obtain payment on this scale, Chopin might remain short of wealth but could never be poor.

In Majorca, meanwhile, the skies had begun to be blue again. The warmth began to dry up the dampness. Sand, years later in her untrustworthy *Histoire de ma vie*, declared that she would have been happy to remain at Valdemosa two or three years with Maurice and Solange. But Chopin wanted only to get away from the accursed place, while Sand's later statement was forgetful or deceitful. For they all embarked at Palma on the afternoon of February 13, and two days later she was writing to her friend Mme Manuel Marliani from Barcelona: "God grant that I may leave soon and that I never set foot in Spain again." (Mme Marliani's husband was the Spanish consul in Paris.) She went even further the moment she reached French soil, saying that both Chopin and she would have died had they remained one month more in Spain, he of melancholy and disgust, she of fury and indignation.

The trip from Valdemosa to Palma and thence to Marseille swarmed with the paraphernalia of a nightmare. At Valdemosa the natives were so thoroughly frightened by the possibility of tubercular infection that Sand was unable to hire a carriage to take her party to the port. Chopin was therefore forced to make the bumpy journey in a springless wagon devoid of upholstery. At Palma, probably weakened by the jolting he had just undergone, he suffered a hemorrhage. Desperately eager to get away, he could not be persuaded to rest awhile in Palma, but insisted on boarding the Barcelona packet, which was ready to sail with a cargo of one hundred swine. The master of the tiny vessel was no less frightened than the Valdemosans. He would not grant Chopin one of the few reasonably comfortable cabins aboard because, he insisted, any mattress would have to be burned if the sick man lay on it. So the weary, terribly ailing man had one of the poorest of the accommodations, located so that both the stench of the swine and their grunting and squealing added to his discomfort. The bleeding could not be stopped, and by the time the vessel approached Barcelona Chopin was gravely weakened. Sand then took matters firmly in hand. With the assistance of the local French consul, she had the patient transferred to a French ship lying near by in the harbor. There the ship's physician was able to stanch the bleeding. But immediate departure on the Marseille ship was out of the question: the party had to remain an entire week in Barcelona.

By the time they boarded the S.S. *Phénicien,* Chopin had so far recovered that its captain (also probably less timorous than his Spanish counterpart) gladly ceded his own cabin to the greater comfort of the patient. On February 25, 1839, one hundred and eleven days after leaving Perpignan, the somewhat bedraggled little group arrived at Marseille. They took lodgings at the Hôtel de Beauveau.[9] Chopin at once began to feel better. In a letter dated March 7 and continuing detailed financial instructions to Fontana, he stated his uncertainty of returning to Paris at all during the coming summer. Sand, it would seem, had already invited him to remain with her at Nohant. Turning to the subject of his health, Chopin wrote:

Embrace Yas [Matushinski] for me; tell him that I'm — or, I mean, that they were not permitted to bleed me, that I have vesicants, that I don't cough badly except in the morning, and that I'm not yet at all classed as consumptive. I drink neither coffee nor wine, but only milk; I keep warm and resemble a girl.

Soon he was bombarding Fontana with querulous and then enraged letters about the refusal of publishers to agree to all the arrangements and payments he desired. He accused them of being thieves, hurling at them, Pleyel included, the worst epithet he knew — "Jew" — and descending to the scatological with words such as the one polite translators have rendered as "offal," but

---

[9] The fact that George Sand had correspondents address her in care of the doctor who attended Chopin rather than at the hotel has always been cited as proof of her discretion. It is at least likely that she took this precaution not for benefit of the public but to keep the contents of letters, including words about his illness, from her recuperating lover. At no time was Sand notably discreet.

which is more honestly translated as "shit." To Pleyel, at the same time, he pretended to be annoyed at Fontana — that much-importuned and unfortunate young man, he said, should not have been troubling Pleyel! He blandly reported also that he had sold "or practically sold" the piano that Pleyel had sent to him in Majorca. In fact — without notifying Pleyel of his plan — he had turned the piano over to a firm of Palma bankers on an ill-defined preliminary promise that they would eventually send either its owner or himself twelve hundred francs. As late as March 28, in fact, he was writing to these bankers urging them to forward the payment to Paris, directly to Pleyel. And even in the midst of denigrating the publisher to Fontana, Chopin stopped to order the Préludes dedicated "à mon ami Pleyel." The way in which these devious negotiations parallel certain actions of Beethoven and Wagner suggests that great composers have at times regarded the placing of their creations as above the rules of ordinary business decency.

Despite enthusiastic invitations from prominent citizens of Marseille, Sand and Chopin refused to be lionized. On March 8, however, Chopin's friend the great tenor Adolphe Nourrit committed suicide in Naples by jumping from a window. On April 24 his body arrived at Marseille and he was honored with a memorial service in Notre-Dame-du-Mont. Chopin was persuaded to play the organ. He chose Schubert's *Die Gestirne*, a favorite with Nourrit, but played it so softly and simply that many of those present — each had paid fifty centimes for a ticket of admission — were disappointed. They were even more disappointed by the failure of the notorious George Sand, hidden in the organ loft, to put in an appearance.

Chopin's first recorded mention of George Sand to one of his friends occurred in a letter to Voitsyekh Gzhimala, dated at Marseille on March 27, 1839. Here he refers to her as "my love." To Gzhimala he mentioned her again in a letter of April 12: "My Angel is finishing a new novel: Gabriel. Today she is writing in bed all day. Do you know, you would love her even more than you do if you knew her as I know her today." Whatever the Majorcan winter had done to him, it had not diminished his love. Sand, on her part, was contented to have found at last a man whom she could simultaneously desire, dominate, care for, and praise to herself and to others. There is no reason to doubt that in 1839 and for some time thereafter their relationship was wholly pleasing to them both.

Chopin had regained sufficient strength by May to be able to join Sand in a trip by sea from Marseille to Genoa. He had never before visited Italy, and she was perhaps eager to revisit the scenes of happy days with Musset. Maurice accompanied them, going off with his mother on the sightseeing that Chopin felt unequal to doing. The passage back to Marseille was windy and rough. Although this time he suffered no hemorrhage, Chopin was pitifully seasick. He again rested briefly in Marseille, but on May 22 the entire entourage set out by way of Arles for Nohant. It was the first of many trips that Chopin was to make there.

At Nohant Chopin was examined by Gustave Papet, George Sand's family physician. Papet announced that, though Chopin had a chronic laryngeal complaint, he was not tubercular. This diagnosis it is impossible to believe. The doctor recommended that his patient spend the whole summer in the country, not attempting to return to Paris until autumn — almost certainly the advice that Chopin and Sand wished to hear. Writing *Histoire de ma vie* years later, the lady tried to convince herself and the world that her attachment to Chopin at this time was entirely that of a maternal vicar, that she struggled successfully against succumbing to real love or to passion, and that she accepted the care of the invalid as a terrifying duty. Her attitude toward Chopin eventually did cool into something like the state thus described, but in the summer of 1839 her interest in having Chopin at Nohant was that of a passionate woman in having her lover with her.

Chopin's creative life cannot conveniently be divided into the three traditional periods of juvenilia, works of early and middle maturity, and final fruits. Yet there is little doubt that most of the music he composed from 1838 on is fuller, firmer, more richly designed, more beautiful than most of what he had composed earlier. I see no reason for questioning that his love affair with George Sand played a real part in this deepening and widening of his art, particularly as it is more than probable that she was the first woman with whom he enjoyed full sex relations.[10] His ill-

[10] I can find nothing to justify the belief, held by William Murdoch and others, that Delphine Pototska had been Chopin's mistress.

ness, too, especially as it almost certainly was already tuberculosis, may have driven him to deeper searching within himself. The
mere fact that he was an experienced man of twenty-eight played
its part. Nobody who loves Chopin's music would willingly part
with more than some fragments of it, but few faced with a choice
would not rather have that which he composed from 1838 to the
end of his life than that which he composed before 1838.

During 1837 Chopin had published, in addition to the Études,
opus 25, the following: the Impromptu in A flat, opus 29, the
four Mazurkas, opus 30; the B-flat minor Scherzo, opus 31; and
the Nocturnes, opus 32. In 1838 he saw into print only the four
Mazurkas, opus 33, and the Waltzes, opus 34. In 1839 he published only the Préludes, opus 28, worked over from 1836 to 1839.
Not until 1840 did the list of his publications begin suddenly to
swell with the major works he had started to compose after the
inception of his affair with George Sand. I do not wish to over-
stress the causal connection, but it existed, and their meeting is
more than a useful and memorable signpost. It was a Chopin
physically damaged, but mentally at the portal into his finest period as a creative artist who settled down with his remarkable
mistress at Nohant for the summer of 1839.

X

THERE was one important ground on which Chopin and George Sand could never meet. She was an intellectual, interested in ideas of many sorts, social, political, religious, and artistic. He was not in any appreciable sense an intellectual at all. His letters are almost wholly devoid of any discussion of ideas, of books, of other arts than music, of any music but his own and that of a few operatic composers. He was unique among the composers of his era in not himself having literary pretension: as an adult he wrote nothing but letters, letters charming in their complete spontaneity, but usually lacking in verbal graces. It would be impossible to prove that he understood, or for that matter that he even read, Sand's writings, not to mention those of a dozen other important literary figures whom he met. That he was intelligent, possessed of a sharp and capable mind, his letters prove, as does the complex structural mastery of his best compositions. He altogether lacked the curiosity that marks the true intellectual, however, and his mental energies were almost entirely concentrated on the business under his hands whenever he could have it there — the composition of music.

During his first summer at Nohant, Chopin composed. He built into a Sonata a Funeral March in B-flat minor that he had written about two years before, composing or polishing the other three movements in the comparative peace of the Sand menage. She, all the while, kept her pen busily sweeping over paper: she was fecund, and all her publishers were both critical and insatiable. Together she and Chopin planned their return to Paris. He constantly sent both to Fontana and to Gzhimala requests and specifications for the living-quarters he and Sand would require. Fontana was commissioned to order Chopin's winter wardrobe — a hat, a pair of gray trousers without a belt, and a "plain black

velvet waistcoat, but with a small inconspicuous pattern, something very quiet and elegant." Fontana, finally, was to find him a
manservant.

In Paris the commissions were faithfully carried out. For Sand
and her children and servant two small houses in a raised rear
garden at 16 rue Pigalle were rented, while for Chopin there was
an apartment of two rooms and a foyer at 5 rue Tronchet. It was
to the latter that Chopin went on October 11, 1839, the completed B-flat minor Sonata in his traveling bags. He had been absent from Paris for almost an entire year. His hope was of settling
down at once to composing and teaching. But the distance from
the rue Tronchet to Sand's small domain in the rue Pigalle proved
too great for comfort, and before long he turned his apartment
over to Yan Matushinski and joined the menage in the secluded
rear garden. His love had at last obliterated his sharp sense of
the proprieties: in the full light of Paris he now lived openly with
Sand, even receiving his pupils there.

Shortly after returning to Paris, Chopin attended a party given
by his Jewish friend the banker Léo. There he met Ignaz Moscheles, the renowned pianist whom he had failed to encounter in
London in 1837. The two struck up a friendship, playing their
own compositions to the entire satisfaction of both. In a letter
written at the time Moscheles gave his impressions of Chopin:

His appearance is completely identified with his music — both are
delicate and full of sentiment. He complied with my request that he
play, and for the first time I find his music comprehensible, all the
rapture of the Ladies' world intelligible. The *ad libitum* [Chopin's
ever controversial use of rubato], which at the hands of other inter-
preters of his music degenerates into a constant vagueness of rhythm,
is with him an element of exquisite originality; his hard, inartistic
modulations, so like those of an amateur — which I never can manage
when playing Chopin's music — cease to shock me, for he glides over
them almost imperceptibly with his elfin fingers. His soft playing being a mere breath, he needs no powerful forte to produce the desired
contrasts; the result is that one never misses the orchestral effects demanded of a pianist by the German school, but is carried away as by
a singer who bothers himself very little about the accompaniment, but
follows his own impulses. Enough, he is completely unique in the
world of pianists.

In another place Moscheles described Chopin as lively, cheerful, and extremely comical in giving imitations of Pixis, Liszt, and
a hunchbacked connoisseur. Some time later, describing a visit he
made to Chopin's quarters, Moscheles wrote that "Chopin's excellent pupil Gutmann" had played the manuscript Scherzo in
C-sharp minor, opus 39, Chopin himself the manuscript Sonata in
B-flat minor. To the delight of Count de Perthuis, a member of
Louis-Phillipe's court, Chopin several times joined Moscheles in
playing the latter's four-hand Sonata in E-flat major, which he
thoroughly enjoyed. The Count must have told this to the royal
family, for Moscheles and Chopin were together bidden to court
on October 29. Moscheles described the occasion in detail:

First of all Chopin played a "melange of nocturnes and études," and
was praised and admired as an old favorite of the court. I followed
with some old and new études, and was honored with like applause.
Then we sat down at the instrument together, he again playing the bass,
a thing he always insists on. The small audience now listened intently
to my E-flat major Sonata, which was interrupted by such exclamations
as "*Divin! Délicieux!*" After the andante the Queen whispered to one
of her suite: "Would it be indiscreet to ask for that again?" which was
tantamount to a command; so we played it again with increased abandon, and in the finale gave ourselves up to a "musical delirium."
Chopin's enthusiasm throughout the whole performance of the
piece must, it seems to me, have kindled that of his hearers, who over-
whelmed us both with equally divided compliments. Chopin played
another solo as charmingly as before, and met with the same reception. I then improvised on some of Mozart's sweetest airs, and finally
dashed away at the "Zauberflöte" overture. Better than all the words
of praise that flow so glibly from the lips of princes was the King's
close attention during the entire evening. Chopin and I reveled like
brothers in the triumph achieved by the individual talent of each;
there was no tinge of jealousy on either side. At last, after being allowed to enjoy some refreshments, we left the palace at 11.30, this
time only under a shower of compliments, for the rain had ceased and
we had a clear night.

Moscheles persuaded Chopin to contribute three new Études
to a piano method he was compiling with Fétis. Although often
inaccurately labeled posthumous, these three — in F minor, A-flat
major, and D-flat major — were completed in 1839 and published

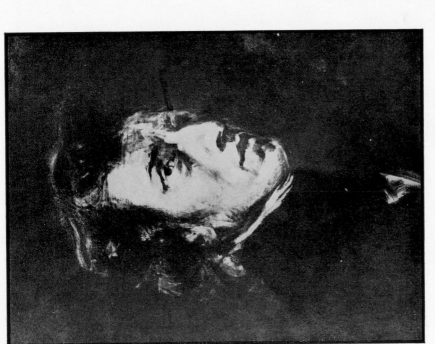

CHOPIN, BY DELACROIX

GEORGE SAND, BY DELACROIX

*Originally parts of the same painting, these portraits were
later cut separately from it.*

JANE WILHELMINA STIRLING
by Deveria

in the Moscheles-Fétis *Méthode des méthodes* in 1840. They
must be added, that is to say, to the impressive list of additions
made in 1840 to the body of Chopin's published works: the B-flat
minor Sonata; the F-sharp major Impromptu, opus 36; the Nocturnes of opus 37; the Ballade in F major, opus 38; the C-sharp
minor Scherzo, opus 39; the Polonaises of opus 40; the Mazurkas
of opus 41; and the A-flat major Waltz, opus 42. Only 1841 was
to match 1840 in the size and caliber of this list. Despite the almost catastrophic stay in Majorca, Chopin had won back some of
his vitality and all of his creative energy. He was benefiting from
his relationship with George Sand. His health, however, continued to worry both his mistress and himself.

In October 1839 a young girl named Friederike Müller, later
Mme Streicher, persuaded Chopin to accept her as a pupil. She
kept a remarkably detailed diary that has proved trustworthy.
Speaking of her early lessons with Chopin, she wrote:

Alas, he suffered greatly. Feeble, pale, coughing much, he often took
drops of opium on sugar and gum-water, rubbed his forehead with
eau de Cologne, and nevertheless he taught with a patience, perseverance, and zeal that were admirable. His lessons always lasted a full
hour, and usually he was so kind as to make them longer. . . . Many
a Sunday I began to play at Chopin's at one o'clock, and only at four
or five o'clock did he dismiss us. Then he also played, and how splen-
didly; but not only his own compositions, also those of other masters
in order to show the pupil how they should be performed. One morning he played from memory fourteen preludes and fugues by Bach,
and when I expressed my joyful admiration over this unparalleled
performance, he replied: "That, one never forgets," and, smiling sadly,
continued: "For a year I have not studied one entire quarter-hour. I
have not the force, not the energy. I always wait for a bit of health in
order to take all that up again, but — I am still waiting. . . ." His
playing was always noble and beautiful, his tones always sang,
whether in full forte or in the softest piano. He took infinite pains to
teach a pupil this legato, cantabile manner of playing. "He — or she —
does not know how to link two notes" was his severest censure. He
also demanded adherence to the strictest rhythm, hated all lingering
and dragging, misplaced rubatos, as well as exaggerated ritardandos.
"I beg you to seat yourself," he would say on such an occasion with
gentle mockery. And it is just in this respect that people make such
terrible errors in playing his works. In the use of the pedal he had also

achieved the greatest mastery, was uncommonly strict regarding its misuse, and repeatedly said to the pupil: "The correct way of using it remains a study for life."

Chopin was too unwell, on April 20, 1840, to attend the matinee in which Liszt, returning from a successful tour abroad, again laid claim to Parisian homage. He plied Mlle Müller with questions as to how Liszt had played. She replied that what had most impressed her was Liszt's artistic self-control, his "calmness in overcoming the greatest technical difficulties." To this, she wrote, Chopin answered:

Then it seems that my advice is good. Simplicity is the final thing. After having conquered all the difficulties, after having played a huge quantity of notes and more notes, it is simplicity that emerges with all its charm, as the final guerdon of art. Whoever desires to reach it immediately will never reach it at all — one cannot begin at the end. It is necessary to have studied a great deal, enormously even, to reach this goal. It is not an easy thing. It was impossible for me to attend the matinee. With my health, one can do nothing. I am always embroiled in my affairs to such an extent that I have not a single free moment. How I envy strong people who have robust health and nothing to do! I am very irritated. I have no time in which to be sick.

This was Chopin's life in 1839 and 1840: he was suffering from the encroachments of tuberculosis (he weighed less than one hundred pounds by 1840), composing at the crest of his powers, teaching. Very probably, too, he was watching George Sand slowly being forced to change, as regarded himself, from a woman in love to a worried woman acquiring an ailing son in the person of her latest lover. Sand had more than Chopin to worry about: her finances were uncomfortably meager. Her play *Cosima*, on which she had begun to count heavily when the Comédie Française had accepted it for production, turned out all but a fiasco, doing nothing to enlarge her income. The play was colored by socialistic ideas of amelioration that she had absorbed from Pierre Leroux, and its failure was at least in part caused by conservative opposition to those ideas. One result of its failure was that George Sand, and Chopin with her, could not afford to spend the

summer at Nohant. It was in Paris that they passed the summer
of 1840.[1]

Chopin did not play in public during 1840. One of the few
glimpses of him vouchsafed during that year was at a lecture
given in December at the College de France by the Polish poet and
critic Adam Mitskyevich. Chopin had imbued George Sand with
some of his own patriotic love for Polish literature, and had supplied her with some of the material — including careful translations — that she had used in her well-known essay *"Goethe, Byron
et Mickiewicz."* The appearance in the hall of the famous novelist
and the rarely seen Polish composer occasioned a burst of applause.[2]

Coming out of retirement on April 26, 1841, Chopin took part
in a semipublic concert at the Salle Pleyel. Others appearing on
the program were the renowned soprano Laure Cinti-Damoreau
and the popular violinist composer Ernst. Cinti-Damoreau sang
two arias from Adolphe-Charles Adam's new opera, *La Rose de
Péronne.*[3] Ernst suffered magnificently through his own *Élégie,*
eliciting from Léon Escudier, in *France musicale,* the comment:
"It is difficult to carry farther the expression of sorrow, misery,
and despair." Most of the evening, however, was Chopin's. He
played Mazurkas, Préludes, Nocturnes, Études, and other pieces
that summoned a flood of praise from such periodicals as *Ménestrel, France musicale,* and the *Gazette musicale.*

The *Ménestrel* critic, after comparing Chopin to Schubert, said:

[1] In addition to preparing and seeing through the press all of his *opera*
numbered 35 to 42 inclusive, Chopin during 1840 completed, composed, or
initiated the Polonaise in F-sharp minor, opus 44; the Allegro de concert in
A major, opus 46; the A-flat major Ballade, opus 47; and the F-minor Fantaisie, opus 49. The A-flat major Waltz, opus 42, was both composed and
published in 1840.
[2] Among the Seventeen Polish Songs published posthumously as Chopin's
opus 74, two are settings of poems by Mitskyevich: *"Precz z moich oczu"*
("Away from my eyes") and *"Moja piesczotka"* ("My sweetheart") — the
latter familiar as Liszt transcribed it under the title of *Chant polonais.*
[3] Adam was one of the most popular composers of the hour. His enormously
successful opera *Le Postillon de Longjumeau* dated from 1836; the first performance of his most enduring work, the music for the ballet *Giselle,* occurred only two months after the concert here described.

The one has done for the piano what the other did for the voice. . . .
It may be said that Chopin has created a school of piano-playing and
a school of composition. Indeed, nothing equals the lightness and
sweetness with which this artist preludes on the piano, nothing again
can be placed alongside his works, which are full of originality, distinction, and grace. Chopin is an exceptional pianist who should not
be, cannot be, compared with anyone.

The long critique in the *Gazette musicale* is more interesting:
it is signed by Franz Liszt, who thus sets the scene in the Salle
Pleyel:

Last Monday, at eight o'clock in the evening, M. Pleyel's rooms were
brilliantly illuminated; to the foot of a staircase covered with carpeting
and perfumed with flowers, innumerable carriages brought the most
elegant women, the most fashionable young men, the most celebrated
artists, the richest financiers, the most illustrious noblemen, a whole
elite society, a whole aristocracy of birth, wealth, talent, and beauty.
    A grand piano stood open on a platform; people crowded about,
eager for the chairs nearest it; they settled themselves, they said to
themselves that they must not miss a chord, a note, an intention, a
thought of him who was about to seat himself there. And people
were justified in being thus eager, attentive, and religiously moved, for
he whom they awaited, whom they desired to hear, admire, and applaud, was not only a clever virtuoso, a pianist expert in the art of
playing notes, not only an artist of great fame — he was all of this and
more than all of this. He was Chopin.

Liszt speaks of Chopin's "repugnance to revealing himself to
the outside world, a sadness that shrinks out of sight beneath an
apparent gaiety; in short, an entire individuality in the highest
degree remarkable and attractive." He continues:

Chopin, who has taken no part in the extreme movement that for
several years has thrown executive artists from all parts of the world
onto and against each other, has constantly been surrounded by faithful disciples, enthusiastic pupils, and warm friends, all of whom,
guarding him from disagreeable contests and painful collisions, have
never ceased to spread his works abroad, and with them admiration
for his name. Further, his exquisite, altogether lofty, and eminently
aristocratic celebrity has remained unassailed. A complete critical silence always reigns around it, as though posterity were here, and in

the brilliant audience that flocked together to hear the too-long-silent poet there was neither reticence nor restriction — unanimous praise was on the lips of all. . . .

His country's element of wildness and abruptness has found expression in bold dissonances and strange harmonies, while the delicacy and grace of his personality were revealed in a thousand contours, in a thousand embellishments of inimitable fancy. . . . Addressing himself to a society rather than to the public, he could with impunity show himself as he is, an elegiac poet, profound, chaste, and dreaming. . . . From the first chords a close communication was established between him and his audience. Two études and a ballade were encored, and people would have asked for a repetition one by one of the pieces on the program had it not been for the fear of the already great fatigue that betrayed itself on his pale face.

"Everyone," *Ménestrel* reported, "went away full of sweet joy and profound meditation."

The story of how Liszt came to write his critique and of Chopin's reaction when he heard of it has been told often, but deserves retelling. The *Gazette musicale* had asked its regular critic, Ernest Legouvé, to cover the concert. Liszt met Legouvé at the Salle Pleyel, however, and insisted that this naturally reluctant man grant him the privilege of honoring his friend's reappearance. Having retired before Liszt's determination, Legouvé reported the incident to Chopin, who at once politely (and perhaps truthfully) answered that he would have preferred a critique by Legouvé. "You must not think that, my dear friend," was Legouvé's comment. "An article by Liszt will be a piece of good luck for the public and for you. Trust his admiration for your talent. I promise that he will create a fine kingdom for you." Chopin smiled at this and said: "Yes, within his own empire." [4]

If Chopin ever enjoyed playing before an audience of more than a few friends or pupils, it must have been at this sort of highly select gathering. Yet he did not appear again before a Paris audience for ten months. But during the summer of 1841 he enjoyed a veritable banquet of music under wholly private

[4] This is the version given by Legouvé in his fascinating, but not entirely reliable autobiography. An earlier version had Chopin replying to the news that Liszt had taken Legouvé's place: "He will give me a little kingdom in his empire."

circumstances. From June on he spent several months with George Sand at Nohant, where another of the guests was Pauline García, now Mme Louis Viardot. This great daughter of Manuel del Popolo Vicente García (and sister of Malibran) was an erudite all-round musician. With her, Chopin read scores, particularly of Bach and Mozart. Certainly he played for her and accompanied her in arias and songs. She was to appear with him at his only 1842 concert. Nor was she the only other Nohant guest whom Chopin found sympathetic. There, either in 1841 or 1842, he came for the first time to know well Eugène Delacroix. The two became fast friends, and in 1849 the great painter was to be a pallbearer at Chopin's funeral. At that funeral, too, one of the singers was to be Pauline Viardot-Garcia.

With the exception of a very brief visit to Paris, Chopin was at Nohant far into the autumn of 1841. It was probably there that he corrected proofs of the numerous compositions that he saw published during that year: the Tarantelle in A-flat major, opus 43; the F-sharp minor Polonaise, opus 44; the Prélude in C-sharp minor, opus 45; the Allegro de concert in A major, opus 46; the Ballade in A-flat major, opus 47; the Nocturnes of opus 48; the Fantaisie in F minor, opus 49; and the Mazurka in A minor dedicated to Émile Gaillard.[5] In 1840 and 1841, that is, Chopin had arrived at the ripeness of his talent and the complete command of his creative power. He had composed many beautiful pieces earlier and was to compose many more; but with the Fantaisie, begun in 1840, completed and published in 1841, he created a single piece unrivaled in the whole corpus of his works for scope and unity, a composition that stands shining at the zenith of his particular universe.

In November 1841 Chopin and George Sand returned to their quarters in the rue Pigalle. No clouds had yet crossed the sky of their relationship, but all estimates of its continuing ardor are conjectural. There exists no reason whatever for supposing that they had ceased to be lovers. There is every indication that her attitude toward him became constantly more protective and maternal. She was, as ever, scraping her pen across ream after ream

[5] This Mazurka, often listed among Chopin's "posthumous" works, was published in 1841 by the small Paris firm of Chabal. It was called opus 43, a number now given to the Tarantelle, which was published the same year.

of paper, answering with book after book her wide public's demand for her novels, her own demand for money with which to care for herself, her two growing children, and probably, to some extent, Chopin. She was, by this period, a woman of international fame, much more sought after, lionized, and discussed than her lover.

Again stepping out of his deepening retirement, Chopin gave another semipublic concert at the Salle Pleyel on February 21, 1842. He was assisted by his friends Pauline Viardot-Garcia and Auguste-Joseph Franchomme, the latter a very well-considered cellist. Viardot-Garcia devoted her incomparable artistry to "*Felice donzella,*" an aria by Josef Dessauer, "various fragments" of Handel, and something billed as *Le Chêne et le Roseau,* in which last Chopin accompanied her. Franchomme played an unspecified solo. The selections played by Chopin indicate either that he considered his recent large-scale compositions unsuitable to the occasion or a desire to husband his physical strength. They included the D-flat Prélude; the G-flat Impromptu; four Nocturnes, including opus 48, no. 2; Mazurkas in B major, A-flat major, and A minor; the Ballade in A flat, and the A-flat, F-minor, and C-minor Études, opus 25. It is more than likely that his increasing ill health, which was to prostrate him intermittently from this time on, made this sort of choice inevitable.

The critic of *France musicale* evoked the scene for his readers:

Chopin gave at the Salle Pleyel a delightful soirée, a fete graced by charming smiles, delicate, rosy faces, small, shapely white hands; a splendid fete in which simplicity was joined to grace and elegance, while good taste served as a pedestal for wealth. Those hideous black hats which give men the ugliest possible appearance were very scarce. Golden ribbons, delicate blue gauze, strings of quivering pearls, the freshest roses and mignonettes — in short, a thousand combinations of the prettiest and gayest colors were grouped and intermingled in every manner on the perfumed heads and white shoulders of the most attractive women whom princely salons fight to entertain. The first success of the gathering belonged to Madame George Sand. No sooner had she appeared with her two charming daughters [6] than she was the observed of all observers. Others might have been upset by having all those eyes

[6] The mysterious second "daughter" of George Sand was undoubtedly her young cousin and (later) adopted daughter, Augustine Brault.

turned on them like so many lights, but George Sand was content to lower her head and smile. . . .

Not all the critics were wholly laudatory in reporting this concert. Jean-Maurice Bourges, in the *Revue et gazette musicale*, called Chopin's ornamentation "constantly novel, but at times mannered," and added that "too much fine and minute overrefinement is not always without pretension and frigidity." But Bourges granted that Chopin evoked enthusiasm, a response less violent than that to Liszt or Thalberg "exactly because it is the most intimate chords of the heart that he makes vibrate." It was the critic of *France musicale* who exploded into dithyrambs:

While listening to all these sounds, all these fine shadings, which follow one another, intermingle, diverge, and reunite to reach one and the same goal — melody — do you not believe that you hear the tiny voices of fairies whispering under silver bells, or a shower of pearls falling on crystal tables? The pianist's fingers seem to multiply *ad infinitum*; it appears impossible that just two hands can create effects of swiftness so nice and so natural. . . .

Three weeks after Chopin's concert a whole musical period came to an end with the death, on March 15, of Cherubini, who, born ten years before Beethoven, had lived to reign as academic musical dictator of Paris. Death struck more bitterly at Chopin when, on April 20, his close friend Yan Matushinski died; his disease had been tuberculosis, from which Chopin too was suffering, and which by 1842 he must have known to be a grave threat, if not to his life, then to his career. He appeared in public no more that year or, in fact, any year until 1848. In the summer he was at Nohant, where he particularly enjoyed the company of Delacroix. Chopin's attitude toward Delacroix's art was his attitude toward every art but music (except for Polish literature): mildly interested indifference resulting in a complete lack of understanding. Delacroix the man, who had an intense and discriminating love of music, and of Mozart especially, he really liked. He was on friendly terms, too, with another of George Sand's friends and guests, Louis Blanc, the Socialist whose *Histoire de dix ans* had vituperated Louis-Philippe. Although Chopin was a congenital royalist, his own interest in non-Polish politics remained rudimentary. Other members of the Nohant household were Maurice, Sand's nineteen-year-old son, and Solange, her thirteen-year-old daughter, neither of whom had yet developed the rampant individualities that later became embroiled in the breaking-up of their mother's relationship with Chopin. Least attractive of those who wandered in and out of the château was Hippolyte Châtiron, Sand's bastard half-brother, her father's son by a maidservant. Châtiron was the sort of man to make Chopin cringe: a heavy drinker, a vulgarian who was gregarious.

In publications of Chopin's music 1842 was the sparsest of his mature years. The only pieces by him that came new from the presses were the Mazurkas of opus 50 and the one in A minor issued in a collection called *Notre temps*. The brief list is a little deceptive, however; during 1842 he was at work on the four major compositions that were to see the light in 1843: the G-flat major Impromptu, opus 51; the Ballade in F minor, opus 52; the A-flat major Polonaise, opus 53; and the Scherzo in E major, opus 54.[7]

When the Sand-Chopin entourage returned to Paris in the autumn of 1842, it was not to remain at the quarters in the rue Pigalle. During the summer they had spent a few days in Paris for the purpose of selecting new ones. By November they were settled into two apartments on the Square d'Orléans. Sand lived at no. 5 rue Saint-Lazare, Chopin at no. 9, and Sand's friend Mme Marliani between them at no. 7. This arrangement has sometimes been interpreted as proof of their desire to preserve an appearance of propriety, though the fact that Mme Marliani had occupied no. 7 before they left the rue Pigalle seems to prove that they had taken the only apartments available.

The year 1843 was an uneventful one for Chopin, so devoid of events, in fact, as to suggest strongly that his health was steadily growing less dependable. During the summer he was again at Nohant. Once he accompanied Sand, Maurice, and some

[7] On December 15, 1842 Chopin wrote to Breitkopf & Härtel in Leipzig, offering them the Scherzo for 600 francs, the Ballade for the same amount, and the Polonaise for 500. He explained that he also had an Impromptu, but was not offering it to them because he had promised a friend that he would allow Friedrich Hofmeister — another Leipzig publisher — to issue one of his pieces.

neighbors on an excursion to the banks of the Creuse, where Maurice — who had taken some lessons in painting from Delacroix — sketched. Sand returned from the excursion unwell, and her letters of the period exude a gloom matched by that in Chopin's. He also made at least one trip to Paris alone, either to take Solange there for some reason or to call for her. Also, he returned to Paris in the autumn before Sand did. Thence he wrote her a letter in which he tried carefully to reassure her about the state of his health. The letter breathes eagerness to see her again. Nothing had yet ruffled the deep, benevolent calm of their relationship.

More shattering than even the death of Yan Matushinski was news that Chopin received in May 1844: his father had died on the 3rd of that month. Nicolas Chopin had been seventy-two, and his famous son had not seen him for nearly nine years. The news therefore struck him with more force. His own health, already seriously deteriorated, became so threatening that George Sand suggested to Yustina Chopin by letter that some member of the family ought to come from Warsaw to see him. The reply was that his sister Ludvika and her husband would come to Nohant via Paris during the summer. Writing to Ludvika from Nohant, Sand specified that "Fritz" would go into Paris to meet them, and that in any case the Yedzheyeviches were to make use of her apartment while there. Clearly realizing that she must arm Ludvika against the shock of seeing the outward signs of her brother's disease, Sand wrote:

You are certain to find my dear boy very weak and much changed since the last time you saw him! But don't be unduly alarmed about his health. It has been almost steady over the past six years, during which I have seen him every day. I have hope that in time his constitution will be strengthened, but at the worst I feel sure that with a regular life and with care it will endure as well as most. . . .

She had not, of course, literally seen Chopin every day since 1838, the year of the trip to Majorca, but it is notable that she should advance a claim to that intimacy when writing to Chopin's sister.

However close Chopin was to the moment at which he would actually begin to die, he was still near the apogee of his creative life at the time when he met the Yedzheyeviches in Paris and returned with them to Nohant. Ludvika seems to have realized exactly what a haven from the world George Sand provided for her brother. Her reaction to the famous writer was unblemished by censure of any sort; their meeting established a genuine friendship. When, in September, the Yedzheyeviches left Nohant to return to Warsaw after a stay of about one month, Sand asked them to take a rosary as a gift from her to Yustina Chopin. As a memento of the visit to Nohant she presented Ludvika with a manuscript of her most recently completed novel, the charming pastoral *La Mare au diable,* not published until two years later. And before accompanying his sister and brother-in-law as far as Paris on their return journey, Chopin must have played to them his nearly completed Sonata in B minor, which was to be issued in June 1845 as his opus 58.

By letter George Sand assured Ludvika that her visit had borne good fruit. "One cannot enjoy such happiness for a month without some trace of it remaining," she wrote. But her most interesting comment on the visit was made in a note to Mme Marliani: "Thanks to his sister, who is much more advanced than he is, Chopin has now recovered from all his prejudices. It is a notable conversion, which he himself has not noticed." This can only refer to Chopin's timidities about the fact of their liaison, fears and shrinkings that he may have displayed particularly when faced by the imminence of Ludvika's arrival. It can only mean that the liberal and intelligent Ludvika understood her brother's position thoroughly, let him see that she both understood and approved it, and thus dispersed his fears and hesitations. Certainly Ludvika continued to address George Sand by letter with a sisterly affection.

During 1844 Chopin published only two works: the Nocturnes of opus 55 and the Mazurkas of opus 56. The following year he likewise issued only two: the B-minor Sonata and the Berceuse. There were sufficient reasons for this sparseness. For 1845, when he again passed the summer at Nohant, was the year that saw family circumstances begin to undermine the orderly, peaceful existence that Chopin had been enjoying with his mother-mistress. It was the year during which the untamed, irresponsible, if altogether explicable characters of Solange and Maurice Sand were to start making untenable Chopin's position in their mother's household. When the complicated emotional cyclones of 1845-6 are untangled and examined closely, and then are judged in relation to Chopin's swiftly declining hold on life, they entirely explain why he composed little in 1845, composed and completed little more in 1846.

George Sand was responsible. But her responsibility for what ensued did not lie, as romantic historians have enjoyed stating that it lay, in her having seduced the frail Chopin, burned the flickering life from him, and then cast him aside. The truth was simpler and less melodramatic: she had been a poor disciplinarian to her children. Devoting herself constantly to writing and public activities, she had brought to approximate maturity a son whom she adored and a daughter she did not. Both began suddenly to be adults and to show the perfectly comprehensible results of a careless, a haphazard, and consequently an evil motherhood.

XI

Writing from Paris on Easter Sunday, 1845, to his old friend Stefan Vitvitski,[1] Chopin found nothing but insignificant daily events to list: he was attending a fete at Prince Chartoriski's on Easter Monday; Adam Mitskyevich was no longer lecturing at the College de France because his attempts to convert some of his students there to a Messianic sect had led to his dismissal; Chopin was going with Delacroix to the Conservatoire to hear a singing of Haydn's *Creation,* and two days earlier had heard the Mozart Requiem; their friend Gzhimala seemed younger than ever, was dancing like a "twenty-year-old," and so on. The whole year that saw the publication of the Berceuse and the B-minor Sonata was stitched together with this sort of outwardly undramatic events. In Chopin's life it altogether lacked overt drama.

The annual sojourn at Nohant had already begun by June. On July 8, writing to Gzhimala, Chopin reported that bridges and mills between Nohant and Paris had been destroyed in floods. Pauline Viardot-Garcia had been staying with them; Louis Viardot, her husband, had come to call for her, but had returned to Paris alone because of the dangerous condition of the roads. In one of his longest surviving letters Chopin gossiped on for pages to his family on July 20. These are typical passages:

I have written three new mazurkas [opus 59] that will probably be issued in Berlin because a man I know has begged me for them: Stern, a good fellow and a learned musician, whose father is starting a music shop. Also I have received an invitation from the committee that is to erect a monument to Beethoven (at Bonn on the Rhine) to come for the inauguration. You can imagine how likely I am to go. . . . Mme Viardot, also, who will be passing through your town, told me that she

[1] Ten of the Seventeen Polish Songs posthumously published as Chopin's opus 74 are setting of poems by Vitvitski.

will call on you. Here she sang me a Spanish song of her own, composed in Vienna last year; she promised to sing it to you. I like it very much, and doubt that anything better of that sort could be listened to or imagined. . . . M. Billard, a *historical painter*, not specially famous, and an ugly man, had a pretty wife, whom [Victor] Hugo seduced. M. Billard surprised his wife with the poet, and Hugo was obliged, because the man wanted him arrested, to show his peer of France's medal in order to gain a moment's respite. M. Billard wanted to bring action against his wife, but it ended in a private separation. Hugo suddenly started off for a several months' trip. Mme Hugo (who is fine) has taken Mme Billard under her protection, while Juliette (an actress at the Porte-Saint-Martin theater, famous here for ten years, whom Hugo has been keeping for a long time in spite of Mme Hugo and his children and his poems about family morality) — this Juliette has gone with him. . . . Donizetti has come to Paris, where he expects to spend the summer and compose a new opera. . . . The wild Indians (Ioways) have already sailed from Havre on the ship *Le Versailles*. The wife of one of them — his name was Shinta-yi-ga: "little wolf," and hers Oke-wi-mi, meaning in Indian "the she-bear who walks on the back of another" — died (poor creature) of homesickness; they are erecting a monument to her in the Montmartre cemetery (where Yasio is buried). Just before she died she was baptized, and the funeral was held at the Madeleine, in her parish; the monument is to be a peculiar one, designed by M. Préault, a fairly well-known sculptor, and M. Lassus, an architect. It is to be of stone, with bronze flowers winding around it and broken off at the top by a spirit (supposed to be the mal du pays), then bronze bas-reliefs with gilded views of their Rocky Mountains, the banks of the Missouri, etc.; their life over there, and some verses by M. Antony Deschamps. . . . Tell Bartechek [Anton Bartsinski] that the electro-magnetic telegraph between Baltimore and Washington gives remarkable results. Often orders sent from Baltimore at 1 in the afternoon are carried out, and the goods and parcels ready to leave Washington by 3; and small parcels asked for at 4.30, arrive by the 5 o'clock convoy, which reaches Baltimore at 7.30, from Washington, seventy-five English or twenty-five French miles; I think that's quick.

This letter ends with a postscript containing a series of French puns intended to amuse Ludvika's husband, Kalasanty Yedzheyevich. A typical one is "Godfroi of Bouillon was thus named because he was the most *consommé* [consummate] captain of his period." The letter is, in general, an outpouring of high spirits.

Its only indication of the troubles that were brewing in the Nohant household is a reference to quarrels between Mme Sand's
maid, Susanne, and Chopin's Polish manservant, Yan, who had
been accusing the girl in bad French of being ugly as a pig, of
having a mouth like someone's behind. "As Mme S.'s maid is
very skillful, quick, and useful, it is possible that I may have to
dismiss him for the sake of peace, which I should hate to do, for
new faces are small joy. Unfortunately, the children also dislike
him. . . ."

Maurice Sand, then twenty-two years old, had developed an
understandable, increasing dislike of Chopin's position in the
household and was instigating trouble over Yan as a method of
attacking his master. There is evidence that this kitchen and
backstairs intrigue was abetted by Augustine Brault, Maurice's
adopted sister and distant cousin, a pretty girl with whom he
flirted, but whom his scatterbrained sister Solange resented exactly as he himself resented Chopin. Solange, for her part, was
not above irritating Chopin and annoying her mother by flirting
with Chopin himself — she, after all, was a young lady of eighteen. The lines were being drawn for the coming battle: George
Sand, her idolized Maurice, and her adopted daughter Augustine
against Chopin and Solange. Poor Yan, Chopin's valet, was the
first victim: he was dismissed as a result of Susanne's complaints.
It could not be long before the position of Chopin himself in the
household would be made untenable. He was weak and unwell,
and it is not possible to believe that he was any longer George
Sand's lover.

Events did not rise to a crisis during 1845. As late as October 1
Chopin was writing a gay, chatty letter to his family,[2] and Sand
was adding a postscript: "Good day, my dear; we love you, we
kiss you affectionately; may the good God bless you always." She
had, nonetheless, already conceived — and probably had begun
to write — her novel *Lucrezia Floriani,* a *roman à clef* in which
the characters and relationship of Prince Karol and Lucrezia

[2] There is no mention in this letter — or elsewhere — of the deaths of Nicolas
Chopin's two sisters, Anne Thomas and Marguérite Bastien, who died,
twelve days apart, at Marainville during 1845. The very survival until this
date of these women seems to have been unknown either to Chopin or to his
family in Warsaw.

Floriani are unmistakably interpretations of Chopin and herself and of their exacerbated, dying relationship. She had also made up her mind, controverting Chopin's expressed advice and wishes, to make legal her adoption of Augustine Brault. The winter of 1845–6 might be got through without an open break between them, but for the Nohant summer of 1846 the portents were increasingly ominous.

In 1845 and 1846 Chopin was working at the great Barcarolle in F-sharp major, the Polonaise-Fantaisie, and the Sonata for cello and piano, as well as the Mazurkas of opus 59, completed in 1845, and the Nocturnes of opus 62 and Mazurkas of opus 63, both completed in 1846. These dates are noteworthy because Chopin was to compose no more music except for three Mazurkas, three Waltzes, and probably one song. His health, intermittently bad for years, had started rapidly to deteriorate during the harsh winter of 1844–5, and now constantly became more desperate. The break in comfort, routine, and safety accompanying the break with George Sand was to intensify his disease and make impossible for him any further composing except on the smallest scale.

Events worth reporting were few in the winter of 1845–6. In April 1846 Chopin went on a short visit to Tours. In May George Sand went to Nohant. Chopin marked the eve of her setting-out with a party, the invitations to which contained the words "Music, flowers, food." The guests included Louis Viardot, Pauline Viardot-Garcia, Prince and Princess Chartoriski, Princess Sapieha, Louis Blanc, Delacroix, and several others. Neither that night nor a short while later, when Chopin left Paris to follow Sand to Nohant, did he realize that he was about to part from her. He was to remain in her château until early November.

On June 25, 1846 the *Courier français* began the serial publication of Sand's *Lucrezia Floriani*, which Chopin had read chapter by chapter as it was written, and about which he had not complained. Sophisticated Parisians, however, were very shortly to be interpreting the novel as a bitter, unkind revelation of his position vis-à-vis its author. She was known to have used Pauline Viardot-Garcia as a model in her successful novel *Consuelo,* and Heinrich Heine, who knew both Sand and Chopin, had no doubt that *Lucrezia Floriani* dealt with her affair with Chopin. Writing in 1850 to his friend Heinrich Laube, Heine said of Sand: "She has outrageously mistreated my friend Chopin in a detestable novel divinely written."

Lucrezia Floriani is the story of a love affair between Prince Karol and the title character, a well-to-do actress and courtesan suffering from ennui and disillusionment. Lucrezia constantly protests the purity of her intentions and the strength of her maternal instincts, which seem indiscriminately aroused by her children and by Karol. He woos her and she succumbs. Her surrender is accompanied by noble speeches about her gift for saving him — he is ill. "In this trial Providence really sent Karol the person most able to assist and save him. Lucrezia Floriani had an almost marvelous instinct for judging the condition of illnesses and the care to give them." The detailed analysis of Lucrezia's character matches, almost point by point, George Sand's analysis of her own character in her *Histoire de ma vie*. In the novel, she wrote of her heroine:

Besides, she had lodged in her soul too many loves at once, which is to say that she had wished to be the mother of her lovers without ceasing to be the mother of her children, and that the two affections, always in combat, had to resolve their struggle by the extinction of the less obstinate. The children had always won out and, to speak in metaphor, the lovers, taken from the orphan asylum of civilization, had been forced soon or late to return to it.

When the love of Lucrezia and Karol has started to cool, he is presented as jealous of her children, ridden by a sick jealousy of everything. He is irritated by the constant presence of the children and by the attention she pays to them. These, again, are charges that Sand made against Chopin in *Histoire de ma vie*. In the novel there is no doubt that in analyzing Karol she was analyzing Chopin, especially in such a passage as:

Prince Karol was sweet, sensitive, exquisite in everything. At fifteen years of age he possessed all the graces of adolescence united to the grave demeanor of maturity. He was delicate in body as in spirit. But this absence of muscular development meant that he preserved a charming beauty, an exceptional physiognomy that had, so to speak, nor age nor sex. About him there was nothing of the male and hardy air of a descendant of that race of ancient magnates who knew nothing but to drink, to hunt, and to wrangle. Nor was there about him anything of the effeminate gentility of a rosy cherub. He resembled the ideal creatures used by the poetic spirit of the Middle Ages for ornamenting Christian temples; he was an angel, beautiful of face, resembling a great sad woman, pure and svelte of body as a young Olympian god, and to crown this combination he was at once tender and severe, chaste and passionate.

The climax of the novelist's charge against Prince Karol can be adopted as it stands for her chief charge against Chopin. There was undoubtedly a large part of justice in it: "He had only one great fault, involuntary and disastrous — intolerance of spirit." In the novel the relationship is wrecked on the distance between their natures, on the shoals of her unshakable attachment to her children. The following passage stands at the crisis of the story:

If she smelled a flower, if she picked up a pebble, if she caught a butterfly for Célio's collection, if she taught a fable to Béatrice, if she caressed the dog, if she cut a fruit for little Salvator, he said to himself: "What an astonishing nature! Everything pleases her, everything amuses her, everything intoxicates her. She finds beauty, perfume, grace, utility, pleasure in the tiniest details of creation. She admires everything, loves everything! Then she does not love me — I who see, admire, cherish, and understand nothing in the world but her. An abyss separates us!"

At the bottom this was true. A nature rich by exuberance and a nature rich by exclusiveness could not lose themselves in each other. One of them had to devour the other, leaving nothing but cinders. This was what happened.

What happens in *Lucrezia Floriani* is that the heroine falls victim to grief in the unlivable world that Prince Karol creates about her and about himself. Only in this did the novel predict badly: "One of them had to devour the other, leaving nothing but cinders. This was what happened." But the one to die was not George Sand. It was Chopin, who did not survive the separation by a full three years. Although no intellectual, and certainly no literary man, and therefore unarmed to criticize the book, Chopin must have read *Lucrezia Floriani* with a sensation of fatality. A judgment was being passed on him: he was to be shut out. In the novel George Sand had symbolized his dismissal from life.

The tension between Maurice and Chopin broke into a violent quarrel on or about June 29, 1846. Similar tiffs had occurred earlier, but in this one George Sand openly took her son's part. Even if she did not at that time drive Chopin into saying (as he has been quoted): "You no longer love me," he must have realized that this was the truth. Scandals and accusations troubled the country air: that Augustine Brault was Maurice's mistress, that his mother — who hoped to see them marry — did not object; that Solange was trying to woo Chopin away from her mother. This last tale was spread by Solange's governess and music teacher, Mlle de Rozières. Solange was an unusually ardent girl in the full flower of physical maturity. Her mother had more than once tried to marry her off, perhaps as much to get rid of her as to forestall the evident possibility that Solange's physical ardors would involve her in scandal.

The guests at Nohant that summer included — besides Matthew Arnold, Delacroix, Emanuel Arago, and Countess Laura Chosnovska — two of George Sand's candidates for Solange's hand. One was Louis Blanc, the other Pierre-Marin-Victor-Richard de Laprade, but neither the Socialist nor the poet had held Solange's easily distracted attention. There were other prospective bridegrooms. Some time after the bitter quarrel between Chopin and Maurice, in fact, there turned up at Nohant a minor local nobleman named Fernand de Préaulx. He succeeded where the others had failed, and Solange's betrothal to him was announced. He was strongly attracted by the girl, and his sincere intensity held her interest for several months.

Maurice, meanwhile, was extending and consolidating his influence over his mother, establishing clearly his position as head of the family, weakening Chopin's condominium. During the autumn a servant named Pierre, who had been at Nohant for forty years, was dismissed; so was a maid named Françoise, who had been there since before Solange's birth. The regime was changing. Chopin recognized that his private world was changing with it. Writing to his family on October 11, he said that because Solange and Maurice did not wish to leave Nohant, he would return to Paris ahead of George Sand. He also predicted that both of the children would marry early in the coming year. Actually he left Nohant for the last time early in November. He

was fully aware of the alterations in his life there, but nevertheless was planning to return the following year. Then, he was still
able to believe, things might take a turn for the better.

Delacroix saw Chopin often during the winter of 1846–7. On
January 27, 1847, for example, the two men met at Mme Marliani's. In his *Journal* Delacroix noted that Chopin had told him
that he was attempting to better his health by a new sort of mas-
sage treatment. "That would be very fortunate," Delacroix remarked. On March 11, again, Delacroix called at George Sand's.
Chopin was there, and the *Journal* records: "That nice good-look-
ing Chopin played for us awhile. What a charming genius!"

In February 1847 George Sand and her children had finally
returned to Paris, leaving the still-faithful Préaulx behind. In
Paris mother and daughter were soon sitting for portrait busts to
Auguste-Jean-Baptiste Clésinger, a sculptor who had attracted
Sand's attention when, in March 1846, he had written to ask her
for permission to name one of his statues after the heroine of her
Consuelo. In 1847 he was formally presented to her by a friend
of both. Immediately he was inflamed by Solange's physical
charms. He was a badly educated vulgarian, and therefore not
so distasteful to Maurice as the somewhat dandified Préaulx.
Further, he was unyielding when his desires were aroused, and
he soon conquered Solange's fickle heart. The result was that
when the moment came for her to sign her marriage contract with
Préaulx, she refused.

In April, hoping to dissuade Solange from marrying Clésinger,
Sand carried the girl back to Nohant. But Clésinger was not to
be balked in his desire: he followed them to Nohant and obtained
Solange's promise to marry him. Sand became frantic. Maurice
was away, visiting Holland. She herself was no match for the
urgent determination of Clésinger and Solange. She asked Maurice to rush home, adding carefully that Chopin was not to be
consulted or drawn into these family affairs. Nonetheless, she was
in frequent and friendly correspondence with Chopin, who was
awaiting her return to Paris. She finally wrote him that Solange
and Clésinger were to be married. Solange herself, in the friend-
liest terms, also wrote him about her impending marriage. In
May, Chopin wrote to the mother: "You will know that among
your friends no one desires the happiness of your child more than

I do," while to the daughter he said: "I have already, several days ago, asked your mother to convey to you my most sincere wishes for your future; and now I cannot refrain from telling you of all the pleasure I have derived from your charming little letter, in which you seem to me to be so happy. You are at the peak of joy, and I hope that you will always remain there. With all my soul I desire your unchanging prosperity."

Those May entries in Delacroix's *Journal* which refer to Chopin have an ominous sound. On May 9: "The poor lad has been ill for a week, and very gravely. He is a little better now." On the following day: "Went to see Chopin this morning without being admitted." Chopin was having an especially enfeebling bout with his disease. Sand, receiving rumors of his condition, added him to her other worries. He was being cared for by Princess Marcelline Chartoriska, who wrote to Sand about him. She could not leave Solange at Nohant with Clésinger and rush to his bedside in Paris; so she wrote pleadingly to Mlle de Rozières for details. And on May 12, 1847 she addressed Chopin's friend Gzhimala, the man to whom she had turned so surprisingly for counsel at the beginning of the liaison. Among surviving documents this one is a key to the attitude George Sand took toward the unfortunate conclusion of that liaison.

Thank you, dear friend, for your good letters. I knew in a vague and uncertain way that he was ill twenty-four hours before the letter from the good Princess [Chartoriska]. Thank that angel for me also. What I suffered during those twenty-four hours it is impossible for me to tell you, and whatever had happened, I was placed so that I could not have moved. Well, once again he is saved, but how dark the future is for me in that quarter! I do not yet know whether my daughter will be married here in a week or in Paris in two weeks. In any case, I shall be in Paris for a few days at the end of the month, and if Chopin can be moved I shall bring him back here. My friend, I am as happy as possible about my daughter's marriage, for she is in raptures of love and joy, which Clésinger seems to me to deserve! He loves her passionately, and will give her the life she desires. Be that as it may, one suffers a lot in making such a decision.

I think that Chopin must have suffered too over not knowing, not understanding, and not being able to give any advice. But his advice on the real affairs of life it is impossible to take seriously. He has never seen facts in their true light or understood human nature in any detail;

his soul is all poetry and music, and he cannot bear anything that disagrees with him. Besides, his influence in my family affairs would mean for me the loss of all dignity and of all love between me and my children.

Talk to him and try to make him understand in a general way that he must give up worrying about them. If I tell him that Clésinger (whom he dislikes) deserves our affection, he will only hate him more, and will incur Solange's hatred. All this is difficult and delicate, and I know no way to calm and restore a sick mind irritated by every attempt to cure it. The evil that gnaws at this poor being morally and physically has for a long time been killing me, and I see him leave without ever having been able to benefit him because the chief cause of his sadness is the anxiety, jealousy, and distrust of the affection he bears me. For seven years I have lived like a virgin with him and with others. I have aged prematurely and without effort or sacrifice, so weary was I of passion, so disillusioned and so beyond recovery. If any woman in the world should have inspired him with the most complete confidence, it was I — and he never realized it; and I know that many people accuse me, some with having worn him out by the violence of my passions, others with having reduced him to despair by my follies. I believe that you know what is what. He complains of me that I have killed him by deprivation, while I was certain that I should have killed him by acting otherwise. See how I am placed in this fatal friendship, in which I made myself his slave whenever I could do so without showing toward him an impossible and blameworthy preference over my children, when the respect I ought to inspire in my children and my friends has been so delicate and so important to preserve. I have, in this matter, achieved prodigies of patience, of which I did not think myself capable — I, who never had a saintly disposition like the Princess. I have been martyred; but Heaven has been inexorable against me, as if I had great crimes to expiate; for in the midst of all these efforts and all these sacrifices he whom I love with absolutely chaste and motherly love is dying, a victim of his insensate attachment to me.

May God in his goodness grant at least that my children may be happy, that is to say good, noble, at peace with their consciences; because, with regard to happiness, I do not believe in it in this world, and Heaven's law is so strict in this regard that it is almost a blasphemous rebellion not to think of suffering from external things. The only strength in which we can take refuge is the will to perform our duties.

Remember me to Anna and tell her the depths of my heart, and then burn my letter. I send you one for the good Gutmann, whose address I don't know. Don't give it to him in front of Chopin, who doesn't know yet that I have been told about his illness, and who will prefer me not to know about it. His worthy and generous heart has a thousand exquisite scruples beside the cruel aberrations that are killing him. Ah! if only Anna could talk to him one day and get inside his heart in order to cure him. But he seals himself hermetically against his best friends. Good-by, my dear, I love you. Rely on me always to have courage and perseverance and devotion in spite of my sufferings — and know that I shall not complain. Solange embraces you.

Perhaps some presentiment that the future would find this letter valuable prevented Gzhimala from burning it as Sand requested. For it is the letter of a literary artist preparing effects rather than the letter of an honest woman. What it says about Chopin killing himself for love is ridiculous as Sand puts it; what was killing him was tuberculosis combined with the knowledge that her love for him had cooled to a point at which she could pose as a loving mother preferring her children's happiness and respect to her own life. But what the letter says in all clarity, what it was certainly intended to say, is that the relationship that had kept Chopin alive, that had allowed him to work and to achieve some of his finest music, was now almost at an end. The message, like *Lucrezia Floriani,* is a dismissal smothered in excuses.

Solange Sand was married to Clésinger at Nohant on May 20. Her presumptive father, Baron Casimir Dudevant, was present, together with her mother and brother. But Chopin, to whom Solange was now closer than ever, was not there. A virulent attack of what was called asthma had confined him to his bed. It was just as well that he remained in Paris, for the open war that immediately succeeded the marriage might indeed have killed him.

On June 12 Chopin wrote a letter to his family. In it he discussed Clésinger with extreme bitterness, George Sand with a frankness that must have astonished his mother and Ludvika. He described Clésinger as heavily in debt, a brute who had been known to beat his mistress, a drunkard excused as a genius. One of his recently exhibited sculptures had been a naked woman in a position so obscene that he had been obliged to twist a snake around her thighs as a substitution for the conventional figleaf.

It was not impossible, Chopin wrote, that at Clésinger's next exhibition the onlookers would behold "in white marble Sol[ange]'s little behind." Speaking of Sand, he wrote: "The mother is adorable, but she has not a pennysworth of good sense." His own prophecy was that Solange and Clésinger would not get along with each other for more than one year after the birth of their first child. But he clung to a belief, a somewhat mystical one, despite the omens, that whatever George Sand dealt with was somehow to her benefit:

Even her quarrels with her husband have turned out to her advantage; she has kept with her the children whom she loves above everything — she has brought them up healthy and happy — she herself enjoys good health, though she works tremendously — after having written so many books (more than ninety) she has her eyesight intact — everyone adores her — she is not poor — she is charitable: instead of having a wedding party for her daughter she gave 1,000 francs to the poor of the parish. It happens, nevertheless, that she does not always tell the truth — but that is permitted in a novelist.

Chopin had begun to judge George Sand more objectively than she was by then able to judge either herself or him. But he was still teetering on the question of spending some part of the summer at Nohant.

Events in the Sand château, meanwhile, were deciding that question for him. Not quite three weeks after Solange's marriage to Clésinger, George Sand announced the betrothal of her adopted daughter, Augustine Brault, to the young Théodore Rousseau, a friend of Maurice and later an outstanding figure in the Barbizon school of painters. This was too much for Solange, who detested Augustine almost as much as she disliked Maurice. Determined to prevent the marriage, Solange told Rousseau that Augustine had been Maurice's mistress. This achieved her purpose, for on receiving this probably false news Rousseau simply ran away. The engagement was officially broken on June 22. There followed two weeks of embattled struggle, with Sand, Maurice, and Augustine arrayed against Solange and Clésinger. At one point Solange, beside herself with rage, openly accused her mother of having had an affair with another of Maurice's cronies.

At the crest of the war, Clésinger started toward Maurice with a hammer in his hand. The presence in the room of the parish priest was not enough to keep Clésinger from what looked to Sand like an attempt at murder. She flung herself between her son and her son-in-law, striking Clésinger in the face. In the melee he in turn punched her in the breast. Maurice had picked up a pistol, and what might suddenly have turned into a double or triple murder was averted only by the priest and some other friends who happened to be present. They succeeded in parting the infuriated participants.

At this point George Sand ordered Clésinger and Solange to leave Nohant immediately and never return. According to her account of the events, they left, failing to pay any of the debts that they had incurred, and bearing off candelabra and counterpanes that were not theirs. Sand frantically wrote Mlle de Rozières that Chopin was not to hear of all this anything beyond what she herself had been forced to write him. "I was afraid," she explained, "that he might arrive in the middle of a scene and that the pain and shock would kill him." Neither Sand's letter to Chopin nor his reply survives. On July 20, however, Delacroix wrote in his *Journal:*

Chopin came in the morning while I was having lunch after my return from the Museum, where I had received the order for the copy of the *Corps de Garde.* He told me about the letter he had received, and he has since read me almost all of it. . . . There is no question but that it is atrocious. Cruel passions and long-restrained impatience come to the surface; and, by way of a contrast that would be amusing if the subject were not so sad, the author intermittently takes the place of the woman and spreads herself in tirades that seem borrowed from a novel or a philosophical homily.

Partly because George Sand would not lend them a carriage for the journey, the Clésingers had not gone to Paris. So Solange wrote to Chopin, probably pouring out her own version of the recent grotesque happenings, and certainly telling him that she was ill and must, in view of her mother's attitude, ask him to lend her and her husband the carriage that he had left at Nohant. Chopin at once wrote Sand that Solange was to have the carriage and told Solange that he had so written her. The effect on Sand of this proof that Chopin was siding with the girl — whom she was at the moment describing to Mlle de Rozières as having caused her nothing but tragedy — can be imagined. It gave her further reason for hardening her heart against a man whom she had ceased to love and no longer wished to mother and to nurse. His lending the carriage to Solange has often been singled out as the one real cause of his break with Sand, which it certainly was not. But it may well have sealed that break with certainty.

As late as July 25, nonetheless, George Sand was expecting Chopin to come to Nohant. Either her anger had cooled or she believed that Chopin would see through the Clésingers and arrive at her view of matters. If this was so, it is impossible to understand what she thought Maurice's attitude to his return would be. Sand was undoubtedly upset over the fact that Chopin, while not writing to her, kept in touch with Solange. Despite her statements to the contrary, it is unlikely that she would have regarded Chopin's arrival at her château as anything but a further, and unwelcome, complication. She was a very tired woman, and a situation could get too complicated even for her.

Chopin continued on friendly terms with Solange and even seems to have altered somewhat his opinion of Clésinger. Solange reported to him a slanderous rumor that was being passed about — that from him Clésinger had borrowed large sums of money to pay for furniture. Chopin answered:

I received your letter with pleasure and read it with grief. What are all these slanders about? Your husband has never borrowed any *large sum* from me *to pay for your furniture*. You returned the five hundred francs to me as soon as you reached Besançon.[3] Also I found the five louis in my purse, and always forgot to thank you for the delicate manner in which you repaid your creditor for *large sums*.

The tone of this letter certainly suggests that Chopin intended to throw suspicion of having invented the slanders onto some definite person or persons. George Sand? Maurice? Augustine

[3] After their dismissal from Nohant the Clésingers had gone first to visit Baron Dudevant, then to visit the elder Clésinger, a sculptor living at Besançon. From the latter place they had then gone to La Châtre, closer to Nohant.

Brault? It is impossible to tell. Chopin's friendly attitude toward Solange never altered: as late as two months before his death he was in correspondence with her.[4]

These protracted upheavals, coinciding with a period when Chopin's health was extremely bad, naturally saw his creative activity sharply reduced. In 1846 he published only the Mazurkas of opus 59; the Barcarolle; the Polonaise-Fantaisie; and the Nocturnes of opus 62. During that year he completed the Barcarolle, the Polonaise-Fantaisie, and the Sonata for cello and piano; composed the Nocturnes of opus 62, the Mazurkas of opus 63, and the Mazurka in A minor, opus 67, no. 4; and began the Waltzes of opus 64. In 1847 he completed the Waltzes of opus 64 and composed one song. The publications of 1847 were the Sonata for cello and piano; the Mazurkas of opus 63; and the Waltzes of opus 64. Chopin was to publish nothing more.

Late in November 1847, hearing from Solange that she had twice fruitlessly visited Nohant in the hope of a reconciliation with her mother, Chopin wrote her a letter that displays the finality with which he had by then accepted his own exile from Nohant:

Every morning for the past fifteen days I have begun to write to tell you how unhappy.I am over the results of your two visits to Nohant. But the first step is made; you have shown affection, and there is a certain rapprochement, for you have been asked to write. Time will do the rest. Also, you know that one must not take too literally everything that people say; and even if, for example, she will no longer *know* an outsider like me, it can scarcely be that way with your husband, who has become a member of the family. . . . I shall attempt to give you some news that will be better than our climate, but for that this *hateful year* must end. . . . That is all. I choke; I have a headache, and I beg your pardon for my erasures and my French. . . .

[4] What well-intentioned friends had said in advance about Clésinger proved well justified. His creditors became importunate toward the close of 1848, and the property that George Sand had deeded to her daughter as a dowry was attached and liquidated to pay them off. At that time Solange was still so bitter toward her mother that she could tell Chopin that it was not in fact Clésinger's creditors, but George Sand herself, who had ordered the property seized!

To his sister Ludvika, on Christmas, Chopin unburdened his mind and heart. After a gossipy opening, his letter proceeds:

Sol is with her father in Gascony. She saw her mother before she left. She was at Nohant with the Duvernets, but her mother received her coldly, telling her that if she will leave her husband she can return to Nohant. She saw her bridal bedroom converted into a theater, her boudoir into an actors' dressing-room, and writes that her mother talked to her only of financial affairs. Her brother played with her dog, and all he found to say to her was: — "Would you like something to eat?" Neither the cousin nor those other people were visible; in short, her two visits were failures. Before leaving, she returned there the next day, but was received even more coldly than the first time. Still, her mother did ask her to write and say what she intends to do. The mother seems to be more bitter against her son-in-law than against her daughter; yet in the famous letter to me she wrote that her son-in-law is not bad; it is only her daughter who makes him so. It seems as though she wanted, at one stroke, to be rid of her daughter and of me because we were inconvenient; she will correspond with her daughter; so her maternal heart, which cannot do without some news of her child, will be calmed, and with that she can stifle her conscience. She will believe that she is fair, and will call me an enemy for having taken the side of her son-in-law (whom she cannot endure only because he has married her daughter — and I did all that I could to prevent the marriage). A strange creature, for all her intellect! Some sort of frenzy has come upon her; she breaks up her own life, she breaks up her daughter's life; with her son, too, it will end badly; I predict and could swear it. For her own justification she longs to discover something against those who care for her, who have never done her any harm, but whom she cannot bear to see about her because they are mirrors of her conscience. Thus she has not written one word more to me, she will not come to Paris, nor has she mentioned me to her daughter at all. I am not sorry that I helped her through the eight most difficult years of her life: the years when her daughter was growing up and her son was living with his mother; I do not regret what I have suffered; but I am sorry that the daughter, that carefully cultivated plant sheltered from so many storms, has been broken at her mother's hand by a carelessness and levity pardonable perhaps in a woman in her twenties, but not in one in her forties. What has been and is no longer leaves no trace on the record. Some day, when Mme S. considers the matter, she can have only kind memories of me in her soul. Meanwhile she is now in the strangest paroxysm of motherhood, acting the role of a juster and better mother than she really is; and that is a fever for which there is no cure in the case of heads with so much imagination when they have stepped into such quicksands. For the rest — "even cypresses have their caprices. . . ."

And on the last day of 1847 Chopin wrote a letter to Solange, who was pregnant. He was certain, he said, that she would soon be receiving "ninety lines instead of nine" from her mother, and that "the grandmother's joy will be the joy of the young mother. You will adore together the little angel coming into the world to restore both your hearts to their normal state." He told Solange that her mother's most recent novel, *François le Champi*, would shortly begin to appear serially in the *Journal des débats*, and that "some sort of memoirs" were being publicly hinted. He seems not to have had a suspicion that George Sand would publish, in her *Histoire de ma vie*, a distorted justification of her attitude toward him and toward the breaking-up of their relationship. It was on this note that Chopin ended the saddest year of his life and began a year that was to be marked by astonishing activity on the part of a man who was already much more than half dead.

XII

Ｏｎ February 16, 1848 Chopin gave a concert at the Salle Pleyel. For this, his last public appearance in Paris, the program read:

1. Trio — Mozart, played by Chopin (piano), Jean-Delphin Alard (violin), and Franchomme (cello)
2. Arias — Mlle Antonia Molina di Mondi
3. Nocturne and Barcarolle — Chopin, with the composer at the piano
4. Aria — Mlle Antonia Molina di Mondi
5. Étude and Berceuse — Chopin, with the composer at the piano

INTERMISSION

6. Scherzo, Adagio, and Finale from the Cello Sonata in G minor — Chopin, played by the composer and Franchomme
7. New aria from *Robert le diable* — Meyerbeer — Gustave-Hippolyte Roger
8. Préludes, Mazurkas, and Waltz in D-flat major, opus 64 — Chopin, with the composer at the piano.

In the rooms on the rue Rochechouart that Wednesday evening at half past eight an audience of three hundred — having purchased tickets to a total of six thousand francs (they could have had as many of the best seats at the Opéra for thirty-six hundred) — heard the visibly ailing sorcerer weave his unique spells. The political situation was darkening: the revolution that overthrew Louis-Philippe broke out the following Tuesday. But nothing of the glamour and glitter of Chopin's Paris was lacking therefor. His close friends, knowing how seriously sick he was, were amazed to see that when he took his place before the keyboard his wasted condition showed only in an exceeding pallor. He walked erect, his dress was that of the eternal dandy. There was no faltering. But there was also no volume beyond a *forte*, and the sorceries were woven among infinite gradations of *piano* and *pianissimo* built up with breathtaking sensitivity to climaxes at the volume where a Liszt climax would have begun. In the Barcarolle the dynamics were reversed by a man conscious of his lack of physical reserve: the piece's tremendous upheavals of sound were replaced by a shimmering *pianissimo* that shook the most musical among his listeners. Again and again in the flower-filled room they called Chopin back. He had to repeat the D-flat Waltz. By then he was holding himself to effort by a fierce expenditure of will. Retiring to the green room for the last time, he all but fainted. He had bade farewell to the great city that was his adopted home. In twenty months he would be dead.

But Paris did not wish to let Chopin go. Subscriptions were begun for another concert, which was announced for March 10. The wind of rebellion, breaking through on Chopin's thirty-eighth birthday, swept away the possibility of that concert, among the least of its victims. Perhaps Chopin had somehow foreseen the Revolution, in fact, for there had been public announcement before it occurred that he would shortly be leaving the city. A Scottish lady six years his senior, Jane Wilhelmina Stirling, had been one of his devoted pupils. With her sister, Mrs. Erskine, she had long been pressing upon the ailing man an invitation to visit Scotland. Now, with the aristocratic society of Louis-Philippe's reign collapsing about him, he had no reason left for remaining in France. He decided to cross the Channel again for the first time in eleven years.

On March 4, while preparing his departure, Chopin called on Mme Marliani and there accidentally encountered George Sand. Their conversation was brief. On February 28 Solange Clésinger had given birth to a daughter. On March 3 Chopin had written her: "The arrival of your little daughter has given me, as you may suppose, more joy than the arrival of the Republic." And on Sunday, March 5, he wrote to Solange again, this time to tell her of his encounter with her mother:

Yesterday I went to Mme Marliani, and as I left I met your mother at the vestibule doorway; she was coming in with Lambert. I said good-day to your mother, and my second phrase was: had she had any news of you lately. "A week ago," she replied. "You have not heard anything yesterday or the day before?" "No." "Then I can tell you that you are a grandmother; Solange has a daughter, and I am very happy that I am able to be the first to give you the news." I bowed and went downstairs. Combes the Abyssinian (who has fallen right into the Revolution on arriving from Morocco) was with me, and as I had forgotten to say that you are doing well, an important thing, especially for a mother (now you will understand that easily, Mother Solange), I asked Combes to go up again, as I could not manage the stairs, and tell her that you are getting on well, and the child too. I was awaiting the Abyssinian at the bottom of the stairs when your mother came down with him and put to me, with much interest, some questions about your condition. I answered that you had written me a few words yourself, in pencil, the day after the birth of your child, that you have suffered a great deal, but that the sight of your little daughter has made you forget it all. She inquired of me whether your husband was with you, and I answered that the address of your letter seemed to me to be in his handwriting. She asked me how I am; I replied that I am well, and requested the concierge to open the door. I bowed, and found myself in the Square d'Orléans on foot, escorted by the Abyssinian.

"I suppose that she is happy in the triumph of republican ideas," Chopin added. But though he received word in a few days that Solange's child had died, he did not see George Sand again. She had returned to Nohant, and he went to England, arriving in London on the night of Holy Thursday, April 20. Mrs. Erskine and her husband had taken lodgings for him at 10 Bentinck Street, Cavendish Square, where he found all manner of details thoughtfully arranged, including chocolate to drink and note-paper with his monogram. He had made the Channel crossing "without much seasickness," he wrote Gzhimala, but he had been forced to rest briefly at Folkstone. He did not long remain in Bentinck Street, but moved to a spacious apartment at 48 Dover Street. By May 6 he was writing Adolf Gutmann that he had three pianos — an Érard, a Pleyel, and a Broadwood — in his rooms. "But what is the use," he complained, "when I have no time to play on them?" His days were being crowded with more social activities than were good for a man who was inter-mittently spitting blood and being forced to rest from wasting attacks.

On May 11 Chopin wrote to Gutmann:

I have just returned from the Italian theater. Jenny Lind sang for the first time this year, and the Queen showed herself for the first time since the Chartists.[1] Both produced a great effect — and, on me, so did old Wellington, who sat beneath the Queen's box like an old monarchical dog in his kennel under his crowned Lady. I have met J. Lind, and she very graciously sent me a most excellent stall with her card. As I had a good place, I heard well. She is a typical Swede, not in an ordinary light, but in some sort of polar dawn. She is tremendously effective in *Sonnambula*. She sings with extreme purity and certainty, and her soft notes are steady and as even as a hair. A stall costs 2 1/2 guineas.

In another letter he told of being invited to play with the Philharmonic, but said that he would much prefer to give a morning recital in a private house, "with admission limited to a certain number of persons." He noted that all the Parisian pianists came to London, but were not all successful: "they want classical things here." And so, to Gutmann and Gzhimala at least, Chopin poured out the small talk of his weary London life. He would not play at the Philharmonic because "there one must play Beethoven, Mozart, or Mendelssohn." Mme Viardot sang her own arrangement of some of his Mazurkas at Covent Garden, and they were encored. On May 12 he dined with Lind, who then sang Swedish folksongs until midnight. By that date he had five pupils.

Chopin's depression was exaggerated by financial worries, particularly because his landlord was threatening to double his monthly rent of twenty-six guineas. Up to June 2 he had had "only two paid evenings at 20 guineas." He was continuing to give a few lessons at a guinea each, and had no plans for a public appearance. At an evening at the Duchess of Sutherland's, however, he played before Victoria, Albert, the Duke of Wellington, and many others of the highest rank. Tamburini, Lablache, and Mario also performed that evening, and Chopin had two short

[1] On April 10 what had purported to be the march of 500,000 people from Kensington Common to Parliament for the presentation of the Chartist demands had turned out to be a meeting of about one tenth that many people — and their leaders had called off the march. The threat, however, had spread considerable fear.

talks with Victoria and one with Albert. He still refused to play
at the Philharmonic, which permitted only one rehearsal — and
that public — paid nothing, and found success synonymous with
Mendelssohn's music.

It would be possible for him to start life afresh, Chopin remarked to Gzhimala, if he had some days free from blood-spitting,
if he were younger, and if his afflictions did not prostrate him.
Finally he succeeded in giving a matinee concert with Mario at
the house of Mrs. Sartoris,² 99 Eaton Place. This was on June 23.
It left him with the wish to give another, and he believed that the
two together might net him three hundred guineas, little enough
in view of his expenses in rooms just off Piccadilly at the zenith
of the London social season.

Finally, one day when spending some time in the company of
Manuel Patricio García, Chopin was offered the drawing-room
of Lord Falmouth's house at 2 St James's Square for another matinee. As García was Mme Viardot's brother, Chopin then felt that
he must invite her to assist him in the concert, though he did not
wish to, apparently because he resented her reporting to George
Sand about his welfare. She again sang some of his Mazurkas,
and things generally went well. This was July 7; three days later
the *Daily News* reported on the "numerous and fashionable as-
sembly":

M. Chopin performed an Andante sostenuto and a Scherzo from his
Opus 31,³ a selection from his celebrated studies, a Nocturne and a
Berceuse and several of his own Preludes, Mazurkas and Waltzes.
. . . His music is as strongly marked with individual character as that
of any master who has ever lived. It is highly finished, new in its harmonies, full of contrapuntal skill and ingenious contrivance; and yet
we have never heard music which has so much the air of unpremedi-
tated effusion. . . .

And yet five days later Chopin wrote to Gzhimala:

After deducting lodging and carriage, all I shall have been able to
scrape together will perhaps not add up to more than 200 guineas

² Mrs. Sartoris was Adelaide Kemble, sister of Fanny Kemble.
³ This was, of course, the great B-flat minor Scherzo, of the performance of
which Wilhelm von Lenz quoted Chopin as saying: "It must be a charnel-
house."

(about 5,000 francs). In Italy you can live a year on that, but here not half a year. The *season* is almost over. I have not yet played at the Queen's palace, though I have played before the Queen (at the Sutherlands'). The Duchess of Suth[erland] has left London. So perhaps the Queen's director has dug a pit for me because I did not return his call or because I refused to play at the Philharmonic. If the season here lasted six months I could gradually get known after my fashion, but as it is, there is no time.

Chopin had met both Thomas and Jane Welsh Carlyle, who heard him play, probably on July 7. Writing from Chelsea on August 5 to his friend the Reverend Alexander Scott, Carlyle said:

If you see M. Chopin, pray offer him my hearty regards. I hope we shall get some language to speak in by and by, and then get into more plentiful communication. An excellent, gentle, much-suffering human soul, as I can at once see without language.

Mrs. Carlyle was deeply impressed both by Chopin himself and by his compositions. Lamenting, like her husband, that the barrier of language made it impossible for her to talk to Chopin, she communicated with him by letter through Jane Stirling, enclosing a mediocre poem by someone else with a request that it be translated and presented to Chopin. "I prefer his music to all others," was her judgment, to which she added that it pleased her particularly by its aristocratic reserve, the way it withheld its inner nature from all but the elect. It is lamentable that no comment by Chopin on either of the Carlyles survives.

Victoria and Albert soon went to Scotland for the summer, and most of society followed them. Chopin's few pupils deserted him. Jane Stirling and her relations were bombarding him with invitations to visit them in Scotland. To Gzhimala he wrote:

My Scottish ladies are kind, and I gave them your letter; but they bore me so that I don't know what to do. They want to insist that I should go to their homes in Scotland; that's all right, but nowadays I have no heart for anything. Here whatever is not boring is not English.

Finally he had no choice. He accepted an invitation from Miss Stirling's brother-in-law, Lord Torphichen, to stay at Calder House, which was located in Midlothian, twelve miles from Edinburgh. He also agreed to play at Manchester in a concert to be shared with Mme Marietta Alboni.

From Calder House, on August 19, Chopin sent to his family in Warsaw a very long report on his experiences in London. Having described his appearances at the Duchess of Sutherland's, Mrs. Sartoris's, and Lord Falmouth's, he added:

After that evening at the Duchess of Suth[erland]'s, I was told that I was to play at the Queen's palace; but I did not play, why I do not know. Probably because I did not apply for it, and here you have to apply for everything, there is such a congestion of things. Not only did I not apply, but I did not call on the Kapellmeister of the court,[4] or rather, the man who arranges concerts for the Queen and conducts the Philharmonic Society's orchestra (which gives the best concerts here, resembling the Conservatoire in Paris). The Philharmonic Society invited me to play for them: a great favor, or rather honor; everyone who comes here tries for it, and this year neither Kalk[brenner] nor Hallé played, despite much effort. But I refused, and this made a bad impression on musicians, and especially on conductors. I refused once because I was not well; that was the reason I gave; but the real one was that I should only have had to play one of my concertos with the orchestra, and these gentlemen give only one rehearsal, and that in public, with entrance by free ticket. How can you rehearse and repeat! So we should have played badly (though apparently they know my concertos, and Mrs. Dulcken,[5] a famous — hm! — pianist here, played one last year there); so I sent regrets to the Philharmonic Society. One newspaper took offense at this, but that doesn't matter. After my matinees many newspapers had good criticisms, excepting the *Times*, in which a certain Davison[6] writes (a creature of poor Mendelssohn's); he doesn't know me, and imagines, I am told, that I am an antagonist of Mendelssohn. . . .

[4] This would have been Sir Michael Costa.
[5] Ferdinand David's sister, Louise Dulcken (1811–50).
[6] James William Davison (1813–85), long critic of the *Times*, had begun by admiring Chopin's compositions. In 1836, however, William Sterndale Bennett introduced him to Mendelssohn, and thereafter Mendelssohn's compositions usurped Davison's universe. He turned rabidly against many of his own former admirations, and was capable of writing, for example: "The entire works of Chopin present a motley surface of ranting hyperbole and excruciating cacophony." He was not, despite this, above accepting payment from Chopin's English publisher, Wessel, for writing an "Essay on the Works of Frederic Chopin," a defense against attacks he had himself launched!

Saying that he had come to know many personages of the great world, Chopin mentioned Carlyle, Samuel Rogers, Dickens, George Hogarth, Lady Byron ("I understand why she bored Byron"), and her daughter, Lady Lovelace. Among his many royal and titled acquaintances he listed Lady Combermere — at whose home he had one evening met the Duke and Duchess of Cambridge — Count Montemolin (the Carlist pretender), Lady Norton (Richard Brinsley Sheridan's granddaughter, famous for her marital troubles and her opinions on divorce), Lady Blessington, and Count D'Orsay.

The letter continues at length with descriptions of Chopin's trip from London to Edinburgh, of Calder House, of what he calls the English *"vie de château."* He mentions having heard from Solange Clésinger, and at once darts off into a long tale about George Sand:

Her biography has been printed and sold in the streets; written and signed by Augustine's father, who complains that she demoralized his only daughter and made her into Maurice's mistress; that she gave her in marriage, against her parents' will, to the first comer after having promised to marry her to her own son. He quotes her own letters. In short, a hideous business that today is known to all the scum of Paris. It is vile of the father, but the thing is true.

He was still blindly and completely on Solange's side in the continuing family quarrel, and therefore opposed to Sand herself and to Maurice, who had more and more become the shining center of his mother's life.

In a letter to Voitsyekh Gzhimala, also written on August 19, Chopin remarked that the Scottish climate was not agreeing with him: for two days he had been spitting blood. Yet he was planning to go to Manchester, eight hours distant by railway, to appear in a concert on August 28. He had September invitations to houses near Stirling and Glasgow. Early in October "if it is not yet cold (they say that the weather is still good then, and it will bring in about one hundred pounds)," he planned to play in Edinburgh again. Then he glanced more than two months ahead: "What to do with myself next, I am afraid to think." It seemed to him that there was nothing for it but to return to republican

Paris, and he therefore asked Gzhimala to speak to his concierge and the woman who aired and cleaned his rooms.

On the day when Chopin sat in Calder House writing to his family in Warsaw and his friend in Paris, the following notice was run in the *Manchester Guardian:*

Concert Hall — The Directors beg to announce to the Subscribers that a Dress Concert has been fixed for Monday, the 28th of August next, for which the following performers have already been engaged: Signora Alboni, Signora Corbari, Signor Salvi, and Mons. Chopin.[7]

In the clean-aired outskirts of Manchester the ailing Chopin was the guest of an industrial potentate named Salis Schwabe. And on August 28 he duly appeared at the "Gentlemen's Concert," only to be outshone by the dazzling Alboni and diminished by the feebleness of his tone in a hall containing an audience of twelve hundred. The program would now be considered a gigantic pudding. An orchestra played Weber's *Rubezahl* and Beethoven's *Prometheus* overtures and that to Rossini's *Il Barbiere di Siviglia.* Chopin played an Andante and a Scherzo, Études, a Nocturne, and the Berceuse. What the singers performed is not recorded, but their accompanist was George Alexander Osborne, an accomplished pianist who had studied with Kalkbrenner in Paris, where in 1831 he had played at Chopin's first concert.

Because Osborne had heard him under more intimate conditions, had known him in happier days, Chopin begged him to leave the hall while he played. Osborne naturally did nothing of the sort. "Notwithstanding this appeal I was present," he wrote, "unknown to him, in a remote corner of the room, where I helped to cheer and applaud him. I heard him then for the last time, when his prediction was in part fulfilled, for his playing was too delicate to create enthusiasm, and I felt truly sorry for him." Chopin appeared thrice during the concert. During the last of these appearances he won the sort of applause that demanded an encore. To the surprise of his listeners, he did not repeat what he

---

[7] Signora Alboni was, of course, Marietta Alboni, the great Rossinian contralto, then at midstream in her remarkable singing career of nearly two decades. Signora Corbari I cannot identify. Signor Salvi was probably Lorenzo Salvi, a tenor who later sang in New York at both Castle Garden and Niblo's.

had just played, but instead performed something brief that was described as "a fragment of great beauty."

Lingering with the hospitable Schwabe for some days, Chopin rested. Then he went north to Edinburgh. There, after a short but uncomfortable stay in a hotel, he became the guest of a Dr. and Mrs. Lishchinski, with whom he was delighted to be able to speak Polish. By sending their children to stay with friends, the Lishchinskis were able to make room for Chopin and his manservant in two rooms, one of them normally the nursery. These were on an upper floor, and Chopin was by then so weak that the amiable doctor had to carry him up the stairs. Mrs. Lishchinski later told Frederick Niecks that her guest rose late and had soup in his room. His manservant, in addition to keeping his master's clothes in the pink of neatness, curled his master's hair each day. More importantly, Mrs. Lishchinski said that after dinner Chopin, frequently suffering from the cold, sat before the open fire. The Scottish climate was undoubtedly bad for a weakening man in the advanced stages of tuberculosis.

From Edinburgh, Chopin went, probably about September 1, to visit another of Jane Stirling's sisters, Mrs. Houston, a widow who lived in some grandeur at Johnstone Castle, eleven miles outside Glasgow. From there, beginning on September 4, he wrote a long letter to Gzhimala. After describing many events and individuals, he suddenly broke out:

This letter was begun yesterday, to be finished today; but the weather has changed; it is bad outside, and I am cross and depressed, and people bore me with their excessive attentions. I can't breathe, I can't work, I feel alone, alone, alone, though I am surrounded [Here, according to Hoesick, seven lines of the manuscript letter are so crossed through as to be illegible.]

Why should I bore you with my jeremiads! You have troubles of your own, up to your ears. I should cheer you up with my letter. Were I in good humor, I should describe to you one Scottish lady, a thirteenth cousin of Mary Stuart (sic!! Her husband, who bears a name different from his wife's really told me that.) Here it's nothing but cousins of great families and great names that nobody on the Continent has ever heard of. Conversation is always entirely genealogical, like the Gospels; who begat whom, and he begat, and he begat, and he begat, and so on for two pages until you arrive at Jesus.

Near the end of the letter, Chopin wrote:

Today is the 9th. I send you my old letter of Sept. 4. Forgive this scrawl; you know what an effort writing sometimes is for me; the pen burns under my fingers, my hair falls out, and I can't write what I want to say, only a thousand futile things.

While still at Johnstone Castle, Chopin received word that Prince and Princess Alexander Chartoriski (she his good friend Princess Marcelline) and their young son were visiting in Edinburgh. Ill and exhausted though he was, he quickly entrained for that city, and was shortly speaking Polish with the Chartoriskis in a glad reunion. After a brief visit with them, however, he had to travel back to Glasgow, where he had undertaken to give an afternoon concert in Merchant Hall. Because of the hour — two thirty p.m. — and the price of the tickets — half a guinea each — his audience was limited to wealthy and unoccupied members of the local aristocracy and the near-by county families. The Chartoriskis also attended, and then dined with Mrs. Houston and Chopin at Johnstone Castle.

Chopin is said to have earned sixty pounds from his Glasgow concert, which took place on September 27. Repeating the pieces that he had played in Manchester, he was assisted by a singer, Mme Adelasio de Margueritte. Among the friends who had visited Glasgow to hear him were Jane Stirling's aged brother-in-law, Lord Torphichen, and Lord and Lady Murray, she formerly his pupil in Paris. And from Glasgow he went to spend some days with the Murrays at their home in Strachur on Loch Fyne. Still expending his small remaining supply of energy on travel, he then went to Keir, in Perthshire, near Stirling Castle, seat of that distant cousin of Jane Stirling who was currently head of the Stirling clan. From Keir on October 1 he wrote Gzhimala the by then usual mixture of gossip and profound lamentation:

If I don't write you jeremiads, it's not because it would not console me, for you are the only person who knows all about me; but because if I once start there will be no end to it, and forever the same. I am wrong to say *the same*, because for me the future constantly grows worse. I am weaker. I can't compose anything, less from lack of desire than because of physical hindrances; every week I bump up against a new tree-branch. And what can I do? . . . The whole morning, until

2 o'clock, I am fit for nothing now; and then, when I dress, everything strains me, and I gasp that way until dinner-time. Afterward one has to sit two hours at the table with the men, look at them talking, and *listen* to them drinking. I am bored to death (I am thinking of one thing and they of another, despite all their courtesy and French remarks at table). Then I go to the drawing-room, where it takes all my strength to be somewhat animated — because then they usually want to hear me — ; then my good Daniel [his manservant] carries me up to my bedroom (as you know, that is usually upstairs here), undresses me, gets me into bed, leaves the light; and I am at liberty to breathe [8] and dream until morning and time to start all over again. And when I get a little used to it, then it is time to go somewhere else; for my Scottish ladies give me no peace; either they come to fetch me or they take me the round of their families (*nota bene,* they make their folk invite them constantly). They are stifling me out of *courtesy,* and out of the same *courtesy* I don't refuse them.

Three days after this despairing letter to Gzhimala, Chopin was again in Edinburgh. There, in the Hopetoun Rooms in Queen Street, he gave, not the conventional singer-assisted concert of the time, but a recital without assistance. The program read as follows:

1. Andante et Impromptu.
2. Études.
3. Nocturne et Berceuse.
4. Grande Valse Brillante.
5. Andante précédé d'un Largo.
6. Preludes, Ballade, Mazurkas et Valses.

To commence at half-past eight o'clock. Tickets, limited in number, half-a-guinea each.

The critic of the *Edinburgh Courant* reported on October 7:

Of his execution we need say nothing further than that it is the most finished we have ever heard. He has neither the ponderosity nor the digital power of a Mendelssohn, a Thalberg, or Liszt; consequently his execution would appear less effective in a large room; but as a chamber pianist he stands unrivalled.

[8] The immediate cause of Chopin's death was to be tuberculosis of the larynx, though his lungs were also deeply diseased.

This precisely summarizes the opinion of Chopin's playing held, and often expressed, by the best-equipped of his contemporaries.

The cold Scottish winter was drawing in. There was an increasing threat of cholera, which had already begun to spread northward from London. Chopin fell deeper and deeper into weakness, ennui, despair. His round of visits, however, went on — to Wishaw, Lady Belhaven's house, to the castle of the Duke of Hamilton. He was stricken with a severe cold, through which Dr. Lishchinski miraculously nursed him with homeopathic nostrums. Finally — perhaps as much to escape from his "Scottish ladies" embattled on their home ground as to begin his return to Paris — Chopin went south to London. There, a desperately sick man, he arrived on October 31. He stopped at 4 St. James's Place. His cold had returned upon him strengthened, and another homeopath, a Dr. Mallan who was a brother-in-law to Lady Gainsborough, treated him. For fifteen days Chopin could not stir from his room. Then, fortified by medicines, he went on November 16 to the Guildhall to take part in a great concert and ball being given for the benefit of Polish refugees. It was his last appearance in public anywhere.

In London the Chartoriskis were still at hand. Jane Stirling and Mrs. Erskine, with paralyzing kindness, had followed Chopin to London. He was acquainted with many of the numerous Polish refugees. But he felt alone. He wrote frantically to Gzhimala, telling him to arrange suitable quarters at once. A week after the Guildhall affair he at last reached the end of his Scottish-English trail: on November 23 he returned to Paris. What would Hector Berlioz, who later said that Chopin was dying all his life, or John Field, who called Chopin's a "sickroom talent," have said if either of them could have seen the emaciated, pallor-dimmed, and dying man who then came back to the city that he had entered with high hopes and jaunty youthful spirits seventeen years before?

XIII

CHOPIN was not dying all his life. A wasting disease had, however, been gaining on his strength for years, and there is no doubt that with the events of 1846–7 — ending in the final rupture with George Sand — he had begun to die. The trip to England and Scotland had been worse than ill-advised on both the physical and the psychological planes. On the physical, the climate of Scotland and northern England in the damp and cutting autumn had added to the drain on the small vitality he still kept. On the psychological plane he had been cut off from scenes and people dear to him, only to find himself faced day after day with the crushing kindness of Jane Stirling, who was unquestionably in love with him, and that of her numerous family. During 1848 he seems not to have composed anything; it is probably significant that in 1849, back in Paris, he did manage to compose at least two Mazurkas — the G minor, opus 67, no. 2, and the F minor, opus 68, no. 4 — though during that year the speed of his physical deterioration became terrifyingly swift.

Jane Stirling was both good and bad for Chopin. She was nearly six years his senior, a woman of commanding physical presence, fine intelligence, and unbounded goodness of heart. She was wealthy. Chopin knew that she was intensely devoted to him not only as a musician but also as a man. He knew that he and she were being discussed as lovers who might soon marry. But he confessed that he did not find her attractive, and said that they were too much alike for love in that meaning. "Imagine," he wrote, "kissing your own likeness in a mirror." His sense of debt to her was not altogether pleasant, and its irritating content was exaggerated by his realization that he could not reciprocate her love. He said again and again that she and her well-meaning relations bored him, smothered him with thoughtful but gagging attentions, swept him from place to place, and were generally a tax on his strength. Yet without her he might not have been able to remain out of poverty during his last two years.

For by the time of his trip from London to Paris in November 1848 [1] Chopin could neither compose enough to earn an income thereby nor take pupils. He was continually undergoing medical treatment — largely by homeopathic physicians — and was constantly weakening. At first he went on living in the Square d' Orléans apartment, which must often have rustled with the absence of George Sand. To that address, early in March 1849, Jane Stirling is said to have sent a gift of twenty-five thousand francs to alleviate his near poverty. The package containing the banknotes bore no sender's name, as Miss Stirling was too delicate to wish Chopin to discover the source of the assistance — or so the story went as she later wished him to believe it. For some reason that was never established, however, the concierge who received it — she had a room in the house — supposedly took the packet to her quarters and stowed it away there without mentioning it. Miss Stirling naturally could not have expected acknowledgment of the receipt of an anonymous benefaction, and therefore would have had no way of knowing that Chopin had never received the money. Other friends must, in the interim, have helped the dying man to pay his bills and cover medical and other uninterrupted expenses. One of these is known to have been Countess Obreskoff, a Russian patroness of musicians.

As summer came in and Chopin's condition steadily became worse, a group of his friends — it probably included Gzhimala and Delacroix, and perhaps Clésinger — helped him to remove to more commodious and airy rooms at Grande rue Chaillot, 74, in the outskirts of Paris. On June 18 he wrote to Gzhimala, who had gone to the country (perhaps to avoid the epidemic of cholera then raging in Paris), that his "Scottish ladies" had just arrived. "They stifle me with boredom," he reiterated. Jenny Lind had called on him one evening and had sung for him. Delphine Pototska had been there, as had Princesse Charles de Beauvau. But Angelica Catalani, the great singer who had presented him

---

[1] He was accompanied on this journey by his manservant Daniel and by a Polish Parisian friend, a book-dealer named Leonard Nyedzvyetski. It is interesting to note that one month after Chopin's return to Paris, Louis-Napoleon Bonaparte became President of France.

with a watch in Warsaw nineteen years earlier, and whom he had seen recently, had died of the plague.

On the night of June 21 Chopin suffered two hemorrhages, news of which brought Princess Sapieha to see him. Finally, on June 25, he wrote to his sister Ludvika:

My Life,

If you [plural] can come, do. I am ill, and no doctor will do as much for me as some of you. If you are short of money, borrow some; if I recover I can easily earn and repay the lender, but just now I am stripped too bare to send you any. My lodgings here in Chaillot are fairly large, and could accommodate you with two children. Little Ludvika would gain from it in every way. Kalasanty the father could run about all day — the produce exhibition is near — in short, he would have more time to himself than he had before, for I am weaker and shall sit at home with Ludvika.

My friends and well-wishers think that the best medicine for me will be Ludvika's presence here, as Ludvika will doubtless see from Mme Ob[reskoff]'s letter. So try for a passport. I heard today from two people, one from the north, the other from the south, that people who don't know Ludvika have said that it would be good not only for me, but also for my sister. So, mother Ludvika and daughter Ludvika, bring your thimbles and knitting-needles, and I shall give you handkerchiefs to mark and stockings to knit, and you can spend two or three months in the fresh air with your old brother and uncle. The trip is easier now. You won't need much luggage. Here we shall manage as inexpensively as we can. Even if it is sometimes far for Kalasanty from the Champs-Élysées to the city, he can stay in my lodgings in the Square d'Orléans. The busses go from the Square right to this very door. I don't myself know why I want Ludvika so much, but it's as if it would give me hope. I guarantee that it will be good for her too. I hope that the family council will send her to me; who knows but that I shall return with her if I recover? We should all then embrace each other, as I wrote you, only with teeth still in our heads, and no wigs. Wives ought always to obey their husbands, so the husband must be asked to bring his wife. So I beg him to do it; and if he thinks about it, he can give no greater pleasure and benefit to her or to me, or even to the children, if he brings any of them (I have no doubt about the daughterkin). It will cost money, that is true, but it could not be better spent, nor could one travel more cheaply. Once you are here, we can find a shelter. Write me a line soon. Mme Ob[reskoff], who was so kind as to offer to write (I have given her Ludvika's address), may be more able to convince you. Mlle de Rozières also will add a letter, and Cochet also has probably done so, for he certainly didn't find me better. His Æsculapius has not called for ten days; he has probably guessed at last that here there is something beyond his science. All the same, praise him up well to your lodger and to others who know him, and say that he did me a lot of good, but that I am the sort of person who is satisfied the moment he gets a little better; that everyone thinks of him as having cured many people here of cholera. The cholera is abating fast; it is almost gone. Today the weather is fine, so I sit in the sitting-room and admire my view over all Paris: the towers, the Tuileries, the Chamber of Deputies, St. Germ[ain] l'Aux[errois], St. Étienne du Mont, Notre-Dame, the Panthéon, St. Sulpice, Val de Grace, the Invalides; from five windows, and nothing but gardens between. You will see when you come. Now about passport and money; begin soon, as it takes time. Write me a line at once. You know, "even cypresses have their caprices"; my caprice now is to see you. Perhaps God will permit things to come out right; and if God doesn't, then at least act as though He would. I have good hope of it, for I seldom demand much, and should refrain from asking this if I were not pressed by all who wish me well. Hurry, Mr. Kalasanty, and I shall give you a good big cigar for it; I know a person who loves to smoke; but in the garden. I hope that my letter for Mamma's name day arrived on time, so that she didn't miss me. I don't want to think about all this or I shall have a fever; I am not feverish, thank the Lord, which confuses and irritates all ordinary doctors.

Your affectionate, but sick, brother
Ch.

That Chopin did not send this letter off to Warsaw at once is indicated by his statement, in a letter to Gzhimala dated July 2, that it was only that day that he had written home about the seriousness of his condition. He adds that though he has not spat blood for two entire days, his legs are swollen and he remains weak and lazy. He cannot go upstairs, he says, and adds: "I suffocate." How far he was in time and space from the Paris of happier days is demonstrated in a letter written to Solange Clésinger two days later. In it he tells her that the cholera epidemic is receding, and then adds: ". . . but according to what I am told, Paris is becoming more and more deserted. It is hot here, and dusty. There is poverty and there is dirt, and one sees faces that belong to the other world."

In another letter to Gzhimala, dated July 10, Chopin tells his friend that he suffers from diarrhea, and that he cannot travel because his doctor forbids it. He had not yet heard from Ludvika, but said that if she did not come to Paris he would have to leave the city, "for everything here is too costly. I play less and less; I can't write anything." Eighteen days later the melodrama of Jane Stirling's undelivered gift of twenty-five thousand francs reached its denouement, which allows at least two interpretations. Through an elaborate piece of mystification involving a spiritualist medium, it was learned that the concierge at Chopin's apartment in the Square d'Orléans had received the package. There was no question of dishonesty; when the event of its delivery was recalled to this woman, she found and delivered the package exactly as it had been handed to her.

Chopin either did not know or pretended not to know, at first, who could possibly have sent him so munificent a gift. But Jane Stirling's sister, Mrs. Erskine, was present through the whole mummery of medium, intermediary, and recovery. And though Chopin flatly told Gzhimala in a letter dated July 28 that he did not "accept the donation," it is a fact that his diary for that date has an entry that reads: "Mrs. Erskine left 15,000 francs." What seems to have happened is that he refused to accept the entire amount, insisting that Mrs. Erskine take 10,000 francs of it away with her and leave but 15,000 for needs he could no longer deny. By August 3, indeed, Chopin himself was of the opinion that the mysterious performance had been rigged up as a method of trying to conceal the donor's identity from him. "There is kind-heartedness here," he commented, "but what showing-off!" Ludvika still had not obtained a passport, and this fretted Chopin the more because her husband's vacation was shortly to end, perhaps making her trip impossible. "I gasp, cough, and am drowsy. I do nothing. I want nothing. That Alexis [the medium] sticks in my head."

Long-gloomy skies brightened for Chopin on August 8: Ludvika and Kalasanty Yedzheyevich and their daughter Ludvika arrived. During the early part of their stay Chopin was strong enough to be taken once or twice to his rooms in the Square d'Orléans. He had heard that his onetime most beloved friend, Tytus Voitsyekhovski, was about to visit Ostend. He wrote Tytus pathetically of his own inability to visit Belgium too, and begged him to come to Paris, which proved impossible for the reason that Tytus could not obtain the necessary permit to enter France. And on August 30 Chopin received from three physicians in consultation an absolute order that forbade him to attempt a journey to Warsaw or anywhere else. On September 17 he wrote Franchomme that he was "rather worse than better," and that the three physicians had advised him to find lodgings with a southern exposure and remain in Paris. The lodgings had already been found, in fact — at 12 Place Vendôme. Although ready to faint from weariness and weakness, Chopin said that he was looking forward to the winter, when he should be able to receive all his friends in his new rooms. His sister Ludvika had decided to remain with him in Paris unless something urgent summoned her back to Warsaw.

Late in September Chopin was installed in the Place Vendôme. There, on October 15, he was visited by Delphine Pototska, his beautiful friend whom some had called his secret love. He asked her to sing to him, and she complied: she sang either an aria by Chopin's friend Bellini or Stradella's "Hymn to the Virgin," or perhaps both. Her singing was the last touch of color in his life. For three nights earlier he had swerved so close to death that one of his physicians had sent for a Polish priest to administer the last sacraments to him. By then, if not earlier, Chopin himself must have understood that his plans to rebegin his life during the coming winter were doomed. He must have realized that he was dying. And two days after Delphine Pototska had sung for him his hour arrived. The physician asked him if he was in pain, and in reply he said his last word — "*Plus*" [no more]. He died during the very early morning of October 17. Some have written that he died in the arms of his pupil Adolf Gutmann, but Gutmann was away from Paris at the time. In his room at the final moment were his sister Ludvika, Princess Marcelline Chartoriska, and Solange Clésinger.

When he had no longer been able to talk, Chopin had taken a pencil in his hand and on a sheet of letter-paper had written: "As this earth [2] will smother me, I adjure you to have my body

[2] In Chopin's original scrawl, this word looks like *terre* (earth), which it has always been taken to be. Nicolas Slonimsky reads it as *toux* (cough), a de-

opened so that I may not be buried alive." This adjuration was
obeyed: his body was cut open and his heart removed. Placed in
a small mortuary urn, it was eventually deposited at Warsaw in
the Church of the Holy Cross. During the day following his
death Solange's husband took casts of his face and hands while
his friend Kviatkovski sketched in profile the head upright and
dead upon a pillow. As his friends passed through the room to
look at Chopin for the last time, arrangements were begun for
his funeral in the Madeleine.

On October 20 Eugène Delacroix wrote in his *Journal:*

After luncheon I learned of the death of poor Chopin. Strange, in the
morning, before arising, I had been struck by that idea. This is one
more time, after several others, that I have had that sort of premonition. What a loss! What miserable rogues fill the marketplace while
that beautiful soul burns out!

Chopin's funeral was delayed until October 30 by a complication. He had expressed the hope that Mozart's Requiem could
be sung then. That meant female singers, not usually permitted
at the Madeleine, and it took time to wangle the extraordinary
permission. The dead man had been eulogized in *La Presse* by
Théophile Gautier, in the *Journal des débats* by Hector Berlioz —
and on October 30 the ceremony in the Madeleine was both vast
and impressive. It began at noon. The orchestra and chorus of
the Conservatoire, with Narcisse Girard conducting, performed
the Requiem, the soloists being Pauline Viardot-Garcia, Jeanne
Castellan, Alexis Dupont, and Luigi Lablache.[3] The *"Marche
funèbre"* from Chopin's B-flat minor Sonata, as orchestrated by
Napoléon-Henri Réber, accompanied the procession of the coffin
up the aisle. During the ceremony, too, the organist of the Made-

---

ciphering I find it all but impossible to make. Nor do I agree with Mr. Slonimsky that the traditional reading "makes no sense." Certainly earth would
smother a man buried alive.

[3] Pauline Viardot-Garcia, friend of both Chopin and George Sand, was, of
course, one of the foremost singers of the time. Jeanne Anaïs Castellan was
almost as famous, and had created soprano roles in Gounod's *Sapho* and
Meyerbeer's *Le Prophète.* Alexis Dupont, a singer noted for his intelligence,
was a friend of Berlioz. Luigi Lablache, the greatest bass of the era, had
known both Beethoven and Schubert. At Beethoven's funeral in 1827 he had
both sung the music he repeated at Chopin's and borne a torch.

leine, Louis-James Lefébure-Wély, played transcriptions of Chopin's Préludes in E minor and B minor. Mingled with the curious throng were the dead composer's friends and admirers, including many of the leading figures of the day: Delacroix, Meyerbeer (who later complained that he had not been invited to orchestrate the *"Marche funèbre"*), Franchomme, Prince Alexander Chartoriski, Prince Adam Chartoriski, and Théophile Gautier.

At Père-Lachaise Cemetery, in accord with Chopin's expressed wish, there was no graveside oration. The names of the pallbearers have always been in dispute. According to Gautier they were Camille Pleyel, Delacroix, Franchomme, and Prince Alexander Chartoriski. J. W. Davison reported them as Gutmann, Delacroix, Franchomme, and Prince Alexander, adding that the chief mourners were Meyerbeer and Prince Adam Chartoriski, and that Meyerbeer had performed on the drums at Beethoven's funeral.

It was Pleyel who shortly later initiated a subscription list for the purpose of erecting an appropriate monument over Chopin's grave. This project was entrusted to a committee headed by Delacroix. The monument, designed by Clésinger, was a botch that pleased no one. It was unveiled on October 30, 1850, after an anniversary Mass at the Madeleine, in which Lefébure-Wély and Franchomme again took musical part. Someone in Warsaw (was it Joseph Elsner, by then eighty-one?) had sent an urn of Polish earth at Jane Stirling's request. This the Polish priest who officiated at the dedication of the monument symbolically sprinkled over the grave.[4]

Ludvika Yedzheyevich, meanwhile, had parted from Jane Stirling and Mrs. Erskine — from whom she had been forced to borrow five thousand francs to cover Chopin's funeral expenses. She had returned to Warsaw, there to console as best she could the sixty-seven-year-old mother who had lost her only son to posterity after not having seen him for so long. Yustina Chopin was to live until October 1, 1861. Ludvika herself died in 1855. Izabela Chopin Bartsinska, last of the four children of Nicolas and

[4] This occurrence gave rise to a baseless story that on leaving Warsaw in 1830 Chopin had been presented with an urn filled with Polish soil, and that this urn, having always been with him, was buried in his coffin with his body in 1849.

Yustina, lived on until 1881. By that year she must have become aware — if she had had any doubt — that little Fritsek, the brother who had disappeared into the great world to die before he was forty, was firmly established among the immortals. Always the name of Frédéric-François Chopin would awaken in men's minds excited responses of expectation and pleasure. By means of his command over the things possible to the black and white notes of a piano Chopin had conquered time.

II

THE MUSIC

An Introductory Note on

MUSICAL FORM

In the pages that follow I have attempted several things
and deliberately avoided others.

My preliminary intention here was to present as complete
a catalogue of Chopin's compositions as possible — first those
with opus numbers and then,[1] in alphabetical order, those issued
without opus numbers during and after his lifetime. In the separate sections, short in some instances and long in others, I
wanted to give the essential results of reliable modern research
into the dates of composition and original publication; the identities of the friends, pupils, and other individuals to whom Chopin
dedicated or inscribed works or groups of works; and the most
relevant and interesting information and lore relating to specific
compositions.

The larger aim of the expanded listings is that of analyzing in
varying detail almost every composition by Chopin that I have
been able to play, to hear in actual performance, by radio, or on
gramophone records, or to read. I have, however, in the main
avoided strictly harmonic analysis, preferring to concentrate on
aspects of form and structure, of which harmonic analysis may or
may not be an essential part.

Chopin was not that inconceivable monster, a wholly original
composer quite free of debt to his predecessors and of influence
by his contemporaries. His harmonic conduct, his kinds of melody, and all his formal, rhythmic, and other procedures grew out
of the music he knew. The musical literature with which he was
familiar was made up of compositions from the baroque, classic,
and rococo periods; the folk, operatic, and salon music of Poland;
the salon music of Vienna and Paris; and the creations of such

[1] In Appendix A, pages 309–28.

of his contemporaries as Field, Hummel, Kalkbrenner, and Moscheles. I have indicated certain of his adaptations and borrowings. But what a composer accepts for use from the general storehouse of musical creation remains less interesting to analysis than the results of that borrowing: what he adds to it and what he himself imagines and invents.

For my concepts of form I am heavily indebted to a book of literary criticism, Kenneth Burke's *Counter-Statement,* from which, with Mr. Burke's permission, I have appropriated, adapted, and altered phrases, sentences, and entire paragraphs. Throughout his remarkable book, and particularly in its seventy-six-page section entitled *"Lexicon rhetoricae,"* Mr. Burke seems to me to have made exciting sense about the agitated problem of form, and to have made it in a terminology that can, with slight shifts of emphasis, be applied as tellingly to music, painting, architecture, dancing, or sculpture as to the literary works he specifically discusses. He himself was aware of some of this, for he also makes numerous references to music.

Kenneth Burke defines form in literature as "an arousing and fulfilment of desires." [2] For this aspect of the definition may be substituted the statement that form is the tautening and relaxing of nerve-responses, the starting and stopping of motor-reflexes, or any other variety of more mechanistic phraseology. But I cannot believe that form in music has a more meaningful or useful definition — or that sonata form, for example, is, in any of its metamorphoses, anything other than a peculiarly successful means by which some composers have aroused and fulfilled desires.

In analyzing Chopin's music I have tried to locate and then point out some of the specific means that he used to arouse and fulfill certain kinds of musical, psychological, or æsthetic desires. I believe that a given composition or movement is successful in so far as it satisfies punctually and without the introduc-

[2] From this point on I have, for the rest of this discussion, omitted quotation marks to indicate my actual borrowings from *Counter-Statement.* To have included them would have been all but impossible, for I have substituted musical words for literary or general words at almost every turn. By omitting them I have, of course, entirely absolved Kenneth Burke from any responsibility in the result.

tion of irrelevant matter or means the desires and expectations it arouses. In the light of this kind of judgment, of course, a folk-song or a Broadway show hit may be as successful as a symphony by Mozart or a ballet score by Stravinsky. The entire difference between an easy success and a great one resides in the justice, complexity, subtlety, and intensity or elevation of the desires and expectations aroused and of the means applied to bringing about their fulfillment.

Thus it seems to me nonsense to say that solely because he did not dominate the sonata — for so a charge against Chopin reads — the man who composed the F-minor Fantaisie, the B-flat minor Scherzo, the Barcarolle, and the F-minor Ballade was a fumbler with large forms. One of my intentions has been to answer that charge sufficiently. W. H. Hadow made the charge against Chopin most forcefully, writing:

His limitations are plain and unmistakable. For the larger types of the art, for the broad architectonic laws of structure on which they are based, he exhibited an almost total disregard. His works in "Sonata form," and in the forms cognate to the Sonata, are, with no exception, the failures of a genius that has altogether overstepped its bounds.

This seems to me to be unadulterated wrongheadedness. Chopin obviously had limitations, and it was again Hadow, expressing himself in less technical matters, who formulated them with straight succinctness:

When he is at his strongest, we miss that sense of reserve power, that quiet irresistible force, "too full for sound or foam," which charac-terises the dignity of the noblest art. He can be passionate, vehement, impetuous, but he expends himself in the effort. He can express agita-tion, challenge, defiance, but he lacks the royal magnanimity that will never stoop to defy. Even his melody is never sublime, never at the highest level. Its more serious mood stands to the great tunes of Beethoven as Leopardi stands to Dante, rising for a moment on a few perfect lines to follow the master's flight, and then sinking back to earth under some load of weariness or impatience.

While it is sensible to question a critic who belittles the role of defiance and then approvingly cites Beethoven, there can be little doubt that Hadow has here summed up the sensation of diminished size that Chopin's music arouses when set beside, say, Bach, Handel, Mozart, and Beethoven.

಄

Kenneth Burke suggests five aspects of form: progressive form (subdivided into syllogistic and qualitative progression), repetitive form, conventional form, and minor or incidental forms. Hereto I subjoin my own adaptations of his five aspects:

1. Syllogistic progression is the form of a perfectly conducted argument. It advances step by step from its premises to its conclusion, and thus has the form of a demonstration in Euclid. To go from A to E through stages B, C, and D is to obtain such form. In so far as the listener to a musical work, from acquaintance with the earlier sections of a piece, feels the rightness of the development and conclusion, the piece is formal. The arrows of his desires are deliberately turned in a certain direction, and the musical unfolding follows the direction of the arrows.

2. Qualitative progression, the other aspect of progressive form, is subtler. Instead of one musical event preparing the listener for another possible event, the presence of one musical quality or atmosphere prepares him for the introduction of a different — perhaps a contrasting — one. Such progressions are qualitative rather than syllogistic, as they lack the pronounced anticipatory nature of the syllogistic progression. The listener is prepared less to demand a certain qualitative progression than to recognize the justice of the sequence after it occurs. The composer using this procedure puts the listener into a state of mind that can appropriately be followed by another state of mind, and then supplies the musical events that create the other state.

3. Repetitive form is the consistent maintaining of a principle or event under new guises, the restatement of the same musical idea or congeries of musical ideas in different ways. A series of variations may be repetitive form or it may be an adjustment of syllogistic or qualitative progression. From the early Variations on "Là ci darem la mano" (1827) to the Berceuse (1843), Chopin's use of the variation technique was nearly always repetitive form, whereas Beethoven's and Brahms's variations are usually a mixture of syllogistic progression (often toward a summarizing fugue) and qualitative progression from incident to incident. Brahms's incidents, in particular, were often

far removed in character from the originally stated subject for variation.

4. Conventional form involves to some degree the appeal of form *as form*. Progressive, repetitive, and minor forms may be effective without making the listener aware of their identity, of their formality. But when a form appeals *as form*, it is conventional. Three-part song form or the symphony as developed by Beethoven can become conventional and be sought for itself. Composers — Chopin is notably one — who write introductions as introductions, and codas as codas, show the appeal of conventional form.

In conventional form there is an important element of categorical expectancy. That is, whereas the anticipations and gratifications of progressive and repetitive form arise *during* the process of listening, the expectations of conventional form may be *anterior* to the listening. If one sets out to listen to a fugue he makes certain formal demands in which the fugue, regardless of other aspects of its nature, must acquiesce; the same thing is true of a waltz, a mazurka, or a polonaise. Similarly, the rejoicing Beethoven finale can become a categorical expectation of the symphony *as symphony*, and be alterable only by such a stroke of genius as the lamenting finale of Tchaikovsky's "Pathetic." When a piece of music is known to be a sonata, concerto, symphony, mazurka, waltz, polonaise, barcarolle, or fugue, the listener "awaits" certain of its procedures before the first measure is performed. And he may, even before hearing that first measure, look forward to an introduction that will proclaim itself such.

5. Minor or incidental forms. When analyzing a musical work of any length, we may find it bristling with minor or incidental forms such as fugato, pedal point, temporary augmentation or diminution of time value, variation, and canonic imitation. And these minor forms can be discussed as happenings in themselves. Their structural effect depends upon their function in the whole, yet they manifest sufficient evidence of episodic distinctness to bear consideration apart from the text, as is proved by the constant use, in musical analysis, of the word "episode."

Thus a passage of canonic imitation may, by carrying logical development one step forward, have its use as progressive form, and by its continuation of a theme may have its use as repetitive form — and may yet be so formally complete in itself that the listener will recognize it as an event apart from its setting. One section of so tightly constructed a musical organism as a Haydn symphony movement (the notable melodic digression for cello in the C-minor Symphony, no. 95, is a good example) can be detached from its context and heard with enjoyment because, however integrally it contributes to the movement and the symphony, it is an independent curve of musical motion enclosed by its own beginning and end.

ॐ

In harmonic theory a chord can often be analyzed various ways. So in the aspects of structure with which I am dealing the appeal or appositeness of one musical event may be explained by various principles. The important thing is not to confine the explanation to one principle, but to formulate sufficient principles to make a cogent explanation possible. A coda, for example, may be syllogistic in that its particular occurrences mark the satisfactory conclusion of events instigated by what has gone before; qualitative in that it establishes a mood made desirable — "necessary," so to say — by the preceding developments; repetitive in that the themes or other musical ideas once again proclaim their identities; conventional in that it has about it much of the recognizably terminal; and minor or incidental in that it contains a discrete structural rise, development, and fall independent of the context.

If the various formal principles can intermingle, they can also conflict. A composer may create a melody or musical atmosphere that should, by the logic of mobile development in a temporal art, be terminated or replaced; but he may also have made this musical event so appealing that listeners will wholly desire its repetition or continuation. This would be a conflict between syllogistic and qualitative progression. Or conventional form may interfere with repetitive form, as when the symphony, in changing from classically consonant to modern dissonant counterpoint, retained the recapitulations present because of the consonance; and conversely, if we today were to attempt regaining some of the graciousness of consonant usage by composing a symphony entirely in Mozart's euphonious style, we should be making use of the appeal of consonance, but we should risk violating a contemporary canon of conventional form — the dissonant counterpoint now categorically expected from a living symphonic composer.

Conventional form has brought about the extremes of æsthetic acuity and æsthetic bluntness. The establishment of musical conventions may be the result of exceptional imaginativeness and accuracy; their preservation may result from the most inaccurate and unimaginative pedantry. A listener may, for instance, have come to expect a given formal contrivance regardless of the effect that it is best able to produce. Further, his expectancy may be so imperious that he will condemn the slighting of this formal usage even when it would be unrelated to the effect at which the composer is aiming. Yet in violating a convention a composer undeniably violates a major tenet of form: he is disappointing the expectations of his audience, and form by the present definition resides in the arousing and fulfillment of the listener's desires and expectations. The only justification that a composer can have for thus breaking faith with his audience is the fact that such categorical expectations are very unstable (*vide* any honest history of music) and that the composer may, by making his use of the repetitive and progressive principles authoritative enough, succeed in bringing listeners to a sufficient acceptance of his own conventions. He must do this because he is himself a living and creating organism.

This issue, too often clouded by epithets, is further complicated by the fact that resistance to a change in convention may be caused by sensitive appreciation of the convention, by thorough training in it and familiarity with it. Ludwig Rellstab intensely resented Chopin's "ear-splitting discords, forced transitions, harsh modulations, ugly distortions of melody and rhythm." The modern listener may simply be insensitive to the issue as Rellstab's training enabled him to feel it. For such reasons an innovator may at first find a more enthusiastic reception among those whose training is defective, particularly if he is aiming at effects more germane to their experiences.

ৡ৶

The forms of music, to summarize, are not exclusively "æsthetic." They can be said to have a prior existence in the emotional, physical and intellectual equipment and experiences of the listener. They parallel processes that characterize his experiences outside music. Form, dealing as it does with the creation and satisfaction of desires, needs, and expectations, is successful when it gratifies or fulfills the desires, needs, and expectations that it creates. The appeal of form in this sense is obvious: form *is* the appeal.

The appeal of progressive and repetitive form as they figure in the major organization of a musical whole needs no further explanation: any composition more complex than a single unaccompanied melodic line (and probably even that) depends for its very existence on the psychology of form. But when we turn to minor or incidental forms, carrying our inquiry down to the individual phrase or modulation or measure, the relation between form and the releasing of created tension (the satisfaction of desire) is less obvious. There are rudimentary sorts of detail in which the factor of expectation or desire is clearly perceptible, however, as when the repetition of a dominant-seventh chord imperiously arouses the need for a resolution to break the tension of monotony and expectation. Formally speaking, a musical event may be a subject demanding a predicate exactly as the first chords of a cadence demand the final chord.

I do not believe in the eternal superiority of one musical form over another. A form is a way of experiencing; and a given form is successfully made to work when, by its way of using and presenting specific musical matter, it enables the listener to experience the composer's musical ideas and their treatment with a feeling that all the desires aroused have been properly and completely satisfied. There are musical ideas incapable of arousing desires: Liszt's music is full of them. When no desires are aroused, none can be fulfilled: the compositions of second-rate men are frequently nothing more than foredoomed attempts to satisfy uncreated desires. A composer may arouse desires and expectations and then fail to satisfy them: many instances from Rimsky-Korsakov could be cited here. And there are satisfactions that overwhelm and stultify the desires and expectations, as happens again and again in the less successful of Schubert's piano sonatas.

It is as a composer capable of arousing, with viable materials and ideas, exactly the desires and expectations he intends — and capable of satisfying those desires and fulfilling those expectations subtly, completely, and with beautiful economy — that I regard Chopin as entitled to the otherwise artistically meaningless adjective "great."

An Introductory Note on

POLISH MUSIC

L EAVING countless anonymous folk musicians out of account, the earliest Polish composers — such men as Nicolas Gomolka (1539?–1609), Nicolas Zyelinski, and Yakob Polak (known also as Jacob de Reys, 1545?–1605) — were wholly international in character and complexion. Zyelinski spent much of his life in Venice, Yakob Polak in Paris. Slightly different in character was Yosef Kozlovski (1757–1831), an enormously prolific composer of everything from Requiem Masses to theater music. But though Kozlovski included polonaises in several of his works (one of them is quoted by Tchaikovsky in *The Queen of Spades*), he spent most of his life in Russia proper, where he composed music lacking in overt national characteristics.

It was at Warsaw in 1778 that the first Polish-language opera was produced: Matias Kamyenski's *Nędza Użcześliwiona* (*Misery Become Happy*). It must have won aristocratic suffrage, for Kamyenski composed five more operas in the national tongue, and all of them were produced. Living from 1734 to 1821, Kamyenski was not following the imported traditions of the Italian *opera seria,* but rather was writing a more vulgar genre, closely approximating the Singspiel and *opéra-comique* in some of their freer aspects. Even more successful was Yan Stefani (1746–1829), whom Stanislaus Poniatovski imported from Vienna. Stefani supplied his adopted city with almost a dozen operas, of which one called *Krakowiaków i górali* (*The People of Krakov and the Mountain People*) became a long-standing hit.

Chopin's master, Joseph Xaver Elsner, another adopted Pole, was generous with cantatas, operas, and ballets on national themes, producing not less than nineteen operas in the Polish language alone. And from 1811 on, Warsaw heard some two dozen operas from the busy pen of Karl Kasimir Kurpinski, who began as Elsner's assistant at the Warsaw Opera and in 1825 succeeded to its conductorship. Kurpinski composed numerous popular mazurkas and polonaises, as did Mikhel Cleopas Oginski (1765–1833), a talented amateur who studied with Kozlovski.[1] But for any nationalistic flowering comparable to the Russian one of Glinka, Dargomizhsky, and the Five, Poland had to wait for the maturity of Stanislav Monyushko (1819–72), whose *Halka* (1858) holds the position in Polish modern musical history held in Russian musical history by Glinka's two operas. Monyushko's numerous songs are as basic to the Polish-language repertoire as Schubert's are to the German.

In view of the difficulty of seeing or hearing most of the music of Chopin's Polish precursors and coevals, his indebtedness to them is uncommonly difficult to measure. His debt to Elsner he admitted freely, while from Kurpinski he quoted both openly and unconsciously. It is certain that he reacted with creative interest to some of Oginski's mazurkas. But despite his patriotism Chopin was no artistic nationalist, and in quantity and manner his music is as much Western as Slavic, as much French, Italian, and Austro-German as it is Polish. This is not to deny the patent Polishness of his mazurkas and polonaises or the Polish turns and usages that crop up elsewhere in his compositions. It is to suggest that in this regard his attitude toward musical nationalism was about that of Tchaikovsky.

[1] Henryk Opieński stated in an article, *"Les Sources polonaises"* (*Revue musicale,* December 1931), that in about 1750 a composer named Dankovski built the introduction to the first *allegro* of a Symphony in D major on the polonaise rhythm, suggesting that non-operatic composers of the mid-eighteenth century had already begun to use folk and popular music for materials.

CHOPIN, A DAGUERREOTYPE MADE IN 1849

[Courtesy Instytut Fryderyka Chopina, Warsaw]

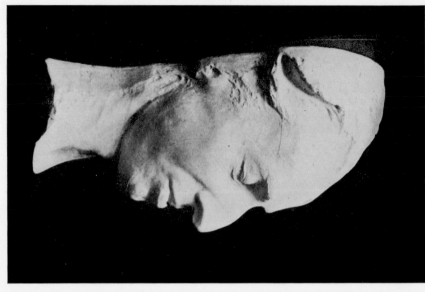

DEATH MASK OF CHOPIN

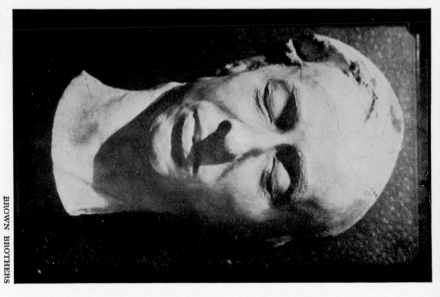

Opus 1

Rondo, C minor

Except for an anonymous March printed in someone else's arrangement for military band, the C-minor Rondo was the first of Chopin's works to be published.[1] It was issued in Warsaw in 1825 by Brzeżina (Bzhezhina), who cleverly timed its appearance to take advantage of public interest in the fifteen-year-old composer, who had played in a Warsaw Conservatory concert on May 27 of that year. The announcement of the publication of the Rondo was made six days later, and the young Chopin again appeared at the Conservatory to play on June 10.

Dedicated to Mme von Linde, wife of the director of the Warsaw Lyceum, the C-minor Rondo is stylistically uncertain and only tentatively and intermittently expressive. It produces an over-all effect of discomfort within its rigid structural walls, a result more of ill-managed procedures than of inappropriate musical ideas. This seldom-played piece has occasional atmospheric touches familiar to anyone acquainted with the great works of Chopin's maturity. But its interest as a musical entity is limited and quickly exhausted, and it is best viewed as a mirror of the concert pieces being composed just before 1825 by other men. Abandoning Chopin's opus 1 to musicologists and collected editions is an established, a good, and by no means a reprehensible custom.

Opus 2

Variations for piano, with orchestral accompaniment, of *"Là ci darem la mano,"* from Mozart's *Don Giovanni*

While visiting friends in the country during the summer of 1827, Chopin began to work at his Variations on *"Là ci darem la mano."* They were completed shortly later, and were published in Vi-

---

[1] Unless the private issuance, in 1817, of the G-minor Polonaise dedicated to Countess Victoire Skarbek be considered publication. See page 319.

enna by Tobias Haslinger in 1830. They are dedicated to Chopin's beloved friend Tytus Voitsyekhovski. The title page of the
original edition reads:*"Là ci darem la mano varié pour le piano,
avec accompagnement d'orchestre,"* a carefully exact description
except that the orchestra, accompanying but spottily, serves
scarcely more than to link the variations. The latter are scored for
piano alone until the final *"Alla polacca,"* a rudimentary polonaise
in which the orchestra and the solo instrument alternate.

The Variations are the comments of a young virtuoso on Mozart's beautiful duet. Except for tiny details they are so respectful
of the melodic line of the duet that they cannot be compared to
the profoundly intellectual acts of variation performed by Beethoven and Brahms. Rather, they are repetitions of the theme
in clouds of arabesques and runs. There is no exploration of the
new themes that might have been elicited from the configuration
of the original. The only passages native to Chopin alone are the
widely broken chords-in-skips in the fourth variation and the Polish dance rhythm on which the final variation is erected.[1] As
Huneker once remarked, Ludwig Rellstab was only a mite too
severe when he said that Chopin, in the Variations, ". . . runs
down the theme with roulades and throttles and hangs it with
chains of snakes."

[1] There is one significant signpost toward the later Chopin in a slight devia-
tion (by way of a passing-note) from Mozart's melody in the first variation.
It begins like this:

When the ear, remembering Mozart, expects it to continue as:

it actually proceeds like this:

Opus 3

Introduction and Polonaise brillante
for Cello and Piano

Joseph Merk (1795–1852), to whom Chopin's opus 3 is dedicated, was a Viennese cellist whom the composer met during either his first (1829) or his second (1830–1) visit to Vienna. In a letter dated May 28, 1831, to his family, Chopin wrote: "Merk tells me that he likes playing with me, and I like playing with him, so together we must produce something good. He is the first cellist whom I can admire on closer acquaintaince. . . ."

The Introduction and Polonaise was published in Vienna before or during 1833 by Pietro Mechetti; it was issued later in Paris by Charles-Simon Richault.

The Introduction was composed after the Polonaise, probably being added to it so as to make a desirable recital piece for Merk. The Polonaise itself was composed at Antonin, Prince Radzivil's estate, in 1829. Writing to Tytus Voitsyekhovski from Warsaw on November 14 of that year, Chopin described his visit to Antonin, interrupting to say: "While there I wrote an Alla Polacca with violoncello. There is nothing in it but glitter; a salon piece for ladies; you see, I wanted Princess Vanda to learn it.[1] I had been giving her lessons. She is quite young: 17, and pretty; really it was a joy to guide her little fingers. But joking aside, she has a lot of real musical feeling; one did not have to say: *crescendo* here, *piano* there; now faster, now slower, and so on."

No reason for disputing Chopin's expressed opinion of the Polonaise is to be discovered in it. The Introduction is no different. The whole is full enough of high spirits so that Wessel, Chopin's London publisher, could entitle it *La Gaîté*, but the tepidity of its invention evokes only a gay vacuity. There is no reason, simply because it is by Chopin, for giving it a respect it could not win on its inherent quality.

[1] Princess Vanda's father, Prince Anton, played the cello.

Opus 4

Sonata, C minor

It was probably during 1827 that Chopin, while a full-time student at the Warsaw Conservatory, composed the first of his three piano sonatas. Certainly it was not later than 1828. It is a student exercise. Not only is it unoriginal, it is also boring, a comment it is all but impossible to make of another of Chopin's extended works. It is dedicated to his teacher, Joseph Xaver Elsner.

Chopin left the C-minor Sonata with Tobias Haslinger, the Viennese music-publisher, in 1828, having labeled it his opus 4. When years passed without Haslinger's issuing the piece, Chopin did not assign the number 4 to another, but was content to leave that number a blank in the list of his published works. Having held the manuscript for thirteen years, in 1841 Haslinger finally got the Sonata as far as the stage of author's proofs. By then Chopin — a famous man and a great composer — evidently looked upon the student Sonata with small love. He never sent the proofs back to Haslinger, who died the following year. Not until Chopin himself had been dead two years did Karl Haslinger, successor to his father, issue the inert work. He was himself a composer and pianist, but he was also a businessman, and by 1851 the publication of any work by Chopin was good business.

Many earnest writers have stated flatly and accusingly that Chopin never mastered sonata form. This is obtuse, if not downright silly, for he composed several pieces in a sonata form as satisfactory in its way, as able to achieve unity in its way, as any of Haydn's or Mozart's or Beethoven's variants of sonata form was in its way. What caused the C-minor Sonata to be born dead and ugly was not that its formal structure was faulty (it is), but that it contained no viable musical ideas.

The C-minor Sonata is cast in the traditional four movements, which are marked *allegro maestoso; menuetto* (*allegretto*); *larghetto,* and *finale* (*presto*). In the *larghetto* Chopin tried a Slavic touch — quintuple time, the $\frac{5}{4}$, familiar as Tchaikovsky used it in the second movement of his "Pathetic" Symphony. This, with its air of being the one stunt permitted a student, does not come off as an effect. By making it necessary for the performer to accent heavily the third beat in each of his first two measures, the composer induces him to convince listeners that he is counting **1-2-3-4-5, 1-2-3-4-5** throughout and a little rushing the **3-4-5**, thus in effect producing duple time, **1-3, 1-3**, etc. The other movements lack even this factitious interest. Nor, except for part of the last movement, do they require brilliant pianism.

Opus 5

Rondo à la Mazurka

Composed in 1826 or 1827, the Rondo à la Mazurka is the most recognizably Polish, the most Chopinesque, of Chopin's very early compositions (though by no means all Chopinesque compositions are recognizably Polish). It was first published in Warsaw by Bzhezhina in 1828, and carries a dedication to Alexandrine de Moriolles, daughter of the tutor to Prince Paul, the son of Grand Duke Konstantin Pavlovich and Princess Lovitska. It then had no opus number, none being assigned to it until it was republished in Leipzig by Friedrich Hofmeister or in Paris by Schonenberger.

The Rondo à la Mazurka opens with a measure that would have sounded wholly reasonable to anyone familiar with Polish folk music, but that would have sounded simply wrong and unmusical to most western European musicians of the time:

The key is F major, and the B naturals should therefore, by contemporary example, have been B flats — for the piece certainly is not conceived in the Dorian mode, equivalent to a normal scale with the fourth tone raised half a step. Furthermore, and this might reasonably have infuriated a sensitive critic, the B natural is insisted upon melodically five times in the first seven measures of the first theme. And no B flat appears in the melody until its eighth measure. This was, if not anarchy, then advanced disorder.

The piece contains other folk-justified diversions from accepted harmonic procedure, one of them occurring in the twenty-first measure:

Here the temporary key is the relative minor, D. In the melodic right-hand part, the G-sharp again represents a raising of the fourth tone of the scale. But here the accompanying left hand simultaneously sounds the regular minor triad (D-F-A), thus producing a sonorous, unmistakable discord with its heart in G-sharp-A. And lest anyone think this accidental, Chopin repeats the combination twice within the next four measures.

The harmonic activity of the Rondo à la Mazurka is far more interesting than its melodies or its architecture. It is no exception to the general rule that Chopin was never to handle the rondo form with mastery. Indeed, he eventually came to disregard it altogether. But the fact that this is a rondo in triple time does indicate a composer not to be bound by precedent: a rondo was typically in $\frac{2}{4}$ or $\frac{4}{4}$ time. The mazurka, however, is typically in triple time. The title "Rondo à la Mazurka" was therefore as eccentric as a sonnet of seventeen lines or a waltz in $\frac{5}{8}$ time (there is one in Tchaikovsky's opus 72). The title, in fact, would have been more exact and less challenging to the sensibilities of academicians as Mazurka à la Rondo. From the mazurka Chopin was to create a firmament of stars and planets all Poland's and his own.

Reviewing the Rondo à la Mazurka in 1836, Robert Schumann rightly discovered in it signs of its composer's extreme youth. But he also found the piece thoroughly Chopinesque, "i.e., lovely, romantic, full of grace." For here, in a piece dating from Chopin's sixteenth or seventeenth year, are the insignia of his mature style, albeit not yet masterfully set down. Here are the sinuous melismas, the chords openly spaced, the chromatically sliding harmonic progressions. The piece, that is to say, has a certain strangeness and charm. It deserves more performances than it gets. But it sins by being too long in despite of its rapid pace: it contains too little musical material and architectural invention to fill out with any sense of satisfaction the length of time it occupies. In over-all effect, therefore, it is loosely strung together and repetitive beyond the right even of a rondo. It produces the sensation of potpourri rather than of integration.

Opus 6

Four Mazurkas

In December 1832 the Leipzig publisher Karl Friedrich Kistner (still operating under the firm name his father had used, Probst-Kistner) issued Chopin's opus 6. This contained mazurkas in F-sharp minor, C-sharp minor, E major, and E-flat minor. The opus was dedicated to Countess Pauline Plater, one of Chopin's pupils.

The first Mazurka in this set, the F-sharp minor, contains with one exception (the drone bass) every minor form out of which Chopin was to build the more than fifty mazurkas that constitute one of the most remarkable of his achievements. Here the melodic triplets are present, the grace-notes so used as to suggest the sound of a nonpianistic instrument, the constant use of broken rhythms — brought about by the most adroit use of rests and tied notes — the wayward disarrangement of normal scales, and the romantic harmonic motions that are already more than half the route from *Fidelio* to *Tristan und Isolde.* The formal structure, though relatively simple, is extremely well conceived. It is the simple ABACA pattern. The A section is always sixteen measures long, but added vitality is given to it each time by its last four measures, which make up a sort of sub-coda; the B section, with its assertive octaves, is eight measures, a perfect example of Chopin's punctuality, for it serves its purpose in that time and would have been unwelcome for one measure more; the C section, the structural climax, is sixteen measures, exquisite in themselves and leading most gratefully to the second repetition of A.[1]

Number two of opus 6, the C-sharp minor Mazurka, is less good than the F-sharp minor. It makes extensive, and finally monotonous, use of a favorite Chopin device derived from Polish folk usage. This is the pedal-bass left-hand accompaniment of a chord resting on the dominant of the scale.

The E-major Mazurka, number three of the set, introduces the true drone bass, in this case with displaced accents that create a welcome rhythmic variety. In fact, the variety in this brief piece is astonishing, but no more astonishing than the assured craftsmanship with which Chopin has managed to give it unity. For the E-major Mazurka is simply and tightly constructed. Its solidity, combined with the beauty and cogency of its musical ideas, makes it vastly superior to its immediate predecessor.

The fourth Mazurka of opus 6, in E-flat minor, is extremely short (only the C-major Mazurka, opus 7, no. 5, is shorter). Yet it manages to suggest harmless monomania, a neurotic insistence that can only appear autobiographical, so far is its refinement removed from the incantatory repetitions of primitive music. That Chopin could proceed so early to the creation of a mazurka lacking any overuse of any of the "characteristic" features of the form is signalized here by the presence of but two triplets — and they identical. It is not possible to think of this intensely personal fragment in E-flat minor as a folk dance: it speaks unmistakably in one of the most sophisticated and personal of voices.

[1] In all my remarks about the length of pieces, movements, or sections, I have purposely avoided referring to repetitions of the kinds that are not written out but are indicated by signs. Unless a pianist, on his own authority, undertakes to vary dynamics or speed during this kind of repetition, it does not seem to me materially to alter the structural design. The signs should, of course, be observed, once their authenticity has been established. Under no condition, on the other hand, should any pianist add unindicated repetitions of his own. In a few cases Chopin's failure to indicate repetition is so interesting that I have commented on it.

Opus 7

Five Mazurkas

On August 8, 1832 Chopin wrote to Ferdinand Hiller, sending the letter to Germany by the hand of a Mr. Johns, an American from New Orleans. Frederick Niecks is authority for the statement that Chopin introduced Johns to Hiller as "a distinguished amateur," but otherwise nothing is known of him. It was to Mr. Johns that Chopin dedicated the five Mazurkas of opus 7, which were composed during 1830 and 1831. The opus was published in Leipzig, simultaneously with opus 6, by the firm of Probst-Kistner.

It was of the five Mazurkas of opus 7 that Ludwig Rellstab said (in addition to the sentence quoted on page 79):

> In the dances before us, the composer indulges a passion to loathsome excess. He is indefatigable, and I might say inexhaustible, in his search for ear-splitting discords, forced transitions, harsh modulations, ugly distortions of melody and rhythm. Everything it is possible to think of is raked up to produce the effect of strange novelty, but especially remote keys, the most unnatural positions of chords, the most perverse combinations with respect to fingering.

It is easy to laugh at this sort of wholly mistaken judgment, but more useful to seize upon it as a way of understanding how unconventional and truly original an effect Chopin's Mazurkas produced on the better-trained and less hospitable of his contemporaries.

In no respectable composition, for example, had musicians of the era previously happened upon such a succession as the following from opus 7, no. 2:

This passage is spoken of by Gerald Abraham as a "succession of sevenths . . . disguised by suspensions producing intermediate transition chords." Viewed melodically, however, it is a chromatic descent by harmonic means that were æsthetically — and almost morally — shocking in 1830–1. An ordinary listener might have been able to accept this sort of novelty at its face value, but Rellstab, thoroughly grounded in musical theory, highly sensitive to what should normally follow certain premises, would have had to be a suppler man than he was to sense the justification for this sort of lawlessness.

The first Mazurka of opus 7, in B-flat major, at once became, and has remained, one of the most widely popular of all the Mazurkas. It is easy to play, and it is notably lighthearted. Its formal structure, perfectly satisfying as revealed in performance, is simple, apt, and easy to grasp. Melody #1 is presented in twelve measures and then repeated verbatim, the only changes being in dynamics. Melody #2 requires but eight measures to achieve its purpose of contrast, whereupon four nonmelodic notes lead to another restatement of Melody #1, again with slight dynamic shifts. Both these first melodies begin with rising, scale-like motions that descend only as a means of beginning to rise again. The third melody, however, to the accompaniment of a drone bass, is predominantly descending, and lasts but eight measures before it is succeeded by the second reintroduction of Melody #1 entire. The piece is, then, a variety of rondo with two differing trios, the formula being ABACA.

The A-minor Mazurka, no. 2 of this set, is built on a more complex plan, the formula being AB [1] ACDC. This is the piece of which Huneker said that "it is as if one danced upon one's grave."

The third Mazurka, F minor, begins with eight measures of submelodic introduction. It is all straightforward vigor and life, widely varied in rhythmic insistence and harmonic color.

The swift Mazurka in A-flat major, fourth in the set, is another notable example of the various fulfillment that Chopin could wrest from the simple ABACA pattern. But this one lacks the captivating profile of the first of the set; it tends, because of absence of distinction in the melodies, to seem tepid.

Last in opus 7 is a wisp of a Mazurka in C major. Not counting four introductory measures consisting of a bass G octave re-

[1] The B section contains the transitional passage on page 185.

peated twelve times in decreasing volume, it contains only sixteen measures, and it breaks off without a true ending, leaving
in the vibrating air a question almost as enigmatic and unanswer-
able as that asked by Schumann's *"Vogel als Prophet."* Like a
fragment torn from some longer composition, it is as extended as
it should be, a fair companion to those other gnomic utterances,
the seventh and twentieth Préludes.

Opus 8

Trio in G minor for violin, cello, and piano

Four times only did Chopin write for solo stringed instruments,
and all four of the pieces contain parts for the cello. Only once
did he add violin: in the Trio composed in 1828–9 and published
in Leipzig by Probst-Kistner on March 6, 1833, with a dedication
to Prince Anton Radzivil. The Trio is now seldom played. It is
conventional in form, harmony, and melodic tournure. Its themes
are pretty, charming, and rarely forceful or Chopinesque. It performs gratefully, but it is not important or foolishly neglected
music.

The G-minor Trio is in four movements. The opening is an
allegro con fuoco. There follows a *scherzo* marked *con moto ma
non troppo,* in G major. It is in the triple-time melody of the
adagio that Chopin's voice may most easily be recognized in this
otherwise somewhat natureless music. The *finale,* an *allegretto,*
returns politely to G minor. I doubt that any perfomance of the
Trio could lend it the vitality it so obviously lacks. Robert Schumann reviewed it in dithyrambs that he would have been wiser
to save for better music.

Writing to Tytus Voitsyekhovski on August 31, 1830, Chopin
said:

Last Sunday I tried the Trio; I don't know, perhaps it was because I
had not heard it for a long time, but I was rather pleased with myself
(lucky fellow, you'll say, won't you). One thing struck me then — that
it would be better to use the viola than the violin because on the violin it's the first string that dominates, and here it's scarcely used. The
viola will be more resonant against the cello, which is in its own regis-
ter — and then to publish.

But an access of the economic wisdom that so often guided Chopin evidently decided him not to expend further energies on this apprentice piece in a genre he did not intend to develop. He allowed it to be published as composed.

Opus 9

Three Nocturnes

A nocturne is, of course, a night-piece. In liturgical music the word refers to the night watches of which a matins service consists. In secular music, however, the term does not antedate the mid-eighteenth century. It was used by Haydn, who produced many *notturni*, including some for hurdy-gurdy. If Chopin was not familiar with Haydn's nocturnes, he probably knew those of Gyrowetz. But the earliest keyboard pieces that we who know Chopin would recognize as nocturnes are those of the itinerant Irishman John Field (1782–1837). Field is a recklessly neglected second-flight master, and by his numerous nocturnes bequeathed to Chopin more than their designation. The E-minor Nocturne, opus 72, no. 1, composed in 1827, has sufficient blood-brothership to one of Field's so that nobody would have questioned the appearance of his name on it. Chopin's best night-pieces can be described fairly as what a genius did with the sort of materials that Field invented and used. Chopin took the essentials of the nocturne nature and intensified them a thousandfold. In the E-minor Nocturne he showed at seventeen that he might some day equal Field, a remarkable achievement in itself.

Mme Camille Pleyel, to whom Chopin dedicated his first published Nocturnes, had been christened Marie-Félicité-Denise Moke. She was an able pianist and a calculating flirt, if not something worse. At eighteen she enchanted Ferdinand Hiller, and at just nineteen became engaged to Berlioz, whom she jilted as soon as he left Paris for Rome. Thereupon she married the forty-two-year-old piano-manufacturer, pianist, and composer Camille Pleyel. On receipt of this news poor Berlioz acquired laudanum, strychnine, and two pistols and set out from Rome for Paris to kill the new Mme Pleyel, her mother, and then himself. This

triple enterprise he abandoned on reaching Nice after a series of
tragicomic mishaps. There he failed to commit suicide, composing instead his overture *Le Roi Lear*. It is assumed that Chopin's
dedication of his opus 9 to Mme Camille Pleyel is to the pianist
rather than to the lightheaded seductress.

With the first Nocturne, in B-flat minor, Chopin introduced
the musical world to his own original and sensuously poetic version of the night-piece. This is an astonishing composition in
many ways. After one opening measure, the left hand unvaryingly
plays twelve eighth-notes to the measure for eighty-two consecutive measures! A mood of nocturnal calm is established at the
beginning, but it is a calm capable of sudden disturbances, *appassionato* and *con forza,* capable, too, of dissolving in cascades
of coloratura chromatics that owe much to arias by Rossini and
Donizetti. The first section descends into a deeper part of the
night, where a slow, passionate story is told — a musical and not
a literary story. This is music of a pale and amorous young man,
of puissant and unfulfilled sexuality, and certainly of creatures
who move by night. It is succeeded by a section of awakening,
or a return to less amorous thoughts, and then by a repetition of
the first section. Nothing is more remarkable about the B-flat
minor Nocturne than its unquestioned unity.

Second in opus 9 is the shortest of the Nocturnes, in E-flat
major, long one of the most popular of Chopin's pieces. It was
always in demand, during Chopin's lifetime, whenever he or
another pianist performed his music. It has lost little of its charm
today. Like most of the Nocturnes, but more easily, it can be
rendered nauseously cloying by dragging its tempo or clinging
to any of its emotion-charged notes. Pianists who gaze upward
or close their eyes while playing should eschew the E-flat Nocturne as likely to come out syrup. Only he who plays cleanly, and
fastidiously respects the music's integrity, may perform it without fear. After passing through several series of complicated
modulations, the Nocturne builds up to a thunderous climax,
pauses, breaks into a rocking, repeated, cadenzalike unmelodic
figure in grace-notes, and then closes on two obviously terminal
measures containing no tones but those of the tonic triad, E flat,
G, and B flat.

The B-major Nocturne, number 3 of opus 9, is one of Chopin's least satisfying creations. Being loose-jointed, it sounds overlong even played at a just tempo. Such music as this would not have raised Chopin above the surrounding plain on which dwelt interesting second-rate composers like Field, Hummel, and Kalkbrenner, to each of whom the Nocturne seems indebted for some of its uningratiating mannerisms. It is an example of Chopin the manufacturer of salon pieces for ladies. It is surely a composition that in later years he would have been unable to compose and unwilling to publish. Near its delayed close it unravels into a vocalization or cadenza of the kind that was to bemuse Franz Liszt into a false belief: that with similar adaptations of what singers could do better he could transform banal melodies into the materials for masterworks.

Opus 10

Twelve Grand Études

Everything that Chopin had published up to 1833 was overtopped in quality and importance when, in June of that year, Probst-Kistner of Leipzig issued his *"Douze Grandes Études, opus 10."* Appropriately dedicated to the foremost pianist of the time, perhaps of all time, the composer's friend Franz Liszt, they combined peculiarly modern exploration of the keyboard with first-rate musical ideas to initiate a new period of keyboard music. That period was to end, almost exactly one century later, with the death of Maurice Ravel. Chopin himself later published fifteen more Études, and of the twenty-seven it was to be said truly that he who could play them could play anything.

With the first Étude, in C major, Chopin ushered the music-lovers of his day suddenly into a new world. It was a world that he himself had discovered before his arrival in Paris in 1831, for a fair copy of the manuscript of both this and the second Étude is dated the very day he left Warsaw for the last time, November 2, 1830. Although the C-major Étude contains quiet sections, *diminuendos* of structural importance, it is largely loud, muscular music. It requires strong hands that must either be of unusual span or be trained to perfect aim. For though the space between one note and the next is never unusually wide, the layout of the arpeggios — and in a rapid tempo — requires the hand to be stretched so as to transcend constantly the normal reach of an average hand at rest. The piece is all rushing movement. Huneker quoted a clever jester as calling it "a runaway chorale," a tag as acute as it is amusing. Neither in tempo nor in unaccented sameness must its runaway character be allowed to dominate. Rather, the carefully plotted accents must be decisive in projecting its suavely melodic, choralelike nature.

The second Étude, in A minor, is an essay on how to produce a perfectly even, graduated scale with the third, fourth, and fifth fingers of the right hand. It teaches this mastery of speed and volume by means of forty-nine measures, in only two of which (the thirty-second and the last) does the right hand play anything but sixteen sixteenth-notes in scales, with one or two chordal notes added on most of the counted beats. These chords accent not only the piece's bony structure, but also the technical problem being solved, for they often make it necessary to play swift chromatic passages without the help of the thumb and the second finger, and thus tend to strengthen the naturally less strong and agile fourth and fifth fingers.[1]

Conceivably the most beautiful Étude ever composed is the third of opus 10, the slow marvel in E major. Chopin himself, his pupil Adolf Gutmann stated, said that he had never written another melody like it. Relatively easy to play (except for the cadenzalike middle portion), it is maddeningly difficult to play well. For its apparent simplicity masks complexities of accent, phrasing, and tonal shading that justify its being denominated an Étude. It is all, so to speak, at cross purposes that must be reconciled into smooth, melodious, onward movement. Played by a master, it can be one of music's warmest-hued jewels; no lesser pianist should play it except to himself.

The C-sharp minor Étude, number 4 of the set, is an exercise in balancing staccato chords in one hand against rushing, con-

---

[1] This is especially true if the fingering painstakingly indicated in the first French edition (Schlesinger, 1833) be respected and little attention be paid to the "simplifications" suggested by later editors. Contrarily, those simplifications are of genuine help to many hands when the chief aim is musical rather than pedagogical.

tinuous, even notes in the other; in counterpoising a melody against decorations that are of great interest in themselves. Its difficulties are staggering: for example, in a true disclosure of the piece's nature it is essential to withhold any *fortissimo* from the first sixty-nine measures, and then to play one relentlessly through finger-risking hazards to the end, a dozen measures away. It is music of almost physical excitement. Not one of Chopin's most inspired melodically, it stands best in performance exactly where he placed it, between the seductive E major and the light touch of the G-flat major.[2]

The "Black Key" Étude, in G-flat major, is the fifth in opus 10. Here Chopin was writing a musical study and not a relentlessly pursued stunt — though the right hand throughout remains on the five black notes, the left hand often plays white notes as harmonically required. Once the problem of finger-spacing black notes alone has been solved, it is a mistake to regard the right hand's pentatonic melody as the ruling one. The left hand plays no mere accompaniment here. In fact, its role is so important that it is possible to regard the right hand's as the lesser. The proper division of eminence is a shifting one — and the big guns of piano tone sound only in the three concluding measures. This is salon music by a master.

E-flat minor is the key of the sixth number in opus 10. It could have been published among the Nocturnes without being out of place. The problem involved is that of keeping the incessant, unchanging figure of eight sixteenth-notes (two groups to each measure) from crushing the listener under monotony. This was as great a problem for the composer — who solved it superbly

[2] At the end of the fourth Étude Chopin's manuscript carries the following instruction: "*Attaca il presto.*" The "*presto,*" of course, is the fifth Étude. Chopin undoubtedly intended the opus to be played seriatim and entire. I should guess, further, that he originally intended to have Études in each major and minor key, as he was later to have in the Préludes. Note that the following successive pairs, in the twenty-four Études of opus 10 and opus 25, are indications of that plan: opus 10 — C major, A minor; E major, C-sharp minor; G-flat major, E-flat minor; E-flat major, C minor; opus 25 — A-flat major, F minor. In reverse there is also the F minor, A-flat major pair in opus 10. Not having composed proper pieces to fill out the original plan, Chopin, I assume, used the ones he had, fitting them into series designed on other lines of contrast and complement.

by harmonic invention — as it is for the pianist. It seems likely, though it cannot be proved, that Chopin thought of the figure first and the harmonic pattern next, and only then evolved the simple, morose melody. For it is not so much a melody (is not a melody at all when compared with that of the E major, no. 3) as it is an intermittent highlighting of the harmonies through which the burbling figure passes. Five measures from the end, at the indication *crescendo subito,* Chopin demonstrates his genius for the totally unexpected touch that justifies itself: he passes from E-flat minor to bright, metallic A major, returns to the minor — and terminates on the tonic triad of E-flat major.

The superficial aspect of the seventh Étude, in C major like the first, is that of a toccata with a purpose. Here the reigning melody is half-ridden in a figure that seems to be an expanded variant of the accompaniment of the sixth Étude. It stretches along the upper notes of that tripping alternation of (mostly) thirds and sixths, but it occurs on normally unaccented beats, which must therefore be a little abnormally accented. If performed acutely, the piece has an oblique pertness that must never be drowned in the accompanying left hand except when, as in the measures immediately following the long-held G-octave pedal point, the figure simply marks time. At that point, briefly, the left hand speaks a leading role. Like many of Chopin's early pieces, this C-major Étude has a too perfunctory ending. He was to become exceedingly adroit as time passed in making his terminations interesting in themselves and integral parts of the wholes rather than bald, sudden equivalents of *"Finis."*

The eighth Étude, in F major, is one of the few pieces in which Chopin composed for the left hand with a decorative right hand. The opposite procedure he used often, but here the right hand is rarely entrusted with more than a cascade of pianistic brilliance and harmonic color. Salon music again, but the salon is clearly aristocratic, and nothing can be rushed or pounded. Nor must the F major be subjected to dissection in the search for depths it does not contain. It is just what it pretends to be: a gallant — poised, assured, and impeccable, a very handsome gallant.

Neurotic, confessing frustrations, is the ninth Étude, in F minor. It makes a musical point, repeats the point, repeats the repetition, approaches again from another direction, breaks

abruptly into something very like profane oaths, rapidly insists
again and again on the same detail (the same note or octave
six times in rapid succession), says over in octaves what has already been said more than once in single notes, is out of breath,
and dissolves in a shimmer of *pianissimo* futility. It was composed for Chopin's friend Ignaz Moscheles, who must have been
astonished at its surly and rather unhealthy behavior. This is not
to say that it is anything but a very successful piece of music. Its
technical problems are not difficult of solution from the point of
view of agility, stretch, or accuracy of aim. They are almost entirely questions of touch and of color.

"The whole repertoire of pianoforte music does not contain
a study in perpetual motion so full of genius and fancy as this
particular one is universally acknowledged to be, except perhaps
Liszt's *Feux-Follets.*" So wrote Hans von Bülow of the tenth
Étude, in A-flat major. Chopin did not choose the order of the
set without thought, and he was brilliantly right when he put
this burstingly healthy, youthfully ebullient piece after the F
minor and before the filigree traceries of the E-flat major. This is
a study in rhythm. It does not, as it appears at first glance to do,
alternate between measures containing four groups of three
eighth-notes and measures containing six groups of two eighth-
notes — though both groupings occur. Predominantly it varies between measures of six groups of two — in which accents occur on
the second, fourth, sixth, eighth, tenth, and twelfth beats, as in
the first full measure — and those in which the accents fall on the
odd-numbered beats. The first procedure, of course, requires
phrasing in which the first beat of a measure becomes the weak
close of a rhythmic impulse begun on the strong final beat of the
preceding measure. The result, when nicely calculated with exceedingly careful variation throughout, is far from nervous or
restless. It contributes largely to the happiness that suffuses the
Étude.

The eleventh Étude, in E-flat major, is a study in arpeggios,
with the melody picked out by the last, top note of each arpeggio. It requires tremendous rolling stretches in both hands, an
absolute accuracy of aim, and a rare ability to prevent the constant repetition of wide-spaced chords from growing loud. The
rich harmonic actions must not be allowed to sound either

pseudo-orchestral or muddy: however much they may resemble some of Wagner's (Huneker acutely singled out the fifteenth measure from the end as markedly Wagnerian), they are piano music — and by Chopin. The notes in the arpeggios are not so closely bunched but that space remains between them for both air and light to enter, and the sounds of the piece must be drenched in a good deal of both.

Twelfth and last of opus 10's dozen Études is the so-called "Revolutionary," in C minor. Whether or not it was composed by Chopin in his rage over news that the Russians had taken Warsaw (1831), it is one of his most aggressively masculine, bravura outbursts. Played for its sheer noise-making possibilities, it is a thundering bore. Played with the let-ups, the sighing asides, and the re-eruptions that Chopin built into it, it is electrifyingly dramatic, an honest tragedy in tone. Let him who thinks Chopin a simple fellow toying with only the most rudimentary forms and hitting upon success by happy accident sit down to analyze the formal pattern of the "Revolutionary." He will rise from that fascinating inquiry with a realization that at the age of twenty-one Chopin had an unfailing command, intellectually realized, of the technical resources of harmony, a strict conception of design and proportion, and a store of exact wisdom about what the black and white notes of a piano could be made to do. With the C-minor Étude he had arrived at a grasp of his chosen medium that few composers ever attain. In this exact ability to carry out his intentions punctually, succinctly, and with beautiful nicety, he was the peer of Bach, Handel, Mozart, and Beethoven. Their superiority, if it be phrased that way, lies in the greater extension and complexity of the materials they discovered and organized.

Opus 11

Concerto in E minor for piano and orchestra

The first-composed of Chopin's two piano concertos, that in F-minor, was not published until 1836, about seven years after he had completed it. It became known as his second concerto because the E minor, written a year later, was published three years earlier. As with Beethoven's first two piano concertos, then, the numbers of Chopin's should logically be reversed.

The E-minor Concerto was first performed at the third and last of Chopin's Warsaw concerts, on October 11, 1830. There must have been an orchestration of some sort, probably by Chopin himself: as early as May 15, 1830 he had told Tytus Voitsyekhovski that he had written for it an accompanying part making use of muted violins. When he rehearsed the Concerto with orchestra on September 22, 1830, it was noted that the complement of instruments was full except for trumpets and drums. An original orchestration existed, then. But there is reasonable doubt that the orchestration as published in Paris by Schlesinger in July 1833, or that issued in Leipzig by Probst-Kistner two months later, was exactly that original. The cellist Franchomme was long believed to have "composed" the published orchestration, but it seems more likely that he merely edited Chopin's. In any case, the published orchestration is very thin stuff indeed. It is one of the Concerto's chief weaknesses.

Carl Tausig once tried his hand at improving the E-minor concerto. In his edition not only is the orchestration made richer and less haphazard, but the length and design of the music are altered. Tausig thought the orchestral introduction too long (he was right), so he cut it apart, removed measures, and sewed it together again. Rafael Joseffy thought well of the Tausig edition, which Wagner had examined for the arranger, and often played it. Moriz Rosenthal, according to Huneker, complicated matters further by playing his own compromise between the 1833 version and Tausig's. Richard Burmeister rescored both of Chopin's Concertos. Nowadays conductors, resigned to the realization that the 1833 version seems to have persisted, content themselves with fortifying the orchestration and making discreet cuts as they see fit. Nor are pianists averse to adding to the brilliant difficulties with which Chopin strewed the solo part. Critics must therefore be wary of criticizing the composer for everything they hear when the E-minor Concerto is performed.

The E minor was a student showpiece of Karl Filtsch, a prodigy who studied with both Liszt and Chopin. On hearing this boy play, Liszt is said to have remarked: "When he begins to travel I shall shut up shop." Filtsch, who had already given successful

concerts on the Continent and in London, died in 1845 at the age
of fifteen.

The Concerto is dedicated to Friedrich Kalkbrenner. It is in
the traditional three movements, an *allegro maestoso,* a *romanze*
(*larghetto*), and a *rondo* (*vivace*).

The orchestral prelude to the *allegro maestoso* is one hundred
and thirty-eight measures of piano music poorly distributed
among other instruments. In fact, it is an orchestrated potpourri
of music that the piano will play later and better, a fact that tends
to rob the solo of some of the attention it deserves. The solo is
introduced with a *fortissimo* flourish, twice repeated, and followed each time by an upward arpeggio and descending figurations. Then in a quieter mood the piano elaborates on a melody
first heard in the introduction. From that point on, and despite
certain beauties, the movement seems wandering and, at times,
interminable. It lacks all sense of progression and consequently
sags increasingly as it continues.

As a middle movement for his E-minor Concerto Chopin composed an accompanied piano nocturne of the passive sort that only
greater rhythmic resourcefulness and harmonic daring might have
saved from oversweetness. Huneker once dubbed Chopin "the
Polish tuberose," and here that largely inappropriate appellation
fits. The melodies are superb; Chopin's use of them is sentimental.
After this spineless stuff the concluding *rondo* (*vivace*) sounds
more vital than it is (the result of clever foresight on Chopin's
part?), and spins away its rapid tricks most satisfyingly. Even
here, however, bound by models he did not digest because nothing in his nature was sympathetic to them, he held his fancy in
the tight reins of an inept conception of the key relationships of
the classical concerto, or — more accurately — of the concertos of
Gyrowetz, Hummel, and perhaps Kalkbrenner.

In the E-minor Concerto the result of Chopin's composing for
piano with orchestral accompaniment is a botched piece, the absence of which from the corpus of his works would not have diminished his position or present reputation at all.

Opus 12

Variations brillantes

In January 1833 the charming composer of operas and ballets
Louis-Joseph-Ferdinand Hérold died near Paris of tuberculosis.
In 1831 Hérold had won enormous public favor with his opera
Zampa, and the month preceding his death had seen the *première*
of another fine work, *Le Pré aux clercs.* At his death he left another opera, *Ludovic,* all but finished. Jacques Halévy brought it
quickly to completion, and it was produced before Hérold had
been dead four months. It was on an air from this opera, "*Je vends
des scapulaires,*" that, in the same year, Chopin made the error of
composing a set of superficial variations. It was a mistake because
he failed to prove that the concentric, simple-minded melody —
rather like a piece of average passagework — could be successfully
varied at all. What he did do was to break it up and decorate it
with considerable banality and awkwardness. Only in the *lento*
variation (D-flat major) that he placed, for variety, between two
scherzo variations do the shape of the left-hand accompaniment,
the shape of the melody, and a mild strangeness in the harmoniza-
tion remind us at all of Chopin the great composer. Otherwise the
Variations brillantes are a total failure. Huneker's description of
them as "Chopin and water; Gallic *eau sucrée* at that," is too acute
and entertaining to omit.

Chopin dedicated his opus 12 to Emma Horsford, one of his
early Paris pupils. It was published at Leipzig in November
1833 by Breitkopf & Härtel, and in Paris two months later by
Schlesinger.

Opus 13

Grand Fantasy on Polish Airs

The Grand Fantasy in A major on Polish Airs, composed in 1828,
is one of Chopin's least attractive compositions. It has an entirely
perfunctory orchestral accompaniment, but can perfectly well be
played as a piano solo (it is unlikely to reward the effort). It is

dedicated to Johann Peter Pixis, a pianist and composer, like whom it is forgotten by all but historians and musicologists.

The Grand Fantasy begins with an unembellished orchestral introduction in A major, which leads into a burst of fireworks in the same key for the solo piano. Still for the piano, there follows a transcription of a song, "The moon has set," which is then varied in a manner that prefigures the Berceuse composed sixteen years later. For no ascertainable structural reason, this mechanical varying is then succeeded by a "Theme of Charles Kurpinski" — Karl Kasimir Kurpinski, successor to Elsner as chief conductor at the Warsaw Opera. It is probably the melody of an aria from one of Kurpinski's numberless operas. It, in turn, is varied with vacant brilliance. Next a desultory orchestral bridge, one of several, brings us to a kujawiak (kuyaviak). Although this Polish dance is traditionally a very slow relative of the mazurka, Chopin marked this one *vivace*. It supplies the Fantasy's only passage of interest, and sounds not badly as a separate piano solo once the miniscule interruptions of the orchestra have been transcribed into it. It alone is native, though not top-rank, Chopin.

The Grand Fantasy was published in Paris by Schlesinger and in Leipzig by Probst-Kistner, both in the spring of 1834.

Opus 14

Krakoviak — Grand Rondo de Concert

Except for the F-minor Concerto, the Krakoviak is the finest of Chopin's showpieces for piano and orchestra. Composed in 1828, almost simultaneously with the Grand Fantasy on Polish Airs, it was also published in 1834 by Schlesinger in Paris and by Probst-Kistner in Leipzig. It is dedicated to Princess Adam Chartoriska.

The winning qualities of the Krakoviak reside in its spirited melodies and in its harmonic progressions, and not at all in its splayed, sprawling form. After an absurdly irrelevant introduction by the orchestra, a preliminary or fore-theme is stated by the piano, the orchestra intervening now and again with harmony-supporting chords. The melody is in single notes doubled at a two-octave distance, and it has both pungency and attractive

Slavic profile. It is reasonably followed by another brief orchestral preface, and the principal melody [1] of the rondo is played by the solo piano. Gerald Abraham has pointed out that this melody closely resembles the one quoted by Grove as the accompaniment to which, about 1840, the great ballerina Fanny Elssler performed a dance she called a *cracovienne*, a word that — like krakoviak — means a dance from Krakov.

Occasionally in the Krakoviak there are orchestral bridges, and almost self-sustaining orchestral statements, that have a quite un-Chopinesque solidity, indicating either an assistant orchestrating hand or an insight unusual for Chopin into the possibilities of instruments other than the piano and the cello. Like the Grand Fantasy, and despite passages of Slavic minor melancholy, the Krakoviak is predominantly objective and gay. It is music of young pleasure and effervescence. If pianists could now be forced to enclose their volume within a narrow range beginning at *piano pianissimo*, the Krakoviak could be as welcomely performed today as when it was first published in 1834. That would be a musically rewarding experiment.

Opus 15

Three Nocturnes

Of the three Nocturnes that together make up Chopin's opus 15, the first two were composed in 1830–1, the third in 1833. The group is dedicated to Ferdinand Hiller, pianist, composer, teacher, writer, and great friend. It was published almost simultaneously, in January 1834, by Breitkopf & Härtel in Leipzig and by Schlesinger in Paris.

The first Nocturne of the opus, in F major, has all the visible lineaments of a successful Chopin piece. But in performance it evokes a tentative and uncertain effect and never quite comes off. That this may have been wholly or partially intentional [2] does not

[1] It is quoted by Louis Aubert in his curious Chopin score for the ballet *La Nuit ensorcelée*.

[2] The effect is introduced early by the somewhat jerky and indecisive manner in which the upper notes of the melodic figure in the left hand double, repeat, follow, and diverge from the right-hand melody. It is intensified by

make it more satisfying. It cannot entitle the Nocturne to a place among Chopin's best.

Altogether finer is the remarkable second, in F-sharp major. This is a poetically conceived and magisterially carried-out piece worthy of the man who had already published the Études of opus 10. It far excelled anything else Chopin had published up to 1834. Aside from the instantly conquering beauty of the melody first presented, the originality that the whole Nocturne exudes is first made plain in the repetition of that melody. By changing

to

— that is, by substituting five notes for four, and by making the fourth of the five the first note in the piece not native to the key scale — Chopin has subtly, immediately, quickened interest. The Nocturne is everywhere brightened and kept alive by such rhetorical alterations. Much of the *fioritura*-like decoration sounds directly derived from the singing demanded of — and obtained from — performers of Rossini, Donizetti, and Bellini. The *doppio movimento,* which can be played as smoothly as the simplest passage in common time, is in fact a complicated study in cross-rhythms. The accompanying left hand contents itself with eighth-notes and quarter-notes on the beats, but the melodic right hand most often has ten notes to a measure (two groups of five), of which the first, fifth, sixth, and tenth prick out the chief profile of the melody. After the *doppio movimento* the first tempo returns, and the origi-

the manner in which a fragment of repetition breaks off, with an air almost of ennui, just before the *con fuoco* section is introduced.

nal melody is treated briefly, leading with unquestionable cogency into a codalike ending that shows Chopin achieving command of that difficult section. The F-sharp major Nocturne is a great masterpiece in small.

The third Nocturne of opus 15, in G minor, has the appearance and the sound of program music. Chopin noted on the manuscript that it was composed "After a performance of Hamlet," but it is footless to attempt a literary exegesis phrase by phrase — or at all. What the piece seems to be communicating is clearly a musical story. It contains no repeated sections, being designed in three large, successive parts. Despite some daring harmonies, particularly at the end of the first part, the G-minor Nocturne is unfortunately not very interesting to hear. It is not holding its place in popularity with, for example, its predecessor in F-sharp major. Every one of its successors was to eclipse it.

Opus 16

Rondo in E-flat major

Chopin dedicated his opus 16 to Caroline Hartmann, one of his Paris pupils. He composed this Rondo in 1832; it was published early in 1834 by both Breitkopf & Härtel (Leipzig) and Schlesinger (Paris). Except for the Krakoviak it is the longest of Chopin's five published pieces in rondo form. It is, in fact, too long — and very dull. One of Liszt's pupils, Richard Burmeister, who long lived in the United States, and whose many compositions once enjoyed a vogue, tried to improve the E-flat Rondo by adding to it an orchestral accompaniment in the manner of the Schubert-Liszt "Wanderer" Fantasy. This did not help, as the Rondo is now not performed at all.

Chopin produced a certain number of bravura compositions for the use of his pupils, and it is easy to believe that the Rondo belonged among that number. It requires fleet fingers, a taste for self-display, and no poetic or musical insight beyond the most elementary. The first melody of the Rondo itself, especially as it occurs after a vacant introduction, is pretty in a manner that five or six minor composers of the day commanded better than Chopin. There is a plethora of bustle, indicating action without plan. And that is really all. This is an incredible product as coming from a brain capable of producing the Étude opus 10, no. 3, or the Nocturne opus 15, no. 2.

Opus 17

Four Mazurkas

Mme Lina Freppa, to whom Chopin dedicated the four Mazurkas of his opus 17, was a singer. A highly educated and accomplished musician, she held a sort of salon in which Chopin was often one of the many musical visitors. He completed or composed the four Mazurkas during 1832 and 1833, and they were published in May 1834 by Breitkopf & Härtel (Leipzig) and Schlesinger (Paris), bringing the tally of his published Mazurkas to thirteen.

The first of the set, in B-flat major, is real dance music, though a little too sophisticated for the folk. Much of it is courtly and gallant and a little stiff. The middle section (before the *da capo*) is closer to folk music than the Poland-remembered-from-Paris of the main body of the piece.

The E-minor Mazurka, no. 2 of the set, is one of the lyrical type, spottily on the lachrymose side until sixteen measures from the end, when it begins to repeat itself in a vigorous, demanding voice. Here, when things quiet down again, the harmonies become richer while previously unclimbed heights of the keyboard are called into play. The result is a Mazurka of very considerable slow charm.

Many otherwise wary commentators have been trapped into verbal excess by the third Mazurka of the set, in A-flat major. In it, as Niecks wrote, ". . . displacement of everything in melody, harmony, and rhythm is the rule." The melody is constantly accented on normally unaccented beats; the harmony is garishly chromatic, and the rhythm is twisted by the melody. When loud, the piece sounds angry; when soft, it sounds as though preparing for anger. It is entirely Chopin, and only a palpable lack of distinction in the melodies themselves keeps the A-flat major Mazurka from being one of the best.

In opus 17 the best is last. This Mazurka, which existed in rough sketch as early as 1825, is dance music at all only in its middle sections. The outlying parts are darkling poetry charged with

Mazurka

half-lighted magic. The key is A minor, and the piece opens and
closes in hushed incantation. Impersonal, morbid, and suave, the
opening section is unmatched for its hypnotic grace. There is a
long section in A major that slowly rises, falls, and rises to a
thoroughly welcome and satisfying climax. Then the first section
returns, varied with appoggiaturas that intensify its magic. *"Calando"* and then *"perdendosi,"* this changeling among mazurkas
ends on a sigh of vanishing enchantment.

Opus 18

Grand Valse brillante in E-flat major

The first-published (though not earliest-composed) of Chopin's
Waltzes is unique among its companions in several ways. It alone
is denoted *"Grand,"* and it alone is obviously real dance music
exactly as composed. It is clangorous, coarse in texture, and
marked by outbursts of insensitive bravado. Composed in 1831
and published in the summer of 1834 by Schlesinger (Paris) and
Breitkopf & Härtel (Leipzig), it is dedicated to Laura Horsford,
one of Chopin's numerous lady pupils.

The Waltzes composed earlier than the opus 18 — opus 69, no.
2; opus 70, no. 3; E major, no opus, and E minor, no opus — are
shorter than it, simpler, less like ballroom music. In opus 18 all is
bedecked, gala. Couples dressed in high fashion swirl in a bright,
candlelit salon. Hearts and sorrows have been left at home. Only
feet, eyes, and bejeweled hands live to the rhythm of this grandly
superficial music, which unfolds one attractive melody after
another.

At the opening of the E-flat major Waltz four measures suggest
the orchestra announcing the beat. Some of what happens thereafter is as close to Johann Strauss, Jr., as Chopin was ever to approach. Had the composer of this Waltz kept on in this vein he
would undoubtedly have become and have remained popular.
But one thing he certainly would never have been: Chopin.

Opus 19

Boléro in C major

One of the small handful of Chopin's compositions that it is safe to disregard is the Boléro. Chopin had not visited Barcelona or Palma de Majorca when he composed it, and he was no Debussy, able to create an entirely real Spain of his own. The Boléro is superficially Spanish, shows traces of polonaise rhythm, and lies entirely over a monotonous surface.

Writing to Fontana in 1841, Chopin stated that he had received five hundred francs for the Boléro. It seems to have been composed about 1833, during a period in which he put together several glittering and uneven pieces, perhaps with the purpose of playing them in public or having his pupils play them in public, perhaps with the sole purpose of selling them to publishers who would pay five hundred francs apiece for them. The Boléro was issued in 1834 by Peters (Leipzig) and Prilipp et Compagnie (Paris), and is dedicated to Countess E. de Flahaut, one of Chopin's several titled pupils. His English publisher, Wessel, had the inspiration to publish it as *Souvenir d'Andalousie.* But then, Wessel was capable of entitling the B-minor Scherzo *Le Banquet infernal!*

Opus 20

Scherzo in B minor

The first of Chopin's four magnificent Scherzos was composed in 1831–2 and published early in 1835 by Schlesinger (Paris) and Breitkopf & Härtel (Leipzig). It is dedicated to T. Albrecht,[1] an attaché of the Saxon Legation in Paris. Albrecht and his father were both friends of Chopin, who stood godfather to the son's daughter.

The B-minor Scherzo opens with two crashing, dissonant, long-held chords, one at the top of the keyboard, the other near the bottom. They promise musical drama of an intense sort, likely to be melodrama or tragedy; they set up expectations of violence

---

[1] Not F. Albrecht, as printed in some editions.

and action. What follows is all agitated, noisy motion, with inter-
ludes that suggest remembered calms. After repetitions and long
developments (one a constantly modulating scene of mounting
fury) comes a contrasting section marked *molto più lento,* in which
the rocking figure, with the prime melody in an inner voice, suggests Brahms. The melody itself, derived from a Polish Christmas
carol beginning "Sleep, baby Jesus," is one of Chopin's loveliest.
Its lyricism is doomed, and it is at last shattered by a repetition
of the two widely separated dissonant chords of the opening. The
passage of fiery agitation is repeated, and leads to a *fortissimo*
chord struck nine successive times like a denouement of horror.
The curtains close slowly, and then rapidly, and finally with a
tonic *fortissimo* crash.

The B-minor Scherzo is a sufficient reply to those who judge
Chopin largely by the Nocturnes, who therefore call him effeminate and overlanguid. It is powerful music, masculine, direct, and
tragic. Unfortunately, it also gives reasonable chapter and verse
to others who accuse Chopin of structural feebleness. It is overlong, and it is not so much designed or built as pinned together.
Worse, it overfulfills its early promises, presents materials unpre-
pared-for and far from self-justifying while being presented. Only
a sovereign pianist can play it with all of the indicated repeats and
not make it sound like an overtold tale. Others do wisely to omit
the indicated repeats, contenting themselves with the piece's
separate beauties and letting Chopin's ill-conceived structure go
by the boards.

Opus 21

Concerto in F minor for piano and orchestra

In 1829 Chopin composed the Concerto in F minor — actually his
first — which was not published until several compositiions written
later, including the "first," E-minor Concerto, opus 11, had been
issued. The F-minor Concerto was published in April 1836 by
Breitkopf & Härtel in Leipzig, and four months later by Schlesinger in Paris. It is dedicated to Chopin's longtime friend, the
musically gifted and beautiful Countess Delphine Pototska. The

delay in its publication was in part caused by Chopin's having mislaid or lost the original orchestral parts on his way from Warsaw to Paris via Vienna in 1830–1.

The first-published orchestration of the Concerto, whether it is Chopin's own or Franchomme's adaptation of Chopin's, has never wholly pleased anyone. That persistent editor Karl Klindworth rearranged and reorchestrated the Concerto in 1867–8. He was as ruthless as Rimsky-Korsakov tampering with Mussorgsky, and for the same high-minded reasons. The Richard Burmeister who added orchestration to the E-flat major Rondo and revised the E-minor Concerto also published a version of the F-minor. Embarrassed by the opening movement's lack of a coda, he supplied it with a cadenza of his own creation. The Burmeister revision was played by no less a pianist than Paderewski. Enrique Granados also made his own rescoring of the hapless Concerto. Whatever that was, however persuasive, it was not Chopin's F-minor Concerto, which we now customarily hear as less thorough editors (often the performing orchestra's conductor) have touched it up a little here and there. Never are we permitted to hear it exactly as Chopin composed it (solo part) and allowed its publication (orchestration).

The F-minor Concerto, despite mishandling, despite the changes of fashion, and despite not being "Chopin *in excelsis*" (Huneker), is a highly attractive work, superior in every detail to the E-minor. The first movement, marked *maestoso,* has an orchestral introduction little more than half as long as that to the E-minor. The movement itself is vigorous, compact, and full of propulsive invention. Its lack of coda, far from marring its structure, is exactly right: the addition of further material could only have strained the expectations set up and the satisfactions supplied by what has gone before.

The *larghetto* second movement belonged, by Chopin's own statement (letter of October 3, 1829, to Tytus Voitsyekhovski), to his thoughts of Konstantsya Gladkovska. It is a luscious nocturne rich in *fioriture* that resemble the calls of invisible nightbirds. But it has moments of assertive volume, and is saved from swooning by its admirable brevity. Of its middle section, in which the solo piano pronounces dramatically above an orchestral tremolo and doublebass *pizzicati,* Sir Donald Tovey wrote: "This is as fine a piece of instrumentation as Berlioz could have chosen to quote in his famous treatise."

The crown of the F-minor Concerto is the closing *allegro vivace.* It is in triple time. The melody immediately presented by the solo piano is not only very beautiful in itself: it is also a good theme, amenable to development. Follows a section marked *scherzando,* with seductions like those of a superior mazurka. This is presented in exactly twenty-three measures. Then, with the excess of genius, the solo piano sounds, in octaves, a melody that is really the preceding one viewed from a different vantage-point. This supplies one of the most arresting events in Chopin's earlier works. After it he goes on with firmness and punctuality to a not-distant end. To say of the man who designed this movement that he was baffled by structural problems is to demonstrate misunderstanding of the nature of musical architecture. Chopin in 1829 was no fumbling apprentice; he was already a master.

Opus 22

Andante spianato and polonaise,
for piano and orchestra

During 1830–1 Chopin composed a Grand Polonaise in E-flat major for piano and orchestra. In 1834 he wrote an introduction for it, an Andante spianato for piano alone. The entirety was published in the summer of 1836 by Schlesinger (Paris) and Breitkopf & Härtel (Leipzig). An exact translation of the title as printed would read: "Grand Polonaise brillante, preceded by an Andante spianato, for piano with orchestra." It is dedicated to Baroness d'Est, one of Chopin's pupils.

Chopin's opus 22 has seldom been played as Chopin had it published. He himself performed it entire in public only once, at a Habeneck benefit of the Société des Concerts du Conservatoire on April 26, 1835. It is often given as an unaccompanied piano solo, less often in arrangements and versions made by others. Nothing of special value is lost by transcribing the rickety orchestral part of the polonaise into the piano part. But everything is lost when a man like Xaver Scharwenka recomposes both sections, adds

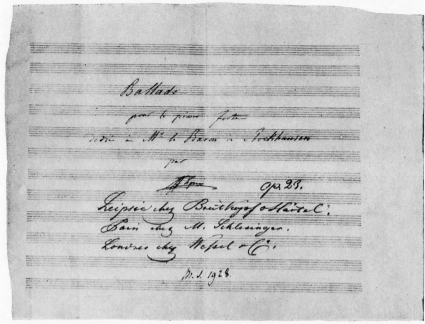

A MANUSCRIPT

*of the G-minor Ballade, opus 23: title page
and first sixteen measures*

A MANUSCRIPT

*of the G-minor Ballade, opus 23: transitional passage
and last thirteen measures*

instrumental accompaniment to the andante spianato, introducing a melody from the Nocturne opus 37, no. 2, and generally remakes the piece in his own image. That the "everything" then lost is not of first importance does not repair the loss.

Not satisfied with "*spianato*" — smoothed out — Chopin added the general direction "*tranquillo.*" And the brief G-major introduction distills the very nature of tranquillity, of Chopin the languorous (sections in $\frac{6}{8}$ time) and moonstruck (those in $\frac{3}{4}$ time). An awkward transition leads to a *tutti* and the polonaise, which is pompous, overproud, and not altogether pleasant to hear. It is difficult. It gratifies virtuoso pianists. But Chopin clearly designed it for show, a process in which he never used half his powers, and the result is not winning.

Opus 23

Ballade in G minor

Chopin seems to have started the first of his four Ballades in 1831 and to have completed it in 1835. Schumann heard him say that both this one and the second were brought to his mind by poems of the Polish patriot Adam Mitskyevich. This report has been connected — later, and on no dependable authority — with Mitskyevich's *Konrad Valenrod* (1828), a poetic narration of battles between the pagan Lithuanians and the Christian Knights of the Teutonic Order. It was published in June 1836 by Breitkopf & Härtel (Leipzig) and Schlesinger (Paris). It is dedicated to the Hanoverian Ambassador to France, Baron von Stockhausen, who probably took some lessons from Chopin.

The G-minor Ballade has always been one of the most widely popular of Chopin's compositions. It begins with seven wholly remarkable introductory measures. At first these speak with great assurance, as though a bard were decisively saying: "This is the way it was." But there is a pause followed by a softer section and another pause: "Well, perhaps I had better start the tale from its beginning." Then two last measures lead to that beginning, eagerly awaited, almost longed for by the moment of its arrival. The last chord of the introduction, an arpeggio, has bred extraordinary arguments. Reading from the bottom up, its notes are D, G, E flat, and B flat. Several editors have removed the dissonance by making the E flat another D, thus substituting banality for the hallmark of invention. But the fact is that Chopin's manuscript, examined with this point in mind, showed the E flat!

It is difficult to hear freshly any composition that has been as hackneyed as the G-minor Ballade or its successor in A-flat major. Its original novelty, however, can be realized. The ballade was, musically, Chopin's invention. In the G-minor he worked out a structural pattern resembling a double mirror image — A(introduction)BCD(development section)CBE(coda).[1] The piece has not so much a formal as a narrative-emotional continuity. Its melodies are too specifically lyrical for actual development of the kind used by Mozart and Beethoven, and Chopin wisely refrained from attempting to force them to it. Instead, he varied and decorated them. The melodies themselves, the sudden rushes of drama, the highlights of gentle dissonance, the conclusive bravura of the coda — these, rather than any perfection of form, have won the Ballade the affection of what must by now total millions of listeners.

Opus 24

Four Mazurkas

The four Mazurkas of opus 24 were composed in 1834–5; they were published late in 1835 by Schlesinger (Paris) and Breitkopf & Härtel (Leipzig). They are dedicated to Count de Perthuis, an aide-de-camp to Louis-Philippe. He was friendly to Chopin, who probably gave lessons to his wife — to whom the B-minor Sonata is dedicated.

The first Mazurka of the set, in G minor, breathes the atmosphere of real folk music, far removed from either the salons of Paris or the introspections of Chopin. Both attractive and popular because it combines exoticism with ease of performance, it is superficial and does not rank among the best.

The second has C major as a courtesy indication only. It is in

---

[1] Gerald Abraham pointed out that this is the design of the first movement of Berlioz's *Symphonie fantastique*, with which Chopin, who disliked Berlioz as a composer, was undoubtedly familiar.

relatively simple ABA form, with a short coda, and most of A is not in C major, but in the Lydian mode,[1] while B is in D-flat major. This is an uneven creation, the outside sections being attractively Slavic in coloring while the trio remains curiously flat and banal.

Brief and winning is the A-flat major, third, Mazurka of opus 24. Some of its persistent effect of newness arises from the fact that its principal melody is presented in groups of six measures rather than in one of the customary multiples of four. Its final eight measures, too — *dolcissimo, perdendosi,* a kind of coda — are like the vanishing of a half-understood vision.

One of the greatest of all the Mazurkas is the B-flat minor, fourth in opus 24. Its introduction, made of alternating and opposed chromatic steps, sets the stage for exactly the extraordinarily various and highly colored music that follows. The amount of rhythmic variety that Chopin here wrings from unchanging $\frac{3}{4}$ time; the amount of melodic beauty he evolves from what are scarcely more than clusters of decorative notes; the amount of harmonic distinction he introduces without appearing to strain after the exotic — these combine to make the B-flat minor Mazurka one of the most gratifying of his short pieces.

Opus 25

Twelve Études

To Countess d'Agoult, Liszt's mistress (whereby she was the future mother of the future Cosima Wagner) and in later life the pseudo George Sand known as Daniel Stern, fell the honor of receiving the dedication of Chopin's opus 25, his second set of twelve Études. These were composed between 1832 and 1836, and were published in October 1837 by both Breitkopf & Härtel and Schlesinger. They contain some of the most difficult and beautiful music ever composed for the piano.

Schumann, writing of how Chopin played the first, A-flat major Étude, said:

---

[1] On the piano an all-white-note scale from F to F gives an equivalent of the Lydian mode.

Imagine an æolian harp having all the scales, and an artist's hand combining them with all kinds of fantastic embellishments, but always with an audible deeper tone in the bass and a softly flowing cantilena in the treble — and you will have some idea of his playing. No wonder, then, that we were charmed most of all by those pieces which we had heard him play, and especially by the first, in A-flat major, more a poem than a study. But it would be a mistake to suppose that he permitted us to hear every one of its small notes.[1] It was, rather, an undulation of the A-flat major chord, strengthened here and there by the pedal; but through the mesh of the harmony there emerged a wonderful melody in big notes. Only in the middle section did a tenor voice break clearly from the chords and join the chief melody.

Here is a sensitive contemporary musician's description of Chopin's *rubato*. For what is the "audible deeper tone" but the firmly regulated bass, played with no rhythmic waywardness, that allowed Chopin to decorate the "flowing cantilena in the treble" with "fantastic embellishments" ever so slightly delayed, ever so slightly hastened? It was the regularity of the bass that made it unnecessary for him to insist with iron insistence that all left-hand and right-hand beats exactly coincide. This — and not over-all waywardness of tempo — is Chopin's exaggerated and reviled *rubato*. It requires acute and unflagging sensitivity if it is not to degenerate into sloppiness or something willful and worse. That sensitivity must also be brought, in the A-flat major Étude, to bear on the pedaling. The piece is a study in contrary motion, in stretching, in accents, in pedaling, in cross-rhythms (measures 17–21), and in control of tone. Its apparent simplicity has lured many to grief; actually it is a piece for gentle giants.

Like the A-flat major, the second Étude of opus 25, in F minor, was composed at Dresden in 1836, while Chopin was visiting the Vodzhinskis. Schumann heard him play it there, and described it as "charming, dreamy, and soft as the song of a child singing in its sleep." It is a study in disparate rhythms: each measure has two groups of triplets in the left hand against four groups in the right. The problem is to avoid accenting every second note in the right hand because it coincides with a note in the left, and to

---

[1] By "small notes" and "big notes" Schumann was calling attention to the unusual manner in which the "Æolian Harp" Étude is printed.

maintain a sinuous line that does not constantly break up at strong accents. The piece has no obvious melody. Rather, it has melodylike progressions that grow out of harmonic patterns. It must not be made to "sing": it is designed to whisper and purl.

A study in accents is the third, F-major, Étude, once widely known as the "Cartwheel" for manifest reasons. All that it requires for producing its full inherent beauty is a minute adherence to the phrasing, accents, and agogic signs. Completely pianistic, it is unimaginable in another medium. Granted the ability to perform it properly, the piece plays itself as a *jeu d'esprit* of flying enchantment.

An avoidance of confusion might be said to be the purpose of the A-minor, fourth, Étude in the set. It is an exercise in persistent syncopation, with the melody carried on off-beats and the harmonic developments constantly delayed by suspensions. It is not, as music to hear, one of the most cherishable of the Études, being somewhat square and unyielding. But this is merely to point out that the A minor is more nearly an unalloyed Étude than the others.

The fifth piece in the opus, in E minor, bristles with technical difficulties, and is once again primarily music. The acrid softness of its opening measures must not be made so lush as to disguise its melody, here carried on the strong beats in contrast to the procedure in the A minor. The *più lento* middle section, in E major, once again presents the chief melody in a relatively bare left hand, and decorates it with constant triplet — and quadruplet — figurations in the right hand. The left hand now demands exactly the right to "sing" denied to the F-minor Étude, no. 2 of this set. The coda is one of Chopin's happiest, and reasserts his mastery over the problem of making a logical ending expressive and interesting in itself. The whole is a small tone poem, as rich in subjective emotion as the A minor is devoid of it.

The toccatalike sixth Étude, in G-sharp minor, unlike its immediate predecessor, will give everything it promises to him who plays it exactly, nicely, and without poetic insight. It is the renowned "Study in Thirds," in which the busy right hand plays nothing (half a dozen chords aside) but thirds for sixty-four measures during which it has only a harmonic relationship to the melody being sounded by the left hand. Fascinating to pianists, the G-sharp minor fascinates listeners only when a rare technical titan plays it. Either it is technique heightened to sorcery or it is nothing but notes.

A mountain on the landscape is the seventh Étude, in C-sharp minor, composed in 1836. Technically, it is a study in bravura for the left hand and in the balancing of two related, diverging, but equally important simultaneous melodies. One melody begins immediately in the left hand, in the first measure after the introduction; the other — its fraternal but not identical twin — begins in the topmost voice of the right hand in the second measure. The result is complex musical poetry of an exalted and heart-shaking sort. Like nothing else in music, the C-sharp minor Étude could easily have justified the title of which Skryabin was so fond — Poem. It was, with the A-flat major and F-minor Études of opus 25, one of the pieces that the enfeebled Chopin felt able to play during his 1848 visit to England and Scotland.

"It might honestly be called 'the pianist's indispensable,' if the phrase had not fallen into disrepute through misuse," Hans von Bülow wrote of the eighth, D-flat major, Étude. "As a remedy for stiff fingers before performing in public, playing it through six times is recommended even to the most expert pianists." This is the study in double sixths, which sometimes move parallel, sometimes move in opposed directions, and sometimes do both alternately. It breaks all sorts of harmonic "laws" (such as those against consecutive fifths and octaves) to achieve music of considerable power. By no means will this piece be satisfied completely by solution of its hand-crippling difficulties. They are but a labyrinth through which the music itself must be entered.[2]

When playing the so-called "Butterfly" Étude, in G-flat major, ninth of opus 25, it is best to forget butterflies. For disregarding that absurd nickname permits concentration on the considerable exigencies and even more considerable beauties of a brief masterwork. Primarily a study in importantly varied touch and accent, it is also a problem in keeping a melodic line distinct from rapid

[2] In *The Oxford Companion to Music* Percy A. Scholes cites the D-flat major Étude as an example of wrong barring. He suggests with cogency that each of its measures might have been cut into two to present a more accurate picture of the necessary accenting.

figures containing notes of equal time value but less interest. The result must whir as no butterfly ever could.

The last three Études of opus 25 are giants, tone poems large in extension, massive in concept, and wholly masculine in poetic content. They would by themselves make it essential to recognize Chopin as great.

First comes the tenth piece of opus 25, the B-minor Étude, a study in the persuasiveness of legato octaves. The opening section and its shortened repetition at the close are full of wild sound, *crescendos, fortissimos,* and crashing *sforzandos.* They must be loud, but nothing could more damage this music than continuous and unvarying volume. The middle section, marked *lento* in contrast to the opening *allegro con fuoco,* is in B major, and is a song of fine strength. But the final section is again all clangor and used power. It ends massively. If John Field ever heard this outburst of glorying in strength, it is impossible to understand how he could have failed to qualify his remark that Chopin's was a "talent of the sickroom."

Composed in 1834, and placed eleventh in opus 25, is the A-minor Étude popularly called "The Winter Wind" because the constant figuration in the right hand resembles what a minor composer might have approximated in an actual effort to depict wind. The nickname, however, must not be taken as an excuse for misunderstanding the music as music. Except for the four measures of introduction (an afterthought on Chopin's part) and the fourth and third measures from the end, the melody is carried in the left hand, while the right hand supplies washes and fountainings of piano tone and melodic color. The last four measures are a masterstroke — a simple cadence followed by the melodic minor scale run upwards in octaves over a range of twenty-nine notes. This extreme harmonic simplicity seems the only possible ending for so richly harmonized a piece, but is exactly the sort of fulfillment that it takes genius to discover.

Magnificent and elemental in one of Beethoven's ways is the twelfth and last Étude of opus 25, surely the greatest of them all. This is the C-minor study in arpeggios. Its grandeur is melodic and a matter of harmony and design, but this gives a performer no leave to overlook nuances of volume, and more especially those of accent, on which the contours depend for their definition. It must not be played as one reasonably imagines the delicate, ailing Chopin to have played it, but as Chopin meant it to be played. It was for years, and with reason, known as the "Ocean" Étude, and there is in it a vast tidal power. No neuroticism here, nothing covert or androgynous, but strength designed and controlled in the creation of a sovereign and conquering beauty.

Opus 26

Two Polonaises

Composed in 1834–5, the C-sharp minor and E-flat minor Polonaises of opus 26 were published in the summer of 1836 by Breitkopf & Härtel and Schlesinger. They are dedicated to the Bohemian composer Josef Dessauer, who lived in Paris and was a friend of Chopin; a song by Dessauer figured on the program of Chopin's concert of February 20, 1842.

The first Polonaise for piano solo that Chopin published during his adult life is marked *allegro appassionato,* and begins with two measures marked *fortissimo* and two marked *forte-fortissimo.* But it is not a noisy piece. The C-sharp minor Polonaise, in fact, is lyric, a little overlyric for all its rhythmic and melodic charm. It has not the authority of some of its more vigorous brothers. In passage after passage it has the character of a nocturne, and awakens to full polonaise-hood only by fits and starts that do not always seem appropriate in their surroundings. The piece is in three large sections, the Polonaise proper, a *meno mosso* trio, and a complete repetition of the first part. Hugo Leichtentritt has cleverly noted that the last measure but one of the trio is a happy additional stroke, the sort of apparently nonessential touch that a lesser composer would have failed to conceive. Try playing the last six measures of the trio with that measure omitted.

More Polish, more vigorous, and generally better achieved is the second, E-flat minor, Polonaise. Niecks well said that "it is full of conspiracy and sedition." Chopin the inflamed patriot unable to succor his oppressed country otherwise than through his music is here proclaimed. The superiority of its musical ideas over those of the C-sharp minor has enabled the composer to give it a much more tightly meshed formal structure. Without being one of the magnificent bardic Polonaises, this one in E-flat minor more than foreshadows their sonorous poetry.

Opus 27

Two Nocturnes

During 1834–5 Chopin composed the two most nocturnal, in the sense of velvety black, of his Nocturnes, that in C-sharp minor [1] and that in D-flat major. They were published in the spring of 1836 by Breitkopf & Härtel and Schlesinger. They are dedicated to Countess Apponyi, wife of the Austrian Ambassador to Paris, whose guest Chopin often was.

The C-sharp minor Nocturne is an architectural curiosity. It has an opening *larghetto* section of twenty-eight measures; a middle *più mosso* section twice that long, ending in a cadenzalike passage in octaves; and a concluding section, in the tempo of the opening — and in reality a condensation of that opening — of only eighteen measures. The last eight measures of the conclusion, moreover, are a cadenza, in which a new, though closely related, melody is introduced. The repetition of the introductory section is therefore actually condensed into ten measures.

Nowhere else is Chopin so night-marmoreal, so smoothly and effetely glimmering, as in the first and last sections of the C-sharp minor Nocturne. About this night there is something hushed, airless, and miasmic. Not an atmosphere in which breath comes without effort, this one is conjured by simple black magic. It is all of a damped and pictorial magnificence, a silent splendor of ebony and jet. The middle section is more human, more powerful, and builds a positive opposition of mood in a *fortissimo* passage in A-flat major. There are moments of defeated gayety before the transitional cadenza is announced in a series of *fortissimo* chords neurasthenic in their insistence. The suave, black, extrahuman mood of the opening is presented briefly, and then the coda speaks peace of an airier and cooler sort. The persistence even here of the accompanying figure — to each measure two groups of six notes, each group rising and falling — gives the Nocturne a rhyth-

[1] For the so-called posthumous Nocturne in C-sharp minor, published in 1875 as an Adagio, see page 317.

mic unity that transforms monotony into an evocative virtue. In short, this is a masterpiece: many have thought it not only the finest of Chopin's Nocturnes, but even the sign of his greatest mastery.

Even less varied [2] is the left-hand accompaniment to the second Nocturne of this pair, the D-flat major. In a piece marked *lento sostenuto* and extending to seventy-seven measures, seventy-five measures have a single-note accompaniment of which the very first sets the unvarying pattern:

Above this rocking figure, however, Chopin works small miracles of melody, harmony, figuration, and gradations of volume, so that no piece is less monotonous than the D-flat major Nocturne honestly played. Here, if anywhere, Chopin's love for the most luscious and flowery Italian-opera music is manifest, though the Nocturne contains many passages of purely instrumental aspect, impossible to the voice. Beginning on a sigh and ending on a satiated whisper, this is music of romance perfumed but not hallowed. Near the mood of its mate in C-sharp minor, the D minor also lives by night, some sensuous night of Chopin's musical imagining.

Opus 28

Twenty-four Préludes

Chopin is known to have composed at least twenty-six Préludes, the twenty-four of opus 28, the C-sharp minor of opus 45, and one in A-flat major first published in Switzerland in August 1918. The series forming opus 28 contains one Prélude in each of the major and minor keys — beginning with C major and A minor, and then in ascending numbers of sharps and descending numbers of flats. They were composed over a long period of time, the final

[2] I am speaking, not of the actual notes or their harmonic implications, but of the shape of the figures.

additions to the set being made — and the set polished — in Majorca in 1838–9. They were published in September 1839 by Breitkopf & Härtel (Leipzig), with a dedication to Joseph Christoph Kessler, a German pianist whom Chopin had met in Warsaw and who had dedicated a set of twenty-four préludes to him. The French edition, issued in two volumes and without an opus number by Catelin et Compagnie, and most English editions are dedicated to the man who had bought them from Chopin for two thousand francs, Camille Pleyel.

Bach's *Präludien* were exactly named: they were prefatory pieces to be played before other pieces of more importance, customarily fugues. César Franck used *prélude* in this fashion in his *Prélude, Choral et Fugue* and *Prélude, Aria et Final.* Chopin's use of the word — repeated since by Debussy, Rachmaninoff, Skryabin, Shostakovich, and others — has no such definite significance. It has been suggested that by *"prélude"* Chopin meant a piece of somewhat improvisatorial character that might be placed before the rest of a program, a description that fits about one third of the twenty-four pieces in his opus 28. More likely, it seems to me, is the suggestion that he was thinking of Bach and the total gamut of keys. Certainly there is no Chopin "prélude character" as there is clearly a Chopin nocturne, scherzo, and impromptu character. Here, to misquote Schumann, Chopin has simply yoked together two dozen of his maddest children.

The C-major Prélude, marked *agitato,* goes in thirty-four swift measures through a tonal range from *mezzo-forte* to *fortissimo* to *pianissimo.* It contains a *stretto,* and is pure Chopin, but it somehow suggest a generic relationship to the first of Bach's forty-eight. It is a superb example of melody evolved from, supported by, and contributing to a figuration: the two elements cannot, in fact, be separated, though the melody must be heard. To play it at all is difficult; to play it well is one of those difficulties which repay all effort.

Composed at Majorca despite traditions to the contrary was the A-minor Prélude, a brief dirge in which there is neither surcease nor hope. Its fragment of damned melody four times closes on the tolling figure that opens both the *"Marche funèbre"* of the B-flat minor Sonata and the "Winter Wind" Étude — quarter-note, dotted eighth, sixteenth, and quarter (or half) — a figure of ominous import, and not only to Chopin. The A minor is difficult to love and impossible not to respect, though it is one of the few published pieces in which Chopin's endless store of originality brought him close to the willful.

Vivace, the G-major Prélude, one flash of thought without time for contrast, purveys moments of sun- and breeze-swept delight. The unchanging left-hand accompaniment figure (doubled one octave higher by the right hand in measures 6–2 from the end) has in itself an almost melodic quality. It must flash in its revolutions like the lightest of eccentric wheels. The whole passes in a small burst of rapture.

Of Chopin's music only his renowned *"Marche funèbre"* and the E-minor and B-minor Préludes were played at his funeral in the Madeleine in 1849. Certainly the E minor is stately and elegiac. But if it is music of grief, it is of grief already resigned. Its musical means fascinate: watch both the single-note melodic right hand and the chordal left proceed by grudging semitones, some full tones, a few therefore highly noticeable wider intervals. Watch the resulting effect of regretful holding back, produced by suspensions and modulations-in-part. Not so modern as the A minor, which almost succeeds in avoiding its tonic altogether, this Prélude, for all its now plane beauty, presents Chopin as a harmonic iconoclast.

The D-major Prélude is pure pianism, its very nature and lineaments having been distilled from abilities exclusive to the piano as a percussion instrument. At three points of major rhythmic interest there are irregularly displaced accents (four groups of six notes accented respectively on the fourth, the second and sixth, the fourth, and the second). Additionally, a constant disagreement about direction of motion between the two hands dizzies the complexities. Not beautiful in any ordinary sense, the D major has the distinction of purposefully controlled intricacy.

According to an anecdote told by George Sand in her *Histoire de ma vie*, one of the Préludes was composed in Majorca as Chopin's dreamlike response to rain dripping on a roof. The story is baldly melodramatic and quite unlikely to be accurate. The honor, if such it be, of being the very Prélude of this anecdote has been evenly divided by commentators between the B-minor and the D-flat major Préludes. And certainly a pianist wishing to be fair to the repetitive figures of either could do it no better than by attempting the impossible task of imitating by piano tone the dripping of Majorcan rain. The B-minor Prélude is a melancholy and beautiful short piece. It has always enjoyed extreme popularity.

A miniature of feminine grace is the sixteen-measure, mazurka-like Prélude in A major, the very essence of slightly exotic poetry. Sentimental, it must not be freighted with extraneous longueurs or its fragrance will prove synthetic and overbearing.

The F-sharp minor Prélude, though marked *molto agitato*, asks to be held within a tempo at which its extremely rich harmonies cannot become a muddy blur. The whole piece has a serviceable melodic profile, but appears to have arisen from the regulated accidents produced by trained hands straying on the keyboard. It would not have been a stranger among the Études.

Solemn, majestic, a trifle grandiloquent, is the ninth Prélude, in E major. Huneker discerned in its twelve measures traces of both Beethoven and Brahms. That Chopin intended it to express solemnity, if not tragedy, is guaranteed by the repetition, more than a dozen times, of the tolling figure mentioned above in discussing the A-minor Prélude. But the spirit of the E major is not damned like that of the A minor; rather, it is brightened through harmonic cartharsis and ends in a *fortissimo* that is like a challenge.

Arpeggios of rhythmic and harmonic, but almost no melodic attractions alternate, in the C-sharp minor Prélude, with less swift measures of semimelodic aspect. This is fragmentary music, a true *prélude*, left incomplete by being an introduction to nothing. It is brief, and it is one of the least among the twenty-four.

The eleventh, B-major, Prélude is a wonderful fragment of young melody that seems to be cut off suddenly before fully expressing itself. Chopin's inexhaustible command of variety for maintaining interest is here simply demonstrated: the single *acciaccature* in measures 3, 4, 7, and 8 become double in the repetition (measures 15, 16, 19, 20), lending the approach to the climactic F sharp a stimulating element of waywardness. Further interest is added to the repetition by the shape and harmony of the left-hand figure of the eighteenth measure, so like a deep-fetched sigh, and by the subtle substitution, in measure nineteen, of an eighth rest on the second left-hand beat for the F sharp of measure seven.

Cousin germane to the A-minor Étude, opus 10, no. 2, is the G-sharp minor Prélude, no. 12. Beginning at *forte*, it seldom descends to *piano* and mostly finds *fortissimo* its true home. It is a rush of passionate volubility in which one assertion is repeated and repeated, and it has no isolable melody, but only a flow of semimelody. The rhythm is insistent, and enduring interest resides chiefly in the swift, endless harmonic changes.

Another piece in which the principal melody seems to grow out of the harmonic investiture of a figure is the nocturnelike F-sharp major Prélude. But here the semimelody becomes a melody of intense interest in itself — indeed, one of great beauty. After the ecstatic quiet of the *più lento*, middle section, the repetition of the first section is more an inspired variant than a true repeat. Nothing is exactly as it was, and chords much wider than one octave, too wide to stretch, add a rhythmic nuance (as they are arpeggioed) as well as a nuance of piano color. The last three measures begin by urging the shape of the opening figure, but suddenly achieve a structural masterstroke as they recall, also, the *più lento*.

A sketch for the *presto* finale of the B-flat minor Sonata is the fourteenth, E-flat minor Prélude. Here, too, an unvarying figure in triplets supplies excellent thematic material without flowering into melody. Unlike the susurrous finale of the Sonata, however, this Prélude possesses a hot and assertive spirit. To play the E-flat minor delicately is to destroy it. Its agogic indications are as important as the harmonic risings and fallings of its broken-chord figure.

Often known as the "Raindrop" Prélude, the fifteenth, in D-flat major, is physically and emotionally widespread. The opening section, in which it is now impossible *not* to hear water dripping, is bland almost to banality. Its pretty, but somewhat flaccid melody is prevented from sounding more banal than it is, not by the harmonic usages — quite un-Chopinesque in their flatness — but by the turns with which it is embellished in measures 11, 15, 17. They are not quite enough. The long middle section is better. It is a marching vision, vague at first, but becoming close and ominous, and then dissolving. There is the briefest

return to the opening — six measures — at the end of which eight
descending notes introduce the coda.

Another strayed Étude is the B-flat minor Prélude, no. 16. By
means of six *forte* chords, three of which contain pungent minor
seconds, and the purpose of which (they are followed by a pause)
seems that of pounding on the stage to center an audience's attention, the piece is launched on a career of frenzy, *presto con
fuoco.* By a paradox, it seems to pause for a moment of consideration at the *stretto,* only to sweep downwards in chromatic octaves
and begin again. No conclusion is reached: near the end a figure
of more widely spaced octaves soars aloft toward the two final
chords, *fortissimo.* The motion of the left-hand accompaniment
appears to pump up energy as though furiously bent on self-
destruction. Huneker was surely correct in calling the B-flat minor
"the boldest of the set."

The A-flat major Prélude, no. 17, has an often remarked resemblance to a Mendelssohn *Lied ohne Worte.* Mendelssohn,
saying that he loved the piece, justly added that he could never
have composed it. Its remarkably beautiful melodic patterns are
shored up on harmonic foundations far too daring for him. The
detail that marks this Prélude most distinctly is the *pianissimo*
(and *piano-pianissimo*) *sotto voce* section running for twenty-six
measures to the end. Eleven times the A flat below the bass clef
is sounded with force, like a cannon shot repeated or the mina-
tory booming of a huge signal.

Eighteenth, and in F minor, is a Prélude with a curious resemblance to the second of Schumann's *Fantasiestücke,* "*Aufschwung.*" They are in the same key, and open with highly similar
melodic statements. Schumann, however, proceeds to develop his
piece at some length and introduces an exquisite *espressivo* contrast, whereas Chopin gives vent to enraged outbursts that skirt
incoherence. "*Aufschwung*" is the better achieved entity, but
Chopin's F-minor Prélude, like a great dramatist's pages of rhetorical indulgence, has beauties of its own.

In the E-flat major Prélude, no. 19, a study in triplets in contrary motion becomes, at the hands of Chopin, a small, luminous
poem of quiet rapture. It does not require contrast (or receive
it until the two loud closing chords), for it is a single impulse of
the heightened praise that might arise from rapture.

An impressive and unforgettable masterwork, the twentieth Prélude, in C minor, contains exactly thirteen *largo* measures. Except for the whole note of the close, the measures rhythmically repeat without variation the pattern established in the first:

By harmonic mastery alone, Chopin builds the repetition and variation of this figure into a composition of genuine grandeur. The verbatim repetition, *pianissimo-crescendo-decrescendo*, of the section originally marked *piano* and finally *decrescendo* is what I understand to be described by the hackneyed phrase "stroke of genius."

A nocturne is the B-flat major Prélude, no. 21. The melody, of absorbing beauty, is at first supported by a left-hand figure of varying profile. The upward, aspiring form of this figure at last prevails and is doubled below the melody by the right hand. The ending, with an aimless and inconclusive message, is not one of Chopin's happiest and tends retroactively to rob the Prélude of power.

Molto agitato, *forte* and *fortissimo*, the twenty-second Prélude, in G minor, is a black storm in which only the nearest forms have visible shape. All compact and sudden in movement, the music seems hinting at a musical message too expansive for so concentrated a manner. Its chief purpose — or, at least, its chief effect — is to offer welcome moments of contrast between the nocturnelike B-flat major and the blue air and sunlight of the F major.

The penultimate Prélude of opus 28 is a marvel of swinging delicacy. In it the attractions of a continuous figuration quite outshine those of a full-fledged melody of very considerable beauty. The piece is all aerial movement. Happy and moderately rapid, it could have closed as it began, unambiguously in F major. But look at the last measure but one: the E flat in the left hand is Chopin:

Try the passage with a C replacing the E flat: that is banality. What seems about to happen, once the E flat is struck, is a modulation to B-flat major (the neighboring A's supplying the leading tone). But the E flat is merely a mote of color, supplying ambiguity, and the signature key is insisted upon by the closing measure, in which there are exactly two notes, four octaves apart, both F's.

Last, the most melodramatic of the Préludes, is the D minor, *allegro appassionato*. Much nonsense has been written about it in the incorrect belief that it was composed at Stuttgart, together with the C-minor Étude of opus 10, on Chopin's hearing of the fall of Warsaw. Actually it is of a later date, and there is nothing specifically Polish or patriotic in it. The revolt it signals is purely musical. The first section is repeated, beginning at the indication *sempre f,* a fourth lower, but almost like a transposition, so exact is the repetition. The transitional section that follows the conclusion of this section on an E-in-altissimo is extraordinary. It modulates all but continually, rising back to the reintroduction of the opening, this time with the right hand in octaves, and followed by an infuriated downward run in thirds. There is more — and all of it wonder-working — before a *forte-fortissimo* chord and a final swift descent of single notes over five and one half octaves lead to three cavernous D's signifying that both the Prélude and Chopin's opus 28 have run their course.

Opus 29

Impromptu in A-flat major

The A-flat major Impromptu, composed in 1837, was published late that year by Schlesinger (Paris), and in January 1838 by Breitkopf & Härtel (Leipzig). It is dedicated to Countess Lobau, one of Chopin's Paris pupils.

The A-flat major, though not a wholly successful piece, has very palpable attractions. The opening section shows Chopin practicing his legerdemain of avoiding a full melody while forming approximate melody out of the harmonic changes in a repetitious figure. The *sostenuto* section that ensues has a full melody, but an undistinguished one, and is interesting mostly for its off-beat accents and coloratura ornamentation. The first section is recapitulated. There is a coda that brings everything to a reasonable end. But the piece does not hold together even under the fingers of the most careful pianist. Its designation as an impromptu allows it a certain freedom — certainly that of having no specifically formal interest — but it exceeds that freedom by failing to pass convincingly from one of its sections to the next. In few pieces does Chopin indulge in the perfunctory bridges that he here substitutes for his often magical transitions.

In George du Maurier's once popular *Trilby*, Svengali makes the hypnotized girl sing this Impromptu, a feat that most sopranos could not perform even under hypnosis. It is a piece whose first measure, with its three clashing D naturals, promises more than the entirety ever supplies. I am willing to admire details throughout, the separate sections even. But to the Impromptu as an entity the only possible over-all reaction is a disappointment tinged with the sensation of having been cheated. Recommending the free use of rubato in it, Klechinski wrote: "Here everything totters from foundation to summit, despite which everything is so clear, so beautiful." But music that totters from foundation to summit must do so under firmer control, with less slips, small lacunæ, and collapses, if it is to be trusted.

Opus 30

Four Mazurkas

During 1836–7 Chopin composed the four Mazurkas that make up his opus 30. They were published late in 1837 by Schlesinger (Paris), and early in 1838 by Breitkopf & Härtel (Leipzig). The opus is dedicated to the Princess of Württemberg, who had been born a Chartoriska.

The first of the set, in C minor, is one of the least grateful of the Mazurkas to listen to or to play. This is owing to lack of distinction in its melodic patterns. The harmonies have touches of Chopin at his most advanced, and must have sounded positively anarchic to most 1837 ears. The following two measures — numbers 3 and 32 — derived though they may be from Polish folk practice, have traveled very far from earlier composed music:

The Mazurkas in opus 30 are arranged in climactic order. The second — in B minor — wins more quickly and more permanently than the first. Klechinski stated, on unknown authority, that the noticeable figure consisting of adjoining octaves descending either a whole tone or a half tone "perfectly realized the character of Uyeyski in his little poem 'The Cuckoo.'" The Mazurka is in ABCB form, though C is really an altered form of A. Most interesting is the fact that B, which first leads to a section in the opening B minor, closes the piece in F-sharp minor without reannouncing the signature key.

The third, D-flat major, Mazurka is better yet, a courtly display of great melodic persuasiveness, harmonic richness, and rhythmic variety. Its introduction consists of eight measures of subtle preparation for the rhythmic patterns to come. It oscillates between major and minor, thus producing a chiaroscuro that suggests wavering lights or easily shifting moods. In the final two measures the wholly unexpected change from F flat to F natural, a last sudden motion back to major from minor, is a masterly touch.

Best of the set, and one of the most powerful of the Mazurkas, is the fourth, in C-sharp minor. Almost every measure offers some detail to admire, but it is the total effect of solid unity that raises this piece to a high position among short piano works. Its bravado close, in which what Huneker called "bare-faced fifths and sevenths" die consecutively away, has often been remarked. Its musical justification is instantly clear, however incorrect it may still look to some eyes. Also, with conquering mastery, Chopin in the coda, beginning seven measures before the end, combines his two chief themes to produce a perfect dying fall. This is no longer an adapted folk dance: it is a musical composition of intellectual strength and sensible tragic power.

Opus 31

Scherzo in B-flat minor

To one of his pupils, Countess Adèle de Fürstenstein, Chopin dedicated his opus 31, the B-flat minor Scherzo composed in 1837. It was published late that year by Schlesinger, and in February 1838 by Breitkopf & Härtel. It has always held a place among the most often played of Chopin's compositions. Long and structurally complex, it demonstrates a grasp of musical architecture of a higher order than any Chopin had essayed earlier. In this respect he was to excel it only in the E-major Scherzo, the last two Ballades, and the F-minor Fantaisie.[1] This would be of little more than technical interest if the formal edifice were not constructed of musical materials of the most viable and beautiful sort.

The B-flat minor Scherzo opens with a summons almost as famous as the four horn-notes that stand before Beethoven's C-minor Symphony. Of this twice-repeated call Wilhelm von Lenz, who knew Chopin personally, said: "For Chopin it was never question enough, never soft enough, never sepulchral enough, never important enough. 'It must be a charnel-house,' he once said." And indeed that reiteration of the *sotto voce* or *pianissimo* query and its *fortissimo* reply for forty-six measures, including six of silence and followed by two more, besides being of extraordinary beauty in itself, is a flawless portal to a big-scale work. It is followed by sixteen measures of related shiftings from *fortissimo* to *piano* and *pianissimo,* with thrilling sweeps downward from an F a dizzy two octaves above the treble clef and supported on an open D-flat octave below the bass clef. Notice how the left-

---

[1] Gerald Abraham classes the Polonaise-Fantaisie with the four compositions here mentioned. With this judgment, though recognizing the complexity of the Polonaise-Fantaisie, I disagree for reasons later detailed (see pages 278–82).

hand chords that follow this cavernous octave repeat the opening question in less mystified tones.

The *con anima* is graced by one of Chopin's finest melodies, a cantilena above a rolling figure in single notes. This is worked up to a thoroughly expressive climax, after which two measures of silence prepare again the suggestive question that began it all. The treatment diverges slightly from the opening section, however, as does that of the descending sweeps, which is now brilliantly foreshortened. But the lyrical *con anima* is restated almost intact. Thus far — and with sufficient material for a composition by itself — we have a formal structure that might be represented by ABCabC.[2]

If Chopin was to increase the extent of this partial edifice with more structure, it had, æsthetically speaking, to be of less motile nature, something able to establish a center of repose. His manner of giving exactly that is what, more than any other single detail, raises the Scherzo to its fulfilling greatness. The *sostenuto* section is spread out in the tellingly apt key of A major. Its long-breathed chords and ornamental rhythmic figures supply precisely the relaxation required before the chief business of the piece may be effectively rebegun. At the indication *espressivo* (C-sharp minor) a semimelody is introduced and given piquancy by a repeated five-note arabesque adapted from the quarter-note figure in measures 2 and 3 of the *sostenuto.* This is the subtle reflection of detail from one section in another that strengthens unity.

Leggiero announces a passage of fluid arpeggios, *crescendo ed animato,* leading at last to a deep-bass E and a moment of silence. These soundless pauses are, it is clear, an integral element of the piece's over-all design. Now the *sostenuto, espressivo,* and *leggiero* sections are recapitulated almost unchanged, and lead to a rearrival at the deep-bass E. To this point, then, the Scherzo might be plotted as ABCabCDEFDEF. To this point, also, the structure is completely sound, right, and well-balanced. Except for what next occurs I should be tempted to say that it is all of those things throughout.

But after another silent measure Chopin begins to comment on and to develop, first the arpeggio passage, then the *espressivo,* now marked *agitato,* and finally the downward-sweeping passage

[2] I have here used small letters to indicate shortened sections.

that originally preceded the *con anima.* And some of his treatment is mechanical, some of it both awkward and disproportionate. In modulations Chopin seems suddenly unsure of himself. The fabric momentarily develops a perilous sag. Only at the indication *sempre con fuoco,* again manipulating the originally *espressivo* passage, does he regain his footing. Here the alternating of chords and the reinforced five-note arabesque is apt and astonishing, especially as the arabesque itself takes on more and more (*diminuendo*) the character of the prefatory question. Another measure of silence. Thus far the complex pattern might be represented as ABCabCDEFDEF*FEBE.*[3]

Now the opening section is repeated, intact as to length, but with small changes that are recognizably growth — not fussy variation, but true development. The first note is omitted; the F at the end of the question is held for six beats instead of one, thus ruling out the measures of silence in favor of measures of diminishing tone; the double measure of silence that originally followed the section has now become bass rumblings with a double trill. A whole element of architecture is repeated, that is, but with the variants that appertain to its new position. Next the B and C sections are repeated, largely in their second form. Nineteen measures before the change from D-flat major to A major a brilliantly light new modulation occurs. The figure of downward sweeps reappears briefly, and the coda begins. Almost complete, the pattern is now ABCabCDEFDEF*FEBE*AB*c*B.

The coda, B-flat minor going again to D-flat major, is brilliantly satisfying and structurally intricate. Because it has a recognizably terminal quality that sets it off from the body of this Scherzo, it is in itself a musical incident. Its eight measures have, in the left hand, a version of the left-hand accompaniment to the original passage of downward sweeps; its right hand looks newly introduced, but turns out to be a variant of the opening question, originally a triplet and one quarter-note, here four eighths and one quarter. The *fortissimo* chord-figure that originally satisfied the questioning now becomes less melodic, more emphatic. On its second repetition, *stretto crescendo,* it leads through eight measures of centripetal modulation to a *fortissimo* iteration of the downward-sweeping figure, harmonically altered and de-

[3] I have here used italic letters to indicate sections as developed.

prived of its answering upward runs. In measures 11 and 10 from the end new use is made of the chordal pattern first presented in the *crescendo* climax of the original *con anima*. It requires five measures, each of one chord, to reach a chord in the D-flat major dominant. A silent measure. The same chord repeated one octave lower. The last silent measure. And then an *acciaccatura* chord is followed by the end, a final crashing assertion of the high F and low D-flat octave with which the section of downward sweeps had first started.

The entire structure might be represented as

ABCabCDEFDEF*FEBEA*BcB$_b^a$-bc-(b).

The Scherzo, that is to say, is built with six prime elements, of which the second three — D, E, and F — play no part once they have been repeated, developed, and succeeded by the opening three. The result is a gently curving, uneven, archlike pattern that brings out the whole expressiveness latent in Chopin's melodic, rhythmic, and harmonic ideas. It succeeds because its succession gratifies progressively the expectations that it arouses. That it begins in B-flat minor and ends in the relative D-flat major is unimportant except as it is the proper result of the pervasive over-all design. It balances, it will not collapse, and it gives, as masterly buildings give, a sense of simultaneously being solid on the ground and soaring upward easily and aptly. Chopin gave it, to use an accurate phrase once much misused, significant form. Alone, the B-flat minor Scherzo refutes the often parroted judgment that Chopin remained an architectural fumbler who could create firm units of nothing more complex than simple song or dance forms.

Opus 32

Two Nocturnes

The two Nocturnes of Chopin's opus 32 were composed during 1836–7 and published, probably late in 1837, by Adolf Martin Schlesinger in Berlin and Moritz Adolf Schlesinger (son of Adolf Martin) in Paris. The opus is dedicated to Baroness de Billing, born Courbonne, probably one of Chopin's Paris pupils.

The B-major Nocturne of opus 32 opens with a melody of saccharine flavor; this might be unbearable but for the delicious

manner in which Chopin varies it with turns and other ornaments. Also, having brought in accessory materials, he seems to
have realized that a restatement of that opening melody might
leave his piece formless or bathetic. He proceeds emotionally,
harmonically — and at last by means of a trill and a turn — back
to exactly the point at which that repetition might be expected.
Then he presents a coda of apparently unrelated, recitativelike
material that, with numerous uncertainties and pauses, leads to
a closing B octave. The coda is an action worthy of a better composition.

The second Nocturne of opus 32, in A-flat major, might fittingly
have been dedicated to John Field, so closely does it resemble
Field's fifth Nocturne, in B-flat major. For purposes of comparison
— and because Field's music is not now often played or owned —
I have herewith reproduced that B-flat major Nocturne intact.

The resemblance of the earlier piece to Chopin's is clear in mood, melodic profile, and rhythmic structure, though Chopin's might accurately be called a superior reconception of Field's. Notice particularly the passage beginning with measure 15 in the

234

Field and that beginning the ¹²⁄₈ section in the Chopin. I do not mean by this comparison to indicate that Chopin's Nocturne seems to me remarkable either in structural proportion or in musical ideas. It represents a great composer using half his powers to play with the salon-music atmospheres of Hummel and Field.

Opus 33

Four Mazurkas

Mademoiselle la Comtesse R. Mostowska, to whom Chopin dedicated the four Mazurkas of his opus 33, may well have been a daughter of Mostovski, that Polish Minister of Education of whom Chopin had had to ask permission before arranging to have Konstantsya Gladkovska and Mlle Volkov as his assistants at his last Warsaw concert. Both Niecks and Ludwik Bronarski place her among Chopin's pupils, on what evidence I do not know. The opus with which she was honored was composed during 1837–8 and issued in November 1838 by Breitkopf & Härtel and Schlesinger. Although attractive, its four Mazurkas are a swift decline from their most immediate predecessors, the C-sharp minor and D-flat major of opus 30.

The first, G-sharp minor, Mazurka of the set is folklike, too simple to hold the interest long. Chopin's flat, unaltered repetition of the opening section after the more interesting middle one is unsuccessful in recalling attention not held by any melodic or harmonic interest.

One of the most familiar of all Mazurkas is the D major, no. 2. It is sprightly and thoughtless dance music (*vivace*) engaged in making a cumulative virtue of reiterations. Of all Chopin's Mazurkas it is closest to being a waltz, particularly a waltz by Chopin. Its final two and one third measures — a sustained fifth in the left hand, over which the right hand rises two octaves in eight skips — supply another example of the exactitude with which Chopin learned to conceive superbly apposite endings for even relatively simple pieces. It is interesting to know that the passion for transcribing Chopin from his beautifully calculated piano version to another, wholly unsuitable, version is not modern: Pauline Viardot-Garcia arranged the D-major Mazurka for voice.

In that malformation it once had great popularity with French sopranos.

The third, C-major, Mazurka of opus 33 is again folklike and again is made on the barest ABA pattern. It possesses, however, melodic character superior to that of the G-sharp minor.

Most responsive and ponderable of the set is the fourth Mazurka, in B minor.[1] Its suggestion of narrative has often been remarked, though the apocryphal statements of what Chopin had in mind while composing it are all egregious. Its pattern is complex and pleasing. The way in which passagework and continuations rise organically out of melodic fragments produces very convincing unity. Of particular interest is the longish passage in single notes that leads to a final repeat, tellingly abbreviated in the interest of balanced weight, of the opening section. This is succeeded by a brief coda planned to a nicety so as to ease the structural stress set up with matched nicety by what has gone before.

Opus 34

Three Waltzes

In December 1838 Breitkopf & Härtel published Chopin's opus 34, and it was published at almost the same time by Schlesinger in Paris, being called *"Trois Valses brillantes."* It has no dedication as an opus, each of its three Waltzes being indited to a different person. Nor were the three composed as a group: there is a distance of seven years between the earliest and the latest.

First comes one of Chopin's five published Waltzes in A-flat major, this one dedicated to Mlle de Thun-Hohenstein. In September 1835 Chopin and his parents had visited the Thun-Hohenstein family at Teschen, and there — on September 15 — he had copied down this A-flat major Waltz for his hosts. As there were

---

[1] It is interesting to speculate on Chopin's reason, if it existed, for so often placing the more impressive and carefully wrought pieces at the end of an opus containing three, four, or five Mazurkas. It suggests that, long before Browning's "The best is yet to be," Chopin wisely reasoned against the practice of catching the eye and ear immediately only to disappoint them, however slightly, as matters proceed. He was not a journalist.

two daughters in the family, it is now impossible to be specific
as to the dedicatee. Indeed, it is possible that Chopin wanted
each girl to believe that it was for her. Like the "Grand" Waltz
of opus 18 it begins with an introduction designed especially to
attract attention, equivalent to taps on the floor from a master of
the dance. This Waltz, in fact, remains within the ballroom type,
but its materials have more flavor and distinction than those of
the E-flat major. The longish coda, too, approaches music to
which the only dancing possible would have to be designed in
advance by a choreographer. Chopin was on the verge of distill-
ing from the ballroom waltz an essential, personal sort of waltz-
poem.

The second, A-minor, Waltz of opus 34 is dedicated to Baroness d'Ivry, probably one of Chopin's aristocratic Paris pupils. It
was composed in 1831, and its spirit suggests that it predates
Chopin's familiarity with the Parisian ballroom waltz, from which
opus 18 and opus 34, no. 1, clearly grew. It is marked *lento,* and
it is all melancholy seductions. Except for the absence of certain
rhythmic and harmonic stigmata, it would not be misplaced
among the Mazurkas. Certainly it is their spiritual kin. Nowhere
is it brilliant, and its structure is poorly laid out to give any sensation of expanding unity. After fifteen and one half measures of
introduction, in which the right hand gives out an unvarying
figure on beats 2 and 3 while the left hand develops a sinuous,
self-centered melody, there is a nineteen-measure section developed from a curiously spavined four-measure melody. This in
turn is followed by a monotonous insistence, for sixteen measures,
on an idea that would become definitely irritating if it lasted four
measures more. On time, however, there arrives a *sostenuto* division in A major, lasting for sixteen measures and then repeated
in A minor. This merges into a repetition, intact, of everything
from measure 16 to the point where the repetition began. Then
Chopin closes the piece with restatement and variation of the
very beginning, producing from that introduction, at one point,
the half-defined outline of a new melody. The total impression
is that of an inspired, but unworked, sketch.

The third Waltz of opus 34 is in F major, and is dedicated to
Mlle d'Eichthal, likely to have been a Chopin pupil. For reasons
too absurd to discuss, it has sometimes been called the "Cat"

Waltz; those who wish to hear miaowings in its appoggiaturas may do so. Here once again are the poundings for attention. What they summon is a typical perpetual-motion semimelody, unaccompanied at first, then with the most indifferent of rum-tum-tum basses. Its shape is determined by displaced accents, not marked as such — and certainly not intended to be emphasized — but growing out of the constant restarting of downward movement on every fourth eighth-note. The rest of the piece has vigorous high spirits. It ends noisily. Only brevity saves it from empty boredom.

Opus 35

Sonata in B-flat minor

The shortest of Chopin's three Sonatas for piano solo is the best known as a whole. It also contains, as its third movement, the *"Marche funèbre"* that is one of the most familiar of all musical selections throughout the Occidental world. Its first, second, and final movements were composed in 1839; the *"Marche funèbre"* almost certainly dates from late 1836 or from 1837. The Sonata was published in the late spring of 1840 by Breitkopf & Härtel. Almost simultaneously it was issued in Paris, not by Schlesinger — who did no more Chopin until opus 44 — but by Troupenas et Compagnie. It bears no dedication.

The most-quoted remark about the B-flat minor Sonata is Schumann's: "The idea of calling it a sonata is a caprice, if not a jest, for he has simply bound together four of his most reckless children; thus under his name smuggling them into a place into which they could not else have penetrated." This entertainingly phrased comment means, I suppose, that the B-flat minor is not a sonata by classical rule; that it really means more is unlikely. I have heard the Sonata played so that it sounded like four separate pieces; the fault was the pianist's. Schumann was no pianist, and the Sonata may have been antipathetic to Clara. But I have heard it played (most recently by Guiomar Novaës) with the complete, over-all, four-movement structural and æsthetic-emotional unity of a Mozart piano concerto or Beethoven piano sonata; then the achievement was Chopin's [1] — and the pianist's. The literary-minded Schumann would have been less disturbed if Chopin had given the four separate movements coined romantic names. But is terminology weakened when a composer chooses to alter an established form with variants of his own? *Pamela, Pride and Prejudice, Vanity Fair,* and *Ulysses* are all novels. Calling the B-flat minor a sonata was neither caprice nor jest: it is a sonata by Chopin.

The first movement opens with four measures, marked *grave,* of introduction. With moving solemnity they prepare the listener for a large-scale composition in B-flat minor, then pause on a dominant-seventh chord. The awaited resolution to the tonic triad occurs (*doppio movimento*), and is insisted upon without an additional note except for doublings through four measures. This, again but at a swifter tempo, prepares the listening mind for an extended composition. Only at the indication *agitato* does the first important melody appear. Once stated, the melodic figure and its accompaniment begin to inch upward. At *forte* in the seventeenth measure new linear development begins, while the shape of the accompaniment changes for the first time in measures 21–4. Now there can remain no doubt: despite the rapid motion, this is to be a piece laid out on spacious lines. Sufficient expectation, sufficient desire for more, has been aroused. Chopin has achieved the formal purpose of any beginning.

At the indication *sostenuto* the second important melody appears. It is elegiac, will do as prefiguring the kind of melodic material we shall encounter in the trio of the *"Marche funèbre."* This increases in power and luminosity until it breaks into the wonderfully apt section in quick triplet chords. There is a repeat of everything but the *grave* introduction (it is not lost — it will be heard of again). From its second ending, the chordal section emerges into a rhythmic reminiscence, in left-hand octaves, of the opening melody, its *sotto voce* taps lengthened by broader interruptions in which the right hand borrows an idea from the introduction. There is then a longish passage of remarkable modula-

[1] It must be remembered that Chopin designed the other three movements to go with the *"Marche funèbre."* He conceived them, that is, as belonging together.

tions toward B-flat major, in which key the broad melody of the *sostenuto* reappears. Developed and varied, this leads to a shortened version of the section in triplet chords.

At this point to have proceeded to restate the *agitato* first melody at length would have been traditional. But Chopin really understood the nature and the weight of what he had already written into the movement. And so by a structural act of wisdom he let his triplet chords work into a *stretto* in which that melody is merely outlined by the left hand while the right moves upward spaciously and chromatically in chords. Then, with seven measures of heavily accented chords, the movement concludes in B-flat major. I cannot conceive how, as one of the four sections of a large composition, it could have been bettered.

Native to the keyboard as though it had grown from it (which it very likely did) is the mighty *scherzo* that follows with instantly accepted inevitability. Its structure is clear to the eye, though to the eye it looks more square than it sounds to the ear. It is full of pure, expertly contrived piano music. The melody of its *più lento* section, again elegiac, is as closely related to the second melody of the first movement as to the trio of the "*Marche funèbre.*" It has the last words in the *scherzo,* too, as it dies away [2] to a chord held for four and one third measures. Thus this most agitated and brilliant of movements finds within itself a perfect bridge to the mournful pomps to come.

This is "the" Funeral March, for which it seems to me likely that Chopin found a remote ancestry in the *allegretto* of Beethoven's Seventh Symphony. Few are the listeners who can now peel away from it the extraneous associations accreted onto it for more than a century of personal and public grief. It is nonetheless beautifully made music. Only the strictest propriety, the most surefooted nicety of taste can preserve its trio from the bathos it too easily supports and expresses. But it can be done: this is no place for rubato or indulgence in self-expression. Huneker wrote of the movement as a whole: "We do know, however, that the March when isolated exerts a much profounder effect than when played in its normal sequence." A profounder extramusical effect, yes, a greater associational and pseudoliterary effect –

[2] *Smorzando* means, literally, killing off.

which is every reason for playing it as the third movement of the B-flat minor Sonata, where musical effect remains predominant.

"Winds of night sweeping over churchyard graves" was Anton Rubinstein's phrase for the concluding *presto*. I have no objection to the tag if it is not allowed to cover up the music. Certainly it is wordless, swift, and terrible. From some level below consciousness, under deliberation, Chopin dredged up the concept of this swirl of unison octaves that alone could have followed the "*Marche funèbre.*" They rush the Sonata to a wholly satisfying conclusion. All passion spent, this spectral music does not trifle with grief: its business is with form, with perfecting a structure, and it triumphs. Every expectation aroused has been fulfilled, every tautening released.

As far as imaginable from the inept fumblings that many honest men have found in it, the B-flat minor Sonata seems to me one of the perfect formal achievements of music. So, and because it is no easy trifle, but a massive and enormously varied work, I believe that by itself, had Chopin written little else, it would entitle him to a position as peer of the greatest artistic creators.

Opus 36

Impromptu in F-sharp major

Like opus 35 and opus 36 the F-sharp major Impromptu bears no dedication. Composed at Nohant during 1839, it was published by Troupenas et Compagnie and Breitkopf & Härtel in the spring of 1840.

Chopin left little or no commentary on or explication of his music except in the memories of his friends and pupils. This is regrettable because a composer's own reasons and conscious motivations, though not always entirely reliable, often supply keys to problems that otherwise must remain unsolved. Why, for example, did Chopin call this F-sharp major piece an Impromptu? As the word itself makes clear, the impromptu is not a musical *form.* Nor is it necessarily a specific musical mood. Only it must be not too formally self-conscious. It must, that is to say, retain some appearance of guided improvisation. But the F-sharp major is half a nocturne and half a ballade, and it would be rewarding to know why Chopin left it in its somewhat unsatisfactory state rather than utilizing its extraordinarily persuasive musical ideas otherwise. For it is an entity only because of its materials and despite the crippling awkwardness of its pattern and of the transitions that scarcely succeed in holding it together.

The principal melody of the Impromptu is foretold, half presented, in the top notes of the left hand in the six-measure introduction, an opening that surely promises to lead into a nocturne. Then the right hand is given the melody, a luscious and songlike one, in single notes. It is varied in profile, decorated with *fioriture*. A submelody in chords then approaches two measures in which the second main melody is foreshadowed. The key changes to D major, and the processional melody is introduced *forte, sostenuto*. A ringing climax then settles down to a notoriously inept and disturbing transition back to the opening melody. Not wishing, however, to restate the opening in the key of the signature, Chopin presents it in an unexpected — and, after the arbitrary *a tempo* transition, an unsatisfactory — F major, with an unsettled and unsettling accompaniment in triplets. This whole part of the Impromptu is feeble and poorly designed, so amateurish that I for one should be happy to learn that it was composed much earlier than 1839.

The transition, *crescendo,* from the unwelcome F major to the much-desired F-sharp major is managed suavely. The protracted section of development awarded to the opening theme, and particularly the melodic variations in thirty-second notes, are interesting, though not of Chopin's best. The left hand alternately accompanies and introduces melodic fragments of its own, suggestions growing out of the harmony. After a measure in which thirty-second-note G sharps and F sharps are in reality a trill, the submelody in chords is restated intact through the first rhythmic intimation of the processional section. The piece ends abruptly. I can think of few more easily understood lessons in how failure to give musical thoughts the extension, development, and formal pattern they require by nature can deprive a composition of full life. Despite separate beauties, the F-sharp major Impromptu must, for these reasons, be listed among Chopin's failures.

Opus 37

Two Nocturnes

The G-minor Nocturne, opus 37, no. 1, was probably composed in 1838; its companion in G major was certainly written out at Nohant in the summer of 1839. The opus was published by Breitkopf & Härtel and Troupenas et Compagnie in the late spring of 1840. It has no dedication. It was later issued by Wessel in London under the title *"Les Soupirs,"* with the result that during his English and Scottish visit of 1848 Chopin was often invited by ladies to play his "second Sigh."

The G-minor Nocturne gets along with the simplest ABA pattern. The first section is given flavor by extremely artful use of grace-notes and of rests, as well as by a manipulation of triplets more characteristic of the Mazurkas. All these ornamental usages lend this section a definitely Polish coloration. The middle section, a mere twenty-four measures, is solemn and quasi-religious. No tempo indication differentiates it from the opening *lento sostenuto,* but it is often played somewhat slower. Adolf Gutmann suggested that Chopin had simply forgotten to insert an instruction for a more rapid tempo. I am inclined to believe him — and certainly the piece is improved if the E-flat major section is not sentimentalized, but is played in a nicely judged *andantino.* The transition back to the opening section is not especially happy, though not a botch like the D-major-F-major event in the opus 36 Impromptu.

Altogether better is the G-major Nocturne. A sort of barcarolle, it is couched in a $\frac{6}{8}$ time that sways back and forth over the first and fourth beats of many measures. The opening melody, presented in alternating sixths and thirds, is highly decorated. The second melody, *sostenuto,* suggests a gondola song even more strongly, and belongs among Chopin's best. Like the G minor, this Nocturne ends almost without preparation. In its fluctuations between activity and happy somnolence, however, it is the superior. Although Niecks's style now seems antique, he expressed something sharply felt when he wrote of the G-major Nocturne: "But let us not tarry too long in the treacherous atmosphere of this Capua — it bewitches and unmans."

Opus 38

Ballade in F major

Chopin began to conceive his second Ballade in 1836, in which year he played a preliminary version of it to Schumann. He worked at it in his cell at Valdemosa in 1838, altering its close. It still does not seem to have satisfied him, for he polished it further in 1839, probably then adding the *presto con fuoco* sections that Schumann had not heard in 1836. It was issued by Breitkopf & Härtel and Troupenas et Compagnie in September 1840, and is dedicated to Schumann, who had dedicated his *Kreisleriana* (1838) to Chopin.

The belief that the F-major Ballade is program music grew out of a statement by Schumann that Chopin had told him of being inspired to write it by "some poems of Mitskyevich." From this small but indefinite beginning Huneker somehow evolved the positive statement that it is based on Mitskyevich's poem "The Lake of Willis." [1] I cannot trace any Mitskyevich poem of that title, though he wrote at least two ballads dealing with enchanted lakes. In any case, I do not see how the Chopin Ballade is improved or damaged by such literary props.

There is certainly a barcarolle lilt to the opening *andantino* of the F-major Ballade. This section a little outstays the expressiveness of its contents, which are, for Chopin, bare and unvaried. After an exquisitely designed measure of dallying, the *presto con fuoco* erupts passionately and noisily, only to slide back to the opening at *Tempo I*. There are *strettos* and other developmental incidents before a *crescendo-fortissimo* passage in chords again produces the *presto con fuoco*. The right hand settles into a reiterated figure like an expanded double trill, while the left, *marcato*, marks a variation on the first melody. Four trilled octaves open into A minor, an *agitato* section of intense transitional interest, a repetition of the *presto con fuoco* idea, a tiny return of the *Tempo I* section — now also in A minor — and the close of the piece. A harmonically notable chord is the one that immediately precedes the final *Tempo I*. The key is A minor, and the

[1] The willis are the ghostly maidens to be seen in the ballet *Giselle* or Puccini's first opera, *Le Villi*.

chord is made up of F, A, B, and D sharp, forming the so-called "French" form of the chord of the augmented sixth. Chopin did not make much use of this chord, which here arises naturally out of what has preceded it. It has the interesting effect, since it moves very easily into the tonic triad (of which, however, it contains only the tonic A), of freighting the A octaves that follow it with an aroma of the missing C and E. This makes the first appearance of those notes, two measures later, seem like the fulfillment of an implied demand.

Enormously more accomplished and satisfying than the G-minor Ballade, the F-major, rich in itself, shows Chopin on the road to using this seminarrative form as the vehicle of some of his richest thoughts. Its promise was to be carried out with magisterial certainty in its two successors, the A-flat major and F-minor Ballades.

Opus 39

Scherzo in C-sharp minor

The C-sharp minor Scherzo was begun in Majorca and completed at Nohant in the summer of 1839. It was published late in 1840 by Troupenas et Compagnie and Breitkopf & Härtel. It is dedicated to Chopin's favorite pupil, Adolf Gutmann.

When Ignaz Moscheles called on Chopin in Paris in 1839, he heard at least two large manuscript works performed — the B-flat minor Sonata and the C-sharp minor Scherzo. Chopin himself played the Sonata for his noted guest, but he entrusted the more physically demanding Scherzo to the large-handed and massively built Gutmann, then about twenty years old. Wilhelm von Lenz later wrote that Chopin decided to dedicate the Scherzo to Gutmann because that "giant" could "punch a hole through the table" with the *forte* left-hand chords in measures 6 and 7. Lenz is a reliable witness, and this testimony should dispose of the ridiculous belief that Chopin wished all of his music to be played in the *pianissimo, piano,* and *mezzoforte* realms to which he himself was confined by illness and lack of muscular development.

The *presto con fuoco* introduction to the C-sharp minor Scherzo presents another example of Chopin's acquired mastery over beginnings. Its whole purpose (aside, as Gerald Abraham pointed out, from placing a "tonal curtain" before the piece) is to interest the listener and arouse large expectations. It achieves this purpose flawlessly, preparing for the size and general nature of what follows. The first main melody arrives *risoluto*. It is vigorous in its octave figures, and it is lengthened and commented upon with firm, undeviating grasp. The second section, in D-flat major, is an adventure in contrasts, and is surely derived from Bach's treatment of chorales.[1] It alternates sections of a beautiful chorale-like melody with falling sprays of rapid, broken chords. It has a middle section in arpeggios, and is then altered somewhat as it returns to the first chief section in octaves. The structure is complex in an impromptu- or caprice-like manner (it has not, for example, a trio in the exact sense) in which nothing is excessive, nothing boring. Apt detail is added to apt detail, and it all ends, not in C-sharp minor, but in what sounds like the enharmonic D-flat major, here written as that rare key, C-sharp major. Only by the limitation of scope imposed by its melodic materials does the C-sharp minor Scherzo stand somewhat below the B-flat minor and considerably below the E-major. It is, nonetheless, one of Chopin's unflawed successes.

Opus 40

Two Polonaises

The A-major Polonaise ("*Militaire*") was composed in Paris in 1838, and originally bore a dedication to Tytus Voitsyekhovski. The C-minor Polonaise was probably begun in Paris, but was completed in Majorca in 1839. Combined as opus 40, the two were issued by Troupenas et Compagnie and Breitkopf & Härtel late in 1840. As published, the opus was dedicated to another of Chopin's Polish friends, his longtime Paris factotum — and later his unwise and unofficial musical executor — Yulyan Fontana.

Until recent years the most popular of the Polonaises (a position now temporarily occupied by the A-flat major, opus 53), the "*Polonaise Militaire*" was the first Polonaise of Chopin's maturity

[1] Chopin passed part of his time at Valdemosa trying to remove editorial changes and additions from the volumes of Bach that he had brought with him from Paris.

to be in a major key. It is the most brilliant, most frank, and most flaunting of his treatments of Polish materials. It is a very noisy piece, shot through with pomp, pride, and male assertiveness. Its powerful rhythms and simple harmonies give it a pervading glitter that is quite irresistible. To say that it lacks subtlety or secondary significance is merely to say that it is this Polonaise and not another. Its design is square and simple. A coda would have been superfluous and oversophisticated, and so it has none. No wonder that Liszt loved to play it! It is music only the piano can produce.[1] No Poland of tragedy here, but a Poland of well-fed, magnificently dressed, and unquestioningly self-assured young aristocrats enjoying themselves with no thought of tomorrow — with, in fact, no thought at all.

Worlds away is the second, C-minor Polonaise of opus 40. Gloom, struggle, and tragedy are its atmospheres, and its wayward harmonic shiftings almost shatter its continuity. The lordly dance melody introduced by the left hand in the third measure is one of Chopin's most elegant and dark,[2] but the Polonaise as a whole fails to measure up to it. Here the listening mind is awakened to anticipation of something more than — or, at least, something different from — the quite unpolonaiselike variation or development that follows. The most interesting portion of the C-minor is its ending, the last eighteen measures. The opening melody is repeated almost intact. But to the first four measures the right hand adds a moaning, contrapuntally conceived melodic fragment that all but denatures it. Then the moaning disappears, soon enough not to become bathetic, leaving a backward-cast light over the whole piece. The closing cadence, in its relation to what has gone immediately before, is exceedingly curious. It leads properly to a tonic C-minor chord. But who can hear this

---

[1] Numerous orchestrations and transcriptions exist to prove this statement.
[2] But is it originally Chopin's? For Alexander I, visiting Warsaw, Karl Kasimir Kurpinski composed a polonaise with words ("Be thou welcome, O King") that begins as follows:

Alexander I died in 1825, and Chopin's opus 40, no. 2, was not composed until fourteen years later.

without a half-conscious feeling that what is about to happen, but never does, is a further step to a tonic G-major chord? Deliberate or accidental, this is an effect of sorcery.

Opus 41

Four Mazurkas

"You know that I have four new mazurkas," Chopin wrote to Fontana from Nohant in August 1839, "one, E minor, from Palma, three written here, B major, A-flat major, and C-sharp minor; they seem good to me, as younger children always do to parents growing old." All four, then, were composed in 1838–9. The opus was published in December 1840 by both Breitkopf & Härtel and Troupenas. It is dedicated to Étienne (really Stefan) Vitvitski. About ten years older than Chopin, this poet of Polish countrysides was his close friend in both Warsaw and Paris. Several of the Seventeen Polish Songs of Chopin's posthumous opus 74 are settings of verses by Vitvitski.

Keeping its Slavic pungency [1] for today's ears is the C-sharp minor Mazurka, first and finest of the four in opus 41. It is elaborately constructed, and its structure is proportioned with entire success. It has a brilliantly invented coda (final twenty-one measures), in which a clangorous version in octave chords of the opening theme is followed by a *piano-pianissimo-smorzando* variation on a harmonic-rhythmic pattern found, in slightly different form, in the subsidiary sections of the two larger divisions of the piece proper. Thus the pattern is closed as happily as opened, to the listener's gratification.

The manuscript of the E-minor Mazurka was dated at Palma on November 28, 1838. Less interesting than the C-sharp minor, the E minor lays less claim to interest. It has the seemingly persuasive wrong convictions of a neurotic, and is more pleasant to play than to hear played. Here, as in the C-sharp minor, an exotic effect is declared by consistent flattening of the second note of the key scale: the expected F sharp is constantly an F natural.

The title that Rossini gave to one of his piano pieces, "Miscar-

[1] The source and potency of this pungency can be isolated. Play the first four measures with B and D both sharpened.

riage of a Polish Mazurka," would have suited the B-major, third, Mazurka of opus 41. Ponderous, lacking appeal to a deadening degree, it begins awkwardly, ends foolishly, accomplishes little along the way.

A slim waltz lost among mazurkas is the A-flat major, fourth in this set. Its ending — an unadorned breaking-off in the middle of an idea from its second section — is apt and witty. But its totality has prettiness only, and the impression it leaves is footling. In this opus, for once, that is to say, Chopin won his victories at the beginning and retreated later.

Opus 42

Waltz in A-flat major

The Waltz in A-flat major, opus 42, was composed in 1840, and was published without dedication in July of that year by Breitkopf & Härtel. Later it was issued by Antonio Francesco Gaetano Pacini of Paris.

In reality a potpourri of, or free fantasy on, waltz melodies, the A-flat major is held together very loosely by recurrences of the chief melodies and by constant reappearances of the promenadelike interlude first introduced at measure 41, a device very like that used by Schumann in *Carnaval.* The Waltz opens in the manner of several pieces by the Johann Strausses, father and son. It is certain that Chopin was familiar with waltzes by the elder Strauss, and by 1840 he could have heard early works by the younger. Here is that Straussian cliché, the prolonged trill (eight measures) into which the accompaniment finally inserts rhythmic outlines. The first melody, *leggiero,* with its most important notes the first and fourth of each measure, supplies cross-rhythms to the unvarying one-two-three beat of the left hand. The promenade follows, and is succeeded by a second melody lasting almost sixteen measures. Again the promenade, for another sixteen.

The third sixteen-measure chief section is built on a most dashing melody of superbly danceable rhythm. The promenade again, in its unvaried sixteen-measure length. At *sostenuto* the tensile brilliance is dimmed in favor of a gentle, pensive melancholy. And this time Chopin expands for forty-four measures before bringing in once again the promenade passage, by now a weak prop for the structure, suggesting, as it must, not so much unity as monomania. At last the opening, cross-rhythmed section repeats with a new close that inevitably conducts us to the fifth appearance of the promenade, this time considerably altered. Now the third chief section is repeated, also much changed. It works up, through four measures of an upward-moving, scalelike passage, to a *crescendo* and a large climax. The last, beneficently the last, repetition of the promenade then leads into the coda, marked *accelerando, forte,* and *crescendo.* This is based on the opening melody, here treated so as to recall the upward-downward motion of the promenade. The close is passably apt.

The pattern of this Waltz might be represented as ABCBDBE-BABCBA(B). On paper, in the mind, or as used with other musical ideas, this pattern may succeed in producing a unified musical fabric. But the A-flat major Waltz is too long for the power of its melodies and for their treatment, and the pattern is meaningless for them. It is, of course, possible to succumb to such charm as the materials have in themselves, and thus to avoid listening for a formal satisfaction that the piece quite fails to supply.

Opus 43

Tarantelle in A-flat major

Chopin's Tarantelle in A-flat major — the title, like those of the Barcarolle, Berceuse, and Boléro, is unique among his compositions — was composed at Nohant in 1841. From there he wrote Yulyan Fontana as follows:

I send you the tarantella. Be kind and copy it out; but first go to Schlesinger or, better, Troupenas, and look at the collection of Rossini's songs edited by Troupenas, in which there is a Tarantella (in F). I don't know whether it is written in $\frac{6}{8}$ or $\frac{12}{8}$. People write both ways, but I should like mine to be the way Rossini has it. So *if* it's $\frac{12}{8}$ or common time with triplets, make one measure of two when you copy. You understand, my dear. It will be

I beg you also to write it all out instead of giving repeat signs. Be quick and give it to Léo with my letter to Schubert[h]. You know that he leaves for Hamburg before the eighth of next month, and I don't want to lose the 500 francs. As for Troupenas, you have time. And if my manuscript is not metrically correct, don't give it to him, but copy it out again and also make a third copy for Wessel. It's a bore for you to copy the beastly thing, but I hope that it will be a long time before I write anything worse. So please look at the number of the last work — that is, the number of the last mazurkas, or perhaps the waltz that Pacini brought out, and give the tarantella the next number.

The piece was published by Troupenas in the autumn of 1841. It was also made ready for publication late in 1841 by J. Schuberth of Hamburg, who advertised it as for sale on New Year's Day 1842.

As Chopin himself hinted at the possibility, it is unnecessary to insist that his unattractive Tarantelle is heavily in debt to Rossini's *"La Danza,"* musically its superior in every detail. Chopin's second-hand version of the furious Neapolitan dance is well written for the piano, but it tends to weary rather than enliven, and it lacks definite profile or structural interest. It is at least probable that Chopin wrote frankly rather than coyly to Fontana, and that he composed the thankless piece entirely to earn the five hundred francs from Schuberth. Certainly the Tarantelle stays among the least heard of his works.

Opus 44

Polonaise in F-sharp minor

It was during 1840–1 that Chopin composed the fifth of his published Polonaises, in F-sharp minor. It was issued on November 28, 1841 by Pietro Mechetti of Vienna and at about the same time by Schlesinger. Mechetti, whom Chopin had known in Vienna, had published his opus 3 eight years before; Schlesinger was again publishing Chopin after about three years. The Polonaise is dedicated to Princesse Charles de Beauvau, a sister of Delphine Pototska. She had been his pupil, and was to remain his faithful friend during his final illness.

On August 24 or 25, 1841 Chopin wrote to Fontana: "Offer him

[Mechetti] a new manuscript (a sort of polonaise, but it's more a fantasia)." The date makes almost certain that this refers to the F-sharp minor Polonaise — which, further, is "more a fantasia" because there is set into it a full-fledged mazurka. Chopin's phrasing suggests that he was perhaps beginning to be somewhat disinterested in the polonaise form and was searching for a way to expand or vary its naturally rather square outlines. He was, in fact, to compose only one more strict Polonaise — the great A-flat major of opus 53 — and within five years he was to publish a piece entitled Polonaise-Fantaisie.

The F-sharp minor Polonaise, nearly twice as long as any earlier example, is one of Chopin's most original conceptions, formally speaking, and one of his mighty successes. Eight measures of introductory material, moving rapidly from a calm *piano* to a furious, stentorian *fortissimo*, exactly prefigure the large scope of the piece. The long, wavering line of the principal polonaise melody further heightens the auditor's sense of potential extension. The succeeding eight measures, in B-flat minor and A-flat major, serve perfectly the intention served badly by the promenade passages in the A-flat major Waltz, opus 42. They provide a firm platform of repose, structurally viewed, though in volume and emotional import they are agitated. Next, after being presented in a harmonically thickened form, the wavering first melody, still in the original key, is set out in octave chords with an upward-sweeping decoration in the left-hand accompaniment. After eighteen measures of development this section leads into four excellently planned and placed measures of transition.

This transition broadens into one of Chopin's wholly original conceptions, a marchlike melody in which groups of four thirty-second-notes serve the emotion-tautening purpose of drum snares. Excellently played, this passage can be one of the most affecting in music. The punctuality of genius at its keenest brings into the midst of this relentless rhythm an eight-measure appearance of the melody first heard in B-flat minor and A-flat major, now in C-sharp minor and B major. Then the inexorable march dies away, *poco a poco diminuendo*, but still rhythmically insistent, to the *doppio movimento*, a mazurka in A major.

The mazurka is given a character of wishless melancholy by the constant downward tendency of its melodic figures, the first

of which seems to have a subtle, integrating resemblance to component parts of the opening melody of the Polonaise proper:

Chopin was to put this deliberate similarity to magical use. The
eighteen transitional measures that close the mazurka, before the
return of the polonaise materials (*Tempo I. — di polacca*), weave
together fragments that might come from either — and a clear
quotation of the introduction — with such deftness as to tighten
musical and structural interest, producing a transitional passage
that only an intellectually musical mind could have evolved.[1]

Notice what Chopin does to bring his already extended piece
to a well-proportioned and timely close. Using the figures of the
introduction, he contrives their effect in six instead of eight measures, and follows them with the first chief melody — not in its
original dress, but as first repeated in octave chords. The interval
in B-flat minor and A major is reiterated intact, as is the section
in which the first chief melody was originally presented with upward-sweeping decoration in the left hand — for seventeen measures, or long enough to re-establish its primacy and bring the
arched fabric of the whole composition to rest comfortably on the
ground again. The final sixteen measures, *stretto,* constitute a
coda that descends, *ritenuto, diminuendo, pianissimo,* to skele-
tonic rhythmic recollections of bustle and activity. The whole is
abruptly concluded by a *fortissimo* F-sharp octave. G C. Ashton
Jonson took that octave for a "convulsive shudder," but it sounds
more like an uncontrollable shout of well-earned triumph.

Opus 45

Prélude in C-sharp minor

Like the F-sharp minor Polonaise, opus 44, the single Prélude in
C-sharp minor, opus 45, was published in Vienna by Mechetti on

---

[1] It would undoubtedly repay pianists to study these measures, the *fortissimo* passages excepted, one hand at a time with the closest attention. Nothing by way of untoward accenting should point at the superior carpentry of
the joining, but awareness of that joining is essential.

November 28, 1841, and at about the same time by Schlesinger
in Paris. It was composed at Nohant in 1841, and is dedicated to
Princess Elisabeth Czernicheff, for the proper spelling of whose
name Chopin appealed by letter to Fontana. In that letter Chopin stated that he had composed the Prélude expressly for Schlesinger, who "ought to give me 300 francs for it, don't you think?"
He stated that it was short and "well modulated" — an un-
derstatement, for the piece has the greatest difficulty in remaining in one key long enough to establish its color in the listener's
mind.

Although composed three years after the latest Prélude of opus
28, this one in C-sharp minor is inferior to most of the earlier ones.
It is sentimentalized harmonically in a fashion that was to become
familiar in some of the piano music of Brahms, and even more
familiar in the Chopinesque early piano pieces of Alexander Skryabin. As a subject for strict academic harmonic analysis it is fascinating. But its outlines shift spinelessly, and no melodic distinction cures its harmonic feebleness. Its cadenza, daring and
successful in exploiting ups and downs moving chromatically,
belongs in a whole conception with more sharpness and dash than
this one. Its resemblance to the orchestral passage that reflects
Alberich's threat immediately before sunlight falls upon the
Rhinegold has often been remarked.

Opus 46

Allegro de Concert in A major

During 1840–1 Chopin recast as a piece for piano solo materials
he had intended, in 1832, to work into a third concerto for piano
and orchestra; they may be the same materials he had considered
even earlier for a concerto for two pianos. The resulting solo composition was published in its present form by Breitkopf & Härtel
on November 28, 1841 and shortly later by Schlesinger. It is dedicated to Chopin's pupil Friederike Müller, who became a concert
pianist of high reputation before her marriage to Johann Baptist
Streicher, the Vienna piano-manufacturer; she also assisted Mikuli
in preparing his edition of Chopin. The German composer Jean
Louis Nicodé, who knew better than Chopin what the music was

good for, twice rearranged the Allegro de Concert, once for two pianos, once for piano and orchestra, adding some seventy measures of his own invention. The piece is now all but unheard in any version whatever.

Because the strictly æsthetic musical interest of the Allegro de Concert is small, the pastime of pointing out passages that sound like full orchestra transcribed, those which resemble piano solo, and those which indicate the entrances of other instruments has often been resorted to in attempts to make it sound better than it is. The thrifty Chopin had simply allowed the late publication of early materials, thus earning some much-needed francs. The music clearly shows that it had been conceived in connection with his long-discarded intention to shine as a piano virtuoso. It might have been hard on his slender purse, but it would not have been hard on his well-earned reputation if he had decided to burn the Allegro de Concert instead.

Opus 47

Ballade in A-flat major

Chopin's third Ballade is dedicated to Mlle P. de Noailles, whom Antoine-François Marmontel, listing Chopin's pupils, called one of his *"disciples affectionnées."* It was composed during 1840–1, and was published late in 1841 by Breitkopf & Härtel, early in 1842 by Schlesinger. Like its three companions, it narrates a musical story and perhaps remotely reflects a literary story, from a poem by Mitskyevich.

The eight-measure introduction at once sets a calmly joyful mood; it ends with the first of the numerous telling silences that are a structural feature of the entire piece. The chief melody, *forte,* enters on an unchallenged statement, repeated and commented upon without rancor. After twenty-seven measures of lighthearted development, this is followed (*diminuendo*) by one transitional measure and an exact repeat of the first five measures of the introduction, which is now lengthened as leading to a chord held for two and one sixth measures. The "one sixth" is important: it supplies the rhythmic key to the F-major section that follows, for it initiates Chopin's means of throwing accents onto the third and sixth beats of each measure, with rests on the second and fifth, weak or tied notes on the first.

With subtle, light-colored harmonies the second principal melody of the Ballade is presented, pruned, expanded, repeated, and developed at length — for sixty-four measures. Then a submelody, in which the key notes are approached by upward appoggiaturas, makes its graceful entrance, soon deliquescing in cascadelike runs. Trills on four ascending notes lead to the one deeply dramatic (*sostenuto*) incident. But this is no tragedy, and in nine measures' time we are back at the rocking figure in broken octaves that can reintroduce the luscious melody in cross-rhythms. When the key changes to C-sharp minor it momentarily seems that tragedy may after all darken a halcyon day, but quickly the right hand enters upon a rapid series of ninety-six G sharps, while the left prepares for excitement that suggests hilarity. The right-hand accompaniment becomes more and more brilliant, and then recedes to an eighth rest.

Now the left hand, using mostly B's, mocks the pattern of those repeated G sharps and their enlargement, while the right pounds a repeated B with an A-sharp appoggiatura. The rocking, off-beat rhythm reappears; so (*sotto voce*) does a semblance of the introduction. The transition back to A-flat major is neatly achieved — and Chopin begins one of the most glorious of his fine codas. This one is a pæan of satisfaction in achievement; it is vigorous, young, and blazingly happy. Nowhere is Chopin less a "sickroom talent," less neurasthenic or sickly. At the *stretto*, in fact, the heavy *crescendo* chords, inching upward again in chromatics, pass almost from coherence to ecstasy. But a clear mind is in control, and the *più mosso* close is the most satisfying of structural capstones.

Nowhere marred by a formal flaw, quite free of sentimentality (except as sentimentality is applied to it by wrongheaded performance), and airily solid, the A-flat major Ballade is one of Chopin's masterpieces. Of more ambivalent materials, of richer and more various means, he was still to make greater music. Nothing else he composed has the special quality of exultance, of radiant jubilation that makes this Ballade seem to glow upon the piano.

Opus 48

Two Nocturnes

In Wilhelm von Lenz's memoirs the following passage describes his waiting in the anteroom of Chopin's Paris quarters:

I always made my appearance long before the hour of my appointment, and waited. Ladies came out, one after another, each more beautiful than the others. On one occasion there was Mlle Laura Duperré, daughter of the admiral,[1] whom Chopin accompanied to the head of the stairs. She was the most beautiful of all, and as slender as a palm tree. To her Chopin has dedicated two of his most important Nocturnes (in C minor and F-sharp minor, opus 48); she was his favorite pupil at the time.

The two Nocturnes, composed in 1841, were published late in that year by Schlesinger and in January 1842 by Breitkopf & Härtel.

The C-minor Nocturne is Chopin's major effort in that genre. So big, so varied, and so narrative-seeming a piece would not, in fact, have been appreciably misplaced as a fifth ballade. Plunging into mid-career in its very first measure, it varies a single melodic pattern for a little more than twenty-three measures by way of subtle rhythmic accents, ornaments, and slight harmonic shifts. Then it dies away easily to an episode marked *poco più lento — sotto voce*. Here a melody suggesting refined pomps is presented in C major, working up through passages in double-octave triplets to a vaunting grandeur. This in turn subsides, in its twenty-fourth measure, to a *piano* marked *accelerando*, and C minor returns in the *doppio movimento*.

And here is one of Chopin's great compositional triumphs. Continuing the well-established triplet rhythm of the preceding section, he uses the opening melody as the basis of a section so entirely new in effect as to produce the requisite novelty, but so meshed in with what has been presented as to give the whole a structural firmness that Beethoven himself would surely have appreciated. Perhaps it is possible to listen to this *doppio movimento* without recognizing its melodic tie to the first section or

[1] Victor-Guy Duperré (1775–1846), who, with Marshal de Bourmont, commanded the French forces at the siege of Algiers in 1830.

its rhythmic continuation of the second; but not to sense in it some special justice and inevitability is impossible. This solution of a formal problem is performed with such assurance that it could be made the text of Chopin's achievement as a master of form. It begins *pianissimo agitato,* and though it includes several *crescendos* and *diminuendos,* its proper proportion is preserved only when the *fortissimo* is withheld, as Chopin intended and indicated, until its final measure — the sixth measure from the end of the piece. The rest is a superbly correct coda.

The F-sharp minor Nocturne is conceived on a smaller scale. Its constructive ideas are less attractive, and its melodic materials are not of Chopin's best. Its outlying sections in F-sharp minor and its middle section in D-flat major have no apparent organic connection, as a result of which the contrast seems to be of the wrong sort. Even extremely able pianists cannot avoid making it sound a little like one piece interrupted halfway for the interpolation of another. Why is this? The outlying sections are flowing, unresting, of a constant tonal ambiguity. Their melodies are not so much true melodies as themes on which to pivot key-colorings in a Wagnerian, sometimes almost Debussyan, way. But the middle section, *molto più lento,* is square-toed and noncommittal, an extended passage of transition from nothing to nothing. From it, also, Chopin returns to his first ideas by a peculiarly unsatisfactory and arbitrary two measures. The F-sharp minor Nocturne does not supply the C minor with a worthy partner; few of the Nocturnes could.

Opus 49

Fantaisie in F minor

The F-minor Fantaisie is not only Chopin's greatest single composition, but also the crowning formal achievement of romantic piano music. Its melodic and harmonic ingredients are so superbly imagined and so magisterially handled as to make inevitable the conclusion that in 1840–1, the years of its composition, Chopin was at the zenith of his creative dominion. These were the years of his greatest happiness in his relationship with George Sand. The Fantaisie is both inherently and actually the music of a man on whom exterior circumstance and inward need have momentarily relaxed their grip, a man able to release his energies in love and creativeness.

Only Chopin's intense observance of public propriety can have prevented him from honoring George Sand with a dedication. Alone among the names of his closest friends hers is missing from the list of his dedications. And so the name that stands with his at the top of the Fantaisie is that of Princess Catherine de Souzzo, one of his Paris pupils. The Fantaisie was published late in 1841 by Schlesinger; Breitkopf & Härtel brought it out in January 1842.

Marked *tempo di marcia,* the Fantaisie opens with as much provocative, forward-tending interest as the B-flat minor Scherzo. The opening page is built mostly on two reciprocating melodic ideas, a two-measure phrase moving downward in open octaves (theme A1) and a chordal phrase with an upward tendency (A2). These alternate, slightly modifying their contours, for nineteen measures, whereupon a single terminal-and-transitional measure — the first in which there are chords on the four beats of the time signature and nowhere else — leads to the march itself (B). The march is unmistakably child to A1 and A2, having visible features of both. With extraordinary beauty and nice estimate of its welcome, this march stays for sixteen measures. The six closing measures of the section are, in effect, its coda, serving exquisitely to round it out, but also building a bridge to the next section. In its last two measures the bass quotes A1 in a flattened-out version that makes its introductory nature clear, as it makes clear that what is to come is certain to be different from A2.

Poco a poco doppio movimento, a new melodic idea (C) is brought forward insinuatingly. What promises to be charming passagework turns into a strophic melody capable of development. It works up to a *fortissimo* climax, only to be broken off by three descending B-flat double octaves. Rebeginning, it works more thoroughly to another *fortissimo,* which this time bursts into a lightning downward plunge from the F two octaves above the treble clef to the C in the second octave below the bass clef. Now, *agitato* and in curiously broken rhythms that include the continuous triplets of what has just passed, comes a section in which a warm single-note melody (D) expands first into thirds and then to four repeated C octaves. The triplet accompaniment, which from the inception of D has taken the form either of three rising

notes followed by a rocking on the second and third of them (1 in
the figure below) or that of three rising notes followed by three
descending (2 in the figure below), takes on a galloping form (3
in the figure).

Above figure 3 a new melodic motive (E) exfoliates plantlike
from the stem of the already growing piece, and interest is heightened by rhythms of four against two groups of three and by occasional dotted notes and rests. Eight measures of the gay E-theme
halt at a bridgelike passage (F), in which the triplets, translated
to the right hand, become a submelody closely related to section
C; this lasts for eight measures given profile by the accompaniment, in which arpeggioed chords play an important rhythmic
role. At the *forte* indication the triplets take on again the form
indicated at 1 in the figure above. The new melody insisted on
above them (G) is angry and explodes in two-measure gusts. The
first gust is followed by a two-measure development of the melody-
in-thirds from section D. When this development arrives the second time, it extends through a climax worked up to *fortissimo.*

Now (H) comes a passionate outburst not quite eight measures
long, in which the top notes of a chordal melody are constantly
approached and reached by rapid passages of octaves in counter-
motion. In the eighth measure the melody thins to a mere outline
of itself, and at the twelfth the rhythm of the countermoving
octaves becomes an insistence on the same chord seven times repeated. This is one of Chopin's most engaging transitions, and
ends in seven successive half-note chords of purposeful harmonic
color. At the indication *piano* the second truly marchlike passage
(I) enters. This is a directionless march that turns round upon itself to suggest marching backwards or sidewise. It breaks off,
forte, at the beginning of the seventeenth measure.

At this point, then, the pattern of the structure might be indicated as A1-A2-B-A1-C-D-E-F(C)-G-D-H-I.

With the exception of one brief new section, the Fantaisie now
grows on apt, welcome, and telling variation, repetition, or de-

velopment of much already presented. First there is a twelve-measure version of C, but without the held whole-notes that had given it a strophic pattern on its first appearance. Brief reminiscences of D, E, F, and C, with C extended in length by wistful and evocative halts on broken chords, now crowd in. Three measures after the indication *slentando* the triplet figure of C becomes a continuous slope upward, *accelerando, diminuendo, calando, rallentando,* and at last (with the characteristic figure of the three descending double octaves), *pianissimo.* Now for the first time the four-flat key-signature changes (it has stood before much besides F minor!) to five sharps (B major), the time to $\frac{3}{4}$. There is a twenty-four-measure interlude of new material (J) of a nostalgic but never bathetic cast. Back to four flats — and to a crashing dissonance followed by another version of C, again ending, *fortissimo,* in the three descending octaves. D is reiterated with its chief melody in octaves. E, F, G, and H lead once more to I, now *più mosso* and *forte,* and again broken off by a loud chord.

The last repetition of the C section mounts to the A natural in the second octave above the treble clef. For three measures a cascade of downward chromatics is given shape by repeated emphasis on D natural and A flat. A bridge measure leads to a repetition of $\frac{3}{4}$ time for the two measures needed for a last brief reminder of J. There is a small cadenzalike declamation growing out of its profile. The four-beat measure reasserts itself and the development, first suggested three measures after the *slentando* that originally led to the first change in key-signature, of the triplet figure of C, now *allegro assai, crescendo, forte, diminuendo,* establishes the key of A-flat major. Two *fortissimo* whole-note chords end the Fantaisie in that key.

The entire pattern of the Fantaisie's structure might, then, be indicated as A1-A2-B-A1-C-D-E-F(C)-G-D-H-I-C-D-E-F-C-J-C-D-E-F-G-H-I-C-J-C. Once the C section is presented, that is, the A and B materials are never reintroduced. C, however, appears in one form or another seven times, D four times, E three times, F (which is intimately related to C) three times, and the other sections only twice. The B section, which on its first projection might have seemed likely to be the chief material of the piece, never reappears at all!

And the point of this structural pattern is not that it can be taken from the Fantaisie to be applied to the building of another composition. It is that Chopin worked it out with piercing intellection to satisfy the demands and possibilities of his material. Not by stretching and contracting his musical ideas to fit an established form did he create this wonderful piece, but by performing with entire success the effort of creating a unique pattern suitable to his own unique materials.

Opus 50

Three Mazurkas

Chopin's opus 50 is dedicated to his friend Leon Shmitkovski, who, having played an active part in the insurrection of 1831, took refuge in Paris. In September 1833, writing to Franchomme from Paris, Chopin ended a letter: "Hoffmann, the corpulent Hoffmann,[1] and the slender Shmitkovski also embrace you." In 1841, too, Ludvika Yedzheyevich mentioned Shmitkovski in a letter. According to Ludwik Bronarski, Shmitkovski, taking part in the 1848 insurrection in Posnan, died there.

Composed in 1841, the three Mazurkas of opus 50 were probably published on November 28, 1841 by Schlesinger, though the edition may have been delayed; Mechetti issued them in September 1842.

Turning the pages of a collection of Chopin's Mazurkas and happening upon the G major of opus 50 immediately after the A-flat major of opus 41 is like going from a Paris ballroom of Louis-Philippe's time back to the villages of Mazovia. For here the dance is again close to the folk-feeling. In such passages as the following, the Slavic Chopin predominates:

[1] This was probably Charles Alexander Hoffmann (or Hofman), husband of Klementina Tanska.

Otherwise the G-major Mazurka is a light-colored and charming piece without incisive character.

No folk music is the second, A-flat major, Mazurka, which is clearly a stately dance of countesses and uniformed officers. It is marked by great rhythmic elegance and a melodic manner of uninterrupted superficiality. Its outlying sections are excelled in interest by its trio — in D-flat major and B-flat minor — which, once saved by neat interpretation from the monotony of its unvarying rhythm, is insinuating and attractive.

A giant among the Mazurkas is the third of this set, in C-sharp minor. Its more earnest and serious character is established in its fine sixteen-measure introduction, in which canonic imitation produces Chopinesque harmonic flavors. This is followed by a remarkable twenty-eight measure section in which a brash rhythmic opening gradually gives way to more gentle moods. Interest mounts by means of a section in which approximate monotony is turned to fascination by small mutations. On a large scale, the C-sharp minor has a veritable development portion in lieu of a small coda. The combining of melodies in almost Bach-like counterpoint is repeated, and the Mazurka ends as a particularly graceful arch achieves completion on three *fortissimo* open octaves. This is altogether Chopin: no one could think of it as either folk music or a salon dance in folklike terms.

Opus 51

Impromptu in G-flat major

Composed in 1842, the "Allegro vivace — Third Impromptu, in G-flat major," was published in February 1843 by Friedrich Hofmeister of Leipzig, on July 9 of the same year by Schlesinger. It is dedicated to a Countess Esterházy, one of Chopin's pupils.

This is salon music with a slight difference. It aims at nothing more complex or — for Chopin — more difficult than charm. But it does not mistake free banality for charm, and its nuances of rhythm and, even more, of harmony are legion. It flows, not in strophes or stanzas, but like a stream slowed by curves, in which it momentarily deepens. Despite this accomplishment, it presents itself, structurally speaking, with rather too much rigidity, and inspires little reply because it speaks its little too flatly. The G-flat major is the least heard of the four Impromptus, and with good reason.

The skittish single-note melody with which the G-flat major Impromptu opens bears a curious generic resemblance to the more clear-profiled melody that opens the A-flat major and to its sister, the opening melody of the Fantaisie-Impromptu. This suggests that Chopin sensed a certain melodic character to be native to the impromptu. Only the F-sharp major, the most definite and accomplished of the four, avoids this rippling indication in its opening. Even the F-sharp major, however, comes to it in the section following the curious passage in F major.

Opus 52

Ballade in F minor

To the key of the great Fantaisie in F minor Chopin returned for the fourth, last, and best of his Ballades. This magnificent narration was composed at Nohant in the summer of 1842 (George Sand and Delacroix may well have been the first to hear it). Dedicated to Baroness C. de Rothschild, it was issued by Breitkopf & Härtel in February 1843, by Schlesinger on December 24 of that year.

Although it has three chief themes — for that of the introduction cannot be called less — the F-minor Ballade, a longish piece, has the monolithic sort of unity more often possible to a short piece with only one theme. Its sad, even hopeless tone is relieved from lachrymosity and self-pity by its unceasing effort and enormous vigor. It begins with a suggestively quiet seven-measure introduction. This melody is to be heard again and is no mere harmonic or rhythmic gateway to the main body of the Ballade.

At the indication *a tempo* the principal melody is brought forward, running a little over four measures. This is then repeated at various altitudes and in varying harmonies, with touches of canonic imitation and with some tentative production of submelodies. A long *crescendo* rises to a *fortissimo* climax, followed by a breakdown into semimelodic figurations, with the successive indications *in tempo, diminuendo, accelerando, leggieramente,* and

ritenuto. This brings the first exploration of the principal melody
to an end after more than seventy measures. Now, *in tempo* again,
the secondary or countermelody is brought forward. This rightly
lacks the sharply defined profile of the principal melody — which,
not to be stilled entirely, is briefly echoed in the tenor-voice
eighth-notes of the following measure:

Not more than nineteen measures are allotted to establishing
the character of this countermelody, which through a *ritardando*
enters its period of exploration at the indication *a tempo.* This
section is much shorter than the exploration of the principal melody: not quite thirty measures as against nearly seventy-three.
This second developmental passage also finds a *ritardando;* then
a *diminuendo* leads to the reappearance of the original introduction, much changed, and now bursting, after a held chord, into a
showerlike cadenza. It is the principal melody that is now re-established and redeveloped, first by canonic imitation and then by
the application of rapid scalelike passages having the effect of
fioriture. Only after thirty-four measures of this further searching
of the principal melody does the countermelody reappear (D-flat
major) in its strongest, most sharply outlined avatar. Twenty-two
measures suffice for the conviction of its power.

A slack composer might well, at this point, have again made
reference to the introduction. Not Chopin, however, sensitive to
its limitations and to the present necessity of being on time. He
inserts a twenty-measure transition of broken chords and whole
chords. This closes, *pianissimo,* on a long-held C-major chord and
a pause. Punctuality satisfied, Chopin then erupts into the most
astonishing of his passionate codas, which here is nothing less
than an entirely new incarnation of his principal melody. Everything latent in, or established as possible by, what has gone before is here flung, under pressure but with unyielding control, at
the listener. Progressively, the Ballade increases its stature almost

to the last measure. What had set forth on this magnificent journey calmly in the dominant of F major blazes to a swift, thunderous close in F minor.

As demonstrating Chopin's organizational powers, the F-minor Ballade stands only a little below the Fantaisie, and that little because the complexity of materials is greater in the Fantaisie and is conquered with equal success.

Opus 53

Polonaise in A-flat major

A phenomenon of recent years, caused entirely by a movie, has been the suddenly increased popularity of Chopin's sixth published Polonaise, the crushingly difficult A-flat major. José Iturbi's brash, insensitive performance of this flashy and vital piece in the "Chopin picture," *A Song to Remember,* was at once taken to the hearts of thousands of people who had otherwise only a remote — and either awed or disdainful — interest in serious music. Record shops were besieged by eager customers who asked for "Iturbi's Polonaise," and the sales of recordings of the A-flat major by Iturbi and other pianists became huge. That this particular Polonaise should thus be singled out for swiftly increased fame more or less as Chopin composed it was noteworthy. Some years earlier, its chief melody had achieved a perhaps even wider dispersion as adapted in a song entitled "Cheek to Cheek." And it is a moot question whether what led otherwise unmusical people to a sudden passion for the A-flat major Polonaise was their recognition backwards of that chief melody as a popular song only recently forgotten.

Karasowski stated, on what authority he does not reveal, that this Polonaise was composed in 1840 after Chopin's return from Majorca. This is unlikely to be true, and it seems actually to have been composed in 1842, along with the G-flat major Impromptu, the F-minor Ballade, and the Scherzo in E major. It was published in December 1843 by Breitkopf & Härtel and Schlesinger, and is dedicated to Chopin's maligned and useful banker friend, Auguste Léo.

Marked *maestoso,* the A-flat major Polonaise is now universally played too fast. It can be made to sound fiendishly brilliant by too fast a tempo — in which it loses, not everything, but only what is best in it. It begins with one of Chopin's masterly settings of the stage, a sixteen-measure introduction of rhythmic and harmonic harshness and some violence. Here the groups of seven chromatically rising sixteenth-note chords (in measures 1, 5, and 9) establish a phrase-pattern that Chopin uses as one of the means of unifying the whole. At measure 17 the first principal melody is begun. It consists of a three-measure statement, one transitional measure, the three-measure statement repeated a half tone higher, and two semimelodic measures of partly transitional nature.

If the Polonaise's sixteen-measure introduction be denoted as A, and the eight-measure presentation of the first chief melody as B, then the succeeding five measures could be C, the second melody, derived from B, but of less importance. This section leads via a swift rising-scale passage in octaves and two bridgelike measures to a complete re-presentation of everything but A, all of it intensified. This time the terminal scale, rushing up more than four octaves, breaks into ten measures of episodic, fragmented material directly derived from what has already occurred. Of these the third and fourth, seventh and eighth measures (D) present a rhythmically and harmonically interesting figure that distills the most obvious polonaise characteristics.

At the indication *sostenuto* the second chief melody (E) is introduced for eight measures strongly reminiscent of the thundering D-major melody of the *"Militaire."* On the third beat of the eighth measure Chopin reintroduces the rising-scale passage, this time in single notes spread over only one note more than an octave. This leads to another presentation, in sixteen measures, of B, complete with both its transitional or submelodic passages. In the fourteenth measure the rising scale in octaves is repeated intact, as are the two measures that originally followed its second appearance.

To this point, then, just before the change to E major, the pattern could be indicated as ABCBCDEBC.

The famous middle section (F) of whirling left-hand octaves follows, and has in reality two introductions. The first consists of two measures of arpeggiated quarter-note chords firmly establishing the key of E major. The second brings forward the *ostinato* octaves, four descending sixteenth-notes to a beat, and also lasts for two measures. Then, *sotto voce,* the new melody is spoken above an unrelenting continuation of the rotating octaves. This increases in urgency and volume for twelve measures, at which point Chopin adroitly changes the key to D-sharp major for three measures. The following measure recalls the rolled chords that originally introduced this middle section; it uses the tonic D sharp as the dominant seventh of E major, thus moving to four measures reproducing that double introduction in its original key.

Now the F section is repeated intact, except that the last measure is cut in half. Its second half, the key-signature having returned to A-flat major, serves to begin the introduction to the G section, an introduction that extends through the following measure. The actual melody of G occupies the next eight measures, the last of which, in turn, serves as a bridge to H, a twenty-six-measure passage of semimelodic runs. H begins *piano* and proceeds through a *diminuendo* and a *smorzando,* but it is highlighted by numerous *sforzatos.*

To this point, then, the pattern of the Polonaise could be indicated as ABCBCDEBCFGH.

With the most brilliant effect possible, B is now thundered in octaves (as on its second appearance), and is intact for fifteen measures. In the sixteenth, however, the Polonaise begins to end. Following the fourth occurence of the rising octave scale passage, the familiar first transitional measure is as before. The second, however, now consists of octave chords moving downward. Then the coda (I) begins, *sempre forte* (but not *fortissimo* until its fifth measure!), making use of wonderfully cemented fragments and echoes from earlier sections, and producing for eleven measures the most persuasive of perorations. In the fourth measure from the close the whirling left-hand octaves of F make a brief reappearance, while the final three measures subtly refer back with solidifying effect to the rolled chords that originally preceded those octaves.

The A-flat major is a long piece (among the Polonaises only the F-sharp minor and the Polonaise-Fantaisie are longer). But its over-all structure is apt, cumulative, and simple — ABCBCDEB-CFGHI — a pattern that would surely descend into the merely rhapsodic were it not for the constant reminiscences in later sections of materials from earlier ones. The piece is striped with bright color, polished surfaces, gallantry accurately and objectively presented. Little in it suggests introspection or sorrow, but much — and perhaps everything — hints at exalted anger. The temptation, therefore, is to play not only too fast but also too loud. It is a temptation often succumbed to, but the A-flat major renders all its power only in a just tempo and a wide, but certainly not a finicking, variety of volume and coloration. No match for the marvelous chiaroscuro of the F-sharp minor, this Polonaise nonetheless unmistakably belongs with what Huneker was the first to call "the greater Chopin."

Opus 54

Scherzo in E major

The last of Chopin's four Scherzos was composed in 1842. Breitkopf & Härtel and Schlesinger published it in December 1843. It is dedicated to Clotilde de Caraman, one of Chopin's pupils (and not, as Chopin himself made clear, to Mlle J. or Jeanne Caraman, as some editions still have it).

The E-major Scherzo is happiness made manifest. Less attention is demanded by happy people than by unhappy ones; often there is less to say about them. Also, there is a sense in which the sunny motion of the E-major Scherzo is aimless — by which I do not mean that it is formless, but that it seems spontaneous and lacks portentousness. Perhaps it is for these reasons that the E-major has been neglected. There is little musical cause for its relative unpopularity among its companions, for it is rich in invention, pleasant to play, and generous with intensely interesting structural and harmonic ideas. Only, it may be, it has a sameness of emotional color.

Lacking an introduction, the E-major Scherzo begins with its most important materials. Two chief melodies are presented, explored, and developed. Then the first of them is repeated and led by interesting routes to the relative minor key, C sharp, in which new material (the trio) is presented. This is followed by a repetition of the opening, two-melodied section and its development. Capping the structure brilliantly is a dashing coda. Looking at the generating ideas themselves, then — and disregarding their extensions and variants — this Scherzo is planned on the simple ABACAB-coda formula. It is not used, however, to build a composition flowing tendentiously in one direction, but is discovered to be one way of constructing a piece that may intermittently start off in pursuit of a thitherto unnoticed objective or turn aside merely to savor some fragment of melody or harmony. Its success for Chopin's purpose is beyond question.

Opus 55

Two Nocturnes

During 1843 Chopin composed the F-minor and E-flat major Nocturnes that were published, with a dedication to Jane Wilhelmina Stirling — his adoring nemesis — as his opus 55. They were issued by Breitkopf & Härtel and Schlesinger in August and September 1844, respectively.

The F-minor Nocturne is a marvel of miniature construction. The idea contained in its first measures

recurs more than a dozen times in the course of this relatively brief piece. And the simple amount of diversity injected into it without strain clarifies the meaning of a genius for composition. On the first repetition, one grace-note is added. On the second, the five melodic notes of the second complete measure become a half-note, a trilled quarter-note, two grace-notes, a dotted eighth, and a sixteenth — leading over the bar-line to a new, if fragmentary, melodic subidea. Only after this subidea is Chopin content to repeat the opening measures intact. But his new ways of seeing them are not exhausted. Perhaps the most remarkable of them all is the following, in which, as Gerald Abraham showed, notes added for decorative purposes become integral constituents of a slightly different melody:

This melodic idea and subidea, with one other idea of matched importance, supply all the subject matter of the piece as far as the *più mosso.* The middle section is more agitated, building to a climax over the impelling drive of a figure in alternated triplets and single notes. Through a notably complex and successful transition this leads back to a restatement of the opening section, which is now spoken with a brevity that gives it newness before its figured variation begins with a flourish of triplets. This becomes, in a sense, its own coda, though those who wish may regard the chords of the last four *in tempo* measures as the true coda.

There is no arguing that the musical concepts of the F-minor Nocturne came from Chopin's best store. What makes the piece successful is that they are treated at the length and in the ways that display them completely before they outstay their welcome. It is because of the nature of these materials, and not because of what Chopin did with them, that the Nocturne easily becomes hackneyed.

Simpler and less well accomplished is the second, E-flat major, Nocturne. Because it has no middle section, and is, in fact, simply one idea carried out without variation (structurally speaking), it has little formal interest. It could be likened to a simple non-repetitive song if it were not so obviously piano-created music. It is, so to speak, a nocturnelike impromptu, a studied impromptu in which all joints and links are smoothed out with miraculous artistry. The melodic periods are very long, and in a *lento sostenuto* would overtax even a well-trained singer. They do not require any sustaining of tone that the piano cannot perform perfectly. There can be little doubt, however, that, unlike its immediate predecessor, the E-flat major Nocturne is more interesting to look at or to play than to hear played. It lacks distinction and, in the final sense, character.

Opus 56

Three Mazurkas

The three Mazurkas of opus 56 were composed during 1843. Breitkopf & Härtel issued them in August 1844, Schlesinger one month later. They are dedicated to one of Chopin's pupils, Mlle C. Maberly. The keys are B major, C major, and C minor.

On a large scale are the first and third Mazurkas of this set. The first, in B major, is overlong: its thematic components are not ductile enough for so extended a fabric. Its second section, *poco più mosso,* spins arid passagework, and the entire piece lacks all pungency.

Consistently more incisive is the brief C-major Mazurka. Its first section of twenty-eight measures has a dronelike left-hand accompaniment that has two related rhythmic patterns, both in two-measure groups. The first one has beats on the first count of its first measure and the second and third counts of its second; the other has beats on the first count of the first measure and all three counts of the second. Above these the melodic right hand traces a rising and falling figure of exotic dark coloration. The middle section has highly attractive passages of canonic imitation (*legatissimo*). The ABA pattern is completed by an altered repetition of the opening. A clear intention has produced complete command of the means for carrying it out.

The C-minor, third, Mazurka of the set is big and full of technical mastery. Its harmonic movements are daring, and have often been called Wagnerian. There is, of course, no doubt that Wagner's harmonies descended in part from Chopin's, and from exactly such passages as this Mazurka contains. The Mazurka, however, presents itself better on paper than in performance, where it tends to sound deficient in character. Its improvisatory air and inconsequential manner suggest Chopin expending on rather inferior ideas more science and effort than would have been necessary if the ideas themselves had been more vivid. The result is a piece more likely to win admiration than liking.

Opus 57

Berceuse in D-flat major

Chopin's only Berceuse was composed in 1843. It was published
in May 1845 by Breitkopf & Härtel and at about the same time
by Joseph Meissonier, Chopin's publishing relations with Schlesinger having terminated. It is inscribed to one of Chopin's favorite pupils, Elise Gavard. She and her brother Charles were
among the friends who assisted him in many ways during the last
stages of his final illness.

Chopin's peculiar greatness has often been said to have arisen
from his realization of the special properties of the piano as a
sound-producing instrument. No better composition than the D-
flat major Berceuse exists in which to isolate this profound realization in action. Harmonically, melodically, and in basic rhythm
the Berceuse is fundamentally simple. Its structural harmonies
are almost wholly diatonic; it has, strictly speaking, only one melodic idea, though this is intermittently joined by a contrasting
semimelody; its controlling rhythm, set by the left hand, is established in the two-measure introduction and is never varied for
sixty-eight measures:

Above this hypnotically rocking figure — which in a cradle-
song suggests the backward-forward tilting of a cradle — Chopin
puts his quiet melody through a series of variations that flower
directly from its nature as a melody for the piano, variations that
lend it the very nature of piano music itself. Chopin had first hit
upon this idea in his opus 13, the Grand Fantasy on Polish Airs,
wherein he exploited the decoration and variation of a simple
melody played above a rocking, largely unvaried rhythmic bass.

In the Berceuse it is not only the rhythm that remains unchanging: its harmonic structure (the chord of the tonic triad for the

first three beats of each measure, that of the dominant seventh
on the second three) is altered only once, when in the two measures anticipating the final *diminuendo* the subdominant triad is
briefly heard. The piece is made continuous and continuously
interesting by means of strict pianistic manipulation of the melody, a treatment making use of grace-notes, roulades, *fioriture*,
trills, chromatically ascending and descending arabesques. It is
not composed in indicable sections, for it constitutes a lyric impulse of uninterrupted motion. As a demonstration of pianistic invention, of taste in exploiting the keyboard, it has few rivals. The
dying fall of its ending — whether or not it be intended to indicate
falling asleep — is perfect, as is the final resolution of the dotted
half-note dominant seventh chord to the tonic triad. This is sorcery, the distillation before us, from beginnings all but commonplace, of a bright fabric of piano tone as light as air and solid
enough to endure forever.

Opus 58

Sonata in B minor

During 1844 Chopin composed little. That little, however, completed at Nohant during the final summer and early autumn of his
happiness with George Sand, was the B-minor Sonata, one of his
greatest works. It was published in June 1845 by Breitkopf & Härtel and probably somewhat earlier by Joseph Meissonier, and is
dedicated to Countess E. de Perthuis, a pupil and friend of Chopin's, and wife of an aide-de-camp to Louis-Philippe, the man to
whom Chopin had dedicated the Mazurkas of opus 24.

The first movement, *allegro maestoso,* opens with a theme sufficiently broad and ample in character, sufficiently arresting in
rhythmic and harmonic implications, to serve as the opening of
a long composition. One moment's consideration of the impos-
sibility of beginning a short composition in this way will throw
light on Chopin's conception of musical architecture. Thence the
movement flings itself forward with all-but-embarrassing richness
of musical ideas. Many critics have felt that the movement is
*over*burdened with ideas, poorly constructed to support them,
but this is in part the old insistence that Chopin never learned

how to use sonata form. The movement, properly performed, sounds unitary, proceeds like the presentation, joining, and proper handling of viable musical materials. It moves. It is never clogged. It has a recognizable and satisfying pattern. I cannot detect in it any point at which the composer can justly be accused of fumbling or miscasting his subject matter, and I therefore find it a perfectly satisfactory movement.

As in the B-flat minor Sonata, the second movement is called a scherzo, this time marked *allegro vivace.* But this scherzo is brief, and has with some appositeness been called Mendelssohnian. Certainly it is lighter in texture and less like Beethoven than any other Chopin scherzo except the E-major of opus 54. As contrast to the thematic richness and the clamor of the opening movement, however, it is welcome.

The *largo* third movement is the least well conceived of the Sonata's four. Its opening section, somewhat marmoreal and funereal, harks back to the *"Marche funèbre,"* but soon gives way to a cloying section in E major, *sostenuto,* which the usually prompt Chopin permits to outstay its possibilities. Nor does the gradual improvement in timing as the movement proceeds wholly wipe out the damage of that unfortunately established sensation of imbalance. The movement has considerable beauties, but does not, as one of four, contribute well to the solidity of the Sonata.

The finale, marked *presto, non tanto,* is exorbitantly difficult to play. Its master must be not so much a virtuoso as a giant. Sixteen *forte, crescendo* chords summon him to battle. Then the indication is *agitato,* placed above one of Chopin's most beautiful and developable ideas. Countless pianists have suffered shipwreck on what follows, and their accidents have left the movement with a bad name. But it *can* be played — and without resort to deception — and therefore all criticism of it as unplayable merely assumes that everything should be playable by anyone. Nor is it difficult by intention or for mere display: its perils grow out of the sweetly reasonable treatment of pianistic conceptions. The movement cannot, unhappily, improve the *largo* retroactively, but it can — and does — rescue the Sonata, raising it back to the plane of the opening *allegro maestoso,* and then higher still. Nothing else in the corpus of Chopin's works, the F-minor Fantaisie alone excepted, is so uninterruptedly, waxingly, and unmistakably great music as this finale. In subject matter, in handling, in scope, and in sheer sonorous beauty it is one of the major musical achievements after Beethoven. It entitles Chopin to a place with all masters of imagination and form.

Opus 59

Three Mazurkas

The A-minor, A-flat major, and F-sharp minor Mazurkas of opus 59 were composed in 1845. They were published in Berlin by Stern & Co. in January 1846 and at about the same time in Paris by Schlesinger's successor, Brandus et Compagnie. They are without dedication.

The A-minor Mazurka, though interestingly made, has little vitality or allure. When, after considerable handling of other matters, the first melody is restated, it is not in the original A minor, but in G-sharp minor, and this turns out to be a happy way of extending the size of the structure. Otherwise the A-minor is scarcely one of Chopin's successes.

Hadow called the A-flat major "perhaps the most beautiful of all the Mazurkas," and certainly its melodies and harmonies are essential Chopin on a high level. Into its brief compass he has compacted an astonishing amount of poetry derived from expressive juxtapositions, harmonic vagaries, and the intertwining of motives. Few compositions are so entirely made of melody.

Very exotic-sounding and very beautiful is the larger Mazurka in F-sharp minor. Harmonically and rhythmically complex even among the Chopin Mazurkas, it has the *sound* (what matters) of means directed sharply to musical ends. It closes with a magic coda. Without pretense to serious elevation, it shows, as Huneker wrote, Chopin at "the summit of his invention."

Opus 60

Barcarolle in F-sharp major

Chopin started his only Barcarolle in 1845 and completed it at Nohant during the summer of 1846. It was issued in December of the latter year by Brandus et Compagnie, and two months later by Breitkopf & Härtel. The dedicatee is Baroness von Stockhausen, wife of the Hanoverian Ambassador to Paris; her husband had received the dedication of the G-minor Ballade.

The typical barcarolle — supposedly an adaptation of the songs of the Venetian *gondolieri* — is in $\frac{6}{8}$ time, with a strong beat on 1 and a weaker beat on 4. Chopin, however, cast his version in $\frac{12}{8}$ time, with strong beats on 1 and 7, weaker beats on 4 and 10, thus enabling himself to present the melodic overlay in a longer, more flowing line. The piece has two introductions, serving two purposes. The first three measures establish the possibility of an extended composition and hint at Italianate melodic and harmonic richness by alternating thirds and fourths with fifths and sevenths. Then there is a pause, and the accompanying left hand establishes the dominating rhythm for two measures:

In the next measure, at *cantabile*, the chief melody is introduced in thirds. It is conceived in two-measure units so artfully linked as to appear continuous. The variants through which this melody and submelodies arising out of it pass are as constantly inventive and attractive as those in the Berceuse. The use of trills and double trills is especially effective. At the indication *poco più mosso* a transitional passage four measures long wonderfully leads from the atmosphere of the first principal theme to that of the second, which is foreshadowed in the octaves that just precede the new indication of key. This second prime melody, in A major, is supported on a new rhythm in the bass, important accents now falling on the first, fourth, seventh, and tenth beats of each measure. The melody itself, with its intermittent ornamental figure of a broken chord strummed upward in sixteenth-notes, at once suggests the probability of *crescendo* and development to a climax. Presented in alternating single notes and sixths, it is restated in alternating single notes and octaves. Increasing importance is allowed to a submelody first introduced in the ninth and tenth measures of this section (last three top notes of the ninth, first top note of the tenth — F-sharp, E, F-sharp, D).

This submelody bears an intimate relation to the more important new melodic idea introduced in the *poco più mosso,* and comes into its own in the *meno mosso* interlude, a transition passage as natural as an expelled breath. At the indication *dolce sfogato,* a dallying episode is made of hints and pieces of preceding sections. The rhythm of the first section gradually reasserts itself, and at the return to F-sharp major (*tempo primo*) is defiantly asserted in octaves above which — beginning with a double trill — the *cantabile* first melody is presented in triumph. The listener is momentarily led to believe that this will be a full and climatic restatement of the first section.

By an unorthodox, self-justifying motion, however, Chopin, at the indication *più mosso,* continues with ten measures of the second melody of the second section, likewise in triumphant voice, before (again with the instruction *tempo primo*) leading his first melody into its last metamorphosis. The Barcarolle truly begins to end at this *tempo primo,* the start of a long, nostalgic peroration full of telling quotations and evocative figuration. At *leggiero,* while the right hand swims through a rippling figure of delicate sparkle, the left sounds a series of chords that mark out a new melody, one evolved from the general shape of the second theme of the second section. The termination, which may strike abruptly, immediately becomes satisfying.

Not again was Chopin to exercise with complete success the large scope that marks the design and the architectural details of the Barcarolle. It is one of his greatest victories because it gratifies as much by the logic of its design and unity as by the singular beauty of its melodic contours and their harmonic raiment. Only a very great composer could produce a piece so inevitable in its progress.

Opus 61

Polonaise-Fantaisie in A-flat major

The last of Chopin's big compositions for piano solo, composed in 1845–6, is the Polonaise-Fantaisie in A-flat major. The piece was published in the autumn of 1846 by Brandus et Compagnie, before the end of that year by Breitkopf & Härtel. It bears a dedication to Mme A. Veyret. This woman is mentioned several times, in relation to the publication of Chopin's posthumous works, by Ludvika Yedzheyevich, Yulyan Fontana, and Jane Stirling, but her exact relation to Chopin remains unclear.

Although Chopin was seriously ill by the time he completed the Polonaise-Fantaisie, this unique composition in no way indicates the senescence of his powers. Indeed, it is as certain proof as could be sought that his command of the materials he already had in hand was so final that he had begun to seek new ones. Harmonically the Polonaise-Fantaisie is the most unconventional of his compositions. Structurally it is *sui generis,* as far removed from the Polonaises of opus 26 or opus 40 as Beethoven's Ninth Symphony is from his First.

Weakness is suggested in the Polonaise-Fantaisie only by the fact that Chopin, having laid out so shiningly original a harmonic and structural plan, failed to dominate it completely, with the result that the piece, as music heard, somehow fails to satisfy completely. It produces no relaxing belief in its overall unity. Not content with the reiteration of easy success, Chopin had begun to expand and explore; the Polonaise-Fantaisie unhappily stands at the end of his great pieces for solo piano. It points toward achievements he died too soon to attempt, but it certainly promises that those achievements would have been more magnificently organized than even the most original and personal of the many large achievements already his. Over the Polonaise-Fantaisie lies the same historic glow of bright, unfulfilled promise that lights Schubert's great C-major Symphony.

The reaction of one of Chopin's foremost contemporaries to the Polonaise-Fantaisie shows how difficult a composition it was, at first, to accept. Of it Liszt wrote:

The Polonaise-Fantaisie is to be classed among the works that belong to the latest period of Chopin's compositions, all more or less marked with feverish and restless anxiety. No bold and brilliant pictures are to be found in it; the loud tramp of a cavalry used to victory is no longer heard; no more resound the heroic chants muffled by no visions of defeat, the bold tones suited to the daring of those who are always victorious. A deep sadness, broken constantly by startled movements, by sudden alarms, by disturbed rest, by stifled sighs,

reigns throughout. We are surrounded by such scenes and sensations
as might arise among those who have been surprised and surrounded
on all sides by an ambuscade, the vast sweep of whose horizon reveals
not a single reason for hope, and whose despair has giddied the brain
like a draught of that Cypriote wine which gives a more instinctive
rapidity to all our gestures, a keener point to all our words, a more
subtle flame to all our emotions, and excites the mind to a pitch of
irritability approaching madness.

Such pictures possess but little real value for art. Like all evocations
of extreme moments, of agonies, of death-rattles, of contractions of
the muscles when all elasticity is lost, where the nerves, ceasing to be
organs of the human will, reduce man to a passive victim of despair,
these serve only to torture the soul. Deplorable visions, which the
artist should admit with extreme circumspection into the graceful
circle of his charmed realm!

Commenting on part of this famous outburst, Niecks added:

Thus, although comprising thoughts that in beauty and grandeur
equal — I would almost say surpass — anything Chopin had written,
the work stands, on account of its pathological contents, outside the
sphere of art.

It is difficult, in fact it is impossible, to find in the measures of
the Polonaise-Fantaisie what Liszt found there. Niecks's findings,
on the other hand, were made in Liszt's comments rather than in
Chopin's music. Both men were reacting partly against his new
violations of convention, his refusal to do again what he had already done perfectly. With more cogency they might have reacted against his failure to do a new thing with the complete
mastery of his manipulation of earlier formal components.

As interesting as the free pattern of the Polonaise-Fantaisie are
its proportions. It contains 289 measures, which are divided into
an introduction — 23 measures and 2 of repetition, a total of 25 —
a principal theme originally presented for 42 measures, repeated
once for 24 and again for 12, thus accounting for 78; a second
theme presented for 26 measures and never repeated; a third
theme presented for 32 measures and never repeated; a fourth (or
second principal) theme (*più lento*) given in 33 measures and
repeated first for 8 measures and then, as the end of the piece, for
35, thus accounting for 76; a fifth theme presented for 26 meas-

ures, interrupted by the repetition of 8 measures of the fourth theme and by the two-measure quotation from the introduction, and then continued for 10 measures, thus accounting in itself for 36; and one purely improvisatory, transitional passage (marked *a tempo primo*) of 16 measures.

Assigning the letter A to the introduction, B to the first melody, etc., the pattern looks like this:

A — 23 measures	E — 8 measures
B — 42 measures	A — 2 measures
C — 26 measures	F — 10 measures
B — 24 measures	— 16 measures of transition
D — 32 measures	B — 12 measures
E — 33 measures	E — 35 measures
F — 26 measures	

Thus the largest spatial importance is given to the first chief theme (B):

This proves remarkably ductile and malleable. Alone among the prominent elements of the structure, it has an instantly recognizable polonaiselike cast, also asserted by the sixteenth-notes in the accompaniment (second quoted measure above).

The only comparable spatial importance is given to the *più lento* theme (E), of which I omit four introductory measures:

This is also a musical idea or group of ideas containing developmental possibilities commensurate with the emphasis put upon it. When it is repeated for eight measures, in fact, the emphasis is brilliantly shifted to the rising and falling figure of its accompaniment, which proves capable of a life of its own.

Third in the space allotted to it, — less than half that allotted to either B or E — is F:

This is closely derived from or related to B, but by its brevity and shape is clearly less suited to long comment or expansion.

It is in the 16-measure transition and what immediately follows it that the structure of the Polonaise-Fantaisie begins to sound fragmentary, loosely tied together. This fracturing lends the final transfigurings of B and E a willful and determined air. They cannot arrive as the inevitable climax that they appear, on the printed page, to assure, for they have been awkwardly and improperly prepared for. It is as though, here at the end of an otherwise wholly admirable effort, Chopin had been induced (by illness?) to relax his concentration, to force to its end what should have reached a logical conclusion in another way.

Had the Polonaise-Fantaisie been perhaps twenty-four or thirty measures shorter, or had it proceeded from the repetition of F to that of B and E by other routes, it might have won fully and without faltering the unexampled triumph that — up to the transition — it promises to win. As Chopin published it, it belongs among the flawed works to which unusual interest is lent by the very fact that, for the most part great, they are in some detail less than they should be.

Opus 62

Two Nocturnes

The B-major and E-major Nocturnes, the last published by Chopin during his lifetime, were composed in 1846. Brandus et Compagnie issued them as his opus 62 in September of that year,

Breitkopf & Härtel in December. They are dedicated to Mlle R. von Könneritz, later Mme von Heygendorf. This pupil of Chopin lent Hermann Scholtz, who prepared the Peters edition of his works, three volumes of his pieces with considerable corrections in his own handwriting.

The B-major Nocturne, which Huneker always referred to as "The Tuberose," is of some technical interest. Even when played with nice propriety, however, it is a composition to justify Chopin's mostly undeserved reputation for effete or overripe creation. Peculiarly satiated, it is not rescued from unpleasant pallor by its coloratura vocalizing or its famous — and very difficult — chains of trills. The trills all but completely disguise the principal melody when it is repeated, in shortened form, after the middle section. The whole is feverish, self-pitying, and less than ingratiating.

More vital, though not great Chopin is the second, E-major, Nocturne. Its structure is both interesting and justified. Its main theme, announced immediately, is worked over for nearly thirty measures. Then an episodic second melody is pronounced above a rapidly moving left-hand accompaniment. This extends to eight measures, when it is succeeded (*agitato*) by a middle section of some vigor. This (sixteen measures) is followed, after two transitional measures, by a restatement of the main theme, now foreshortened to twelve measures. Codalike (*a tempo*), the rapidly moving left-hand accompaniment brings back the episodic second theme for nine measures that satisfactorily complete the structural arch. Punctual as ever, Chopin then ends the Nocturne with three collapsing measures that he may have considered to be the actual coda. The pattern is thus ABCAB-coda.

Opus 63

Three Mazurkas

It was in 1846 that Chopin composed the three Mazurkas published as his opus 63 in September 1847 by Breitkopf & Härtel, on October 17 of that year by Brandus et Compagnie. The B-major, F-minor, and C-sharp minor Mazurkas are dedicated to Countess Laura Chosnovska, whom Chopin seems to have met first in Warsaw.

The B-major Mazurka, marked *vivace*, has a beautiful first section that promises a richer composition than the feeble middle section permits this one to become. The final impression is of a composition started bravely and with energy, but completed by rote and in exhaustion.

Scarcely more than an undeveloped fragment is the F-minor Mazurka. *Lento*, it glides by with aimless and purposeless melancholy.

The justification of opus 63, and one of the finest of all the Mazurkas, is the third, in C-sharp minor. Not containing many more measures than its immediate predecessor, and taking no longer to play (it is marked *allegretto*), this one contains many times as much substance. Wonderful to hear and remarkable under close examination are measures 12 to 3 from the end, which show a superbly easy command of canonic imitation as a resource of musical beauty:

Opus 64

Three Waltzes

The three Waltzes — in D-flat major, C-sharp minor, and A-flat major — that make up Chopin's opus 64 were composed in 1846

and 1847. The opus was published in September 1847 by Breitkopf & Härtel, on October 17 of that year by Brandus et Compagnie. In a usage rare with Chopin, each of the Waltzes has an
individual dedication.

To Countess Delphine Pototska is dedicated the D-flat major
("Minute") Waltz, also foolishly called the Waltz "of the Little Dog." Needless to say, this remarkable effusion of pure
charm should not be performed in one minute; nor should its re-
volving right-hand melody be played in imitation of a dog chasing its own tail, even if it be true that Chopin improvised it at
George Sand's suggestion for a dog doing just that. The pattern
of the D-flat major Waltz is of the simplest: ABCAB. In addition
to its enchantment as euphonious melody, however, it contains
many small touches of the variation that Chopin used so brilliantly
to maintain interest. One of these is the constantly fresh manner
in which its first melody, above the starkest oom-pah-pah bass,
carries accentual attention across the bar-lines.

More complex is the C-sharp minor Waltz, dedicated to Baroness Nathaniel de Rothschild. Here the pattern is ABCBAB. In a
Chopin manuscript quoted by Édouard Ganche, the first G sharp
is missing, and the Waltz begins squarely, thus:

In this manuscript, also, the C section, *più lento*, in D-flat major
is very different from the published form, and thus supplies a
sample of the ways in which Chopin polished his means and forms
before publication:

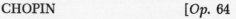

The greatly improved published version of this section points directly at the means — skillful use of ties, unusual periods of melodic phrase, use of a group of eleven notes on four beats — by which Chopin wrests rhythmic subtlety from his three-quarter time.

Dedicated to Countess Katarina Bronitska is the very elegant A-flat major Waltz. Its opening section of forty-eight measures consists of one eight-measure melodic idea (or combination of ideas) six times repeated, but repeated with such shifting harmonic coloration as to remain far from danger of monotony. The succeeding twenty-four measures contain a related submelody that, with notable sophistication, puts forth, in the sixth and second measures before the key-change to C major, the main rhythmic-melodic idea of the second chief division. This middle section holds the interest for thirty-six measures before retreating to the original key for a twenty-four measure condensation of the first section. This in turn makes way for seven measures in E major devoted to further exploration of the first melody. When A-flat major reasserts itself for the final page, it is for thirty-two measures that are not quite new material and not quite quotation from earlier passages. There is a long *accelerando,* and the last of the eight Waltzes that Chopin published flashes brightly from view.

Opus 65

Sonata in G minor for piano and cello

During 1845 and 1846 Chopin composed his only Cello Sonata. It was issued in October 1847 by both Breitkopf & Härtel and Brandus et Compagnie. Chopin dedicated this last of his large compositions to his longtime cellist friend Auguste-Joseph Franchomme, with whom he had unquestionably consulted concerning technical aspects of the cello part. He had worked on the Sonata at Nohant in the summer of 1846, but there had found progress very difficult. This slowness has often been attributed to the disheveled condition of the Sand household and to Chopin's ill health, but it is as likely to have been caused otherwise. The Sonata was a formal attempt as unprecedented as the Polonaise-Fantaisie. Also, Chopin had no cellist at hand to consult. The first public performance of the Sonata, with the opening movement omitted, was given by Franchomme and Chopin at the latter's concert of February 16, 1848. Never from that day to this has this wonderful composition had either the reception or the frequency of performance that it deserves.[1]

The first, *allegro moderato,* movement of the Sonata opens with a passage for piano alone that is reminiscent of the orchestral introductions to the two much earlier Piano Concertos:

[1] As I write, however, the Cello Sonata is being played in New York three times in three weeks by Gregor Piatigorsky, with whom I have had a graciously offered opportunity to discuss it.

Four measures later the cello enters as follows:

From this point on, Chopin develops this chief melody and other relevant materials in an unquestionable demonstration of one way to make the most of sonata form. The musical ideas are always superbly placed with reference to the capabilities and natures of the cello and the piano. A study of this movement or a careful listening to it will fully explain what Sir Donald Tovey meant when he wrote of Chopin: "Some critics would go farther, and say that he had but little talent for the sonata style; but no judge of composition would say this of Chopin's Violoncello Sonata, nor can any serious critic explain away the masterly and terse first movement of the B flat minor Sonata." The *allegro moderato* is reasonably long, but nothing in it is excessive to its well-conceived and brilliantly executed design.

The second movement of the Cello Sonata is a scherzo, the chief theme of which is immediately pronounced by the cello:

This is exploited and explored for one hundred and thirty-two measures, in the course of which such quintessentially Chopinesque figures as the following turn up in the piano part:

The key then changes to D major for a *cantabile* middle section of extraordinary romantic loveliness:

At the close of this section the melody of the scherzo proper re-appears and the key changes back to D minor for an abbreviated repetition of the opening of the movement.

The third movement is a *largo* marked *cantabile*. It is very short and somber. Introduced as follows:

the brief movement, a structural novelty of persuasive power, often recalls the trio of the *"Marche funèbre"*:

The finale of the Sonata, marked *allegro,* begins:

Like the *allegro moderato*, this finale unfolds cogently and with no sense of surplusage or strain, a magnificently achieved handling of materials according to the real sense and direction of sonata form, if not by its uncodified rules. Like the rest of the Sonata, it is grateful for the cellist, but by no means a cello solo with piano accompaniment. It serves its terminal purpose admirably.

The Cello Sonata is a saddening work, but not for reasons often cited, such as that it represents Chopin's powers in decline. All to the contrary, it is a harbinger of newly conceived compositions of large scope, an earnest of their quality. The sadness is not intrinsic, but extrinsic: Chopin was to live long enough after completing it to compose only a few comparative trifles. The magnificent Piano Sonatas, peers of the great Ballades and Scherzos, unique mates to the Berceuse and the Barcarolle — these were not to be created. And so the G-minor Cello Sonata stands, with the Polonaise-Fantaisie, at the pass into a new realm, one that, with Chopin dead, no one else could enter.

Posthumous opus 66

Fantaisie-Impromptu in C-sharp minor

In 1855 Yulyan Fontana, with the authorization of Chopin's family, proceeded, contrary to Chopin's expressed wishes, to publish several pieces that Chopin had desired destroyed after his death. These included all the opus number from 66 through 74. The composer may have had varying reasons for preferring that these works remain unpublished, but there can be little doubt that one reason was his belief that they were, at least in their existing form, below the standard of his mature compositions. In the case of the so-called Fantaisie-Impromptu, best-known of these pieces, that reason may well have been joined by another, a full realization that the piece was not entirely his own.

The Impromptu in C-sharp minor (to which the tasteless Fontana added the senseless, qualifying "Fantaisie") was probably composed in 1834. In January 1834 Chopin's opus 15 — Nocturnes in F major, F-sharp major, and G minor — had been published, and he had sent a copy of the publication to his family in Warsaw. With his own Nocturnes were included pieces by other composers.

These included variations on *"Je vends des scapulaires,"* the air from Hérold's *Ludovic* on which he himself had composed the Variations brillantes in B-flat major, opus 12, and also Ignaz Moscheles's opus 89, an Impromptu in E-flat major of which the principal theme is:

While no one can doubt the similarity of Chopin's opening theme to this one, I cannot entirely accept Arthur Hedley's belief that Chopin did not publish his Fantaisie-Impromptu because "the plagiarism would have been too obvious." There was no contemporary reason why Chopin might not have issued the piece (the superiority of which over Moscheles's he must have realized as clearly as we can) with a note acknowledging its indebtedness to the Moscheles Impromptu. It is more likely that he failed to publish the piece — which was probably fifteen years old when he died — because he considered it unsuccessful. With this opinion, whether he held it or not, it is easy to agree.

For the Fantaisie-Impromptu did not acquire its patent banality in the process of becoming hackneyed or by having the melody of its *moderato cantabile* middle section dressed up as an American popular song, "I'm Always Chasing Rainbows." It is poorly constructed on the ABA-coda pattern. The transitions from A to B and from B back to A are as unconvincing as though Fontana rather than Chopin had arranged them. The flowing, self-generating melody (Moscheles's) of the opening *allegro agitato* is pleasant enough, if rather frivolous and lightweight. But the *moderato cantabile* is both mawkish and recalcitrant to any development. Chopin soon becomes discouraged with it and limps back to the *allegro agitato*. Gerald Abraham believes that this melody "just contrives to avoid banality by the premature entry of the second four-bar clause, half a bar too soon"; he is referring to the melodic B-flat in the fourth measure of the middle section. To me, on the contrary, this "rubato of phrase conception" (Abraham's words) has a ring of false, saccharine urgency that makes the passage embarrassing. Nor am I tempted to raise my judgment of the piece as a unit when, ten measures from its ending, Chopin closes his coda with a quotation of this same insipid melody, now pulled stickily out of shape.

Posthumous opus 67

Four Mazurkas

The four Mazurkas that Fontana put together as Chopin's opus 67 cover a period of fifteen years. The first, in G major, and the third, in C major, were composed in 1835; the fourth, in A minor, was completed in 1846; the second, in G minor, belonged to 1849, the year of Chopin's death, and was probably the last but one of his compositions.

The G-major Mazurka is uninteresting. Originally inscribed to a Mlle Mlokosyevichova, it looks like a pure *pièce d'occasion*.

The G-minor Mazurka reads and sounds like a sketch. It contains good preliminary musical ideas. Had Chopin lived, he could have made it into one of the better Mazurkas by polishing and elaborating it with a care it does not, in its published form, exhibit.

The C-major Mazurka is familiar to balletomanes for its important role in *Les Sylphides*. It has considerable charm. Having stated his opening eight measures of melody with the right-hand theme in single notes, Chopin repeats it effectively for another eight in sixths and thirds (producing, in the second measure of this section an astonishing chord containing D, E, F-sharp, G, and A), and then repeats the entire sixteen measures. Then, by way of contrast, he introduces a two-measure phrase of no definite character, repeating it four times with slight variation, only to return to one repetition of his opening melody in each of its eight-measure forms. The charm of the piece, then, resides not in any formal attraction, but in the peculiarly Chopinesque profile of that six-times-repeated theme. The Mazurka was originally inscribed to a Mme Hoffmann, probably Klementina Tanska.

Most rewarding of the quartet is the A-minor Mazurka. Here the pattern has its own interest. It is ABCAB, and each section

consists of sixteen measures. The insertion of the C middle part
saves the whole from the fault of squareness. That Chopin had
already worked this material considerably is proved by the existence of a complete manuscript in a simpler and less satisfying
version. It is one of the few among the posthumous works that
Chopin himself might have been glad to publish as it now appears.

Posthumous opus 68

Four Mazurkas

Like opus 67, opus 68 is a catch-all of Mazurkas written by Chopin over a long period of years — in this case, twenty-two. The
first, in C major, and the third, in F major, were written in 1829
or 1830; the second, in A minor, dates from 1827; and the fourth,
in F minor, was composed in 1849 — on Fontana's testimony, it
was Chopin's last composition.

The C-major, first Mazurka, if it is really Chopin's — and I
should prefer to learn that it is not — is conceivably the poorest
piece of music legitimately to bear his name.

In all possible contrast, the second, A-minor, Mazurka is very
fine in every detail, a piece so expertly conceived and so wrought
of peculiarly mazurkalike and Chopinesque materials that it is
impossible to understand why Chopin himself did not publish it.
Here, as in the Rondo à la Mazurka, opus 5, dating from about
the same period, he produces unfailing magic by sharpening the
fourth degree of his scale (producing the Lydian mode). Here,
too, he rests his final chord on the unaccented second beat, by the
floating duality of this feminine cadence giving the ensuing silence a real role in the music itself. Neither the harmonies nor the
form are Chopin at his most courageous, but within these limitations the A-minor Mazurka is a perfect achievement.

The third, F-major, Mazurka is a curiously disjunctive and uneven composition. Its outer sections are unimaginative, but they
enclose a trio (*poco più vivo*) that produces an exotic effect of
some power by a drone bass with displaced accents and a skitter-
ing single-note melody making use of the sharpened fourth. This
seems to be that rarity, Chopin quoting an actual folk melody.

Fontana's footnote to the fourth, F-minor, Mazurka reads: "This

Mazurka is the last inspiration that Chopin put on paper a short time before his death; he was already too ill to try it at the piano." It is dispirited and despondent, and therefore too reasonably allows all sorts of biographical interpretation. Which is to say that it is exactly the music a novelist might have wished his protagonist to compose if that hero had been a relatively young man dying and remembering with faraway love the Poland he had once known but would never know again. Its formal facture does not display in full possession of his creative strength the man who, only three years earlier, had composed such a masterpiece as the Barcarolle.

Posthumous opus 69

Two Waltzes

The two Waltzes of opus 69 are in A-flat major — composed in 1835 — and B minor — composed in 1829.

The A-flat major Waltz is the one that Chopin wrote out as a farewell gift to Marya Vodzhinska and presented to her on September 23 or 24, 1835. It has potent attractions that would not be appreciably misplaced, triplets and all, among the Mazurkas. An interesting opportunity to watch Chopin at work improving first — or, at least, early — thoughts is provided by the existence of two distinct manuscripts of this Waltz. I append hereto excerpts from each of its principal sections as they appear in the first and second manuscripts:

OPENING MEASURES, FIRST MS.

OPENING MEASURES, SECOND MS.

OPENING MEASURES, SECOND SECTION, FIRST MS.

OPENING MEASURES, SECOND SECTION, SECOND MS.

OPENING MEASURES, THIRD SECTION, FIRST MS.

OPENING MEASURES, THIRD SECTION, SECOND MS.

TRANSITIONAL MEASURES, THIRD SECTION, FIRST MS.

TRANSITIONAL MEASURES, THIRD SECTION, SECOND MS.

It will be seen at once that both manuscripts differ from the common published version, which is almost certainly the latest and is undoubtedly the best. Camille Pleyel turned a neat phrase by referring to this Waltz as "the history of D-flat," a witticism whose relevance even a superficial glance at the music instantly confirms.

Run-of-the-mill early Chopin is the second, B-minor, Waltz, rather commonplace in melodic character except in its D-major section, very superior ballroom music of the sort that was to be the fortune of the E-flat major Waltz, opus 18. This section, again, is so different in manuscript, so lacking in the subtle highlights of its later version, that it provides clues to Chopin's working methods:

Posthumous opus 70

Three Waltzes

With his usual disregard for the dates of composition, Fontana put together in opus 70 Waltzes composed in 1835 (G-flat major), 1843 (F minor), and 1829 (D-flat major).

The G-flat major Waltz, which functions importantly in *Les Sylphides,* is all sprightliness and superficial sparkle. It is squarely constructed, having a first section of thirty-two measures, a *meno mosso* section of forty-eight measures, and (*tempo primo*) a six-teen-measure repeat of the first section. It ends suddenly without a coda. The following quotation from a manuscript version reveals a lack of almost all the bright motion of the published version. Note particularly the absence of the opening ornament and of the trill on the first D flat of the next measure. Note also the spavined effect of the sixteenth-note rests preceding the upward melodic skips:

The second, F-minor, Waltz should properly carry a dedication, for its manuscript is inscribed: *"A Mlle Elise Gavard, son vieux professeur et ami, Chopin."* It lacks all profile and distinction.

The D-flat major Waltz is the one that, in a letter dated October 3, 1829, Chopin told Tytus Voitsyekhovski he had composed that morning while thinking of Konstantsya Gladkovska. It is very carefully composed, has more solidity of structure than any other of the posthumous Waltzes. Chopin borrowed from it several ideas for later Waltzes, greatly improving them in the process. The opening measures, for example, are a tentative assault on the problem brilliantly solved in the A-flat major Waltz, opus 42 — in the remarkable cross-rhythms after the end of the introductory trill. And who can fail to recognize in

what later became

in the wholly superior Waltz in A-flat major, opus 34, no. 1?

Posthumous opus 71

Three Polonaises

The earliest of his Polonaises for solo piano that Chopin himself published dated from 1834–5. But the three Polonaises that Fontana strung together as the opus 71 are earlier, belonging respectively to 1827 (D minor), 1828 (B-flat major), and 1829 (F minor).

The D-Minor Polonaise starts like an unfledged version of the A-flat major Polonaise, opus 53. But it carries none of the intensity of that great piece. It is jerrybuilt, inclined to splay out helplessly when it should stand firm. Its composer was still trying to find himself in a form that eluded him. The piece was originally inscribed to Tytus Voitsyekhovski.

The B-flat major Polonaise shows Chopin trying to infuse a personal sort of stately melancholy into an essentially impersonal and virtuosic sort of piece. It is otherwise devoid of interest.

The F-minor Polonaise is the one that so pleased Princess Eliza Radzivil that Chopin had to send her a copy of it. That its trio in A-flat major always particularly pleased her seems to prove that she had a taste for the music of Weber. No proof beyond this Polonaise would be needed to prove that Chopin originally derived his conception of the form not from native Polish sources alone, but also from the polaccas of Weber and Polish imitations of them.

Posthumous opus 72

Nocturne in E minor; Funeral March in C minor; Three Écossaises

Fontana made a catch-all of the opus 72: it contains a group of entirely unrelated pieces.

The E-minor Nocturne was composed in 1827. It is pretty in a style that John Field managed more expertly than Chopin, but it is also thin and watery. Only as a tentative flexing of untrained muscles by a seventeen-year-old boy — in the light of history, that is — can it be found interesting.

The small C-minor Funeral March dates from 1829. The fact of its existing has been almost obliterated by the fame of the one in the B-flat minor Sonata, and it has usually been dismissed as a footling trifle. Nonetheless, it has an individual sort of luscious, marmoreal beauty, particularly in the melody of its A-flat major trio. Curiously for the ever pianistic Chopin, it sounds more like a sketch for orchestration than like music conceived for the keyboard.

The three Écossaises — in D major, G major, and D-flat major — were probably what Fontana considered the best of a larger group of them composed by Chopin as early as 1826. Despite all older statements to the contrary, the écossaise does not seem to carry any traces of Scottish origin, and Chopin's examples are no more national in character than Schubert's or Beethoven's. They have long supplied virtuoso pianists with a restful encore number, but they are musically flat, stale, and unprofitable.

Posthumous opus 73

Rondo for two pianos in C major

On December 27, 1828 Chopin wrote Tytus Voitsyekhovski that at Sanniki on September 9 of that year he had rewritten his C-major Rondo for two pianos. What he had actually done was to arrange for two pianos a Rondo he had composed earlier for piano solo. In its published form it is long and extremely wearying. It is display music, and vacuously conceived even for that purpose, being often clogged with uninteresting decoration. It belongs, with the C-minor Sonata and several of the other post-humously published pieces, to a class of music that it is impossible to love and difficult to concentrate on long enough to hear through attentively.

Posthumous opus 74

Seventeen Polish Songs

Into the last of the nine posthumous *opera* that Fontana arranged he crowded together all but two of the surviving examples of Chopin's vocal music. Two additional songs by Chopin were to be published later. Those issued in opus 74 were:

1. *Życzenie* (zhichenye, wish or desire), original in G major, to a text by Stefan Vitvitski
2. *Wiosna* (vyosna, Spring), original in G minor, to a text by Vitvitski
3. *Smutna Rzeka* (smootna rzehka, sorrowful river), original in F-sharp minor, to text by Vitvitski
4. *Hulanka* (hoolanka, revelry), original in C major, to text by Vitvitski
5. *Gdzie lubi* (gdzye looby, where [she] loves), original in A major, to text by Vitvitski
6. *Precz z moich oczu* (prech zmoikh ochoo, away from my eyes), original in A-flat major, to text by Adam Mitskyevich
7. *Poseł* (posel, almost posehw, messenger), original in D major, to text by Vitvitski
8. *Śliczny chłopiec* (slichny khlopyets, handsome lad), original in D major, to text by Bogdan Zaleski
9. *Melodya* (melodya, melody), original in E minor, to folk, anonymous, or original text
10. *Wojak* (voyak, warrior), original in A-flat major, to text by Vitvitski
11. *Dwojacki Koniec* (dvoyatski konyets, double ending), original in D minor, to text by Bogdan Zaleski
12. *Moja piesczotka* (moya pyeschotka, my sweetheart), original in G-flat major, to text by Mitskyevich
13. *Niema czego trzeba* (nyema chego tzheba, there is no reason why it must be), original in A minor, to text by Bogdan Zaleski

14. *Pierścień* (almost pyershtsyen, ring), original in E-flat major, to text by Vitvitski
15. *Narzeczony* (nazhechony, bridegroom), original in C minor, to text by Vitvitski
16. *Piosnka litewska* (pyosnka litevska, little Lithuanian song), original in F major, to text by Vitvitski
17. *Spiew grobowy* (spyev grobovy, sepulchral song), original in E-flat minor, to folk, anonymous, or original text

Handily the best-known of the seventeen is the first, often referred to as "The Maiden's Wish," and familiar in Liszt's inflated piano transcription. It is a simple, mildly charming waltz — or perhaps mazurka — consisting of an eight-measure introduction for piano, twenty-one measures for the voice, and a repetition of the introduction. Harmonically and rhythmically extremely simple, it was composed in 1829.

Dating from 1838 is the second song, sometimes called "Spring." This is singularly monotonous, consisting of a four-measure melody sung fourteen times, eleven in its original form, three in slight alteration. Further, the voice throughout doubles the melodic right hand of the piano.

The third song, commonly called "Troubled Waves," is one of three composed in 1831. It is written with some care, but tends to monotony.

Fourth, dating from 1830, is the so-called "Drinking Song" or "Bacchanal," which clearly demonstrates Chopin's small talent for the robust sort of conviviality. It is falsely bibulous and quite unconvincing. It has a four-measure introduction and a twelve-measure solo-piano interlude consisting of eight mazurkalike measures of new material and a repeat of the introduction. As an instrumental tailpiece the first eight measures of the interlude are repeated. They are far more attractive than the undistinguished melody given to the voice.

The fifth song, known as "What a young maiden loves," and composed in 1829, has considerable variety within a small structure. After four measures of solo-piano introduction come eight for the voice. These end on a pause followed by four measures marked *scherzando*, these last bringing welcome rhythmic variety. Then, *tempo primo*, come eight measures of vocal material derived from the first section, but omitting its opening four measures.

The song ends with four piano measures of closely related, but newly phrased matter.

The sixth song, composed in 1830, is sometimes called "Out of my sight" or "Out of thy presence." It is mostly a rather flat waltz-with-words, but achieves some poignancy in a second, *andantino espressivo*, section in $\frac{2}{4}$ time.

"The Message" or "The Messenger," seventh in the opus, is merely a sketch, and has a curiously Teutonic cast in which Chopin's use of the sharpened fourth seems willful. It dates from 1830.

A mildly Chopinesque song is number eight, "My Sweetheart," composed in 1837. It is a mazurka, complete with triplets and sharpened fourth. Although fundamentally unvocal, it can be sung with considerable effect.

The ninth number in opus 74, composed as late as 1847, is "Melody" or "The Promised Land." It is saved from the crushing squareness of its vocal line by an aptly various accompaniment, which makes good use of continuous triplets against duple time or merely strikes chords as though supporting recitative.

A complete fiasco with materials that Schumann could have conquered is the tenth song, "The Horseman before the Battle." Its imitation of horn- or bugle-calls is almost comically flat. There is not one detail to lift this song even momentarily out of commonplace. It dates from 1830.

The "double ending" of the Polish title of the eleventh song (1845) refers to the deaths of a girl and her soldier lover. The song is sometimes known in English as "Two Corpses." Despite its minor key, however, it is neither tragic nor even very expressive.

Twelfth in the opus is "My Delight," the best, and musically the most Chopin's own, of the seventeen. Despite its instrumental introduction, which could easily lead into a full-fledged solo mazurka, it proves to be a real song. It is very carefully worked out and wonderfully expressive. In Liszt's transcription it is the familiar *Chant polonais*. Chopin composed it in 1837.

The thirteenth song, dating from 1845, is "Melancholy," slightly Schubertian, a little persuasive.

A captivating miniature is the fourteenth song, "The Little Ring," another waltz-with-words. It was probably composed on September 8, 1837, for Marya Vodzhinska.

Banal in a blatant way that makes attributing it to Chopin unpleasant is the fifteenth number of opus 74, "The Homecoming." This song opens and closes with a senseless rush of octaves and unmercifully agitates a dull melody. It dates from 1831.

Sixteenth, "Lithuanian Song" or "Sweet was the morning," is a very beautiful and raptly expressive work. It has some of the best qualities of folksong, from which it is directly derived. A rare quality among the seventeen, it has grateful material for a singer. Chopin composed it in 1831.

Bad, grandiloquent, and embarrassing is the final song, known as "Poland's Dirge." It pulls out all the worst pseudopatriotic stops, saws away at heroism, and swims through bathos. Chopin's love for his native land was expressed with blazing sincerity and artistic surefootedness elsewhere, but here he reacted with overemphasis to words unfit for musical setting. This appalling song dates from 1836.

Chopin was attracted by beautiful singing his whole life long. What songs he might have composed if he had directed his full powers onto the problem will never be known. All that is certain is that he never regarded the writing of songs as more than a byway of his activity. The results, charming in part, are minor both absolutely and relatively to the rest of his compositions. It is sometimes argued that non-Poles cannot fully appreciate Chopin's songs. Is this not to say kindly that he failed to create them *as music*?

Appendix A

WORKS WITHOUT OPUS NUMBERS

Albumblatt in E major

In 1927 there was published an Albumblatt in E major, the original manuscript of which, dating from 1843, was inscribed to Anna Szeremetieff. I have not seen a copy of this.

Andante dolente in B-flat minor

An Andante dolente in B-flat minor was composed by Chopin in 1827. It does not seem to have survived.

Grand Duo Concertante for cello and piano

On November 21, 1831 Louis Véron presented to a highly enthusiastic Paris audience a new opera by Giacomo Meyerbeer. It was a setting, in the very grand grand-opera style that Meyerbeer was perfecting, of a libretto entitled *Robert le diable,* by Scribe and Delavigne. This patchwork of false and true grandeur, of nonsense and shrewd sense, of inspiration and hackwork, became epidemically popular and remained so for years. Arrangements for various solo instruments and combinations of instruments were made of selections from it and rushed to press by composers eager to earn ready money. To these tributes to Meyerbeer's success Chopin and Auguste-Joseph Franchomme added, in 1833, by publishing their jointly composed *Grand Duo concertante sur des thèmes de l'opéra "Robert le diable."* It was also issued as a piano duet with the opus number 15. This was either intended to be its number in the list of Chopin's works or was its actual number in the list of Franchomme's. In any case, Chopin later gave the number 15 to three Nocturnes, while Franchomme's compositions — and cello-and-piano pieces composed in collaboration with George Alexander Osborne and others — have now been forgotten.

It is just as well to forget the Duo Concertante also. It is empty, flashy, overdressed music that does scant justice to the juicy Meyerbeer tunes and no justice at all to Chopin himself. A reasonable guess would be that most of the structural layout of the piece is Chopin's, while the cello figurations and the general relation of the two instruments are Franchomme's. The piece was published by Schlesinger in Paris on July 6, 1833, and some time during that same year was brought out in Berlin by A. M. Schlesinger.

"Enchantments"

In 1912 there was published a Chopin song to which the title "Enchantments" had been given. Dating from 1830, it is poor stuff.

Three New Études

It was in 1839 that Chopin, at the invitation of Ignaz Moscheles, composed the Études in F minor, A-flat major, and D-flat major. They were included in the *Méthode des méthodes,* a general piano-playing text by Moscheles and Fétis issued in August or September 1840. As published separately by the Schlesinger firms of both Berlin and Paris, they were described as *"études de perfection"* extracted from the Moscheles-Fétis volume. They are now included in nearly all general editions of the Études of opus 10 and opus 25. They are often described as "posthumous," which they most certainly were not. They are short, all of them are musically attractive, and two of them are exceedingly beautiful.

The F-minor Étude, in common time, is written throughout (except for its four closing measures) as a single-note melody with a single-note accompaniment. Mostly the melody is six quarter-notes to a measure — two groups of triplets — and the accompaniment eight eighth-notes. The problem for study, then, is the familiar one of "three against four." But the listener to this sinuous and enchanting *andantino* may never realize at all that there is a problem, so emotionally expressive of pure charm is its musical answer. The piece has been compared to the F-minor Étude, opus 25, no. 2, in which the problem is four eighth-note triplets in the right hand against two quarter-note triplets in the left. But though the one in opus 25 is longer and more popular, this one has more to say and says it more persuasively.

Least interesting of the Three New Études is the second, in A-flat major. Here the study problem is similar to that of the first: in $\frac{2}{4}$ time there are two eighth-note triplets in the melodic right hand against four eighth-notes in the left — another version of cross-rhythm, this time "two against three." Despite artful nuances, however, this piece skirts monotony. More surprising, it verges several times on a banal and Brahmsian sentimentality.

Finest of the three, and one of the great Études, is the D-flat major, a waltz in disguise. Here the problem is more difficult to solve: the simultaneous playing of staccato and legato. The upper notes in the right hand must be legato throughout, as must some of the single notes and chords in the left; all of the lower notes in the right hand, with some of the chords and single notes in the left, must be staccato. Without performing this difficult feat — difficult, at least, in a nicely conceived *allegretto* — a pianist can still make a considerable musical effect with the piece, but the perfect carrying out of Chopin's intention heightens that effect many degrees. Its apparently continuous melodic line calls forth a light shimmer of harmonic shiftings that lays a lovely glow of color over the whole Étude.

Fugue

The genuineness of a Fugue published with Chopin's name on its title page has now been established. The manuscript is at present in the collection of Arthur Hedley.

Largo in E-flat major

In 1937 the *Polski Rocznik Muzykologiczny,* or *Polish Annual of Musicology* (Warsaw) discussed and analyzed two previously unpublished pieces by Chopin, a Largo in E-flat major and a Nocturne in C minor. Both were published in 1938 by Towarzystwo Wydawnicze Muzyki Polskiej (Warsaw).

The E-flat major Largo is dated *"Paris, le 6 juillet,"* but bears no year. It is a curiously bare manuscript, and contains no agogic signs or other markings, unless wavy-line arpeggio signs in the third and seventh measures be so considered. It suggests the possibility that Chopin may have been pondering a new national anthem, so closely does it resemble that usually square and self-satisfied musical hybrid:

Lento con gran espressione in C-sharp minor

See the Nocturne in C-sharp minor, page 317.

Mazurka in A minor (to Émile Gaillard)

Originally issued in 1841 as Chopin's opus 43 was the A-minor Mazurka dedicated "*à son ami Émile Gaillard.*" It was probably composed in the year of its publication. Ludwik Bronarski, who has seen a copy of it as published by Chabal of Paris, suggests that the reason why it was republished without an opus number is that a mistake had been made in giving the same number to the Tarantelle, published at about the same time. In any case, it is not a posthumous work. The first German edition, issued in 1855 by Bote & Bock, has no opus number. The identity of Émile Gaillard was unknown until 1934, when Albert Déchelette published in the *Journal des débats* (December 28) an article identifying him as a Chopin pupil. Déchelette had known Gaillard at the end of his life, when he had retired from a banking position in Paris, and the only way to persuade him to return to the piano was to play a Chopin piece badly in his presence.

The "Gaillard" Mazurka is a work of intense interest, one of the finest of all Chopin's pieces of this class. Its first section divides chief melodic interest alternately between the hands in a most attractive way. Its second section wrings semimelodic charm out of thirty-six measures in which the rhythm is unvarying: each measure has, in the melodic right hand, two eighth-notes, one quarter-note, and two eighth-notes. The third division repeats the first for twenty-six measures and then diverges from it through a passage leading to a trill that lasts for ten measures. Below this trill a new melodic-rhythmic idea is fadingly introduced. The trill evaporates into a rapid leap upward of an octave and another octave — and the Mazurka is done. No folk music, no dance music, this is pure Chopin, as personal as his face or his signature.

Mazurka in A minor ("*Notre temps*")

In 1842 or 1843 B. Schotts Söhne of Mainz published as a Christmas album a collection of twelve pieces by Czerny, Chopin, Kalliwoda, Rosenhain, Thalberg, Kalkbrenner, Mendelssohn, Bertini, Wolff, Montski, Osborne, and Herz. The album was called *Notre temps*, and Chopin's contribution to it, announced as early as February 1842, was a Mazurka in A minor. It begins with the following four-measure phrase:

Probably composed in 1840, this Mazurka fails to rank with Chopin's best, and its tendency to a numb sameness is not of the sort with which he was able to work small, continuous miracles in such a piece as the F-minor *Méthode des méthodes* Étude. This A-minor Mazurka was republished in 1845 as *Mazurka élégante*.

Mazurka in F-sharp major (false)

Several nineteenth-century editions of Chopin include a Mazurka in F-sharp major. Ernst Pauer, an Austrian pianist who wrote many books about playing the piano (he was a pupil of Mozart's son Wolfgang Amadeus, Jr.) was unable to believe that so dull a piece could really be Chopin's. And on July 1, 1882 he happily published in the London *Musical Record* news that he had found the putative Chopin

Mazurka to be by Charles Mayer (1799–1862), a pupil of John Field. As its first attribution to Chopin, by the publisher J. P. Gotthard, occurred after Mayer's death, it is ridiculous to blame Mayer for the error, which, curiously, was perpetuated by Klindworth in his edition of Chopin.

Various Mazurkas

There are in existence, in both published and unpublished versions, several Mazurkas by Chopin of which I have been able to see either only unreliable copies or none at all. Confusion arises from the fact that different writers who have examined manuscripts (some of which seem no longer to exist) have referred to what may be the same pieces in widely varying ways. There are, or may be, Mazurkas in A major, A minor, A-flat major, B-flat major, C major, D major, and G major.

In 1902 a Chopin Mazurka in A major was published from a manuscript in the possession of descendants of Elsner. This I have never seen.

The Oxford University Press edition of Chopin contains an uninteresting Mazurka (called #42) in A minor that dates from about 1829.

In 1851 a Chopin Mazurka in A-flat major was published in two different versions — or two different Mazurkas by Chopin, both in A-flat major, were published. In 1930 an A-flat major Mazurka, possibly identical, was published with word that the manuscript carried an inscription to Marya Szymanowska. I assume this to be the one published in *Die Musik* (Berlin), Volume XXIII (1931) page 417, for both were said to have been composed in 1834. The Mazurka published in *Die Musik* begins:

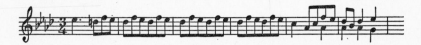

In 1825 Chopin composed Mazurkas in B-flat major and G major (see page 17). These may have been published, perhaps privately, in 1825 or 1826, but the first reliable record of their publication is that they were issued in 1902. I have not seen either one.

Several writers refer in vague terms to an additional Mazurka in C major, of which I can find no clear record.

In 1829 Chopin composed a D-major Mazurka that he revised three years later. It is possible that both the original version and the revision were published two years after his death. One or the other version was certainly issued in 1902. I have been unable to see either one.

Nocturne in C minor

In 1938 there was published a C-minor Nocturne that Chopin had composed in 1827, and of which a manuscript survived in the Paris Conservatoire. The editor of the published version stated that he had made in it only absolutely essential changes. I should have preferred to see the Nocturne as Chopin wrote it. It is a mildly interesting piece, which I reproduce here *in toto* because it is otherwise unobtainable:

Nocturne in C-sharp minor

In 1830 Chopin gave his sister Ludvika a composition headed *"Lento con gran' espressione,"* inscribing it "To my sister Ludvika as an exercise before beginning the study of my second Concerto." Six years later, when he was visiting the Vodzhinski family at Dresden, Marya Vodzhinska gave him an album in which to note down some of his music for her. Into it he copied eight of his songs and the 1830 Lento. The piano piece escaped the busy hands of Fontana and was not published until 1875, when the Posen publisher Leitgeber issued it as an Adagio. It is clearly an early sketch for a Nocturne, however,[1] and it has more recently been published as a Nocturne in C-sharp minor.

The Nocturne contains fragments of the sorts of material and ideas that Chopin was to use for constructing his best essays in this genre. They are not in their optimum condition, however, and are treated with maiming brevity and utter lack of co-ordination. Into sixty-four measures Chopin has crowded a four-measure introduction, sixteen measures of a leading melody, eight measures of a *più mosso* second melody derived directly from the opening melody of the finale of the F-minor Concerto, a three-measure extension marked *lento,* a transitional measure in $\frac{5}{4}$ time, an eleven-measure *animato* in $\frac{3}{4}$ time, two transitional measures marked *adagio,* and nineteen measures, *tempo primo,* repeating and developing the first leading melody with too much unintegrated decoration. The piece — which, remember, Chopin himself did not publish — is ungrateful in performance, appearing to be shards glued together without sense of balance or design.

[1] Only the C-minor Nocturne published in 1938 and the E-minor Nocturne of opus 72 are earlier.

Polonaise in A-flat major

In 1899 the Warsaw *Musical Echo* printed in facsimile a thitherto un-published A-flat Polonaise by Chopin. I have not been able to see a copy of *Musical Echo*, but the Polonaise is probably the one published in 1902 in what Arthur Hedley has called a "barbarous transcription." If so, it was composed to honor Zhivny's birthday on April 23, 1821, Chopin then being eleven years old. Huneker, disdaining grammatical elegance, wrote of it: "Written at the age of eleven, this tiny dance is a tentative groping after the form he later conquered so magnifi-cently." Its principal melody begins as follows:

Polonaise in B-flat major

Of this Polonaise I know nothing except its existence, and that it was inscribed to one Alexandra Polinska. It seems to have had some sort of publication in 1937.

Polonaise in B-flat minor
(*Adieu à Guillaume Kolberg*)

According to footnotes in the Breitkopf & Härtel edition, the B-flat minor Polonaise dates from the days just preceding Chopin's departure in 1826 for Bad Reinertz with his mother and his sisters. Its manu-script title was *"Adieu à Guillaume Kolberg,"* while its trio (D-flat) was headed *"Au revoir!* after an air from *Gazza Ladra."* The statement is made that "some days before Chopin's departure the two friends had been present at a performance of Rossini's opera."

Wilhelm Kolberg was the son of Jules Kolberg, an engineer who was friendly with Chopin's father. The "air from *Gazza Ladra*" is the aria beginning *"Vieni, vieni fra queste braccia, mi balza il cor nel sen!"* Un-fortunately, the piece seems to have been rather too thoroughly "ed-ited" by Klechinski before publication, and it cannot therefore really be judged as wholly Chopin's. It begins with the following melody:

The Rossini melody, originally in D major, is transcribed as follows:

Polonaise in G minor (Victoire Skarbek)

In *La Revue musicale* (Paris) for March 1, 1927 Zdislas Jachimecki (Yakhimetski) published an article entitled *"La Première Composition Imprimée de Chopin (1817)."* This was a section from his book *Fryderyk Chopin, rys życia i twórczości*, issued at Krakov in 1927 and reissued in Paris in 1930 as *Frédéric Chopin et son œuvre.* In this article he first publicly revealed the discovery of the G-minor Polonaise composed by Chopin in 1817 and published that year with a dedication to the young Countess Victoire Skarbek. In the article Yakhimetski reproduced the music and its title page — the latter reading: *"Polonoise [sic]/pour/le Piano-Forte/Dediée/ a Son Excellence Mademoiselle la Comtesse/Victoire Skarbek/faite[*scratched out]*/par Frédéric Chopin/ musicien[*scratched out]* Agé de huit Ans/ a Varsovie Chez l'Abbe J. J. Cybulski a la Nouvelle Ville dans la Maison de Cure de Notre Dame."*

The existence of this Polonaise had been established by the discovery of a notice in the January 1818 issue of a Warsaw literary monthly, *Pamietnik Warszawski.* In a section headed "Literary News," under the subheading "Memento of Polish works published in 1817," there was a sectional "Note on Frédéric Chopin, native of Warsaw who, being but eight years old, is already the composer of musical works." The notice read:

Although we do not list musical composers among the writers — they are authors for all that — we cannot in silence pass by the following composition published by friendly hands: *Polonaise* for pianoforte, dedicated to her Excellence Mme the Countess Victoire Skarbek, by Friderik Chopin, aged eight years. The composer of this Polish dance, an adolescent of scarcely eight years, is the son of M. Nicolas Chopin, professor of the French language and literature at the Warsaw Lyceum; he is a true musical genius who not only performs at the piano with the greatest ease and extraordinary taste the most difficult pieces, but has already composed some dances and variations that provoke the greatest astonishment among experts, above all because of the author's youth. If this adolescent had been born in Germany or France he would have attracted to himself the interest of all the societies. The mention we make is intended to demonstrate that under our sun also geniuses are born, and that only the lack of a glittering publicity keeps them hidden from the great public.

It was the Polish poet Joseph Galuszka of Krakov who lent Yakhi-metski a four-volume collection of the piano music published in Warsaw between about 1816 and 1830, thus allowing him to discover the "Polonoise" in question. This particular copy, further, contained, on its last page, Chopin's autograph inscription to his friend Yan Bialo-blotski. The first part of the piece as published follows:

The trio of the Polonaise follows as published

Several passages contain what are obviously errors in music of this nature and texture. That they are errors in the publication is almost certain, for it is unlikely, even if the boy Chopin had been capable of making them, that Zhivny or some other mentor would not have corrected them in the manuscript. In the first part there are five of these errors: (1) second measure, bottom note of the first right-hand chord should be C rather than B; (2) eleventh measure, bottom note of last left-hand chord should be E flat rather than F; (3) twelfth measure, bottom note of second left-hand chord should be D rather than F; (4) thirteenth measure, second left-hand octave should probably be F's rather than G's; final measure, bottom note of second left-hand chord should be F rather than G. In addition, in the fifteenth measure the sixth left-hand note should conceivably be A rather than B flat.

In the trio it seems likely that the half-note chord in the fourth measure should have a horizontal line through its staff, indicating — as in the preceding measures — that it is to be repeated as though it were four eighth-note chords written out.

There is a more understandable error about Chopin's age in both the January 1818 article in *Pamietnik Varshavski* and the title page of the Polonaise itself. Chopin was seven, and not eight, when the piece was published, but of that we can now be more certain than the people of Warsaw could in 1818 or 1817. Certainly the misstatement of the boy's age was not deliberate: who ever heard of wishing a child prodigy to be older than his true age?

Of the G-minor Polonaise itself there is little to say. Yakhimetski, whose knowledge of Polish music is encyclopedic, says that it shows the influence of the "Polonaises of Prince Michel Oginski, the true founder of the polonaise, which became national through the tendency to penetrate into the domain of the heroic and tragic." He points out, for example, the crossing of hands in the eighteenth and nineteenth measures of the first section, saying that this device was much used by Oginski and appeared in all the eight Polonaises composed by Chopin earlier than the C-sharp minor, opus 26, no. 1. Unfortunately, however, Oginski's music is today as unknown as Chopin's Polonaise in G minor.

Polonaise in G-flat major

In 1872 B. Schotts Söhne of Mainz published a G-flat major Polonaise that was attributed to Chopin. Of it Niecks wrote:

> Nothing but the composer's autograph could convince one of the genuineness of this piece. There are here and there passages which have the Chopin ring, indeed, seem to be almost bodily taken from some other of his works, but there is also a great deal which it is impossible to imagine to have come at any time from his pen — the very opening bars may be instanced.

The hint that the G-flat major Polonaise might be a pastiche has proved to be unjustified, for there is no longer any doubt of the genuineness of the work, which appears to date from 1829, thus being contemporary with the F-minor Concerto. There is no reason, however, to revise Niecks's judgment of the music as music.

Polonaise in G-sharp minor

First published in 1864 was a G-sharp minor Polonaise by Chopin, issued with a dedication to one Mme Dupont, identity unknown, whom Ludwik Bronarski supposes to have been a French friend, in Warsaw, of Chopin's parents. In the Breitkopf & Härtel *Gesamtausgabe* edition, in which it is no. 15, it is dated 1822, an assignment that Niecks and Huneker were reluctant to accept on grounds of stylistic development, both stating that it was too advanced for Chopin at twelve. This it does not seem to me to be, and I fully agree with Gerald Abraham that it could have come just as it stands from a talented boy of twelve. It is mostly made of rather vacuous figurations, it is restless to show off its cleverness — and such a passage as the following (from its trio) is pure imitation Weber:

Mr. Abraham was wrong, however, in referring to this Polonaise as the "earliest known work of Chopin's": the G-minor (Victoire Skarbek) Polonaise, the B-flat major (Alexandra Polinska) Polonaise, and the A-flat major (Zhivny) Polonaise are all earlier.

Prélude in A-flat major

In August 1918 the Swiss periodical *Pages d'art* (Geneva) published a Chopin Prélude in A-flat major bearing the inscription *"A son ami Pierre Wolff, Paris, 10 juillet, 1834."* It was later published by Édition Henn (Geneva) and Édition Rossignol (Paris). The identity of Pierre Wolff is not clear, but he may well have been a brother or son of Chopin's longtime friend Édouard Wolff, French pianist and composer, whom he met first in Warsaw and later knew in Paris. I have been unable to see a complete copy of the Prélude, which is described at some length in the fifth revised edition of Ganche's *Frédéric Chopin, sa vie et ses œuvres.*

Souvenir de Paganini

In 1829 Chopin composed a set of variations that he called *Souvenir de Paganini*. This was published in 1881, but I have been unable to see a copy of it.

Variation in E from the "Hexameron"

In 1837 Princess Cristina Belgiojoso invited six composers to write an equal number of variations on the March from Bellini's *I Puritani*, allowing her to have them performed at a charity concert and published together for the benefit of the poor — specifically, Italian refugees in Paris. The composers whose variations were published were Chopin, Czerny, Herz, Liszt, Pixis, and Thalberg. The full title of the published "Hexameron" was: *Hexaméron: Morceau de Concert. Grandes variations de bravoure sur la marche des Puritains de Bellini, composées pour le concert de Madame la Princesse Belgiojoso au bénéfice des pauvres, par MM. Liszt, Thalberg, Pixis, H. Herz, Czerny, et Chopin.*

Chopin's contribution was a *largo* in common time in the key of E major. The "Hexameron" was published in 1841. Liszt, who had composed the introduction, the passages connecting the separate variations, and the finale, also arranged the whole as a work for piano and orchestra. He was fond of playing the solo-piano version.

Variations in E on a German National Air

It was probably during the summer of 1824 that Chopin began to compose a set of variations on a German song entitled *Der Schweizerbub* (*The Swiss Boy*). He sent the completed work to Tobias Haslinger of Vienna in 1828 or 1829. Haslinger temporized with it as he did with the C-minor Sonata, neither composition being published by him — or at all — during Chopin's life. It was Haslinger's son Karl who, in 1851, eventually issued both the Sonata and the Variations.

The Variations are considerably simpler and much easier to play than the opus 2 Variations on "*Là ci darem la mano.*" They have a flashy but uninteresting introduction. The theme itself, twelve measures in length, is one that Beethoven might have used for another set of piano variations — and, indeed, some of Chopin's texture suggests Beethoven's variations on melodies by Paisiello, Dressler, Winter, and Süssmayr, not to mention those on a Swiss song and *God Save the King.* Chopin's first variation makes considerable use of triplets. The second, *scherzando,* is particularly Beethoven-like. The third merely breaks the left-hand harmonies into sixteen sixteenth-notes to a measure. The fourth variation, with displaced accents, is the most interesting, though it sounds completely un-Chopinesque. The fifth is an unsuccessful *tempo di valse,* in which the theme is unconsciously caricatured. This variation is extended to and beyond the point of monotony, and thus closes the piece weakly.

Here, as in the opus 2 Variations, Chopin confined himself to varying the rhythm and the harmony of his theme and never brought forth from it the secondary ideas made primary that would have enriched Beethoven's or Brahms's comments.

Variations in F major for piano duet

Never published, and perhaps no longer in existence, is a set of Variations in F major for piano duet. It was composed by Chopin in 1826 and inscribed to Tytus Voitsyekhovski.

Variations for flute on a theme from *La Cenerentola*

A set of flute Variations on a melody from Rossini's *La Cenerentola* exists in an edition bearing Chopin's name. There is no evidence whatever that it is actually his work.

Waltzes in A-flat major and E-flat major

In 1902 there were published, from manuscripts discovered in the possession of the Elsner family, a Mazurka in A major and two Waltzes — in E-flat major and A-flat major. I have never been able to see any of these.

Waltz in C major

In 1826 Chopin composed a C-major Waltz that seems never to have been published, and of the present survival of which I have no information.

Waltz in E major

Composed in 1829, the E-major Waltz seems originally to have been a companion to the B-minor Waltz, opus 69, no. 2. I have been unable to determine when it was first published, but it was issued both by Gebethner & Wolff (Warsaw) and W. Chaberski (Krakov). It has, in its principal melody, a rather faded sentimental charm, derived largely from the modulations, which permit the bottom voice in the right hand to progress downward from E to G sharp by semitones:

Otherwise the E-major Waltz is tentative and banal and fails to adumbrate Chopin's best efforts in the form.

Waltz in E minor

In 1868 B. Schotts Söhne of Mainz published a Waltz in E minor by Chopin. This was composed in 1830. It is difficult to guess why Chopin himself never published it, for it is not only one of the most attractive and densely composed of the Waltzes, but belongs among the best of his pre-Paris compositions.

After eight measures of waxing introductory material, ending on a two-beat pause, a four-measure melodic-harmonic idea of predominantly upward direction is propounded and then answered by another four-measure idea of contrary tendency. Both are then repeated, establishing themselves with complete certainty as the prime thematic condiments of the piece. Then Chopin presents sixteen measures of comment and exploration, these being conceived and written with such sensitivity as to make them a subordinate continuation of what has preceded. Then for sixteen measures the prime material is repeated, arriving at a first ending that leads back to an entire repetition beginning with the sixteen measures of comment. When this repetition is completed, there is a change to E major.

The trio is music very characteristic of Chopin at the hour when he was about to abandon Warsaw for Paris. In the beginning it consists of two mirror-phrases of four measures each, the constellation of eight measures being stated, with some variation, four times. Interest shifts to the left hand, which thus far has had only rhythmic and harmonic duties, with notes only on the signature beats. Now for eight transitional measures it plays a semimelodic role while the right hand carries an echo melody on inner voices. Then, by a merging stroke of real cleverness, Chopin returns to the opening mirror-phrases of the trio, allotting them two complete restatements. The eight transitional measures are repeated and lead again to reiteration of the mirror-phrases. First they have their usual accompaniment, but then the left hand takes up six rocking eighth-notes to the measure for the second eight measures. The key shifts back to E minor, and the prime material of the first section is reintroduced as though to be recapitulated entire. It gets through one eight-measure statement, but at the fourth measure of the second statement breaks off, a structural shrinking that has a fine effect. The twenty-three-measure coda is a perfect conclusion for this eminently danceable and pervasively lighthearted Waltz.

Waltzes written in the album
of Mme the Countess P—

The two Waltzes listed in many catalogues of Chopin's works as *"Valses mélancoliques sur l'album de Mme la Comtesse P—"* are in reality the B-minor Waltz, opus 69, no. 2, and the F-minor Waltz, opus 70, no. 2. It is probable that Chopin wrote them in the unknown Countess's album, and that after his death the publisher Wildt (Krakov) derived them therefrom, perhaps without knowledge that Fontana had published them or was about to publish them.

Appendix B

CHOPIN'S BIRTH REGISTRY AND BAPTISMAL CERTIFICATE

The registry of birth (original in Polish) reads as follows:

In the year 1810, on the 23rd of the month of April at three o'clock in the afternoon. Before us, the parish priest of Brokhuf, district of Sokhachev, department of Warsaw, Nicolas Chopin, father, aged forty years, living in the village of Zhelazova Vola, presented himself and showed us a male child born in his house on February 22nd at 6 o'clock in the evening, this year, and declared that the child was born of himself and of Yustina Kzhizhanovska, his wife, twenty-eight years old, and that his wish is to give the child two Christian names — Frédéric and François. Having made this statement, he showed us the child in the presence of Yosef Vizhikovski, steward, aged thirty-eight years, and of Frédéric Gesht, aged forty years, both living in the village of Zhelazova Vola. The father and the two witnesses, having read the birth certificate, which was showed to them, declared their ability to write. We have signed the present document:

Abbé Yan Dukhnovski, parish priest of Brokhuf,
fulfilling the function of civil servant

Nicolas Chopin, father

The baptismal certificate reads:

Ignatius Maryanski Vicarius Ecclesiæ
23 Aprilis 1810

Ego qui supra supplevi ceremonias super infantem baptizatum ex aqua bini nominis Fridericum Franciscum, natum d. 22 Februarii Maficorum [Magnificorum] Nicolai Choppen [*sic*] Galli et Justinæ de Krzyzanowska Legi [Legitimorum] conjug [conjugum], Patrini Maficus [Magnificus] Franciscus Grebecki de villa Ciuliny [?, illegible] cum Mafica [Magnifica] Anna Skarbkowna Contessa, de Zelazowa Wola.

329

Appendix C

GENEALOGY OF CHOPIN

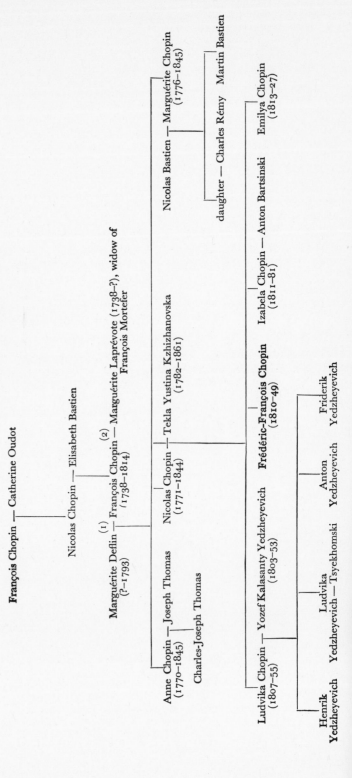

BIBLIOGRAPHY

THE FOLLOWING LIST *includes only books — and a few monographs and periodical pieces — dealing directly or indirectly with Chopin that I have consulted while writing the present book. It does not include general background reading in Polish, French, or music history. Nor does it include very numerous highly specialized periodical and monographic sources that can be consulted only in the largest reference libraries, where they are in the main excellently catalogued.*

ABRAHAM, GERALD
  Chopin's Musical Style. Oxford University Press, London, New York, Toronto, 1939. An excellent chronological study of Chopin's evolving style, marred only by an acceptance of some now incredible datings.

AUDLEY, MME A.
  Frédéric Chopin, sa vie et ses œuvres. E. Plon et Cie, Paris, 1880.

BARBEDETTE, H.
  F. Chopin: Essai de critique musicale. Heugel, Paris, 1869.

BIDOU, HENRI
  Chopin. Félix Alcan, Paris, 1925. (*Chopin,* translated by Catherine Alison Phillips. Alfred A. Knopf, New York, 1927.)

BINENTAL, LÉOPOLD
  Chopin (Polish). W. Lazarski, Warsaw, 1930. (*Chopin,* translated into French. Éditions Rieder, Paris, 1934.)

BRONARSKI, LUDWIK
  Chopin's Harmony (Polish). Warsaw, 1935.
  Études sur Chopin. 2 vols. Éditions La Concorde, Lausanne, 1946. Valuable highly specialized essays dealing with fine historical and musical points.

CHOPIN, FRÉDÉRIC-FRANCOIS
  Nearly four hundred of Chopin's letters survive in whole or in part, in manuscript and in transcription. No satisfactory collected edition of them exists in any language. The Opieński-Voynich American edition is untrustworthy as to dating. Also not all known texts are included, and of those used, not all are complete. The book should be consulted with intense wariness.

BIBLIOGRAPHY

Chopin's Letters (binding reads *Chopin's Collected Letters*), collected by Henryk Opieński, translated from the original Polish and French with a Preface and Editorial Notes by E. L. Voynich. Alfred A. Knopf, New York, 1931.

Friedrich Chopins gesammelte Briefe, edited by Bernard Scharlitt. Breitkopf & Härtel, Leipzig, 1911.

Les Lettres de Chopin, "Collection Polonaise." Société française d'éditions littéraires et techniques. Paris, 1933.

DAVISON, JAMES WILLIAM
Frederick Chopin: a Memoir. Boosey & Co., London, n.d.

DRY, WAKELING
Chopin. John Lane, New York, 1926.

DUNN, JOHN PETRIE
Ornamentation in the Works of Chopin. Novello, London, 1921.

EGERT, PAUL
Friedrich Chopin. Potsdam, 1936. An important study for its revisions and for its close study of manuscripts.

FINCK, HENRY THEOPHILUS
Chopin and other Musical Essays. Charles Scribner's Sons, New York, 1889.

GANCHE, ÉDOUARD
Dans le souvenir de Frédéric Chopin. Mercure de France, Paris, 1925 (5th edition).

Frédéric Chopin, sa vie et ses œuvres. Mercure de France, Paris, 1921 (5th edition).

Souffrances de Frédéric Chopin, Essai de Médecine et de Psychologie. Mercure de France, Paris, 1935.

Voyages avec Frédéric Chopin. Mercure de France, Paris, 1934 (2nd edition).

Ganche was the first modern scholar to make use, in a Western language, of the magnificent researches of Hoesick and other Polish scholars. His own original research was wide, deep, and deftly handled. Although I have disagreed with some of his conclusions, I have found few occasions to disagree with his factual statements.

HADDEN, J. CUTHBERT
Chopin. J. M. Dent & Sons, London, 1903. (Revised edition, J. M. Dent & Sons, London, and E. P. Dutton & Co., New York, 1934.) A volume in "The Master Musicians," this has been superseded by Hedley, q.v. below.

HADOW, SIR WILLIAM HENRY
Studies in Modern Music, Second Series. Seeley & Co., London, 1895.

BIBLIOGRAPHY

HEDLEY, ARTHUR
  Chopin. J. M. Dent & Sons, London, 1947. A volume in "The Master Musicians," this is an admirable highly condensed biography and critique.

HOESICK, FERDYNAND
  Chopin, His Life and Works. 3 vols. (Polish). Warsaw and Krakov, 1911. The great modern sourcebook, particularly on the Polish period, and the best biography between Niecks and Ganche.

HUNEKER, JAMES GIBBONS
  Chopin, the man and his music. Charles Scribner's Sons, New York, 1900. A bravura study, valuable for enthusiasm but careless of data, this enduringly famous book has a life of its own.

JACHIMECKI, ZDISLAS
  Frédéric Chopin et son œuvre. Librairie Delagrave, Paris, 1930.

JEAN-AUBRY, GEORGES
  Hommage à Chopin. Paris, 1916.

JONSON, GEORGE CHARLES ASHTON
  A Handbook to Chopin's Works. William Heinemann, London, 1905.

KARASOWSKI, MORITZ
  Frederic Chopin, His Life and Letters, translated by Emily Hill. William Reeves, London, 1939 (3rd edition). The original, *Fryderyk Chopin, Życie, Listy, Dzieła,* issued at Warsaw in 1882, was a ground-clearing work; the English translation is badly translated and execrably edited.

KARÉNINE, WLADIMIR (pseudonym of Mme V. D. Komarova)
  George Sand, sa vie et ses œuvres. 4 vols. Plon-Nourrit, Paris, completed 1926. The definitive life of George Sand.

KARLOWICZ, MIECZYSŁAW
  Souvenirs inédits de Frédéric Chopin, translated into French from the Polish by Laura Disière. Welter, Paris and Leipzig, 1904. The Polish original, published by the Chopin section of the Warsaw Musical Society, contained numerous Chopin and George Sand letters that were curiously omitted in the French translation.

KELLEY, EDGAR STILLMAN
  Chopin the Composer. G. Schirmer, New York and London, 1913.

KLECZYŃSKI, JEAN
  Chopins grössere Werke, Breitkopf & Härtel, Leipzig, 1898.
  Frédéric Chopin: De l'interprétation de ses œuvres. Noël, Paris, 1880.
  The Works of Frederic Chopin and their Proper Interpretation, trans-

lated by Alfred Whittingham. William Reeves, London, n.d. (5th edition).

LEICHTENTRITT, HUGO
Analyse der Chopin'sche Klavierwerke, 2 vols. Berlin, 1921. A painstaking and thorough analysis along strictly academic lines.
Friedrich Chopin. Berlin, 1905. (Later edition, Schlesische Verlaganstalt, Berlin, 1920.)

LENZ, WILHELM VON
Die grossen Pianofortevirtuosen unserer Zeit. Berlin, 1872.

LISZT, FRANZ
Life of Chopin, translated from the French by Martha Walker Cook. Oliver Ditson & Co., Boston, 1863 ("fourth edition revised"). Actually a collaboration with Princess Carolyn von Sayn-Wittgenstein, Liszt's "biography" of Chopin was dated at Weimar in 1850. Its first appearance was as a serial in *La France musicale,* Paris, in 1851. It is wholly unreliable.

MAINE, BASIL
Chopin. Duckworth, London, 1933.

MURDOCH, WILLIAM
Chopin: His Life. John Murray, London, 1934. The distinguished Australian pianist unfortunately died before writing his companion volume on the music. The existing biographical volume is sensitive and generally dependable.

NIECKS, FREDERICK
Frederick Chopin as a Man and Musician. 2 vols. Novello, Ewer & Co., London and New York, 1888. The first complete life of Chopin. A great work of nineteenth-century scholarship, this book has had a baneful influence because it has been accepted as standard when modern research had proved it incorrect in hundreds of points.

OPIEŃSKI, HENRYK
Chopin. Levous, Altenberg, 1910.
See also Chopin, Frédéric-François.

POIRÉE, ÉLIE
Chopin. Laurens, Paris, 1907.

PORTE, JOHN F.
Chopin, the Composer and His Music. William Reeves, London, n.d.

PRINCET, MAURICE
Frédéric Chopin. No publisher, Paris, 1932.

SAND, GEORGE (pseudonym of Amandine-Aurore-Lucile, Baronne Dudevant)
Correspondance. 4 vols. Paris, completed 1884.

Histoire de ma vie. 3 vols. Paris, completed 1855.

Journal intime (posthumous), edited by Aurore Sand. Calmann-Lévy, Paris, 1926 (3rd edition).

Lucrezia Floriani, Calmann-Lévy, Paris, 1888.

SCHARLITT, BERNARD

Chopin. Leipzig, 1919.

See also Chopin, Frédéric-François.

SIKORSKI, JOSEF

Recollections of Chopin (Polish). In *The Warsaw Library,* Vol. XXXVI. Warsaw, 1849.

STRENGER, HENRYK

On Chopin's Life and Genius and the Spirit of His Music (Polish). Wende, Warsaw, 1910.

SZULC, M. A.

Fryderyk Chopin and His Musical Compositions (Polish). Zupanski, Posen, 1873.

TARNOWSKI, COUNT STANISLAS

Chopin: as Revealed by Extracts from His Diary, translated from the Polish by Natalie Janotha. William Reeves, London, n.d.

TOESCA, MAURICE

The Other George Sand. Dennis Dobson Limited, London, 1947. A fascinating, if slightly ludicrous, attempt to remake a reputation.

VALETTA, IPPOLITO (Giuseppe Ippolito Alessandro Desiderato Pio Maria Franchi-Verney, Conte della Valetta)

Chopin: La Vita, le opere. Fratelli Bocca, Turin, 1910. From a literary point of view, one of the best books on Chopin ever written though some of its factual material has now been rendered obsolete.

VUILLERMOZ, ÉMILE

La vie amoureuse de Chopin. Ernest Flammarion, Paris, 1927.

WEISSMAN, ADOLF

Chopin. Schuster & Loeffler, Berlin, 1912.

WILLEBY, CHARLES

Frédéric-François Chopin. Sampson Low, Marston & Company, London, 1892.

WINDAKIEWICZOWA, HELENA

Fundamental Forms of Polish People's Music in the Mazurkas of Chopin (Polish). Krakov, 1926.

WINWAR, FRANCES

The Life of the Heart: George Sand & Her Times. Harper & Brothers, New York, 1945.

BIBLIOGRAPHY

WODZIŃSKI, COUNT ANTON
   Les trois romans de Frédéric Chopin. Calmann-Lévy, Paris, 1886.
   Mistaken for fact, this novel has infested Chopin biography with
   considerable nonsense. It is straight fiction.
ZALESKI, ZYGMUNT L.
   La Patrie musicale de Chopin. B. Roudanez, Paris, 1917.

In December 1931 the *Revue musicale* (Paris) issued a special number devoted entirely to Chopin. It contained the following: "Frédéric
Chopin," by the Comtesse de Noailles; "Chopin," by Paderewski;
"Notes sur Chopin," by André Gide; "Ce que Chopin doit à la France,"
by Alfred Cortot; "Frédéric Chopin et la musique polonaise moderne,"
by Karol Szymanowski; "Frédéric Chopin et la Pologne," by Stanislas
Niewiadomski; "Itinéraire de Varsovie à Paris," by Mat. Glinski; "Plus
tard, à Paris," by Cyprien Norwid; "La vie musicale de Frédéric Chopin à Paris," by Édouard Ganche; "Chez un élève de Chopin," by
Ernest Schelling; "Les sources polonaises de la musique de Chopin,"
by Henryk Opieński; "Le sens expressif des tonalités dans la musique
de Chopin" — notes by Louis Aguettant, published by Henri Rambaud;
"Considérations sur les éléments du style de Chopin," by Bronislawa
Wojcik-Keuprulian; "Sur l'orchestre latent' dans le piano de Frédéric
Chopin," by Georges Migot; "Chopin et l'ancienne musique française,"
by Wanda Landowska; "A propos d'un manuscrit," by Yvonne Le-
fébure; "Chopin et la musique contemporaine," by Stéphanie Loba-
czewska; "Documents et souvenirs," by Léopold Binental; "Quelques
disques de Chopin," by H[enry] P[runières], and "'Édition de travail,'"
by Fred. Goldbeck.

General Index

INDEX

INDEX

i v

INDEX

INDEX

INDEX

INDEX

INDEX

Index of Chopin's Compositions and Literary Juvenilia

A NOTE ON THE TYPE USED IN THIS BOOK

The text of this book is set in Caledonia, *a Linotype face designed by W. A. Dwiggins. Caledonia belongs to the family of printing types called "modern face" by printers — a term used to mark the change in style of type-letters that occurred about 1800. Caledonia borders on the general design of Scotch Modern, but is more freely drawn than that letter.*

The book was composed, printed, and bound by The Plimpton Press, Norwood, Massachusetts. The binding is based on designs by W. A. Dwiggins.